A Jussi Björling Phonography

2nd Edition

Enlarged and Revised
by
Harald Henrysson

Svenskt Musikhistoriskt
Stockholm 1993

Cover photo: Sven Åsberg/Pressens Bild AB

One of the last pictures of Jussi Björling, taken at his last public performance, the Stockholm Skansen recital on August 20, 1960.

MUSIK I SVERIGE
Music in Sweden

Publications issued by Svenskt Musikhistoriskt Arkiv
& Svenska Samfundet för Musikforskning

6

1st edition by Harald Henrysson & Jack W. Porter, 1984

Printed 1993 by Tabergs Tryckeri AB, Taberg, Sweden
ISBN 91-85172-10-3

Photo: Musikmuseet, Stockholm

An early picture of Jussi Björling as Rodolfo in La bohème at the Royal Opera in Stockholm.

Table of Contents

Section 3: Indexes

Section 4: Bibliography

Foreword to the Second Edition

The second edition of the *Phonography* contains numerous additions and corrections. It has increased in size mainly through the expansion of the Chronological Table of Jussi Björling's Life and Career, which now includes dates and other details for a great number of performances. Statistical information about JB's opera, operetta and oratorio repertoire has been removed from the Chronological Table and is now arranged in a separate list. The introduction of the CD record has made a new part of Section 2 necessary; of the more than 300 new disc and tape numbers listed in this edition, about half represent CDs. A bibliography of sleeve texts and record booklets dealing with JB has been added whilst three short lists in the former edition have been omitted (List of Disc and Tape Issues Based on Secondary Information; Currently Available Issues; Tape Copies of Live Opera Recordings).

In principle, the content of this volume is otherwise arranged in the same way as in the previous edition with one exception: all performances of which recordings cannot be proved to exist have been moved from the main list in Section 1:B to an appendix. Eight recordings which have been discovered since the previous edition was published are now included in Section 1:B. As a result, certain numbering changes in that section became necessary. The Key to Index Numbers on pp. 237 clearly demonstrates which numbers have been changed and I hope this re-numbering will not cause too much inconvenience to owners of the former edition. There are also several changes in the sub-numbering system used for opera excerpts (both in Section 1:A & B).

I am pleased that the interest in Jussi Björling's life and recordings, the reception of the first edition of this work and the continued support from people all over the world, have made this second edition possible. I am greatly indebted to a number of people and would have liked to include each and every one in the list below, but that would have been impossible.

Australia:	Ken F. Lester; David R. Morgan
Brazil:	Dorian Bruzzi
Canada:	Charles Hooey; E. Lacombe
Denmark:	Peter Kjærulff
Finland:	Helen Aminoff, YLE; Henrik Christiernin
Germany	Adolf Brune; Karin Burger, BMG Classics
Great Britain:	Jack Allott; Joseph Colley; Richard Copeman; Stephen J. Crowley; Ruth Edge, EMI Music Archives; Alfred Gardner; Ken Jagger, EMI Classics; Michael Letchford; John Parry, Decca; Karl Pike
Hungary:	Lajos Heiner
Italy:	Alessandro Sciocchetti
Japan:	Christopher N. Nozawa
Netherlands:	Klaas Morcus
Norway:	Aase Nordeng

South Africa: Roy Edmonds, EMI S.A.

Sweden: Olle Andersson; Bertil Bengtsson; Anna-Lisa Björling-Barkman; Lars Björling; Märta Björling-Kärn; Thomas Boltenstern, Konsertbolaget; Bergljot Bucht, R. Opera Archive; Lennart Ekman; John Erik Eleby; Björn Englund, ALB; Tommy Eriksson; Axel Falk; Tony Franzén; Lars-Göran Frisk; Thomas Gorne, Sw. Radio; Hanna Hedman; Lars Hemmingsson, Sw. Radio; Lennart Holmgren, Malmö Municipal Theatre; Per Åke Körvell, Sw. Radio; Hans Lindquist, BMG Ariola; Harold Löwing; Kjell Nilsson; Jan Norin, Sw. Radio; Göran Söderwall; Carl-Gunnar Åhlén; Lars-Henrik Österholm

USA: Kevin Barry; Silvana Di Marco, PolyGram Records; Andrew Farkas; Gene Gaudette, BMG Classics; Don Goldberg; Paul Gruber, Metropolitan Opera Guild; Otto Haberer; Thomas M. Hines; Lawrence F. Holdridge; Nathaniel S. Johnson; Barney Mitzman; Kendall Svengalis

I am also grateful for the active support of my publisher, the Swedish Music History Archive.

Any additions and/or corrections to this new edition will be much appreciated.

March, 1993

Harald Henrysson
c/o Svenskt musikhistoriskt arkiv, Box 16 326, S-103 26 Stockholm, Sweden

Photo: Bild & Text Harry Berger

Jussi Björling recording Swedish songs on September 25, 1957 at the Europafilm Studio in Stockholm

Forewords to the First Edition

Foreword by the Editorial Committe

In April 1982 "A Jussi Bjoerling Discography" by Jack W. Porter and Harald Henrysson appeared in Indianapolis, USA. The circumstances surrounding this publication were complicated, notable and in part unpleasant; indeed, the work can best be described as a "non-authorized" edition. In letters-to-the-editor in three international record magazines Henrysson criticized Porter's departures from the agreements previously reached between the two compilers, and *Stereo Review* printed a retort by Porter. In publishing a revised and enlarged version of the originally intended edition, the Music in Sweden Committee wishes therefore to present its assessment of the situation.

At an early stage in the authors' work on the phonography Porter stipulated, as condition for his continued participation, that he be named co-author on the publication's title page. However, the agreement on this point between the two parties cannot be taken as justification for the publication in the United States of the abovenamed "non-exclusive" edition (Porter's designation), which Porter put out entirely without our or Henrysson's knowledge. No other publisher than the Music in Sweden Committee/Swedish Music History Archive had ever been in question. In fact, publication occurred during our contract negotiations with Porter, negotiations which at that point were broken off. Porter's edition reverses the previously settled order of authors' names on the title page and changes the wording of the title itself. In an entirely new preface Porter presents his own somewhat vague and in no way binding account of the authors' relative share in the work. No economic arrangement has been made nor any compensation been paid either to Henrysson or the Committee.

Thus the Music in Sweden Committee feels free to publish the present version of the phonography, prepared by Harald Henrysson alone. In his own foreword Henrysson explains the relationship between the current work and the American edition of 1982 as well as the extent of Porter's contribution.

The order of authors' names on the title page and the title of the work (apart from the supplementary subtitle) are now in accordance with what the two compilers themselves had settled upon earlier; in the opinion of the Committee they present a more accurate picture of the actual state of affairs. Henrysson is the principal author of the work. He has, apart from minor exceptions which he describes himself, compiled the manuscript. He has also, while giving consideration to Porter's views, worked out the system for the disposition of the information and attempted to improve current methods for registering recordings.

As regards copyright, Henrysson's and Porter's mutual copyright remains in force for those portions of the contents which are common to the American edition of 1982. For the revised and newly written sections the Music in Sweden Committee/Swedish Music History Archive hold joint copyright.

Special thanks are due the Swedish Research Council for the Humanities and Social Sciences for a grant for printing the work and for sympathy with the circumstances which significantly delayed publication. Preparation of the manuscript for copy has been made possible through a generous grant from the Längmanska kulturfonden.

The Music in Sweden Committee

Foreword by Harald Henrysson

For the initial impulse for this work, going back to 1972, I am much indebted to the late Eyvind Skandrup Lund, one of the two persons behind "Jussi Björling: A Record List" (1969). In 1973, when it became clear that no second edition of the Danish work would appear, I began to prepare a new publication and received Skandrup Lund's supplementary material. Since J.W. Porter in Indiana, USA, had informed Skandrup Lund about his interest in these matters, I contacted Porter who offered his assistance in my work. In 1975, when I had found a publisher in the Swedish Music History Archive, Porter asked to be regarded as co-author of the work, if he were to continue his assistance. I did not reject this proposal; the cooperation of an interested American seemed natural to me.

Not until 1981 did financial support for the publication become available. During the intervening years, I had collected information from many sources. Porter was the most important one as regards American recordings and issues, and his access to American collections (including the large one brought together by himself) as well as his contacts helped to make the manuscript more complete and accurate on many points. I discussed several problems with him in correspondence, and he received my manuscript at different stages for comments, corrections and additions. At the beginning of 1982, I sent Porter my final typewritten draft for checking. A few months later, I learnt that it had not only been published by him behind my back as "A Jussi Bjoerling Discography", but that he had also reversed the names of the authors and written a new foreword. The intentions behind these manipulations are evident and made further cooperation between us impossible. The circumstances also makes it necessary for me to stress that since the beginning, I led the compilation of this work, and that I was mainly responsible both for the arrangement of the information in the lists (except the present Section II:C) and for the introduction and most of the commentary (except "Additions and Corrections"). Nonetheless, Porter's contribution was substantial. I did not question his presentation as co-author, and in the end, I had accepted all his demands concerning the planned publication which were in my power to influence (including the original wording of title page and foreword and the sharing of royalties). The pretext Porter has publicly given for his action (in the Stereo Review) that I would have "failed to comply with earlier understandings that we would be presented unequivocally as co-authors" is incomprehensible to me.

Under these circumstances, I am alone responsible for all additions and changes in the earlier manuscript. Some of them could not be included in Porter's edition because it was published without my knowledge; by far the largest part, however, is the result of my continued research during the past 2 1/2 years. Compared with the American edition, two introductory chapters ("A Chronological Table of JB's Life and Career" & "A Summary of JB's Recording Career and Repertoire") and two short tables (Section II:D,E) are wholly new, as are the illustrations and most of the much enlarged commentary. Nearly half of the recording reference numbers have had to be changed, due to additions and corrections and a slight change in the numbering system.

The term "phonography" was intended all along for the title of this work. Like corresponding words in other languages, "phonography" has previously been used for lists of sound recordings dealing to a large extent with unissued material. When listing all types of recordings - issued or not - with the same accuracy, I prefer this term to "discography" with its more restricted original associations.

I am greatly indebted to many persons and institutions for information and other help; under the most unusual circumstances described above, I would hardly have been able to produce a new edition acceptable to me without all the personal support I have received. The assistance from Anna-Lisa Björling-Barkman, Lars & Ann-Charlotte Björling - widow, son and daughter of the late tenor - has been very valuable. My cooperation with Porter was against their advice, and if that cooperation should have associated their names with his activities in the name of the so-called "Jussi Bjoerling Memorial Archive", I would like to stress that no member of the Björling family has any connection with this organization. - For the improvement of my English, I am especially grateful to Stig Sahlin and Ruth Hansell. Despite its size, the list of contributors below is incomplete, and I hope that no one will feel unjustly neglected. The list includes (1) persons and institutions with whom I myself have been in contact; (2) those reported by Porter in 1981 as having given him assistance; (3) persons whose additions and corrections to "A Jussi Bjoerling Discography" came indirectly to my knowledge.

Argentina:	Marcelo A. Montarcé; Horacio José Sanguinetti; Rudi B. Sazunic
Australia:	Laurie Gravino; Ken F. Lester; Joseph A. McDonough; David R. Morgan; Val Napthine (ABC); Bill Robertson (EMI); R.L. Wills (RCA)
Austria:	Hildegard Frank (EMI Columbia); Herbert Kotrnoch; Österreichische Nationalbibliothek; Franz Pfrogner (ORF)
Belgium:	F.A. Willems
Brazil:	I. Barroso (EMI-Odeon); Edgar de Brito Chavez, Jr.
Canada:	Charles Hooey; Ruby Mercer; Bernard B. Power; Patrick Tee; Harry Woo
Chile:	Juan Dzazópoulos
Denmark:	Hans Hansen; Knud Hegermann-Lindencrone; Alfred E. Olsen; Herbert Rosenberg; Eyvind Skandrup Lund; Tivoli, Musikafdelingen
Finland:	Pekka Gronow; Lars-O. Landén (Yleisradio)
France:	Phonothèque Nationale
Germany (East):	Deutsche Schallplatten
Germany (West):	Dietmar Achenbach; Peter Aistleitner; Adolf Brune, Uwe Carstens; Bernd Holzförster; J. Landgraf (EMI Electrola); RIAS-Berlin; Teldec Schallplatten; Hugo Thielen
Great Britain:	Norman Brown; George F. Burr; Joseph Colley; Leonard D. Court; James H. Crawley; Bryan Crimp; Stephen J. Crowley; John Culshaw; Ruth Edge (EMI Music Archives); J.D. Gilbert; Syd Gray; Christopher Griffiths; R. Holder; Robert

Howarth; John L. Jones; Alan Kelly; Michael Letchford (Decca); Colin A. Pryke; Christopher Raeburn (Decca); John Thompson; Michael D. Varcoe-Cocks; John Watson (EMI); Victor R. Watts; H. Wilkinson; Cliff Williams; Eric Wimbles

Italy: Ezio Reali; Alessandro Sciocchetti; Benito Vassura (RCA)

Japan: Christopher N. Nozawa; K. Uji (Toshiba-EMI)

Netherlands: Jan Broere; Ali Groenhuizen; H.A. van den Klinkenberg (EMI-Bovema); Klaas Morcus; Anthony G.H. Wanders

New Zealand: Bruce Anderson (EMI); Gordon K. Canning; R.A. McFarlane (WRC)

Norway: Frode Skulstad (EMI Norsk)

South Africa: H. Friedman (Teal); Dorothea Jackson (EMI Music); J. Nofal (EMI Record & Tape Centres); Denys Schorn; Ivan Schwartz

Spain: Arturo González Guerra (Radio Nacional)

Sweden: Bertil Allander (Sveriges Television); Bibliotekshögskolan; Anna-Lisa Björling-Barkman; Ann-Charlotte Björling; Lars Björling; Bertil Bokstedt; Carl L. Bruun; Karin Byström (Sveriges Radio); Harry Ebert; John Erik Eleby; Mats Elfström; EMI Svenska AB (Staffan Carlweitz, Anne-Mor Noring, Ture Söllsnes & Gun-Britt Winnert); Björn Englund (ALB); Tommy Eriksson; Lars-Göran Frisk; Ove Hahn (Gröna Lunds Tivoli); Frank Hedman; Gunilla Henrysdotter; Meg Henrysson; Sune Hofsten (Stockholms Konserthusstiftelse); Kungl. Teatern (Bertil Hagman, Veronika Holmberg & Klas Ralf); Karleric Liliedahl; Birgit Nilsson; Kjell Nilsson; Arne Ohlin (Sveriges Television); Nils-Göran Olve; Stig Sahlin; Sven Scheme; Barbro Skarin (SF-arkivet); Olle Söderholm; Stiftelsen Jussi Björling-gården; Sveriges Riksradio (many members of the staff, incl. Bengt Brännland, Claes M. Cnattingius, Carl G. Friedner, Ruth Hansell, Lars Hemmingsson, Lars Bampe Karlsson & Dagmar Söderbäck)

Switzerland: Fritz Schärer

Uruguay: Rossanna Gioscia (Palacio de la Música R. & R. Gioscia)

USA: Kevin P. Barry, Sr.; Jack Belsom; The Chicago Tribune; J.A. Christensen; William Collins; John J. Corbett; Fernando A. Córdova; Stanley A. Cory; Philip C. Curtis, Jr.; Richard W. Douglass; Thomas Fitzpatrick; Richard V. Flynn; George G. Fowler; Harry F. Heun; Idabelle Firestone Audio Library; Indiana University Music School Library; The Indianapolis Star; Edmund Juszczyk; Clifford B. Kincaid; John Kunish; Henry F. Kurtz; Warren Lawrence; William W. Lemonds; Lyric Opera of Chicago; Donald A. McCormack; G. Mauerhoff; Paul Messal; The Metropolitan Opera Guild; Richard Mohr; W.R. Moran; Anthony & Donna Jean Morawski; Museum of Broadcasting; Michael Nevin; Newberry Library; Robert Parylak; Thomas E. Patronite; James R. Peters; John F. Pfeiffer (RCA Records); Leonard Phillips; Herbert J. & Paula Gerard Renison; Marty Robinson; Kenneth Rocek; Andre G. Ross; Walter Rudolph; Fred C.

Schang; Frederick Schauwecker; Rupert P. Seemungal; David Shahin; Dan Shea; Martin A. Silver; Edward J. Smith; Nancy M. Sorensen; William F. Stineman; Stephen M. Stroff; Kendall Svengalis; William Violi; Thomas C. Willis; Hans H. Wurm.

August, 1984
Harald Henrysson

Symbols and Abbreviations

>	refers (in Section 2) to an earlier (or parallel) issue with identical contents, under which number the included JB recording(s) are specified
=	separates (in Section 1) issues with identical contents on different labels; indicates (in Section 2) that the issue also has a parallel number, under which details are found; separates (in Section 2) parallel sleeve titles in different languages
*	symbol for stereo recording or, in brackets, for electronically reprocessed mono recording (see p. 71 for further explanation)
^{1}	indicates the first (mono) issue in a group of issues with identical contents (for example, "*HMV* (GB) ^{1}RLS 715")
8T	8-track stereo cartridge
a.	ante (before); indicates that a record was issued before, or at the latest in, a certain year (& month)
A	Austria
Ace Diam.	Ace of Diamonds
ALB	Arkivet för ljud och bild [Swedish National Archive of Recorded Sound and Moving Images], Stockholm
Ar	Argentina
ATRA	The Arturo Toscanini Recordings Association
ATS	The Arturo Toscanini Society
Au	Australia
AV	audiovisual (used for film and video recordings)
bar.	baritone
beg.	beginning
bn	bassoon
Br	Brazil
c.	circa
Ca	Canada
Cap.	Capitol
CBS	Columbia Broadcasting System
cel	celesta
CFP	Classics for Pleasure
Ch	Chile
cl	clarinet
Col.	Columbia
coll.	collection
cond.	conductor
cont.	contralto
D.	Deutsch (numbers of Schubert's works)
Dan	Danish
db	double bass

Dk	Denmark
Elec.	Electrola
EMI	Electric & Musical Industries, Ltd.
Eng	English
eng hn	english horn
Excel.	Excellent
Fi	Finland
Firestone Libr.	Idabelle Firestone Audio Library, New England Conservatory of Music, Boston
fl	flute
Fr	France, French
G	(West) Germany (also used for Teldec issues outside Germany)
Golden Age	The Golden Age of Opera
Hist.Op.Perf.	Historical Opera Performances Edition
HMV	His Master's Voice (& translations of the label)
hn	horn
ips.	inches per second
Ir	Ireland (Eire)
It	Italy, Italian
J	Japan
JB	Jussi Björling
JBD	A Jussi Bjoerling Discography (1982)
JBRL	Jussi Björling: A Record List (1969)
Magn.Ed.	Magnificent Editions
MC	[music] cassette tape
Met	The Metropolitan Opera, New York
MFP	Music for Pleasure
m.-sop.	mezzo-soprano
NBC	National Broadcasting Company
NL	The Netherlands
Nor	Norway, Norwegian
N.Y.	New York
NZ	New Zealand
ob	oboe
Op.Arch.	Operatic Archives
orch.	orchestra
p.	page
	post (indicates that a record was issued after a certain year (& month)
perc	percussion
perf.	performance
pf	piano
Pl.Mus.	Plaisir Musical
pseud.	pseudonym
R.	Royal
RCA	Radio Corporation of America
Read.Dig.	Reader's Digest
Rich.	Richmond
rpm.	revolutions per minute

s.	side
SA	South Africa
sax	saxophone
Sel.Read.Dig.	Selezione dal Reader's Digest
Sera.	Seraphim
S.F.	San Francisco
sop.	soprano
Sp	Spain
Sto.	Stockholm
Sv.Favoriter	Svenska Favoriter
Sw	Sweden, Swedish
Sw.Radio	Swedish Broadcasting Corp.
Sw.Society	Swedish Society (Discofil)
ten.	tenor
timp	timpani
tpt	trumpet
Tr	transcription (discs)
trbn	trombone
Unique	Unique Opera Records
Ur	Uruguay
US(A)	United States
v.	version
va	viola
vc	cello
VC	video cassette tape
Vic.	Victor
vn	violin
Vocal Rec.Coll.	Vocal Record Collectors' Society
Voix Ill.	Voix Illustres
Westm.	Westminster
WRC	World Record Club

A Chronological Table of Jussi Björling's Life and Career

This table gives all JB recording dates (in the phonography itself arranged in two separate chronological lists) together with other dates from his career in one sequence. JB did not keep any appointment-book, and the information in this table has been gathered from many sources, including the five JB biographies in Swedish, collections of press cuttings (the most important of which are found at Jussi Björling-gården, Borlänge, and at the Music Museum, Stockholm), correspondence with opera and concert institutions and private individuals and discussions with Mrs. Anna-Lisa Björling-Barkman. Stockholm Royal Opera performances have been checked in the Opera Archives. Valuable information about performances at certain other opera houses has been received especially from Mr. Tommy Eriksson. While the list of opera performances is complete (though some performances such as with local US companies may be missing), many Swedish recitals, especially outside the larger cities, are missing, and the information about US recital tours is only fragmentary. Researching JB's career has been rendered especially difficult by the fact that he many times cancelled solo appearances and operatic engagements. Whenever possible, it has been my ambition to verify that scheduled performances actually took place. Printed programmes exist of some scheduled appearances which never took place (one such example is a *Don Giovanni* performance in 1948 in Los Angeles). Performances followed by "(?)" are regarded as uncertain. I will be grateful to receive corrections and information, especially from the US, which may contribute to the knowledge of JB's career.

The contents of the table may be described as follows: (l) Introductory presentation of family and background. - (2) Brief references (numbers in bold) to all recordings listed in Section 1 of the phonography, and to performances listed in the Appendix to Section 1:B. - (3) Information about all known opera performances. For every month, the operas performed, the respective cities (opera houses), the dates for the first and last performance in a city during the month, and the number of performances are shown. When an opera is performed for the first time, it is treated separately. For example, the table shows for October 1931 that JB, in Stockholm, (a) between the 3rd and the 28th gave four performances of three operas already in his repertoire; (b) on the 16th performed *La notte di Zoraima* for the first time and then gave two more performances of it up to and including the 24th. Notes on JB's first opera performances together with certain famous singers are also given in the text. For a survey of all JB's operatic roles with indication of how many times he sang them at various opera houses, see the separate list of Opera, Operetta and Oratorio Repertoire (pp. 53). - (4) A comprehensive selection of dates and places for concerts and recitals ("concert" stands for orchestral accompaniment, "recital" for piano or unknown accompaniment). - (5) Some other important dates of biographical interest.

Country is not given for Swedish or American cities. For other cities, the country is indicated in brackets the first time they appear on the list. Premises for concerts and recitals are as a rule indicated only for cities where JB appeared more frequently.

Background

JB's great-grandfather, Lars Björn (1809-96), and his grandfather, Lars Johan Björn (1842-1909), were both blacksmiths in the central Swedish province of Hälsingland. The latter moved in 1861 to Finland. At the same time, he changed his surname to Björling, as one of his brothers had already done, thereby giving birth to one of the Swedish families with that name (the baritone Sigurd Björling came from another family). In 1864, Lars Johan Björling married a Finnish girl, Matilda Lönnqvist, and in 1866 he returned to Sweden, where he lived most of the time at Strömsbruk in the parish of Harmånger in Hälsingland. There David Björling, JB's father, was born in 1873. In 1880, David moved back with his parents to Finland but came to Sweden again in 1893 to try his father's profession. He was later followed by his parents. In 1899 or 1900, David Björling crossed the Atlantic and spent some years in the US, working among other things as a toolmaker. In America, he was adviced to train his voice and studied at the Metropolitan Opera School. David returned to Sweden about 1905 but soon went on to Vienna, where he continued his music studies. Back in Sweden a couple of years later, David Björling settled at Borlänge, about 200 km. NW of Stockholm in the province of Dalarna. At that time, Borlänge was a small urban district which had grown up around an important railway junction and was surrounded by the rural district Stora Tuna; today, the municipality of Borlänge includes Stora Tuna, but the latter name is retained for the parish. In Dalarna, David Björling met the nine years younger modiste Ester Sund from the village of Norr Romme in Stora Tuna, who was known for her beauty and musicality. They married on July 19, 1909. Of their four musically gifted sons, JB was the second one.

Karl Johan Olof (Olle) Björling was born in 1909 and died in 1965. Handicapped by rachitis in his youth, he did not have any stage career but earned a solid reputation as a concert and oratorio singer. He was also first tenor of the popular Björlingkvartetten [The Björling Quartet] which was founded in 1934. The third boy, Karl Gustaf (*Gösta*), born in 1912, had like JB an operatic career. Gösta sang at the Royal Opera in Stockholm between 1940 and 1957, when he suddenly died. He was especially successful in character and buffo parts. Gösta Björling was married the second time to the American alto Bette Wermine. Karl, the youngest of the Björling children, was born in 1917. His mother died from tuberculosis shortly after his birth, and he was taken care of by an aunt during his younger years. Unlike his father and brothers, Karl was a baritone, active as a concert singer beside his civil occupation as an electrician. When he died in 1975, not more than 57 years old, he had still lived longer than any of his brothers or his parents.

David Björling was still active as an opera singer when his children were small (e.g., he sang in *La bohème, La fille du régiment* and *Cavalleria rusticana* with the Eklöf-Trobäck Company in 1912), but his expected debut at the Royal Opera never took place. He soon limited himself to giving concerts and to the task of a singing teacher. He trained the voices of his boys from early childhood according to theories which he had learnt and developed.

1911
February
5 Borlänge: JB born at 10 p.m. in a wooden house in Magasinsgatan. Probably David B. was on tour, as his wife preferred to stay with relatives in Borlänge when the child was expected. At that time, the family's own home was situated at Norr Romme, Stora Tuna, but soon - in 1912 - they would move to the house where JB had been born (this building no longer exists, but timber from it was used for the museum "Jussi Björlinggården" in Borlänge). The date and place for JB's birth are noted in the midwife's appointment-book, consulted only after his death. JB himself regarded February 2 as his birthday. This date is noted in the parish register, but it was evidently not inserted there until about half a year after his birth.

March
18 Stora Tuna Church: Christened Johan Jonatan [JB was named after an uncle, living in Borlänge. The name Jussi (originally sometimes written "Josse") is actually Finnish; it was introduced by JB's Finnish grandmother.]

1915
December
12 Örebro, Trefaldighetskyrkan [Trinity Church]: First public performance by JB and his brothers Olle & Gösta (as a trio, they sang "Sjung om studentens lyckliga dag", accompanied by their mother). The family lived from 1914 to 1919 alternatingly in Örebro and in Dalarna.

1917
April
26 Uppsala, Academic Hospital: Ester Björling dies on her 35th birthday, a few weeks after Karl's birth. A few days later, the boys sing at their mother's funeral at Stora Tuna Church.

1919
October
28 New York: David Björling and his three eldest sons (sometimes called "The Bjoerling Male Quartet") arrive for a recital tour in the US. The family would travel from coast to coast, singing mainly in churches in areas with a large Swedish population, the boys being dressed in Dalecarlian folk costumes. [For further details regarding the first part of the tour, see note for Nos. 1-6 in Section 1:A.]

November
20 New York, Gustavus Adolphus Church: First recital in America

1920
February?
New York: Recordings (= **1-6**)

1921
April
21 New York: David Björling and his sons depart for Sweden
May or **June**?
Leksand: The Björling family settles in this town in Dalarna for the next few years

1922
May - August
Tour in northern Sweden
September - December
Tour in central and southern Sweden begins

1923
January - April
Tour in central and southern Sweden continues

1924
July
6 Leksand: The Björling boys sing before the King and Queen outside the church

1926
January
3 Ystad: Recital. Intensive tour in southern Sweden begins, with the headquarters in this town.
April?
Ystad: David B. falls ill with a stomach ailment, but soon continues to lead touring activities from his sickbed
August
9 Västervik: Björling family arrives for convalescence of David B. and for continued touring activities
11 Västervik, Folkets Park: Recital
13 Västervik Hospital: David B. dies from an incorrectly treated appendicitis
17 Stora Tuna Church: David B. buried
Mora: The Björling boys go to stay with a friend of their father, Rolf Lundgren
September
21,26 Mora: Recitals
December
25 Mora Church: Farewell recital by the Björling trio before they try, with little success, to resume touring activities

1927
October
4 Mora: The Björling brothers and Rolf Lundgren leave, hoping to go on to the US. This second US recital tour stopped by US Consulate General in Gothenburg (necessary guarantees lacking); the ensemble dissolves.
October or November
Ystad: JB returns to this town, where he had probably also lived early in 1927. For a period, he has a job as a clerk at a household store.

November

Ystad: Private performance before members of the Royal Orch. paying an occasional visit. Assistance from Salomon Smith (a pharmacist and amateur musician who held an important position in the musical life of southern Sweden), who asks the general manager of the Royal Opera in Stockholm, the baritone John Forsell, to give JB an audition.

1928

January?

Sto., R. Opera: received by J. Forsell, who promises an audition later on. JB in the meantime earns his living from car washing and occasional performances in private societies.

February

8 Borlänge: Concert (?)

March

9 Sto.: First radio appearance (= **A01**)

April?

Sto.: Audition before Martin Öhman (Swedish tenor, at this time active in Berlin but in Stockholm for guest performances). Öhman tells Forsell he has listened to "the best Swedish tenor voice of the century".

July

Sto.: Radio appearance (= **A02**)

August

21,28 Sto., R. Opera: Auditions before J. Forsell. These were JB's 2nd and 3rd auditions before Forsell (the latter one was for entrance to the R. Opera School). The first audition was not dated by Forsell, who wrote in his diary after the second one: "Remarkably good, a phenomenon, 17 years". At one of the auditions, JB was accompanied by the conductor Tullio Voghera, who had been Caruso's accompanist and would become an important teacher for JB. After the entrance examination at the Conservatory, JB was accepted for the only vacant position in Forsell's solo song class. He was soon allotted a scholarship of Kronor 320 a month "besides some money for dress" and in 1929 for a period boarded with the Svedelius family (Carl Svedelius was headmaster of a well-known grammar school, his wife Julia known as an author). Forsell personally accepted to be JB's guardian.

December

25 (Jönköping): Rolf, JB's son with Linnea Hellström (1907-53), born [JB had stayed with the Hellström family before he moved to the Svedelius family. Rolf B. has been active as an opera, operetta and concert singer in Sweden and abroad.]

1929

September

4 Sto.: Recordings, cond. H. Meissner (= **7-8**). First JB recordings as a tenor.

October

4 Sto.: First recording contract signed

5,19 Sto., R. Academy of Music: Concerts by conservatory students

November

2,23 Sto., R. Academy of Music: Concerts by conservatory students

December

12,13 Sto., R. Academy of Music: Concerts by conservatory students

18 Sto.: Recordings, cond. Grevillius (= **9-12**)

1930

February

8,22 Sto., R. Academy of Music: Concerts by conservatory students

March

8,22 Sto., R. Academy of Music: Concerts by conservatory students

April

First *HMV* record issued, X 3377

3 Sto., Radio concert (= **A03**)

12 Sto., R. Academy of Music: *Requiem* (Mozart), in concert by conservatory students

29 Sto., Concert Hall: *Te Deum* (Bruckner), cond. V. Talich

May

11 Sto., Hasselbacken Restaurant: Appearance at Konstnärsringen [Artists' Circle] spring banquet (described in a newspaper as "Jussy Berglund's" first solo appearance before a larger audience)

12 Sto.: Recordings, cond. N. Grevillius (= **13-14**)

July

21 Sto., R. Opera: *Manon Lescaut* (Puccini), first perf., in role of The Lamplighter. At JB's very first opera perf., Des Grieux's role, in which he would only appear in 1949, was sung by E. Beyron; N. Grevillius was the conductor.

25 Sto., R. Opera: *Bellman* (Ziedner), only perf., in role of Näktergal

August

11 Sto., R. Opera: *Manon Lescaut*

20 Sto., R. Opera: *Don Giovanni* (Mozart), first perf., in role of Don Ottavio. This was JB's official debut in a major role; it took place at a special perf. for a congress of pediatricians. Don Giovanni was sung by J. Forsell, Leporello by J. Berglund; A. Järnefelt was the conductor.

September

25 Sto., R. Opera: *Don Giovanni*

29 Sto.: Recordings, cond. N. Grevillius (= **15-19**). Include JB's first opera recordings.

October

8 Sto.: Recordings, cond. N. Grevillius (= **20-22**)

18 Sto., R. Academy of Music: Concert by conservatory students

27 Sto., R. Opera: First opera contract signed

November

1 Sto., R. Academy of Music: Concert by conservatory students

29 Sto., R. Opera: *Louise* (Charpentier), first perf., in role of A Song-writer

December

1-26 Sto., R. Opera: *Louise* (5)

6 Sto., Storkyrkan Cathedral: *Messiah* (Handel), first perf. (with R. Opera ensemble)

12 Sto., R. Academy of Music: Concert by conservatory students

25 Sto.: Radio concert (*Messiah*, part 1 = **A04**)

27,30 Sto., R. Opera: *Guillaume Tell* (Rossini), first perf. (+1), in role of Arnold. This was JB's second official debut role. The successful first perf. brought about JB's probably first newspaper interview.

1931

January

4-27 Sto., R. Opera: *Louise* (1), *Guillaume Tell* (2), *Don Giovanni* (1)

13-18 Sto., R. Opera: *Saul og David* (Nielsen), first perf. (+2), in role of Jonathan. This was JB's third and last official debut role.

February

11 Sto.: Recordings, cond. N. Grevillius (= **23-25**)

13 Sto.: Recordings, cond. H. Bingang (= **26-28**)

20-27 Sto., R. Opera: *Guillaume Tell* (3), *Saul og David* (3)

March

2-20 Sto., R. Opera: *Guillaume Tell* (1), *Saul og David* (2)

14 Sto., Academy of Music: Concert by conservatory students

21,25 Sto., R. Opera: *Engelbrekt* (N. Berg), first perf. (+1), in role of Bishop Sigge

April

5 Sto., R. Opera: *Missa Solemnis* (Beethoven), first perf.

18,25 Sto., R. Academy of Music: Concerts by conservatory students (incl. *Mignon*, act 3)

19,24 Sto., R. Opera: *I cavalieri di Ekebù* (Zandonai), first perf. (+1), in role of Ruster. JB's first perf. of this opera was also his first appearance with K. Thorborg.

29 Sto., R. Opera: *Guillaume Tell*

May

6-9 Helsinki (Finland), Finnish Opera: *Don Giovanni* (2), *Engelbrekt* (1), *Cavalieri di Ekebù* (1 = **A05**) on tour with Stockholm R. Opera. The first *Don Giovanni* was JB's first opera perf. outside Sweden; *Cavalieri* his first broadcast of a live perf.

19 Sto., R. Opera: First permanent contract signed. This contract guaranteed the singer Kronor 500 a month with successive increases but was later revised and improved.

July

22 Gothenburg, Liseberg: Recital

29 Copenhagen (Denmark), Tivoli: Recital. JB was engaged for his first recital outside Sweden on the basis of a recording. His successful debut lead to further engagements in Copenhagen in the following summers.

August

8,17 Sto., R. Opera: *Tannhäuser* (Wagner), first perf. (+1), in role of Walther

14 Sto., R. Opera: *Cavalieri di Ekebù*

30 Sto., R. Opera: *Roméo et Juliette* (Gounod), first perf., in role of Tybalt

September

1-22 Sto., R. Opera: *Tannhäuser* (2), *Manon Lescaut* (2), *Louise* (1), *Saul og David* (2, incl. **A06**)

18,19 Sto.: Recordings, cond. N. Grevillius & F. Winter (= **29-31**)

29 Sto., R. Opera: *Der fliegende Holländer* (Wagner), first perf., in role of Erik

October

3-28 Sto., R. Opera: *Tannhäuser* (2), *Roméo et Juliette* (1 = **A07**), *Manon Lescaut* (1)

16-24 Sto., R. Opera: *La notte di Zoraima* (Montemezzi), first perf. (+2), in role of A Voice in the Night

November

2-22 Sto., R. Opera: *Notte di Zoraima* (1), *Saul og David* (1), *Der fliegende Holländer* (1), *Guillaume Tell* (1)

7-27 Sto., R. Opera: *Il barbiere di Siviglia* (Rossini), first perf. (+4), in role of Count Almaviva. In this opera, JB appeared for the first time on the opera stage together with S. Svanholm (then a baritone).

December

2 Sto., R. Opera: *Barbiere di Siviglia*

5 Sto., Storkyrkan Cathedral: *Messiah*

29 Sto., R. Opera: *Salome* (R. Strauss), first perf., in role of Narraboth

1932

January

3-24 Sto., R. Opera: *Guillaume Tell* (1), *Salome* (2), *Tannhäuser* (2), *Notte di Zoraima* (1)

7-13 Sto.: Recordings, cond. N. Grevillius (= **32-35,37,38**)

12,14 Sto.: Recordings (first ones as "Erik Odde"), cond. F. Winter (= **36,39**)

16-30 Sto., R. Opera: *L'illustre Fregona* (Laparra), first perf. (+3), in role of Tomas

February

1-28 Sto., R. Opera: *Roméo et Juliette* (1), *Barbiere di Siviglia* (3), *Illustre Fregona* (2)

15,17 Sto., R. Opera: *Tristan und Isolde* (Wagner), first perf. (+1), in role of A Sailor

25,29 Sto., R. Opera: *Rigoletto* (Verdi), first perf. (+1 = **A08**), in role of The Duke of Mantua. This was the first of JB's opera roles which would remain in his repertoire after his permanent contract with the R. Opera expired in 1939.

March

2-30 Sto., R. Opera: *Illustre Fregona* (1), *Saul og David* (3), *Barbiere di Siviglia* (1), *Manon Lescaut* (1), *Rigoletto* (2), *Missa Solemnis* (1)

April

3-16 Sto., R. Opera: *Tannhäuser* (2), *Illustre Fregona* (1)

14-25 Sto., R. Opera: *Das Herz* (Pfitzner), first perf. (+2), in role of A Young Cavalier

May

6 Sto., R. Opera: *Illustre Fregona*

June

8-16 Copenhagen, Tivoli: Recitals (4)

July

6 Gothenburg, Liseberg: Recital

August

8,10 Sto.: Recordings (partly as "Erik Odde"), cond. H. Bingang (= **40-44**)

9,12 Sto., R. Opera: *Tannhäuser* (1 = **A09**), *Barbiere di Siviglia* (1)

September

3-28	Sto., R. Opera: *Barbiere di Siviglia* (2), *Salome* (1), *Tannhäuser* (1)
6,10	Copenhagen, Tivoli: Recitals
9?	Copenhagen: Recordings, cond. J. Warny (= **45-46**). First recordings outside Sweden as a tenor.
?	Sto.: Recording (as "Erik Odde"), cond. H. v. Eichwald (= **47**)

October

2-5	Sto., R. Opera: *Illustre Fregona* (1 incomplete + 1 complete perf.), *Salome* (1)
8,16	Sto., R. Opera: *Mignon* (Thomas), first perf. (+1), in role of Wilhelm Meister

November

2-27	Sto., R. Opera: *Mignon* (2, incl. **A10**), *Illustre Fregona* (1)
9,16	Sto., R. Opera: *L'elisir d'amore* (Donizetti), first perf. (+1), in role of Nemorino
24	Sto.: Recording (as "Erik Odde"), cond. H. Bingang (= **48**)
24,28	Sto., R. Opera: *Resa till Amerika* [*Journey to America*](Rosenberg), first perf. (+1), in role of The Bargeman
26	Sto., Royal Palace: Joint recital with J. Forsell and others

December

1-27	Sto., R. Opera: *Resa till Amerika* (2), *Rigoletto* (2, incl. **A11**)
3	Sto., Storkyrkan Cathedral: *Messiah*

1933

January

5-30	Sto., R. Opera: *La traviata* (Verdi), first perf. (+2), in role of Alfredo
14,21	Sto., R. Opera: *Evgeny Onegin* (Tchaikovsky), first perf. (+1), in role of Lensky
17	Sto., R. Opera: *Das Rheingold* (Wagner), only perf., in role of Froh

February

1-19	Sto., R. Opera: *Resa till Amerika* (1), *Elisir d'amore* (4), *Traviata* (1), *Onegin* (2), *Tristan* (1)
2?	Sto.: Recording (as "Erik Odde"), cond. F. Andersson (= **49**)

March

11-30	Sto., R. Opera: *Knyaz Igor* [*Prince Igor*] (Borodin), first perf. (+6, incl. **A12**), in role of Vladimir
12,26	Sto., R. Opera: *Barbiere*, *Missa Solemnis*
?	Sto.: Recordings, cond. N. Grevillius (= **50-53**)

April

5-27	Sto., R. Opera: *Knyaz Igor* (4), *Barbiere* (1), *Der fliegende Holländer* (2), *Traviata* (1)
6	Sto., R. Opera: *Kronbruden* [*The Crown Bride*] (Rangström), first perf., in role of Mats
11?	Sto.: Recordings, cond. N. Grevillius (= **54-56**)

May

5,6	Copenhagen, R. Theatre: *Knyaz Igor*, *Don Giovanni* (= **A13**) on tour with Stockholm R. Opera
8	Kristianstad: *Barbiere* on tour with R. Opera
10	Copenhagen, Tivoli: Concert by Stockholm R. Opera
16,26	Sto., R. Opera: *Knyaz Igor* (2)

June

1? Sto.: Recordings, cond. H. Meissner (= **57-59**)

July

12-21 Copenhagen, Tivoli: Recitals (4)

August

3-30 Sto., R. Opera: *Knyaz Igor* (3), *Cavalieri di Ekebù* (2, incl. **A14**), *Barbiere* (1)

10? Sto.: Recordings (as "Erik Odde"), cond. G. Säfbom (= **60-62**)

22,27 Sto., R. Opera: *Roméo et Juliette* (Gounod), first perf. (+1) in role of Roméo

September

6-14 Sto., R. Opera: *Djamileh* (Bizet), first perf. (+2, incl. **A15**), in role of Haroun

7-27 Sto., R. Opera: *Knyaz Igor* (1), *Roméo et Juliette* (1), *Cavalieri di Ekebù* (1)

10 Sto., Skansen: Recital (Barnens dag)

13 Sto.: Recordings, cond. N. Grevillius (= **63-64**)

30 Sto., R. Opera: *Martha* (Flotow), first perf., in role of Lyonel

October

1-30 Sto., R. Opera: *Djamileh* (2), *Martha* (2), *Knyaz Igor* (1), *Barbiere* (1), *Illustre Fregona* (1), *Roméo et Juliette* (1)

10 Sto.: Recordings, cond. N. Grevillius & S. Waldimir (= **65-68**). Include last "Erik Odde" recordings.

19,27 Sto., R. Opera: *Tosca* (Puccini), first perf. (+1), in role of Cavaradossi. This was JB's first main Puccini role.

25 Sto.: Recordings, cond. S. Waldimir (= **69-70**)

November

6-29 Sto., R. Opera: *Don Giovanni* (1), *Roméo et Juliette* (1), *Mignon* (1), *Djamileh* (1), *Knyaz Igor* (1)

13 Sto.: Recordings, cond. N. Grevillius (= **71-72**) - the first in a series of opera recordings in Swedish

December

1-29 Sto., R. Opera: *Knyaz Igor* (3), *Cavalieri di Ekebù* (1)

15 Sto., R. Opera: *Die Zauberflöte* (Mozart), first perf., in role of Tamino

20 Sto.: Recordings, cond. N. Grevillius (= **73-74**)

30 Sto., R. Opera: *Arabella* (R. Strauss), first perf., in role of Elemer

1934

January

2-18 Sto., R. Opera: *Arabella* (4. incl. **A16**), *Zauberflöte* (1), *Knyaz Igor* (1)

27,29 Sto., R. Opera: *Fanal* (Atterberg), first perf. (+1 = **3401**), in role of Martin Skarp

February

1-26 Sto., R. Opera: *Fanal* (4), *Arabella* (1?)

March

2-28 Sto., R. Opera: *Fanal* (4), *Knyaz Igor* (1)

3 Sto.: Recordings, cond. N. Grevillius (= **75-76**)

13 Gävle: *Barbiere di Siviglia* on tour with R. Opera

22 Sto.: Verdi radio concert with R. Opera soloists (= **A17**)

April

3-8 Sto., R. Opera: *Fanal* (1), *Kronbruden* (1), *Tosca* (1)
7 Sto., R. Opera: Concert by opera soloists, cond. N. Grevillius
18 Sto., R. Opera: *Un ballo in maschera* (Verdi), first perf., in role of Riccardo

May

26,27 Oslo (Norway): *Don Giovanni* (= **A18**), *Fanal* on tour with R. Opera
31 Sto., R. Opera: *Fanal*

June

29 Copenhagen, Tivoli: Concert (excerpts from *Fanal*), cond. N. Grevillius

July

6 Malmö: Festival concert, cond. O. Morales (= **A19**)
11-21 Copenhagen, Tivoli: Recitals & concerts (5)

August

10,14 Sto., R. Opera: *Fanal* (1), *Knyaz Igor* (1)
19 Gothenburg, Slottsskogsvallen: Concert with local choir (= **A20**)
25,28 Sto., R. Opera: *Faust* (Gounod), first perf. (+1 = **A21**), in role of Faust
29,30 Sto., Gröna Lund: Recitals. These appearances were a result of the repeated successes in Copenhagen and would begin a long series of open-air summer recitals up to 1960.

September

3-28 Sto., R. Opera: *Faust* (6), *Fanal* (1), *Tosca* (1), *Barbiere* (1)
7 Sto., Drottningholm Palace Theatre: Soiree (= **A22**)
8 Copenhagen, Tivoli: Recital

October

1 Fagersta: *Barbiere* on tour with R. Opera
5-25 Sto., R. Opera: *Faust* (2), *Tosca* (1, opposite D. Giannini as guest), *Knyaz Igor* (1)
13-29 Sto., R. Opera: *La bohème* (Puccini), first perf. (+3), in role of Rodolfo
20,23 Sto., R. Opera: *Il tabarro* (Puccini), first perf. (+1), in role of Luigi

November

2-30 Sto., R. Opera: *Barbiere* (1), *Faust* (4), *Fanal* (1), *Kronbruden* (1 = **A23**)
17,20 Sto., R. Opera: *Sadko* (Rimsky-Korsakov), first perf. (+1), in role of A Hindu Merchant

December

1 Sto., Storkyrkan Cathedral: *Messiah*
2-26 Sto., R. Opera: *Sadko* (2), *Tabarro* (2, incl. **A24**)
5-8 Malmö, Ystad & Kristianstad: *Tosca* on tour with R. Opera (one perf. in each town)
15 Sto.: Engagement to Anna-Lisa Berg. [JB's future wife, daughter of a Royal Orch. musician, was a lyric soprano whom he had met at the Conservatory. She would travel with him on most of his tours and from 1947, they appeared together in concert and recital many times and a few times also in opera *(Bohème* in Stockholm & Helsinki; *Roméo et Juliette* in San Francisco). Mrs. Björling remains a resident of Stockholm to this day.]
15 Örebro: Recital
16 Sto., Sportpalatset: Water festival (with Anna-Lisa)
29 Sto., R. Opera: *La fanciulla del West* (Pucccini), first perf., in role of Dick Johnson

1935

January

1-28 Sto., R. Opera: *Fanciulla* (6), *Bohème* (2)

16 Gothenburg, Lorensberg: Recital

26 Sto., R. Opera: *Die Entführung aus dem Serail* (Mozart), first perf., in role of Belmonte

February

1-26 Sto., R. Opera: *Traviata* (2), *Faust* (2), *Sadko* (1), *Entführung* (2, incl. **A25**), *Knyaz Igor* (1)

14-22 Sto., R. Opera: *Cavalleria rusticana* (Mascagni), first perf. (+2), in role of Turiddu

18 Östersund: *Tosca* on tour with R. Opera

March

1-25 Sto., R. Opera: *Cavalleria* (1), *Barbiere* (1), *Fanciulla* (1 = **A26**), *Onegin* (3), *Fanal* (2), *Entführung* (1), *Missa Solemnis* (1)

4 Sto.: Recordings, cond. N. Grevillius (= **77-78**)

26,29 Sto., R. Opera: *Fidelio* (Beethoven), first perf. (+1), in role of Florestan

April

1-10 Sto., R. Opera: *Fidelio* (2), *Cavalleria* (2), *Tristan und Isolde* (1)

8-21 Central & southern Sweden: Recital tour with Einar Larson, baritone (incl. Falun, Västerås, Eskilstuna, Karlstad, Jönköping, Gothenburg, Helsingborg, Malmö)

May

1 Sto.: Recordings (for Royal Wedding), cond. S. Waldimir (= **79-80**)

16-19 Riga (Latvia), National Opera: *Don Giovanni* (1), *Cavalieri di Ekebù* (1), *Fanal* (1), on tour with Stockholm R. Opera

23 Sto., R. Opera: Gala perf. at Royal Wedding (*Roméo et Juliette*, act 2 = **A27**)

June

3 Sto., Oskar Church: Wedding of JB and Anna-Lisa Berg (followed by honeymoon in Italy)

19-26 Copenhagen, Tivoli: Recitals (4)

July

2 Brussels (Belgium), World Exhibition: Joint concert with other Swedish artists (= **A28**). JB's first appearance in Central Europe; it also brought him a Belgian order, his first decoration.

10,31 Sto., Gröna Lund: Recitals

August

6-30 Sto., R. Opera: *Faust* (2), *Sadko* (2), *Bohème* (3), *Cavalleria* (1 = **A29**), *Knyaz Igor* (1)

17,20 Sto., R. Opera: *Il trovatore* (Verdi), first perf. (+1), in role of Manrico

September

4-23 Sto., R. Opera: *Bohème* (1), *Fanal* (1), *Cavalleria* (1), *Rigoletto* (1)

15 Sto., Skansen: Recital. This was the first of JB's own open-air recitals here; they soon became an annual event like those at the Gröna Lund situated nearby.

17,18 Sto., R. Opera: *Die Fledermaus* (J. Strauss), first perf. (+1), in role of Alfred

October

2-31 Sto., R. Opera: *Fanal* (1), *Illustre Fregona* (1), *Barbiere* (1, with G. De Luca as guest)

12-27 Sto., R. Opera: *Aida* (Verdi), first perf. (+3), in role of Radamès
23 Växjö: *Tosca* on tour with R. Opera

November

1-29 Sto., R. Opera: *Illustre Fregona* (6), *Fledermaus* (2), *Faust* (1), *Bohème* (1), *Mignon* (1), *Knyaz Igor* (2, with F. Chaliapin as guest)
30 Sto., Storkyrkan Cathedral: *Messiah*

December

1-26 Sto., R. Opera: *Bohème* (1), *Faust* (1, with F. Chaliapin as guest), *Onegin* (1), *Fledermaus* (1)
13 Sto., Berns: Lucia festival
15-17 Malmö: *Mignon* on tour with R. Opera (3)

1936

January

2-6 Sto., R. Opera: *Cavalleria* (1), *Faust* (1 = **A30**), *Fledermaus* (1)
5 Sto., Concert Hall: Popular concert, cond. A. Wiklund
11,19 Sto., R. Opera: *Pagliacci* (Leoncavallo), first perf. (+1), in role of Canio
11 Sto., Fenix-Kronprinsen: Cabaret programme
26 Sto.: *Från Strauss till Lehár*, radio concert (= **A31**)

February

1-25 Sto., R. Opera: *La damnation de Faust* (Berlioz), first perf. (+7), in role of Faust
4 Sto.: Anders, first child with Anna-Lisa Björling, born [Anders B. at present lives in the US as head of the financial administration at Gustavus Adolphus College, St. Peter, Minn.]
9-27 Sto., R. Opera: *Illustre Fregona* (1), *Sadko* (3), *Cavalieri di Ekebù* (1)
15 Sto., Fenix-Kronprinsen: Cabaret programme
16 Sto.: *Från Strauss till Lehár*, repeat of radio concert (= **3601**)

March

2-9 Sto., R. Opera: *Cavalieri di Ekebù* (1), *Damnation de Faust* (1 = **A32**), *Trovatore* (1)
12,13 Vienna (Austria): Radio recital (= **A33**) & Concert Hall recital
17,19 Prague (Czechoslovakia), National Theatre: *Faust*, *Traviata*
23,25? Copenhagen & Århus (Denmark): Recitals
27,29 Sto., R. Opera: *Faust* (1), *Fledermaus* (1)

April

9-28 Sto., R. Opera: *Bohème* (1), *Missa Solemnis* (1), *Fledermaus* (1), *Sadko* (1), *Cavalleria/Pagliacci* (1), *Damnation de Faust* (1), *Zauberflöte* (1)
25 Sto.: New recording contract signed

May

8-16 Sto., R. Opera: *Pagliacci* (1), *Roméo et Juliette* (2, incl. **A34**)
20 Prague, National Theatre: *Aida*
23 Brno (Czechoslovakia), Provincial Theatre: *Bohème*
28 Vienna, State Opera: *Trovatore*. JB's opera debut in Vienna, also his first perf. with M. Németh and A. Svéd

June

1-7 Vienna, State Opera: *Bohème* (1), *Trovatore* (1), *Aida* (1 = **3602**)
12 Prague, National Theatre: *Trovatore*

July

23	Sto., Gröna Lund: Recital
29,31	Copenhagen, Tivoli: Recitals

August

7-29	Sto., R. Opera: *Bohème* (2), *Faust* (2), *Fledermaus* (1), *Roméo et Juliette* (1), *Pagliacci* (1), *Fanal* (1 = **A35**)

September

1-28	Sto., R. Opera: *Aida* (2), *Fledermaus* (1), *Cavalleria* (1), *Bohème* (1 = **A36**), *Trovatore* (1), *Traviata* (1)
5,11	Sto., R. Opera: *Madama Butterfly* (Puccini), first perf. (+1), in role of Pinkerton
26,30	Sto., R. Opera: *La fille du régiment* (Donizetti), first perf. (+1), in role of Tonio

October

2-31	Sto., R. Opera: *Traviata* (1), *Fille du régiment* (4), *Aida* (1), *Butterfly* (1)
7,8	Sto.: Recordings, cond. N. Grevillius (= **81-86**)
22,23	Norrköping: *Roméo et Juliette* on tour with R. Opera
28	Uppsala, University: Recital

November

1	Sto.: Radio concert, cond. A. Wiklund (= **A37**)
1-29	Sto., R. Opera: *Trovatore* (1 = **A38**), *Cavalleria/Pagliacci* (1), *Butterfly* (2), *Fille du régiment* (2)
26,30	Sto., R. Opera: *Rossini in Neapel* (Paumgartner), first perf. (+1), in role of Gioacchino

December

1,3	Sto.: Recordings, cond. N. Grevillius (= **87-90**). First recordings which were not in Swedish and which were intended for the international market.
2-30	Sto., R. Opera: *Rossini* (4), *Illustre Fregona* (1 = **A39**)
5	Sto., Storkyrkan Cathedral: *Messiah*
5	Sto., Fenix-Kronprinsen: Charity soiree
7,8	Malmö: *Zauberflöte* (2), on tour with R. Opera
15	Paris (France), Cité Universitaire: Gala concert (*Bohème*, act 1)

1937

January

2-31	Sto., R. Opera: *Illustre Fregona* (1), *Faust* (2, incl. **A40**), *Roméo et Juliette* (1), *Butterfly* (1), *Mignon* (1)
19,20	Sundsvall & Östersund: *Barbiere* on tour with R. Opera
26	Sto.: Recordings, cond. N. Grevillius (= **91-92**)

February

4	Nuremberg Opera (Germany): *Pagliacci*
6	Berlin (Germany), German Opera House: *Bohème*
8,10	Dresden (Germany), Saxony State Opera: *Bohème*, *Rigoletto*. In both operas, JB sang opposite M. Cebotari
14-25	Vienna, State Opera: *Bohème* (1), *Trovatore* (1), *Butterfly* (1), *Pagliacci* (1), *Fanciulla* (1). *Bohème* was first perf. opposite J. Novotna
27	Budapest, R. Opera: *Aida*

March

2	Vienna, Concert Hall: Recital
5-22	Vienna, State Opera: *Trovatore* (2), *Faust* (1 = **3701**), *Pagliacci* (1 = **3702**), *Ballo* (1), *Rigoletto* (1)
9	Budapest (Hungary): Recital
14	Prague, New German Theatre: *Aida*. First perf. opposite Z. Milanov.

April

1-17	Sto., R. Opera: *Faust* (1), *Roméo et Juliette* (1), *Butterfly* (1 = **A42**), *Aida* (1)
2	Sto., R. Opera: Broadcast to Britain (*Fanal*, act 2) (= **A41**)
8	Sto.: *Parad för millionen*, radio programme (= **3703**)
22	Sto.: Recordings, cond. N. Grevillius (= **93-94**)
28	Sto., Concert Hall: *Requiem* (Verdi), cond. F. Busch (= **A43**)

May

8,14	Gothenburg: *Bohème, Knyaz Igor* on tour with R. Opera
17-29	Sto., R. Opera: *Fille du régiment* (1), *Faust* (1), *Aida* (1), *Knyaz Igor* (1)

June

6	Sto., Skansen: Recital. The first of many appearances on Swedish Flag Day at Skansen or Stadion.
12,13	Paris, Champs-Élysées Theatre: Swedish concerts (with other soloists), cond. N. Grevillius

July

29	Sto., Gröna Lund: Recital

August

5-31	Sto., R. Opera: *Bohème* (2), *Butterfly* (1), *Pagliacci* (1), *Roméo et Juliette* (2), *Faust* (1), *Knyaz Igor* (2), *Cavalleria* (1)
14-29	Torö & Sto.: Production of motion picture *Fram för framgång* (= **3704**) begins

September

1-29	Sto. & Torö: Production of motion picture *Fram för framgång* (= **3704**) continues
3-5	Sto.: Recordings, cond. N. Grevillius (= **95-102**)
4	Sto.: Skanstulls nöjesfält: Recital
5	Sto., Gröna Lund: Concert in connection with *Fram för framgång* production
14-24	Sto., R. Opera: *Don Giovanni* (1, with E. Pinza as guest = **A44**), *Bohème* (1), *Rigoletto* (1, with L. Tibbett as guest)
30	Sto., R. Opera: *Mefistofele* (Boito), first perf., in role of Faust

October

1-18	Sto.: Production of motion picture *Fram för framgång* (= **3704**) continues
3	Sto.: Broadcast greeting before US tour (= **3705**)
3	Sto., R. Opera: *Mefistofele*
27	Uppsala, University: Recital

November

2-10	Sto.: Production of motion picture *Fram för framgång* (= **3704**) finished
11	Sto.: Recording for motion picture *John Ericsson* (= **3706**)
12	Copenhagen, Odd Fellow Palace: Recital
16	London (Great Britain), Queen's Hall: Recital. JB's first British appearance
28	New York, Carnegie Hall: General Motors radio concert (= **3707**). This was JB's American debut as a tenor.

December

1 Springfield: Recital. US tour begins (about 12 performances to follow)
5,19 New York, Carnegie Hall: General Motors radio concerts (= **3708,A45**)
8,15 Chicago, City Opera: *Rigoletto* (1), *Bohème* (1). *Rigoletto* was American opera debut (with L. Tibbett & Beverly Lane)
13 Chicago, Palmer House: recital
20 New York, Waldorf Astoria Hotel: Bagby Morning Concert (joint with L. Pons)
21 Contract with the Met for next season announced

1938

January

4 New York, Town Hall: Recital. JB's first solo recital in this city
16 Sto.: Radio interview after return from US tour (= **A46**)

February

2 Sto., R. Opera: JB gives notice about termination of contract, valid beginning with season 1939/40
4-28 Sto., R. Opera: *Bohème* (1), *Faust* (1), *Cavalleria/Pagliacci* (1), *Rigoletto* (2, incl. **A48**)
14 Uppsala, University: Recital
16 Malmö, Hippodrome Theatre: Recital
17 Copenhagen: Radio concert, cond. N. Malko (= **A47**)
25,26 Gävle: *Faust* on tour with R. Opera

March

2-28 Sto., R. Opera: *Aida* (2), *Roméo et Juliette* (4), *Tosca* (1), *Cavalleria/Pagliacci* (1)
16 Norrköping: *Faust* on tour with R. Opera
20 Sto.: Radio concert, cond. L.-E. Larsson (= **A49**)

April

4-30 Sto., R. Opera: *Der Zigeunerbaron* (J. Strauss), first perf. (+5), in role of Sándor Barinkay
12 Copenhagen, Odd Fellow Palace: Recital
15-20 Sto., R. Opera: *Missa Solemnis* (1), *Cavalleria* (1), *Bohème* (1)
19 Sto., Concert Hall: Charity concert, with chorus
28 Sto.: Recordings, cond. N. Grevillius (= **103-05**)

May

10,11 Malmö: *Roméo et Juliette, Faust* on tour with R. Opera
13-27 Sto., Concert Hall: Opera Evenings with R. Opera (3)
30,31 Sto.: Recordings (partly duets), cond. N. Grevillius (= **106-11**)

July

14 Sto., Gröna Lund: Recital

August

10 Sto.: Recordings, cond. N. Grevillius (= **112-13**)
11-26 Sto., R. Opera: *Aida* (2, incl. **A50**), *Bohème* (1), *Butterfly* (1), *Zigeunerbaron* (1)
31 Malmö, Hippodrome Theatre: Charity recital

September

2-11 Sto., R. Opera: *Bohème* (1), *Traviata* (2), *Faust* (1), all opposite E. Norena as guest

4 Sto., Skansen: Concert, cond. N. Grevillius (Barnens dag)
25 Örebro: Festival soiree

October

4-17 Sto., R. Opera: *L'africaine* (Meyerbeer), first perf. (+5) in role of Vasco da Gama

12 Sto.: Recordings, cond. N. Grevillius (= **114-17**)

20 Västerås: *Faust* on tour with R. Opera

27,30 Gothenburg: *Aida, Bohème* on tour with R. Opera

November

13 Detroit: *Ford Sunday Evening Hour*, radio concert (= **A51**). Probably first perf. on this US tour.

24,30 New York, Met: *Bohème (2)*. The first perf. was Met debut for JB, Mafalda Favero and Marisa Morel.

27 Chicago, Opera House: Recital (?)

December

2,10 New York, Met: *Trovatore* (2, first Met perf:s in this opera)

19 New York, Brooklyn Academy of Music: Recital

1939

January

6 Seattle, Music Hall: Recital

13 Princeton: Recital (?)

15 Detroit: *Ford Sunday Evening Hour*, radio concert (= **A52**)

17 New York, Carnegie Hall: Recital. Last appearance on this US tour.

February

4-25 Sto., R. Opera: *Bohème* (3, incl. **A53**), *Aida* (1), *Faust* (2), *Pagliacci* (1), *Roméo et Juliette* (1)

13 Gothenburg, Concert Hall: Concert, cond. T. Mann

March

7-25 Sto., R. Opera: *Traviata* (1), *Bohème* (2), *Roméo et Juliette* (1), *Faust* (1)

April

1-23 Sto., R. Opera: *Cavalleria* (3), *Missa Solemnis* (1), *Bohème* (1), *Butterfly* (2), *Faust* (1)

4 Örebro: Recital

9 Sto.: *Svenska bilder*, radio concert (= **A54**)

16 Sto.: Lars(-Olof), second child with Anna-Lisa, born [Lars B. at present lives in Stockholm and is active as a tenor singer (opera, operetta, recital).]

May

3-8 Gothenburg: *Roméo et Juliette* (1 = **A55**), *Bohème* (1), *Faust* (1 = **A56**), on tour with R. Opera. *Faust* was last perf. under expiring contract.

12,23 London, R. Opera (Covent Garden): *Trovatore* (2 = **3901,A57**). The first perf. was JB's Covent Garden debut and also his first perf. opposite G. Cigna. He would return to this opera house only in 1960.

17,19 Sto., Concert Hall: Concerts with R. Opera, cond. N. Grevillius

June

8 Hilversum (Netherlands): Radio concert, cond. F. Weissmann (= **3902**)

11 The Hague (Netherlands), Scheveningen Kurzaal: Concert, cond. E. Ansermet

July
14,15 Sto.: Recordings, cond. N. Grevillius or with H. Ebert, piano (= **118-24**)
31 Sto., Gröna Lund: Recital
August
2 Gothenburg, Liseberg: Recital
6 Furuvik: Recital (= **3903**)
10 Sto., R. Opera: *Bohème*. First Stockholm opera perf. as a guest.
16,17 Lucerne (Switzerland): *Requiem* (Verdi) (2, incl. **A58**), cond. A. Toscanini. JB's first perf:s under this conductor.
23-29 Sto., R. Opera: *Roméo et Juliette* (1), *Fanal* (1), *Traviata* (1 = **3904**)
October
19,22 Sto., Concert Hall: Recitals. First own recital here + charity perf.
25 Helsingborg: Recital
27 Copenhagen, KB Hall: Recital
28 Malmö: Radio concert, cond. J. Fernström (= **A59**)
November
4 The Hague: Concert, cond. W. Mengelberg
27 Seattle, Music Hall: Recital. One of the first on this American tour (comprising about 25 recitals).
December
9 Winnipeg (Canada): Recital. JB's Canadian debut
13 Pittsburgh, Carnegie Music Hall: Recital
28 New York, Met: *Faust* (first Met perf. in this opera)

1940
January
1-15 New York, Met: *Rigoletto* (1, first Met perf. in this opera), *Bohème* (2)
2 Philadelphia: *Faust* on tour with Met
21 Chicago, Opera House: Charity recital (for Finland)
30 New York: Recordings with Ebert, piano (= **125-31**) - first Victor recordings
February
2 New York, Town Hall: Recital
9,10 San Francisco, Opera House: Concerts, cond. P. Monteux
March
1 New York: Recordings with Ebert, piano (= **132-36**)
21-29 Sto., R. Opera: *Bohème* (1 = **4001**), *Roméo et Juliette* (1 = **4002**), *Aida* (1 = **4003**)
25 Sto., Concert Hall: Charity recital (for Finland)
May
7 Sto., Concert Hall: Charity recital (for Finland)
13,21 Sto., R. Opera: *Bohème, Roméo et Juliette*
June
16 Sto., Skansen: Recital
July
18 Sto., Gröna Lund: Recital
August
22 Gothenburg, Liseberg: Recital

September

5	Sto., Gröna Lund: Recital with other soloists (Barnens dag)
16	Malmö, Realskolan: Recital
18	Helsingborg, Concert Hall: Recital
26	Sto.: Radio concert, cond. N. Grevillius (= **A60**)
27	Uppsala, University: Recital
30	Lund, University: Recital

October

18-29	San Francisco Opera: *Bohème* (2), *Ballo* (1 = **4004**). First *Bohème* perf. was S.F. opera debut. Second *Bohème* was first opera perf. opposite E. Rethberg.
26	Seattle, Civic Auditorium: Recital. One of the first on this US tour, comprising about 30 recitals.

November

4	Los Angeles: *Ballo* on tour with S.F. Opera
12	Pasadena: Recital (?)
16	Chicago, City Opera: *Rigoletto*
23	New York, Carnegie Hall: *Requiem* (Verdi), cond. A. Toscanini (= **4005**)

December

2-30	New York, Met: *Ballo* (3, incl. **4007** - first Met perf:s in this role), *Trovatore* (2), *Faust* (1). *Ballo* opened the season; *Faust* was first perf. with L. Warren
8	Detroit: *Ford Sunday Evening Hour*, radio concert (= **4006**)
17	Philadelphia: *Ballo* on tour with Met
28	New York, Carnegie Hall: *Missa Solemnis*, cond. A. Toscanini (= **4008**)

1941

January

8,11	New York, Met: *Ballo*, *Trovatore* (= **4101**)
31	New York, Town Hall: Recital

February

8,27	New York, Met: *Rigoletto* (2)
16	Chicago, Opera House: Recital
22	Stillwater: Recital

March

27	Sto., Auditorium: Recital

April

3	Sto., R. Opera: Charity soiree
5-30	Sto., R. Opera: *Roméo et Juliette* (2), *Bohème* (1), *Pagliacci* (1)
8	Sto.: *Honnör för lyssnarna!*, radio programme (= **4102**)
17	Uppsala, University: Recital
23	Copenhagen, KB Hall: Recital

May

3,5	Sto., R. Opera: *Bohème, Roméo et Juliette*
16	Örebro: Recital

June

16,17	Sto.: Recordings (partly duets), cond. N. Grevillius (= **137-40**)

July

1,2	Överluleå & Övertorneå: Recitals (as field artist)
17	Sto., Gröna Lund: Recital

August

1	Solna, Haga: Stockholm Garrison Festival
3	Furuvik: Recital
17	Borås, Ryavallen: Opening concert for sports ground
22	Copenhagen, Tivoli: Recital

September

21-28	Sto., R. Opera: *Bohème* (2), *Aida* (1), *Tosca* (1)
30	Gothenburg, Concert Hall: Recital

October

3	Halmstad: Recital
4	Sto., R. Opera: Charity concert with other soloists (for victims of naval catastrophe)
7	Gothenburg: *Bohème* on tour with R. Opera
12	Östersund: Recital
14	Sundsvall: Recital
21	Helsingborg, Concert Hall: Recital
24	Malmö, Amiralen: Recital
31	Sto.: Scheduled American tour cancelled at the last moment

1942

January

31	Sto.: Radio concert, cond. S. Ehrling (= **4201**)

February

3-23	Sto., R. Opera: *Roméo et Juliette* (2), *Rigoletto* (2), *Bohème* (1)
21	Sto., Concert Hall: Charity concert with other soloists (for Finnish children)

March

5-15	Sto., R. Opera: *Ballo* (4)
17,28	Gothenburg, Concert Hall: Recitals
19	Uppsala, University: Recital
22	Copenhagen, Odd Fellow Palace: Recital
24	Malmö, Realskolan: Recital
26	Helsingborg, Concert Hall: Recital
31	Örebro: Recital

April

9	Berlin, Philharmonie: Recital (= **A61**)
17	Gothenburg, Concert Hall: Recital

May

5	Sto., Concert Hall: Concert, cond. N. Grevillius
9-16	Sto., R. Opera: *Aida* (1), *Roméo et Juliette* (1), *Rigoletto* (1)
18,19	Helsinki: Charity recitals (for disabled soldiers)
23	Furuvik: Recital

June

14	Sto., Skansen: Recital (for Sparfrämjandet)
28	Örnsköldsvik: Recital

July

24	Copenhagen, Dyrehaven: Recital
26	Karlskrona: Recital
30	Sto., Gröna Lund: Recital

August

5	Solna, Haga: Stockholm Garrison Festival
8	Sto., Skansen: Recital
12	Ystad: Recital
26	Gothenburg, Liseberg: Recital
27	Sto., Gröna Lund: Recital
28	Södertälje: Recitals (2)

September

17-20	Copenhagen, R. Theatre: *Rigoletto* (2), *Bohème* (1)
27,29	Sto., R. Opera: *Roméo et Juliette*, *Bohème*

October

2	Sto., R. Opera: *Rigoletto*
8	Sto., Concert Hall: Joint recital with H. Schymberg & E. Larson
12,26	Gothenburg, Concert Hall: Recitals
25	Malmö, Palladium: Recital

November

22,25	Budapest, R. Opera: *Bohème*, *Faust*
27,28	Budapest: Recitals (incl. **A62**)

December

8	Appointed Knight of the Royal Swedish Order of Vasa
8	Sto., Concert Hall: Charity concert, cond. N. Grevillius (for Red Cross)
13	Sto., Town Hall: Lucia festival
24	Period of illness (pneumonia) begins

1943

January

31	Kalmar: Recital (first after illness)

February

2	Gothenburg, Concert Hall: Recital
4	Lund, University: Recital
9	Malmö, Realskolan: Recital
11	Karlshamn: Recital
12	Karlskrona: Recital
17-28	Sto., R. Opera: *Aida* (1), *Rigoletto* (1), *Faust* (1), *Bohème* (1)
21	Helsinki, Finnish Opera: *Bohème* (charity perf.)

March

2	Västerås: Recital
7	Sto., R. Opera: *Roméo et Juliette*
10	Uppsala, University: Recital
21-28	Dalarna province: Recital tour in churches (incl. Mora, Älvdalen, Orsa, Rättvik, Leksand)

April

1-11	Sto., R. Opera: *Faust* (1), *Bohème* (1), *Trovatore* (2)
24,28	Florence, Teatro Comunale: *Trovatore* (2). This was JB's opera debut in Italy; it was also his first perf. with M. Caniglia & F. Barbieri.

May

2,6	Florence, Teatro Comunale: *Trovatore* (2)
10	Sto., Concert Hall: Joint recital with H. Schymberg (private arrangement)

13 Sto., R. Opera: *För Europas barn*, radio programme (= **4301**)
23 Sto., Stadion: Recitals (2) at the Stadsloppet [City Race]

June

4 Sto.: Ann-Charlotte, third child with Anna-Lisa, born [Ann-Charlotte B. at present lives in Stockholm and is active as a singer (opera, operetta, musical).]
6 Sto.: *Sommarens kvart*, radio recital (= **4302**)
30 Sto., Gröna Lund: Recital

July

10 Sto.: *Sweden Calls America*, radio concert transcription (= **4303**)
15 Sto., Gröna Lund: Recital

August

10 Solna, Haga: Stockholm Garrison Festival
18,20 Copenhagen, Tivoli: Recitals
28 Sto., Skansen: Recital

September

3 Sto., Gröna Lund: Recital (Barnens dag)
17-30 Sto., R. Opera: *Rigoletto* (2), *Trovatore* (2), *Aida* (1)

October

7 Helsinki, Messuhalli: Charity recital (= **A63**)
10 Stora Tuna & Falun: Recitals in churches
12 Gothenburg, Concert Hall: Recital
14 Sto., Concert Hall: Recital
22 Sto., Tennishallen: Opening ceremony
26 Malmö, Realskolan: Recital
29 Lund, University: Recital
31 Helsingborg, Concert Hall: Concert, cond. S. Frykberg

November

7-19 Northern Sweden: Recital tour (incl. Luleå, Boden, Piteå, Härnösand, Östersund)

27 Sto., Town Hall: Recital (contribution to charity choral concert)

December

1 Sto., R. Opera: *Roméo et Juliette*
2 Sto.: Illness period begins (appendicitis)
31 Sto., R. Opera: New Year's Vigil

1944

January

25 Sto., Concert Hall: Charity concert, cond. N. Grevillius (for Red Cross)

February

2 Kristinehamn: Recital
12 Gothenburg, Concert Hall: Charity concert, cond. N. Grevillius (for Red Cross)
13 Borås: Recital

March

27-30 Sto.: Recordings, cond. N. Grevillius (= **141-48**)

April

5 Sto.: Recordings, cond. S. Waldimir (= **149-50**)
14-25 Sto., R. Opera: *Faust* (1), *Cavalleria/Pagliacci* (2), *Trovatore* (1)
23 Karlsborg: Recital
29 Sto., Concert Hall: Charity recital with other soloists (for Blå Stjärnan)

May

4 Linköping: Recital
6 Åtvidaberg: Recital (?)
14 Sto., R. Opera: Gala performance for Red Cross (*Aida*, act 3)
21 Sto., Skansen: Recital (at the Djurgårdsmässan)

June

6 Sto., Stadion: Swedish Flag Day ceremony (= **A64**)
16 Sto.: Appointed Royal Swedish Court Singer
29 Sto., Gröna Lund: Recital

July

27 Sto., Gröna Lund: Recital

August

6 Sto., Enskede Sports Field: Recital
10 Ljusterö: Recital
13 Varberg: Recital
15 Falkenberg: Recital
16 Gothenburg, Liseberg: Recital
27 Södertälje: Recitals (2)

September

9 Sto., Eriksdalshallen: Recital at election meeting
19-28 Sto., R. Opera: *Ballo* (1), *Trovatore* (1), *Faust* (1 = **4401**), *Aida* (1)

October

3 Sto., R. Opera: *Bohème*
20 Sto., Concert Hall: Joint concert with H. Schymberg, cond. N. Grevillius
26 Sto., Concert Hall: Charity gala with other soloists, cond. A. Järnefelt (for Finland)
29 Helsingborg, Concert Hall: Concert, cond. S. Frykberg

November

4 Sto., R. Opera: Gala perf. for Swedish Theatre Union (*Roméo et Juliette*, act 2)
10 Sto.: Radio concert, cond. T. Mann (= **4402**)
19-24 Southern Sweden: Recital tour (incl. Växjö, Malmö, Lund, Jönköping)
28 Gothenburg, Concert Hall: Recital

December

5 Uppsala, Cathedral: Joint recital with actor A. De Wahl
13 Sto., Town Hall: Lucia Festival
? Sto.: Transcription of radio concert, cond. N. Grevillius (= **A65**)
31 Sto., R. Opera & Concert Hall: New Year Soirees

1945

January

1 Sto.: *Radiotjänst 20 år*, radio programme (= **4501**)
16 Sto., R. Opera: *Aida* (charity perf. for Belgian children)
28 Sto., Concert Hall: Charity recital with other soloists (for children of Europe)

February

6 Sto., R. Opera: Charity gala for Italian children (*Trovatore*, act 3 + *Butterfly*, act 1)
11 Linköping: Recital
13 Gothenburg, Concert Hall: Joint concert with H. Schymberg, cond. S. Westerberg

17 Helsinki, Conservatory & Messuhalli: Charity recitals
18 Helsinki, Swedish Theatre: Charity recital
22 Sto., Bromma Läroverk: Recital

March

7 Gothenburg, Concert Hall: Gala recital (for Reso)
9 Falun: Charity recital with other soloists (incl. Anna-Lisa, who replaced Gösta Björling)
11 Mora: Recital in connection with the Vasaloppet, a skiing competition
13-25 Northern Sweden: Recital tour (incl. Östersund, Sundsvall, Härnösand, Umeå, Luleå)

April

6-24 Sto., R. Opera: *Faust* (1), *Roméo et Juliette* (1), *Bohème* (2), *Ballo* (1 = **A66**), *Rigoletto* (1)
21,27 Sto., Concert Hall: Charity concerts with other soloists (for Blå Stjärnan and Simfrämjandet)
27 Receives Royal Swedish Medal "Litteris et Artibus"

June

6 Sto., Stadion: Swedish Flag Day ceremony (= **A67**)
15 Sto., R. Opera: Charity gala for Danish Resistance Movement
19 Solna, Råsunda Stadium: Recital (Barnens dag)
27 Sto., Skansen: Recital

July

19 Sto., Gröna Lund: Recital

August

2 Sto., Gröna Lund: Recital
5 Furuvik: Recitals (2)
11 Ljusterö: Charity recital
29 Sto., Skansen: Recital

September

6,7 Sto.: Recordings, cond. N. Grevillius (= **151-54**)
10-16 Sto., R. Opera: *Roméo et Juliette* (1), *Rigoletto* (1), *Trovatore* (1), *Bohème* (1)
20 Sto., Concert Hall: Concert, cond. N. Grevillius
23 Copenhagen, R. Theatre: *Ballo* (= **A68**)
28 Sto.: Radio concert, cond. T. Mann (= **4502**)
JB's autobiography, *Med bagaget i strupen* [My Throat Is My Travelling Bag], is published

October

7 Detroit: *Ford Sunday Evening Hour*, radio concert (= **4503**). This was JB's first American perf. after the war. The American tour would begin on the West Coast, last until May and include more than 70 concerts and recitals.

November

2 Portland: Recital (?)
3 Seattle, Moore Theater: Recital
9 Los Angeles: *Bohème* with S.F. Opera. This was first perf. opposite D. Kirsten.
19 New York: *Voice of Firestone*, radio concert (= **4504**)
29 New York, Met: *Rigoletto*

December

5-29 New York, Met: *Tosca* (2, first Met perf:s in this opera), *Rigoletto* (2, incl. **4506**). First Tosca perf. also first perf. opposite G. Moore.

22 New York: Transcription of Christmas greeting for broadcast to Sweden (= **4505**)

1946

January

1-11 New York, Met: *Bohème* (1), Mizrachi Benefit Concert (1), *Tosca* (1)

8 Philadelphia: *Tosca* on tour with Met

13 Detroit: *Ford Sunday Evening Hour*, radio concert (= **4601**)

15 Quebec (Canada): Recital (?)

17,19 Toronto (Canada): Recitals

21 New York: *Voice of Firestone*, joint radio concert with E. Steber (= **4602**)

25 Atlanta: Joint recital with D. Kirsten

26 Birmingham: Joint recital with D. Kirsten (?)

28 New Orleans: Recital (?)

February

11-26 California: Recital tour (incl. San Francisco, Los Angeles, San Diego, Pasadena, Claremont?)

March

3 Chicago, Orchestra Hall: Recital (?)

6 Ottawa, Capitol Theatre: Recital (?)

25 New York: *Voice of Firestone*, radio concert (= **4603**)

April

2,4 Habana (Cuba): Recitals

15 New York: *Voice of Firestone*, radio concert (= **4604**)

17,20 New York, Met: *Ballo* (1), *Rigoletto* (1)

28 Cleveland: *Bohème* on tour with Met. First perf. opposite L. Albanese.

May

2 Ann Arbor: Concert, cond. E. Ormandy (?)

4 Minneapolis: *Bohème* on tour with Met

9 Montreal (Canada): Recital

12 Detroit: *Ford Sunday Evening Hour*, radio concert (= **4605**)

15 New York, Carnegie Hall: Scandinavian "Pops" Music Concert, cond. S. Parmet (= **A69**). Probably last perf. on American tour.

29 Gothenburg, Liseberg: Recital

July

27,31 Sto., Skansen & Gröna Lund: Recitals

August

12 Sto., Skansen: Concert

20-24 Milan (Italy), La Scala Opera (at Sports Palace): *Rigoletto* (3). First performances with La Scala company.

28 Copenhagen, KB Hall: Recital

September

11-18 Sto., R. Opera: *Tosca* (1), *Trovatore* (1), *Bohème* (1)

13 Sto., Stadion: Greece Festival

October
5,7 Chicago Opera: *Rigoletto*, *Bohème*
14,16 San Francisco Opera: *Bohème*, *Trovatore*
18 Carmel: Recital
25 Spokane: Joint recital with D. Kirsten (?)
26,29 Los Angeles: *Trovatore*, *Bohème* on tour with S.F. Opera
30 Portland: Recital (?)

November
3 Los Angeles: *Roméo et Juliette* on tour with S.F. Opera
6 Omaha: Recital (?)
20 Los Angeles: Concert (?)
23 New York, McMillin Theater: Recital
28,29 Detroit: Concerts, cond. K. Krueger

December
5,7 Toronto: Recitals
19,23 New York, Met: *Bohème*, *Faust*. *Faust* was first perf. with R. Merrill.
21 New York: Transcription of Christmas greeting for broadcast to Sweden (= **4606**)

1947

January
15-27 New York, Met: *Roméo et Juliette* (1, first Met perf. in this opera), *Bohème* (1), *Trovatore* (1)

February
1 New York, Met: *Roméo et Juliette* (= **4701**)
17 Dallas: Recital
23 San Francisco, Opera House: Recital. In all about 35 recitals on US West Coast on this tour.

March
3 Los Angeles: Recital (?)
29 Chicago, Orchestra Hall: Recital

April
5 New York, Met: *Trovatore*
11? Boat to Britain runs aground; British recital tour cancelled

June
17 Solna, Råsunda Stadium: Charity festival (Barnens dag)

July
17,30 Sto., Gröna Lund & Skansen: Recitals
26 Ljusterö: Joint charity recital with H. Theorell, violin

August
14 Sto., Gröna Lund: Recital
18 Oslo: Joint charity recital with J. Berglund
23,30 Sto., Skansen: Recitals (the second for Barnens dag)
29 Gothenburg, Liseberg: Recital

September
5 Illness period (lumbago) begins; British recital tour cancelled

October
10 Sto., R. Opera: Gala for King of Denmark (*Aida*, act 4)
21 Sto., R. Opera: *Faust*. New lumbago period begins.

November

?	Sto.: *En svensk tiger*, motion picture recording (= **A70**)
27	Sto.: Recordings, cond. N. Grevillius (= **155-58**)
29	Sto., R. Opera: *Bohème*

December

1	Sto., R. Opera: *Tosca*
13	Minneapolis: Joint recital with Anna-Lisa. This was the first public perf. with her in several years and one of the first of about fifty recitals on this American tour.
25-31	New York, Met: *Rigoletto* (1), *Trovatore* (1 = **4702**), *Cavalleria* (1, first Met perf. in this opera)

1948

January

3-10	New York, Met: *Bohème* (1), *Ballo* (1), *Rigoletto* (1)
19,21	Habana: Recitals (?)

February

3	San Francisco, Opera House: Recital
7	Seattle, Moore Theater: Recital
11	Portland: Recital (?)
?	Vancouver (Canada): Recital (?)

March

1	New York, Met: *Trovatore*
6	Chicago, Orchestra Hall: Recital
8	Indianapolis: Recital
11	Bloomington: Recital
15	New York: *Telephone Hour*, radio concert (= **4801**)
21	New York, Carnegie Hall: Recital
30	Baltimore: *Bohème* on tour with Met

April

3	Atlanta: *Bohème* on tour with Met
8	Dallas: *Ballo* on tour with Met
16,21	Los Angeles: *Trovatore*, *Ballo* on tour with Met
28	Lincoln: *Tosca* on tour with Met
30	St. Louis: *Cavalleria* on tour with Met

May

4,6	Cincinnati, Music Hall: *Fidelio*, cond. F. Busch (abridged concert perf.) & contribution to other concert
8	Minneapolis: *Trovatore* on tour with Met
13,15	Cleveland: *Trovatore, Ballo* on tour with Met

June

16	Sto., Skansen: Gala concert, cond. N. Grevillius (on King Gustaf V's birthday)

July

4,7	Sto., Skansen: Recitals (first of them on US National Day)
22	Sto., Gröna Lund: Recital

August

4	Sto., Skansen: Joint recital with Anna-Lisa
15	Gothenburg, Liseberg: Recital

24 Sto., Gröna Lund: Recital

30 Sto., R. Opera: *Bohème* (for Red Cross Conference). This was first opera perf. opposite Anna-Lisa.

September

5 Sto., Concert Hall: Joint charity recital with Anna-Lisa

7,15 Sto.: Recordings, cond. N. Grevillius (= **159-62**)

16-26 Sto., R. Opera: *Tosca* (1), *Cavalleria/Pagliacci* (1), *Roméo et Juliette* (1)

26 Sto., Gustaf Vasa Church: Funeral of Count Bernadotte (= **4802**)

29 Copenhagen, KB Hall: Joint recital with Anna-Lisa

October

9 Sacramento: *Trovatore* on tour with S.F. Opera

12,15 San Francisco Opera: *Bohème* (2). First opera perf. with T. Gobbi (Oct. 12).

25 Ontario, California: Recital (?)

31 Los Angeles: *Bohème* on tour with S.F. Opera. Replaced at announced *Don Giovanni* perf. Oct. 28.

November

15 New York: *Telephone Hour*, radio concert (= **4803**)

December

3-25 New York, Met: *Trovatore* (1), *Bohème* (2, incl. **4804**)

21 Philadelphia: *Trovatore* on tour with Met

26 New York, Met: AGMA Christmas party

1949

January

3 New York, Met: *Trovatore*

11 Washington, Constitution Hall: Recital. This was one of the first of about 40 US and Canada recitals during the spring.

20 Cincinnati: Recital (?)

February

6 Chicago, Orchestra Hall: Recital

19 San Antonio Grand Opera: *Bohème*

21 Houston: Joint charity recital with Anna-Lisa (for Scandinavian Club)

22 Houston: Appointed honorary professor at the University of Houston

March

2 Utica: Recital

8 San Francisco, Opera House: Recital

18,19 Detroit: Recitals (?)

29 Boston: *Trovatore* on tour with Met

April

4 New York: *Telephone Hour*, radio concert (= **4901**)

7 Cleveland: *Rigoletto* on tour with Met

11 New York, Carnegie Hall: *Sweden in Music* (= **4902**). Probably last perf. on US tour.

June

4 Sto.: Appointed Knight of the Royal Swedish Order of the Northern Star

16 Sto., Gröna Lund: Recital

19 Sto., Skansen: Festival soiree, cond. S. Waldimir

29 Sto., Skansen: Recital

July

6 Copenhagen, Tivoli: Recital
11 Sto., Sports Exhibition: Joint recital with Anna-Lisa
13,30 Sto., Skansen: Recitals (the second one joint with Anna-Lisa)
21 Sto., Gröna Lund: Recital
31 Furuvik: Recital

August

10,11 Sto.: Recordings (partly duets with Anna-Lisa), cond. N. Grevillius (= **163-66**)
13 Sto., Skansen: Joint recital with Anna-Lisa
15 Sto., Bromma Airport: Interview at departure for the US (= **4903**)
23 Los Angeles, Hollywood Bowl: *Symphonies under the Stars*, joint concert with Anna-Lisa (= **4904**)

September

6 Honolulu: Joint recital with Anna-Lisa
20,25 San Francisco Opera: *Tosca* (opening night), *Bohème* (= **4905**)

October

2,13 San Francisco Opera: *Faust*
7,16 San Francisco Opera: *Manon Lescaut*. First performances in role of Des Grieux (first new role since 1938).
23 San Francisco: *Standard Hour*, joint radio concert with Anna-Lisa (= **4906**)
25 Los Angeles: *Manon Lescaut* on tour with S.F. Opera

November

4 Milwaukee: Recital
7 New York: *Telephone Hour*, radio concert (= **4907**)
13 Ithaca: Recital
19 New York, Hunter College: Recital
23,26 New York, Met: *Manon Lescaut* (first Met perf. in this opera), *Tosca*
29 Philadelphia: *Manon Lescaut* on tour with Met

December

5-15 New York, Met: *Tosca* (2), *Manon Lescaut* (1 = **4908**)

1950

January

8,11 Sto., R. Opera: *Roméo et Juliette, Bohème*. Several scheduled performances were cancelled owing to laryngitis.

February

13 San Francisco, Opera House: Recital

March

6 New York: *Voice of Firestone*, joint radio & TV concert with Anna-Lisa (= **5001**)
11 Chicago, Orchestra Hall: Recital with Swedish Glee Club
19 South Bend: Concert, cond. Hames
28 Washington, Constitution Hall: Recital
30 Boston: *Tosca* on tour with Met (first perf. opposite L. Welitsch)
31 New York, Carnegie Hall: *Night of Swedish Stars*, joint concert with Anna-Lisa and other soloists

April

8,10	Toronto, Eaton Auditorium: Recitals (?)
15	Cleveland: *Manon Lescaut* on tour with Met
20,22	New Orleans: *Ballo* (2, incl. **5002**)
May	
8,12	Chicago: *Tosca*, *Rigoletto* on tour with Met
21	Sto., Skansen: Recital (at the Djurgårdsmässan)
June	
11	Helsinki, Messuhalli: Recital
29	Selected most popular classical radio singer in Musical America vote (date for diploma)
July	
6	Sto., Gröna Lund: Recital (= **5003**)
12	Gothenburg, Liseberg: Recitals (2)
18	Malmö, Folkets Park: Recitals (2)
25	Sto., Skansen: Recital
August	
3	Sto., Gröna Lund: Joint recital with Anna-Lisa
12	Sto., Skansen: Recital
September	
1	Sto.: *Mitt allra bästa*, radio interview (= **A71**)
2	Copenhagen, Odd Fellow Palace: Recital
?	Odense (Denmark): Recital (?)
4	Virum (Denmark): Perf. at private party (= **5004**)
12,19	Sto.: Recordings, cond. N. Grevillius (= **167-70**)
October	
1	Berlin, Titania Palace: *Stars aus Europa*, radio concert (= **5005**)
6	Uppsala, Cathedral: Joint charity recital with other soloists
13	Sto., Concert Hall: Joint recital with Anna-Lisa
23	New York: *Telephone Hour*, radio concert (= **5006**). One of the first concerts on this American tour, which would comprise about 55 recitals and concerts, 15 of them joint with Anna-Lisa.
November	
6-24	New York, Met: *Don Carlo*, first perf., in title role (= **5007**, +4 more, incl. **5008**). Sung on opening night, this was JB's last new role on stage.
9	New York, S:t John's Cathedral: Memorial service for King Gustaf V
20	New York: *Voice of Firestone*, radio concert (= **5009**)
28	Philadelphia: *Don Carlo* on tour with Met
30	New York: Recording, cond. R. Cellini (= **171**)
December	
4-29	New York, Met: *Don Carlo* (2), *Faust* (4, incl. **5010**)

1951

January

1-10	New York, Met: *Faust* (1), *Manon Lescaut* (2)
3,13	New York: Recordings (partly duets), cond. R. Cellini (= **172-78**)
8	New York: *Telephone Hour*, radio concert (= **5101**)
25	Hartford, Bushnell Memorial (Connecticut Opera): *Bohème*
31	Quebec: Joint recital with Anna-Lisa

February

2 Montreal: Joint recital with Anna-Lisa
9 Detroit: Recital (?)
12 Denver: Joint recital with Anna-Lisa
16 New York: *We, the People*, TV programme (= **A72**)
25 Chicago, Orchestra Hall: Recital

March

3 New York, Hunter College: Recital
9 New York: Recordings, cond. R. Cellini (= **179-81**)
12 New York: *Telephone Hour*, radio concert (= **5102**)

April

1? Sto.: Radio interview (= **5103**)
2 Sto., Concert Hall: Joint recital with Anna-Lisa
8-26 Sto., R. Opera: *Manon Lescaut* (2, first perf:s in Sto. in this opera), *Ballo* (2), *Faust* (1)
17 Sto.: Transcription of radio concert, cond. S. Frykberg (=**5104**)

May

19-30 Milan, La Scala Opera: *Ballo in maschera* (4)

June

2,6 Milan, La Scala Opera: *Ballo in maschera* (2)
20 Helsinki, University: Sibelius concert, cond. N.-E. Fougstedt (= **5105**). Visit to Sibelius.

July

5 Sto., Gröna Lund: Recital (= **5106**)
18 Sto., Skansen: Recital
25 Gothenburg, Liseberg: Recital
29 London, R. Albert Hall: Recital

August

10 Sto., Gröna Lund: Recital (= **5107**)
15 Sto., Skansen: Recital
18 Ljusterö Church: Charity recital

September

6,10 Sto., R. Opera: *Tosca, Manon Lescaut*
21,27 San Francisco Opera: *Roméo et Juliette* (2). Second perf. was JB's only American opera perf. with Anna-Lisa.
30 San Francisco: *Standard Hour*, joint radio concert with B. Sayão (= **5108**)

October

8-20 San Francisco Opera: *Bohème* (2), *Tosca* (1), *Rigoletto* (1)
22 Fresno: *Bohème* on tour with S.F. Opera
26,29 Los Angeles: *Bohème, Roméo et Juliette* on tour with S.F. Opera

November

3 Los Angeles: *Rigoletto* on tour with S.F. Opera
5 San Francisco, Opera House: Recital
11 Los Angeles: *Bergen-McCarthy Show* with Anna-Lisa (= **5109**)
19 New York: *Voice of Firestone*, radio & TV concert (= **5110**)

December

2 Los Angeles: *Bergen-McCarthy Show* with Anna-Lisa (= **5111**)
9 Chicago, Orchestra Hall: Recital. Probably last one on this US tour.

1952

January

22 Sto., Concert Hall: Charity recital with other soloists (for Red Cross)

25 Sto.: Transcription for radio programme *Karusellen* (= **5201**)

February

22 New York: *Trovatore* recording begins (= **182**). JB's first complete opera recording. American tour comprising about eighteen recitals begins in February.

March

6-30 New York: *Trovatore* recording continues

10 New York: *Voice of Firestone*, radio & TV concert (= **5202**)

21,24 New York, Met: *Don Carlo*

April

9 New York, Met: *Don Carlo*

11 New York: Recordings with F. Schauwecker, piano (= **183-98**)

May

17 Oslo, Jordal Amfi: Joint concert with Anne Brown, cond. O. Grüner-Hegge (on Norwegian National Day)

25 Sto., Skansen: Recital (= **5203**)

June

15 London, R. Albert Hall: Recital

17 Copenhagen, Tivoli: Concert, cond. S.C. Felumb, & recital

26 Sto., Gröna Lund: Recital

July

2 Sto., Skansen: Recital

13 Malmslätt: Recital at JUF meeting

15 Malmö, Folkets Park: Recitals (2)

17 Sto., Gröna Lund: Recital

20 Gothenburg, Liseberg: Recitals (2)

25,27 Helsinki: Recitals (first one for Red Cross, second one joint with Anna-Lisa)

August

10 Furuvik: Recitals (2, the second one jointly with Anna-Lisa)

13 Sto., Skansen: Recital

31 Ailment (bleeding ulcer)

October

3 Sto.: Transcription of radio concert, cond. S. Frykberg (= **5204**)

7 Uppsala, University: Recital with other soloists (for Folket i Bild)

26 Sto., Concert Hall: Charity concert, cond. N. Grevillius (for Kungafonden)

November

6,10 Reykjavik (Iceland): Recitals

14,23 London, R. Festival Hall & R. Albert Hall: Recitals

16 Manchester (Great Britain): Recital

21 London: Recordings with I. Newton, piano (= **199-202**)

26 Glasgow (Great Britain): Recital

29 Dublin (Ireland): Recital

December

4 Sto., China Theatre: Stjärnnatt [Night of Stars], charity gala

14 Helsinki, Finnish Opera: *Bohème* (opposite Anna-Lisa)

16 Helsinki, Messuhalli: Recital

29 Sto., R. Opera: *Bohème*

1953

January

2	Sto., R. Opera: *Rigoletto*
7-29	New York: *Cavalleria & Pagliacci* recordings (= **203-04**)

February

1	New York: *Cavalleria* recording finished
3,7	New York, Met: *Cavalleria, Rigoletto*
22	Sto., Concert Hall: Charity recital with Anna-Lisa & other artists (for victims of Dutch flooding)

March

12	Paris, Théâtre de Paris: Recital (press gala). Scheduled debut at Paris Opera some days earlier (as Roméo) was cancelled owing to throat problems.
17	Glasgow: Recital
22	London, R. Albert Hall: Recital

April

29	Gothenburg, Concert Hall: Recital

May

5	Örebro: Recital
7	Uppsala, University: Recital
9	Östersund: Recital
15	Sundsvall: Recital

June

6	Sto., Stadion: Swedish Flag Day ceremony (= **5301**)
8,15	London, R. Festival Hall: Recitals
10	Swansea: Recital
12	Cardiff: Recital
25	Sto., Gröna Lund: Recital
28	Helsingborg: Recitals (2)

July

12	Leksand: Recital (at rowing competition)

August

6	Sto., Gröna Lund: Recital
29	Sto., Skansen: Recital

September

6	Gothenburg, Liseberg: Recitals (Barnens dag)
11	Sto., Kungsträdgården: Recital
13	Sto., Skansen: Recital (on Sweden-America Day)
25,28	Sto., R. Opera: *Tosca, Bohème*. *Tosca* was first perf. opposite B. Nilsson
27?	Sto.: *Resan till dej*, motion picture recording
30	Sto.: Recordings, cond. B. Bokstedt (= **205-08**)

October

15	Detroit, Masonic Auditorium: Recital. One of the first on this American tour
20	Hartford, Bushnell Memorial (Connecticut Opera): *Tosca*
31	New York, Hunter College: Recital

November

16-28	New York, Met: *Faust* (3). First perf., on opening night, was also first opera perf. opposite V. de los Angeles.
?	New York: Radio interview (= **5303**)

December

2 New York, UN Building: Soiree. JB could not carry through his part of the programme owing to voice problems.

17 New York, Met: *Faust*. Replaced after act 1 owing to voice problems. Forced by laryngitis to cancel several performances before this one, and a *Ballo in maschera* broadcast under Toscanini. Convalescence in Sweden until end of January.

1954

January

27 Milwaukee: Recital. Followed by radio interview (= **5401**) next day

February

1 New York, Met: *Bohème*. Followed by renewed convalescence in Bahamas.

27 Miami Beach (Opera Guild of Greater Miami): *Trovatore*. Further scheduled performances in Miami Beach and at the Met cancelled; renewed convalescence in Bahamas and in Sweden.

April

21 Copenhagen, Odd Fellow Palace: Recital

23 Jönköping: Recital

25 Borås: Recital

27 Gothenburg: Recital

May

2 Sto., R. Opera: *Bohème*

27 Swansea (Great Britain): Recital

30 London, R. Albert Hall: Recital

June

4 Sto., R. Opera: *Rigoletto* (= **5402**)

6 Sto., Skansen: Recital

9 Bergen: Festival concert, cond. C. Garaguly (= **5403**)

15 Sto., Concert Hall: Recital (for Co-operative Movement)

23 Sto., Skansen: Recital

July

4 Sto., Skansen: Recital (on US National Day)

11-17 Rome: *Manon Lescaut* recording (= **209**)

29 Sto., Gröna Lund: Recital

August

4 Sto., Skansen: Recital

15-29 Johannesburg (South Africa): Recitals (3) & radio concert (= **A73**)

24 Durban (South Africa): Recital

26 Cape Town (South Africa): Recital

September

1 Cape Town: Concert, cond. F. Schuurman

3 Pretoria (South Africa): Recital

October

22 Sto., Town Hall: Soiree (for Finland Associations)

November

6 Stuttgart, Württemberg State Theatre: *Bohème*

11 Belgrade Opera: *Bohème* (= **A74**)

12 Belgrade: Recital

15 Zagreb, Croat National Opera: *Bohème* (= **A75**)
24 Gothenburg, Concert Hall: Recital
28 Sto., R. Opera: *Rigoletto*

December

1,8 Sto., R. Opera: *Cavalleria/Pagliacci* (2, incl. **5404-05**). The first Cavalleria was first perf. opposite E. Söderström.
10 Sto.: *Tomteluverött*, radio interview (= **A76**)
19 Sto., R. Opera: Svenska Dagbladet Christmas Concert
20 Sto., Södersjukhuset: *Pillerdosan*, hospital radio recital (= **5406**)
30 Sto., Beckomberga Hospital: Recital before patients

1955

January

14,27 Sto., R. Opera: *Tosca, Aida*
18 Helsinki, Messuhalli: Recital
20 Tampere (Tammerfors) (Finland): Charity recital
23 Helsinki, Finnish Opera: *Tosca*
29 Sundsvall: Recital

February

3 Sto., R. Opera: *Bohème*
9 Copenhagen, Odd Fellow Palace: Recital
11-20 Southern Sweden: Recital tour (Helsingborg, Malmö, Halmstad, Lund, Nässjö)

March

10,13 Helsinki, Finnish Opera: *Tosca, Rigoletto*
15 Helsinki, Messuhalli: Recital
20 London, R. Albert Hall: Recital

April

22 Sto., Concert Hall: Charity soiree (Barnens dag)
24 Borås: Recital
26 Turku (Åbo) (Finland): Recital
28 Eskilstuna: Recital

May

5,9 Sto., R. Opera: *Bohème, Cavalleria/Pagliacci*
8 Sto., Skansen: Recital (Red Cross 90th Anniversary)
20 Gothenburg, Ullevi: Recital

June

2 Oslo, Jordal Amfi: Joint concert with E. Schwarzkopf, cond. D. Dixon
6 Sto., Skansen: Recital

July

2-13 Rome: *Aida* recording (= **210**)
31 Furuvik: Recitals (2, on Dalarna Day)

August

Sto.: Illness period begins (nervous ailment)

September

24 New York, Carnegie Hall: Recital (= **5501**). One of the first recitals on this American tour, which included about twenty-five recitals.

October

6 Saskatoon (Canada): Recital. One of several Canadian recitals on this tour.
20 Seattle, Civic Auditorium: Concert

November
5-29 Chicago, Lyric Theatre: *Trovatore* (2, incl. **A77**), *Rigoletto* (2), *Faust* (2), *Ballo* (1). *Trovatore* perf:s were only two performances ever opposite M. Callas. The first *Faust* was first perf. opposite R. Carteri.

December
3 Chicago, Lyric Theatre: *Ballo*
8 Atlanta: Recital
10,12 Houston: Recitals
14 New Orleans: Recital (= **5502**)
20 New York, Carnegie Hall: Joint concert with R. Tebaldi, cond. L. Bernstein (last perf. on this US tour)

1956

January
30 New York: *Producer's Showcase*, TV concert (= **5601**). Probably first appearance on this American tour.

February
1 Pittsburgh: Recital
17 New York, Met: *Ballo*
24 Milwaukee: Recital
26 Chicago, Orchestra Hall: Recital
29 Pasadena: Recital

March
10 New York, Met: Gala concert for President of Italy
14 Philadelphia, Academy of Music: Recital
16-30 New York: *Bohème* recording begins (= **211**)
31 New York, Met: *Manon Lescaut* (= **5602**)

April
1-6 New York: *Bohème* recording finished
4-14 New York, Met: *Tosca* (1 = **5603**), *Manon Lescaut* (1), *Fledermaus* gala (1)
10 Baltimore: *Tosca* on tour with Met
17 Boston: *Ballo* on tour with Met. Only perf. opposite Marian Anderson.
19 Appointed member of the Royal Swedish Academy of Music
24,27 Cleveland: *Ballo, Rigoletto* on tour with Met

May
27 London, R. Albert Hall: Recital

June
6 Appointed Commander of the Royal Swedish Order of Vasa
6 Sto., Skansen: Recital
9 Sto., Town Hall: Recital at luncheon given for Queen Elizabeth II of Britain
16-28 Rome: *Rigoletto* recording (= **212**)

July
10 Copenhagen, Tivoli: Concert
19 Sto., Gröna Lund: Recital (= **5604**)
22 Furuvik: Recitals (2, incl. **5605**)

August
1 Gothenburg, Liseberg: Recital
9 Sto., Skansen: Recital

19 Östersund: Recital (on Sweden-America Day)
27,31 Sto., R. Opera: *Rigoletto, Tosca*

September

3 Sto., Skansen: Recital
5 Sto., R. Opera: *Tosca*
13-23 San Francisco Opera: *Manon Lescaut* (2), *Trovatore* (1), *Tosca* (1). *Manon Lescaut* was sung on opening night. *Trovatore* was only opera perf. opposite E. Farrell. *Tosca* was first opera perf. opposite R. Tebaldi.
30 Sacramento: *Tosca* on tour with S.F. Opera

October

3 San Francisco, Civic Auditorium: Fol de Rol concert, "Opera Goes to the Circus"
19 Los Angeles: *Manon Lescaut* on tour with S.F. Opera
23-30 Chicago, Lyric Opera: *Trovatore* (2), *Tosca* (1)

November

2-16 Chicago, Lyric Opera: *Tosca* (2), *Bohème* (1)
7 Detroit: *Rigoletto* on tour with New York City Opera
24 New York, Hunter College: Recital

December

11 New York, Brooklyn Academy of Music: Recital

1957

January

3-29 Sto., R. Opera: *Tosca* (1), *Rigoletto* (1 = **5701**), *Trovatore* (2, incl. **5702**), *Bohème* (2)
19 Zurich Opera (Switzerland): *Tosca* (at Swedish Week)
22,23 Sto.: Recordings, cond. N. Grevillius (= **213-18**)

February

4 Copenhagen, Tivoli: Recital
6 Gothenburg, Concert Hall: Recital
10 Sto., R. Opera: *Aida*
17 New York: *Ed Sullivan Show*, TV programme (= **5703**). One of the first performances on this American tour.
24 Milwaukee: Recital (?)
26 Chicago: Recital (?)
27 New York, Met: *Tosca*
29 Pasadena: Recital (?)

March

7 Philadelphia: Recital
16,29 New York, Met: *Don Carlo* (2)
19 Philadelphia: *Trovatore* on tour with Met

April

4 New York, Met: *Don Carlo*. Several scheduled perf:s at the Met and on tour cancelled.

June

4-19 Sto., R. Opera: *Aida* (1), *Trovatore* (2), *Bohème* (1)
6 Sto., Skansen: Recital

July

2-18 Rome: *Tosca* recording (= **219**)

28 Gothenburg, Liseberg: Recital

August

5 Sto., Gröna Lund: Recital (= **5704**)

September

1-7 Florence: *Cavalleria* recording (+ arias) (= **220-26**)

25 Sto.: Recordings, cond. N. Grevillius (= **227-31**)

29 Malmö, Municipal Theatre: Concert, cond. G. Tronchi (Swedish-Italian Music Week)

30 Malmö, Municipal Theatre: *Bohème* (= **5705**)

October

2 Malmö, Municipal Theatre: *Bohème*

5 Sto.: Transcription of radio concert, cond. S. Westerberg (= **5706**)

7 Sto., R. Opera: *Bohème*

16-25 Chicago, Lyric Opera: *Bohème* (1), *Manon Lescaut* (2). *Bohème* was first opera perf. opposite A. Moffo.

November

4-30 Chicago, Lyric Opera: *Bohème* (1), *Manon Lescaut* (1), *Ballo* (2), *Tosca* (1), *Don Carlo* (1). *Don Carlo* was first opera perf. opposite B. Christoff.

December

4 New Orleans: Recital (?)

5 Greensboro: Recital (?)

8 New York, Carnegie Hall: Sibelius concert, cond. M. Similä (= **5707**)

1958

February

8 Sto., Cirkus: *Stora famnen*, TV programme (= **5801**)

12 Borås: Recital

17 Sto., R. Opera: *Trovatore*

23 Malmö: Recital

March

2 New York, Carnegie Hall: Recital (= **5802**)

23 Fort Lauderdale: Recital. JB forced by ulcer to cancel last part of tour; two weeks in hospital and convalescence in Florida before return to Sweden on April 21.

May

20 Sto., R. Opera: *Tosca* (= **A79**). Replaced after act 1 owing to voice problems. Scheduled British, German, Swiss & Swedish perf:s cancelled.

June

7 Sto., Skansen: Recital

26 Sto., Gröna Lund: Recital (= **5803**)

29 London, R. Albert Hall: Recital

July

8 Copenhagen, Tivoli: Recital

18 Sto.: Radio concert, cond. G.L. Jochum (= **5804**)

29 Malmö, Folkets Park: Recitals (2)

August

11 Ljusterö: Joint charity recital with H. Theorell, violin
13 Gothenburg, Liseberg: Concert, cond. M. Schönherr
14 Gothenburg, Götaplatsen: Recital
19 Sto., Stadion: European Athletics Championship Opening Ceremony (= **5805**)
24 Åtvidaberg: Recital
28 Helsingborg, Concert Hall: Recital

September

26 San Francisco Opera: *Trovatore*. First opera perf. opposite L. Price.

October

2,11 San Francisco Opera: *Bohème, Trovatore*
5 Sacramento: *Trovatore* on tour with S.F. Opera
8 San Francisco, Civic Auditorium: Fol de Rol concert
20-29 Chicago, Lyric Opera: *Trovatore* (3). First *Trovatore* was first opera perf. opposite G. Simionato.

November

2-8 Los Angeles: *Trovatore* (1), *Don Carlo* (1), *Rigoletto* (1) on tour with S.F. Opera
15-29 Chicago, Lyric Opera: *Rigoletto* (2), *Aida* (3). First *Aida* was first perf. opposite L. Rysanek.

December

1 Chicago: Recital (?)
2? New York: Radio interview (= **5806**)
6 Sto.: *För hela familjen*, TV programme (= **5807**)
11 Sto.: Transcription of radio concert, cond. S. Westerberg (= **5808**)
14 Malmö, Municipal Theatre: Concert, cond. S.-Å. Axelson (unfinished owing to voice problems)
20,28 Sto., R. Opera: *Manon Lescaut*

1959

January

4 London: *Sunday Night at the Palladium*, TV programme (= **5901**)
20 Sto., R. Opera: *Manon Lescaut*

February

8 Sto.: Recordings, cond. N. Grevillius (= **232-39**)
12,15 Sto., R. Opera: *Tosca* (= **5902**), *Manon Lescaut*
24 Ithaca: Recital. One of the first on this US tour, which comprised about twenty recitals.

March

4 Boston, Symphony Hall: Recital
7 New York, Hunter College: Recital
19,21 Tulsa Opera: *Trovatore* (2)
28 Corpus Christi: Concert, cond. Singer

April

10 Kansas City: Recital (?)
13 Atlanta: Recital (= **5903**)
20 San Francisco, Opera House: Recital
27? New York: Radio interview (= **5904**)
29 New York, Carnegie Hall: Recital with Uppsala College Choir

May

24	Sto., Skansen: Recital (at the Djurgårdsmässan)
26	Oslo, University: Recital
28	Skien & Porsgrunn (Norway): Recitals
31	London, R. Albert Hall: Recital

June

3	Sto., Town Hall: Co-operative Movement Festival
6	Sto., Skansen: Recital
16	Sto., Gröna Lund: Recital (= **5905**)
27	Siarö: Telephone interview (= **5906**)

July

3-11	Rome: *Turandot* recording (= **240**)

August

11	Sto., Bromma Airport: Heart attack
20	Sto., Gröna Lund: Recital (= **5907**)
24	Sto.: Heart attack, followed by a week in hospital

September

25,26	Rome: *Madama Butterfly* recording begins (= **241**). Delayed by heart attack [see note].

October

11	Rome: *Madama Butterfly* recording finished
16	Copenhagen, Falconer Centre: Recital
30	Sto.: Radio interview (= **5907**)

November

1	Sto., R. Opera: *Manon Lescaut* (= **5909**)
16-27	New York, Met: *Cavalleria* (2, incl. **5910**), *Tosca* (1 = **5911**)

December

8-22	New York, Met: *Faust* (2) (incl. **5912**), *Tosca* (2), *Cavalleria* (1). *Cavalleria* was last Met perf.
27	New York, Hunter College: Recital. Last perf. on this US tour, followed by vacation in Puerto Rico.

1960

March

6	Sto., R. Opera: *Trovatore* (= **6001**). This was JB's last perf. in the opera house where his career began.
10-18	London, R. Opera (Covent Garden): *Bohème* (4, incl. **A80**). The first perf. was JB's first one in this house since 1939; the third one was sung in spite of a heart attack.
29	San Francisco (Cosmopolitan Opera): *Trovatore*

April

1	San Francisco (Cosmopolitan Opera): *Faust*. This was JB's last opera perf.
5	Pasadena: Recital. Heart problems on this occasion.

May

8	Amsterdam (Netherlands): Joint concert with M. Aarden, F. Giongo & Amsterdam Opera Chorus, cond. W. Lohoff

June

6	Sto., Skansen: Recital
9	Sto, Gröna Lund: Recital with R. Opera soloists (= **A81**)

12-19 Vienna: *Messa da Requiem* recording (= **242**) + contribution to *Fledermaus* recording (= **243**)

July

4 Rättvik: Recital on US National Day, followed by radio interview next day (= **6002**)

10 Rome: *Ballo in maschera* recording begins but is soon cancelled [See note for No. **244**]

28 Sto., Gröna Lund: Recital (= **6003**). Gröna Lund perf. scheduled for Sept. 4 was cancelled due to rain.

August

5 Gothenburg: Radio concert, cond. N. Grevillius (= **6004**)

17 Ljusterö: Joint charity recital with H. Theorell, violin

20 Sto., Skansen: Recital. JB's last public perf.

September

9 Siarö: JB dies early in the morning in his sleep from a heart attack

19 Sto., Engelbrekt Church: Funeral ceremony [broadcast live in Sweden: Sw. Radio archive TAN 60/972]

20 Stora Tuna Church: Interment ceremony

Opera, Operetta and Oratorio Repertoire

All Stockholm opera and operetta performances were with the R. Opera. First performance was in Stockholm unless otherwise noted. Operas first performed in Stockholm were originally sung by JB in Swedish. Chicago performances (except those on tour with the Met) were with the Chicago City Opera, the Chicago Opera, the Lyric Theatre or Lyric Opera of Chicago.

Atterberg, Kurt (1887-1974) Swedish
Fanal: Martin Skarp
1934, January 27 (world première of the work) - 1939, August 26
23 performances, all with R. Opera (21 in Stockholm, 2 on tour in Oslo & Riga)

Beethoven, Ludwig van (1770-1827) German
Fidelio: Florestan
1935, March 26 - April 10
4 performances, all in Stockholm. One abridged concert perf. in English (Cincinnati, 1948)
Missa Solemnis
1931, April 5 - 1940, December 28 (New York)
8 performances: 7 in Stockholm with R. Opera (1931-39), 1 in New York

Berg, Natanael (1879-1957) Swedish
Engelbrekt: Biskop Sigge [Bishop Sigge]
1931, March 21 - May 7 (Helsinki)
3 performances, all with R. Opera (2 in Stockholm, 1 on tour in Helsinki)

Berlioz, Hector (1803-1869) French
La damnation de Faust: Faust
1936, February 1 - April 23
10 performances, all in Stockholm

Bizet, Georges (1838-1875) French
Djamileh: Haroun
1933, September 6 - November 26
6 performances, all in Stockholm

Boito, Arrigo (1842-1918) Italian
Mefistofele: Faust
1937, September 30 & October 3
2 performances, both in Stockholm

Borodin, Alexander (1833-1887) Russian
Knyaz Igor [*Prince Igor*]: Vladimir Igorevich
1933, March 11 - 1937, August 30 (Stockholm)
36 performances, all with R. Opera (34 in Stockholm, 2 on tour in Copenhagen & Gothenburg)

Bruckner, Anton (1824-1896) Austrian
Te Deum
1930, April 29 (Stockholm, Concert Hall)
1 performance

Charpentier, Gustave (1860-1956) French
Louise: Le chansonnier [The Song-writer]
1930, November 29 (R. Opera première of the work) - 1931, September 11
8 performances, all in Stockholm

Donizetti, Gaetano (1797-1848) Italian
L'elisir d'amore: Nemorino
1932, November 9 - 1933, February 19
6 performances, all in Stockholm
La fille du régiment: Tonio
1936, September 26 - 1937, May 17
9 performances, all in Stockholm

Flotow, Friedrich von (1812-1883) German
Martha: Lyonel
1933, September 30 - October 11
3 performances, all in Stockholm

Gounod, Charles (1818-1893) French
Faust: Faust
1934, August 25 - 1960, April 1 (San Francisco, Cosmopolitan)
70 performances: 47 with R. Opera (1934-51: 41 in Stockholm, 6 on tour in Gävle, Norrköping, Malmö, Västerås, Gothenburg), 1 in Prague (1936), 1 in Vienna (1937), 15 at the Met (1939-59: 14 in N.Y., 1 on tour in Philadelphia), 1 in Budapest (1942), 2 with San Francisco Opera in S.F. (1949), 2 in Chicago (1955), 1 with Cosmopolitan Opera, San Francisco (1960)
Roméo et Juliette: Tybalt
1931, August 30 - 1932, February 1
3 performances, all in Stockholm
Roméo et Juliette: Roméo
1933, Aug. 22 - 1951, October 29 (Los Angeles, with San Francisco Opera)
44 performances: 38 with R. Opera (1933-50: 34 in Stockholm, 4 on tour in Norrköping, Malmö, Gothenburg), 4 with San Francisco Opera (1946-51: 2 in S.F., 2 on tour in Los Angeles), 2 with the Met in N.Y. (1947). Only act 4 sung 4 times in Stockholm

Handel, George Frideric (1685-1759) German-English

Messiah

1930, December 6 - 1936, December 5

7 performances, all with R. Opera at Storkyrkan Cathedral, Stockholm

Laparra, Raoul (1876-1943) French

L'illustre Fregona: Tomas

1932, January 16 (Swedish première of the work) - 1937, January 2

22 performances, all in Stockholm (+ one containing acts 1 & 3 only)

Leoncavallo, Ruggero (1858-1919) Italian

Pagliacci: Canio

1936, January 11 - 1955, May 9

20 performances: 17 in Stockholm (1936-55), 1 in Nuremberg (1937), 2 in Vienna (1937)

Mascagni, Pietro (1863-1945) Italian

Cavalleria rusticana: Turiddu

1935, February 14 - 1959, December 22 (New York)

31 performances: 25 in Stockholm (1935-55), 6 with the Met (1947-59: 5 in N.Y., 1 on tour in St. Louis)

Meyerbeer, Giacomo (1791-1864) German

L'africaine: Vasco da Gama

1938, October 4 - 17

6 performances, all in Stockholm

Montemezzi, Italo (1870-1952) Italian

La notte di Zoraima: Voce interna [A Voice in the Night]

1931, October 16 (Swedish première of the work) - 1932, January 13

5 performances, all in Stockholm

Mozart, Wolfgang Amadeus (1756-1791) Austrian

Don Giovanni: Don Ottavio

1930, August 20 - 1937, September 14 (Stockholm)

10 performances, all with R. Opera (5 in Stockholm, 5 on tour in Helsinki, Copenhagen, Oslo, Riga)

Die Entführung aus dem Serail: Belmonte

1935, January 26 - March 17

4 performances, all in Stockholm

Die Zauberflöte: Tamino

1933, December 15 - 1936, December 8 (Malmö)

5 performances, all with R. Opera (3 in Stockholm, 2 on tour in Malmö)

Nielsen, Carl (1865-1931) Danish

Saul og David [*Saul and David*]*:* Jonathan

1931, January 13 (R. Opera première of the work) - 1932, March 23

14 performances, all in Stockholm

Paumgartner, Bernhard (1887-1971) Austrian
Rossini in Neapel: Gioacchino Rossini
1936, November 26 (Swedish première of the work) - December 26
6 performances, all in Stockholm

Pfitzner, Hans (1869-1949) German
Das Herz: Ein junger Kavalier [A Young Cavalier]
1932, April 14 (Swedish première of the work) - April 25
3 performances, all in Stockholm

Puccini, Giacomo (1858-1924) Italian
La bohème: Rodolfo
1934, October 13 - 1960, March 18 (London)
115 performances: 61 with R. Opera (1934-57: 57 in Stockholm, 4 on tour in Gothenburg), 1 in Brno (1936), 2 in Vienna (1936-37), 1 in Berlin (1937), 1 in Dresden (1937), 5 in Chicago (1937-57), 15 with the Met (1938-54: 11 in N.Y., 4 on tour in Cleveland, Minneapolis, Baltimore, Atlanta), 14 with San Francisco Opera (1940-58: 9 in S.F., 5 on tour in Los Angeles & Fresno), 1 in Copenhagen (1942), 1 in Budapest (1942), 2 in Helsinki (1943-52), 1 in San Antonio (1949), 1 in Hartford (1951), 1 in Stuttgart (1954), 1 in Belgrade (1954), 1 in Zagreb (1954), 2 in Malmö (1957), 4 in London (1960). Only act 1 sung once in Paris 1936 (Cité Universitaire)
La fanciulla del West: Dick Johnson
1934, December 29 (Swedish première of the work) - 1937, February 25 (Vienna)
9 performances: 8 in Stockholm (1934-35), 1 in Vienna (1937)
Madama Butterfly: B.F. Pinkerton
1936, September 5 - 1939, April 21
12 performances: 11 in Stockholm (1936-39), 1 in Vienna (1937). Only act 1 sung once in Stockholm 1945
Manon Lescaut: Un lampionaio [A Lamplighter]
1930, July 21 - 1932, March 15
6 performances, all in Stockholm
Manon Lescaut: Il Cavaliere Renato des Grieux
1949, October 7 (San Francisco) - 1959, November 1 (Stockholm)
25 performances: 6 with San Francisco Opera (1949-56: 4 in S.F., 2 on tour in Los Angeles), 8 with the Met (1949-56: 6 in N.Y., 2 on tour in Philadelphia & Cleveland), 8 in Stockholm (1951-59), 3 in Chicago (1957)
Il tabarro: Luigi
1934, October 20 - December 13
4 times, all in Stockholm
Tosca: Mario Cavaradossi
1933, October 19 - 1959, December 16 (New York)
51 performances: 23 with R. Opera (1933-59: 18 in Stockholm, 5 on tour in Malmö, Ystad, Kristianstad, Östersund, Växjö), 16 with the Met (1945-59: 11 in N.Y., 5 on tour in Philadelphia, Lincoln, Boston, Chicago, Baltimore), 4 with San Francisco Opera (1949-56: 3 in S.F., 1 on tour in Sacramento), 1 in Hartford (1953), 2 in Helsinki (1955), 4 in Chicago (1956-57), 1 in Zurich (1957)

Rangström, Ture (1884-1947) Swedish
Kronbruden [*The Crown Bride*]: Mats
1933, April 6 - 1934, November 30
3 performances, all in Stockholm

Rimsky-Korsakov, Nikolay (1844-1908) Russian
Sadko: Indiyskiy gost [A Hindu Merchant]
1934, November 17 - 1936, April 13
11 performances, all in Stockholm

Rosenberg, Hilding (1892-1985) Swedish
Resa till Amerika [*Journey to America*]: Pråmkarlen [The Bargeman]
1932, November 24 (world première of the work) - 1933, February 1
5 performances, all in Stockholm

Rossini, Gioacchino (1792-1868) Italian
Il barbiere di Siviglia: Il Conte d'Almaviva [Count Almaviva]
1931, November 7 - 1937, January 20
26 performances, all with R. Opera (21 in Stockholm, 5 on tour in Kristianstad, Gävle, Fagersta, Sundsvall, Östersund)
Guillaume Tell: Arnold
1930, December 27 - 1932, January 3
11 performances, all in Stockholm

Strauss, Johann (II) (1825-1899) Austrian
Die Fledermaus: Alfred
1935, September 17 - 1936, September 2
10 performances, all in Stockholm
Der Zigeunerbaron: Sándor Barinkay
1938, April 4 - August 26
7 performances, all in Stockholm

Strauss, Richard (1864-1949) German
Arabella: Graf Elemer [Count Elemer]
1933, December 30 - 1934, February 14
6 performances, all in Stockholm (it is doubtful if JB sang the role at the last perf.)
Salome: Narraboth
1931, December 29 - 1932, October 3
5 performances, all in Stockholm

Tchaikovsky, Pyotr (1840-1893) Russian
Evgeny Onegin [*Eugene Onegin*]: Lensky
1933, January 14 - 1935, December 10
8 performances, all in Stockholm

Thomas, Ambroise (1811-1896) French

Mignon: Wilhelm Meister

1932, October 8 - 1937, January 31

10 performances, all with R. Opera (7 in Stockholm, 3 on tour in Malmö)

Verdi, Giuseppe (1813-1901) Italian

Aida: Radamès

1935, October 12 - 1958, November 29 (Chicago)

32 performances: 25 with R. Opera (1935-57: 24 in Stockholm, 1 on tour in Gothenburg), 2 in Prague (1936-37, National Theatre & New German Theatre), 1 in Vienna (1936), 1 in Budapest (1937), 3 in Chicago (1958). Only act 3 and only act 4 sung once each in Stockholm

Un ballo in maschera: Riccardo / Gustavus III

1934, April 18 - 1957, November 18 (Chicago)

38 performances: 9 in Stockholm (1934-51), 1 in Vienna (1937), 2 with San Francisco Opera (1940: 1 in S.F., 1 on tour in Los Angeles), 13 with the Met (1940-56: 7 in N.Y., 6 on tour in Philadelphia, Dallas, Los Angeles, Cleveland, Boston), 1 in Copenhagen (1945), 2 in New Orleans (1950), 6 in Milan (1951), 4 in Chicago (1955-57)

Don Carlo: Don Carlo

1950, November 6 (New York) - 1958, November 4 (Los Angeles, S.F. Opera)

16 performances: 14 with the Met (1950-57: 13 in N.Y., 1 on tour in Philadelphia), 1 in Chicago (1957), 1 with San Francisco Opera (1958 in Los Angeles)

Messa da Requiem

1937, April 28 (Stockholm, Concert Hall) - 1940, November 23 (New York, Carnegie Hall)

4 performances: 1 in Stockholm (1937), 2 in Lucerne (1939), 1 in New York (1940)

Rigoletto: Il Duca di Mantova [The Duke of Mantua]

1932, February 25 - 1958, November 19 (Chicago)

56 performances: 24 in Stockholm (1932-57), 1 in Dresden (1937), 1 in Vienna (1937), 7 in Chicago (1937-58), 13 with the Met (1940-56: 10 in N.Y., 3 on tour in Cleveland & Chicago), 2 in Copenhagen (1942), 3 in Milan (1946), 3 with San Francisco Opera (1951-58: 1 in S.F., 2 on tour in Los Angeles), 1 in Helsinki (1955), 1 with New York City Opera (1956, in Detroit)

La traviata: Alfredo

1933, January 5 - 1939, August 29

13 performances: 12 in Stockholm (1933-39), 1 in Prague (1936)

Il trovatore: Manrico

1935, August 17 - 1960, March 29 (San Francisco, Cosmopolitan)

67 performances: 19 in Stockholm (1935-60), 5 in Vienna (1936-37), 1 in Prague (1936), 17 with the Met (1938-57: 11 in N.Y., 6 on tour in Los Angeles, Minneapolis, Cleveland, Philadelphia, Boston), 2 in London (1939), 4 in Florence (1943), 8 with San Francisco Opera (1946-58: 4 in S.F., 4 on tour in Los Angeles & Sacramento), 1 in Miami Beach (1954), 7 in Chicago (1955-58), 2 in Tulsa (1959), 1 with Cosmopolitan Opera in San Francisco (1960). Only act 3 sung once in Stockholm

Wagner, Richard (1813-1883) German

Der fliegende Holländer: Erik

1931, September 29 - 1933, April 24

4 performances, all in Stockholm

Das Rheingold: Froh

1933, January 17

1 performance in Stockholm

Tannhäuser: Walther von der Vogelweide

1931, August 8 - 1932, September 30

12 performances, all in Stockholm

Tristan und Isolde: Ein junger Seemann [A Young Sailor]

1932, February 15 - 1935, April 6

4 performances, all in Stockholm

Zandonai, Riccardo (1883-1944) Italian

I cavalieri di Ekebù: Ruster (a minor role, not in the original Italian version)

1931, April 19 - 1936, March 2 (Stockholm)

11 performances, all with R. Opera (9 in Stockholm, 2 on tour in Helsinki & Riga)

Ziedner, Edvin (1892-1951) Swedish

Bellman: Näktergal, skald [Näktergal, poet]

1930, July 25

1 performance in Stockholm

A Summary of Jussi Björling's Recording Career and Repertoire

The Björling Boys' Ensemble (1911-1927)

It is noteworthy that although JB died before his fiftieth birthday, his recording career comprised forty years, beginning in the acoustical era and ending when stereophonic sound was already well developed. The American Columbia "juvenile trio" recordings from 1920 are unique documents of JB's "pre-career" as a trebble singer together with his brothers. We will probably never know exactly how and when these recordings were made, but they certainly date from the beginning of David Björling's American tour with his three eldest sons [see note for Nos. 1-6]. (According to JB's autobiography, *Med bagaget i strupen*, he had forgotten these records when he heard one of them played on a radio programme where his little son Anders took part. JB was then able to recall "a big horn before which I stood singing somewhere in the States" and how the brothers "were pulled to and fro on a carriage; when we sang loudly, the carriage was drawn away from the horn, but on lower notes it was drawn closer".)

These recordings demonstrate the results of the skilful and purposeful musical education which David Björling gave his sons very early in life - an education which was one of JB's unique assets when he began his training to become an opera singer. Though no solo performances were recorded in 1920, JB contributed with solo singing already during the US tour, and before the ensemble dispersed in 1927, he also performed songs which would remain in his repertoire: "Tonerna", "Mattinata", "M'appari".

Early HMV Recordings (1929-1936)

JB's recording career as a tenor also had an early start. On September 4, 1929, in Stockholm he made his first recordings for the Skandinaviska Grammophon AB, the Swedish branch of "His Master's Voice". According to Gösta Björling, JB had been recommended to the record company by John Forsell. These first HMV recordings should probably be regarded as test recordings and were not approved for publication, but the singer was thought so promising that one month later, on October 4, he could sign his first recording contract. This contract was valid for two years, starting on October 1, and it guaranteed JB a minimum fee of Kronor 1.200 a year, based upon at least twelve recordings at Kronor 100 each. Recordings which were not approved, for one reason or another, had to be repeated without compensation. For "verse and refrain" and "refrain" recordings, the fee was only Kronor 50 and 35, respectively. These conditions can be compared to those in JB's first operatic contract in 1931, which gave him Kronor 500 a month.

Nils Grevillius, who had already been present when JB had his first audition before the Swedish Broadcasting Corporation in 1928, did not conduct on the two first recordings in September, but beginning with the second session in December and to the very end of JB's career, Grevillius would be more closely associated with him than any other conductor. Together they recorded far more than a hundred songs and arias for the HMV and RCA companies, and Grevillius also conducted many of JB's concerts and opera performances in Sweden. In JB's autobiography, he praises Grevillius as "extremely inspiring" and thanks him for "much of my musical education".

In the same book, JB vividly describes his feelings when he received his first own record. "After the record had been pressed, I was very eager to listen to my own voice in mechanical reproduction. I went up to collect the record and also received a gramophone which they offered to send home to me in the afternoon. But I did not want to wait - I took the big parcel in my arms, got it into an automobile and spent the afternoon playing the record again and again. I hope you will excuse this self-complacency on the part of a boy who had never before been able to listen to himself from the outside, so to speak. I did not recognize my voice at all."

In those two first years as an HMV artist, JB recorded romantic songs of various origins but also, about a month after his operatic debut, the first operatic arias. On September 15, 1931, the first contract was prolonged for one year (same terms as before), and a few days later, JB made his first vocal refrain (refrängsång) recording, assisting Fred Winter's orchestra. This recording was issued in JB's own name, but his continued activities as a "refrain singer" during the two years to come were connected with the assumed name of Erik Odde. Gösta Kjellertz, JB's colleague and friend in those days, has described how the two discussed the possibilities of earning more money by recording popular tunes under an assumed name, and how JB invented his pseudonym by free association. In his autobiography, JB unmasked the "whispering jazz singer" Erik Odde, but he did not include Odde records in the discography. Several of the ten original Odde records are now extremely rare; twelve titles were issued in all, and most of the records had Odde on one side only. (In this connection, it is interesting to note that the chapter "In Mechanical Reproduction" in JB's book contains a proposal to create a national sound archive: "Such an archive need not collect everything, but why not? - it would be difficult to exclude anything. Many jazz records are of extremely ephemeral interest now, but might be interesting to scholars in the future." A national Swedish sound archive which receives the legal deposit of produced records, ALB, was not established until 1979.)

In October 1932, when the HMV contract was prolonged for yet another year, the terms were changed and JB now received a 5% royalty on the retail price (up to 1936, all his records were issued in the plum-label X series; in 1932, those records were sold at a price of Kronor 3.50). Though the contract was not prolonged again in 1933, JB remained an HMV artist and his recordings went on for a time as regularly as before. Thus, during twelve months beginning in October 1933, he made twelve recordings, as he had made between eleven and thirteen recordings during each of the four earlier "contract years". These numbers include Erik Odde recordings, so the assumed name did not actually lead to any expansion of JB's recording activities. It seems to have been difficult for the recording company to find a suitable repertoire for him.

Beginning in November 1933, there was a distinct change in JB's recording profile. The series of opera recordings in Swedish which he now began marked his farewell to dance and "hit" tunes; from now on, JB was definitely established as a serious artist also on the record market. However, from 1934, the absence of an agreement with the Skandinaviska

Grammophon AB was mirrored in a marked reduction of his recording activities, and for two years, starting in October 1934, he recorded only two songs and two arias. Though JB and his gramophone company were not able to agree upon a contract at this time, their relations evidently continued to be good. JB stated in 1945 in his autobiography that he had "always had the most pleasant connections with 'His Master's Voice'" and that he was "really attached to the nice little fox-terrier who looks up into the horn".

The International HMV Artist (1936-1950)

In 1936, JB's successful tour to Prague and Vienna gave promises of a world career and helped to bring about a new formal contract with the Swedish HMV representative. There is also evidence that another record company had now begun to show interest in him. The HMV contract was signed on April 25 and valid for two years, beginning in May. The singer was still given a royalty of 5% for twelve titles a year (with Kronor 300 for each title in advance payment), but his introduction into the international "red label" series would soon give him considerably greater revenues than before. It should be noted that the 1936 contract also stipulated that the recordings should be made in Copenhagen if possible, a paragraph which was never respected.

With the new contract a long series of recordings began in Stockholm, with a varied repertoire of arias, duets and songs. The recordings were alternately made in the original language for the international market, and in Swedish for the Scandinavian market. Until July 1939, when the pianist Harry Ebert accompanied a few lieder, all these recordings were made with an orchestra directed by Grevillius. The impression the records immediately made outside Sweden may be exemplified by a quotation from the first review in The Gramophone of a JB record, DA 1548: "Through the medium of this record a young Swedish tenor makes his bow to British gramophiles. Past disappointments are apt to make the reviewer extra cautious of assuming the prophet's mantle; otherwise I might be rash enough to speak of H.M.V. having discovered a 'new Caruso'. I disclaim any such prophecy and dismiss the idea that Björling's voice resembles Caruso's; but I do say that a young singer with such a splendid voice and obvious skill and intelligence should go very far indeed if he takes himself and his art seriously."

The increased demand for JB records was mirrored in the improved terms; when the contract was prolonged in 1938 and 1939 (each time for one year), the royalty was increased first from 5% to 8%, then from 8% to 10% (valid for the international repertoire only). In 1937, the HMV mother company planned to make recordings with JB when he visited London, but the scheduled sessions had to be cancelled [see note for No. 102X]. JB now began his "second" American career, which was from the beginning very successful, and it was natural that recordings were also discussed with the American representative of the HMV company, the Victor company. JB's first contract with Victor was signed in January 1940, valid for one year and comprising twelve selections. For the recordings, which took place at the beginning of the year with JB's Swedish favourite pianist Harry Ebert, lieder and Scandinavian songs were chosen.

Although the Swedish recording contract was not immediately prolonged, a few recordings with orchestra were made in Stockholm in the summer of 1941. A new contract with the Skandinaviska Grammophon AB was signed in January 1943, but during the two war years

1942 and 1943, which JB mainly spent in Sweden, he made no studio recordings. A further contract signed December 1943 was renewed several times. During a period of five years, about two dozen arias, duets and songs from the international repertoire were recorded in Stockholm with Grevillius as conductor under this contract. The royalty was still 10%, but now a paragraph concerning "perpetual" royalty (which would be paid to the heirs as long as the records were sold) was inserted; this agreement seems to have been rather unique on the Swedish record market.

The RCA Period (1950-1960)

Already by the end of 1946, JB's Swedish recording contract had been prolonged through RCA Victor; in March 1949, he signed a new two-year contract with that company. This proved important for the future; while in the 1930's and 1940's JB had been recording almost exclusively for the Swedish EMI branch, he would during the 1950's and until his death be tied to RCA Victor. Up to 1957, when the old partnership between EMI and RCA broke up, JB's new RCA recordings were issued in Europe on the HMV/Electrola label (as his 78 rpm. HMV recordings had been issued on the Victor label in the US and in some other non-European countries), but later they were distributed on the RCA label everywhere.

The new tape recording technique was used from the beginning for JB's American RCA recordings; they began in 1950-51 with a number of arias and duets with the baritone Robert Merrill, conducted by Renato Cellini in New York, and continued in 1952 with the first complete opera recording, *Il trovatore*. During the years 1952-59, ten complete operas which were all originally issued on the RCA label, were recorded either in New York (*Trovatore, Cavalleria rusticana, Pagliacci, Bohème*), or in the summers in Italy (*Manon Lescaut, Aida, Rigoletto, Tosca*, a second *Cavalleria, Turandot*). JB's last complete studio recording, Verdi's *Messa da Requiem*, made in Vienna less than three months before his death, should also be included with this group of recordings.

After the end of its cooperation with EMI, RCA had entered into a new partnership with Decca/London, and as a result of this, artists under exclusive contract to one of the companies were from 1957 also available for recording projects with the other. JB's early complete opera recordings were generally made together with a group of RCA artists including Milanov, Barbieri, Merrill and Warren; in the late 50's, he was also partnered in the recording studio by Decca singers like Tebaldi and Nilsson. In 1960, JB was lent to the Decca Co. for the recording of *Un ballo in maschera*, an opera which RCA did not have any plans to record at that time. (Regarding the cancellation of this project in 1960, see note for No. 244; the recording was realized in 1961 with Bergonzi in Riccardo's role.) The agreement between RCA and Decca also explains some of the complications in JB's discography: though some of his recordings were made by RCA and originally published on that label, the masters were owned by Decca/London and the recordings could be reissued by the latter companies in the 1970's when the agreement had expired (this applies to the *Cavalleria* of 1957, with operatic arias attached, and to the *Requiem*).

During the 1950's, RCA also produced valuable documents of JB's ability as a recitalist together with his American accompanist Schauwecker: an LP of lieder and songs was made in the studio in 1952 and two Carnegie Hall recitals (1955 & 1958) were recorded live but only in part released by the company. Besides the single LP side of arias recorded in 1957 in Italy to supplement the stereo *Cavalleria*, there were in 1957 and 1959 also RCA recordings of arias and songs in Sweden (through Grammofon AB Electra), where JB's cooperation with Grevillius was continued.

JB also made some EMI recordings in Europe during his RCA period: in 1952 in London, four songs in English with piano accompaniment, and in the following year in Stockholm, four Swedish ones with orchestra (his proceeds from the latter recordings went to charity). More important is the fact that he was for the third time to be de los Angeles' partner in a complete opera recording, *Madama Butterfly*, produced in 1959 in Rome. (The two earlier recordings where JB had sung opposite this exclusive EMI artist, *Pagliacci* and the very successful *Bohème*, now also belong to the EMI catalogue, though they were recorded and originally released by RCA; compare the case with RCA/Decca recordings above.)

Recordings which were never realized

The recording companies certainly did not lack interest in a further exploitation of JB's talents but, for different reasons, several large recording projects which were planned or at least discussed during his last decade never materialized. It is open to discussion which of these are most to be regretted, but it is certainly unfortunate that JB did not record any French opera in the studio. *Carmen* was considered as early as 1951, but when this recording was realized, Jan Peerce sang Don José opposite Risë Stevens under Reiner's baton. A later *Carmen* project might have brought JB together with Callas and von Karajan. In 1954, a planned recording of excerpts from *Samson et Dalila* with JB and R. Stevens under Stokowski was cancelled. For the *Manon* recording conducted by Monteux in 1956, JB was invited to sing opposite de los Angeles but declined at the last moment and was replaced by Henri Legay. There were also plans to record JB in the two French roles which he had in his repertoire, but *Faust* was recorded without JB's participation and a *Roméo et Juliette* planned to be conducted by Beecham in 1959 never took shape.

Two attempts to preserve JB's interpretation of one of his best Italian roles, Riccardo in *Un ballo in maschera*, both failed for different reasons: in 1954, he was forced by laryngitis to be replaced at short notice by Jan Peerce in Toscanini's combined broadcast and recording, and in 1969, Solti's recording was cancelled [see note for No. 244]. JB recorded *Pagliacci* in 1953, but he had earlier discussed to record that opera with the La Scala ensemble in Italy. Though he was reluctant to undertake the principal role in *Otello* on the stage, there were plans for a complete recording both in the early 1950s and in 1960. A *Traviata* recording with JB was originally planned in 1957 together with *Tosca* in Rome. There are also rumours of planned recordings of *Don Carlo* (1954) and Puccini's *Il tabarro* (1960). JB's RCA contract was to expire at the beginning of 1961, and one of the projects under a planned new EMI contract was a re-recording in stereo of *Bohème*, again with de los Angeles; but by the time of his death, JB had already withdrawn from the cast, as the soprano also later did.

Finally, the list of opera roles which might perhaps have been recorded by JB in their entirety should also include two in the Wagner repertoire: *Lohengrin* (under Beecham, who considered JB ideal for the role), and Walther in *Die Meistersinger von Nürnberg*. During JB's last years, there were advanced plans for an LP record of operatic duets with

Schwarzkopf (from *Bohème, Mefistofele, Carmen, Otello, Martha, L'amico Fritz* and *Madama Butterfly*). In Sweden, the cooperation with Grevillius in the recording studio would have continued if death had not intervened; a number of re-recordings in stereo of the 78 rpm. repertoire were planned for the beginning of 1961. Still more interesting might have been a series of operatic scenes for the Swedish Television (from *Roméo et Juliette, Faust, Evgeny Onegin, Knyaz Igor, Tosca, Bohème* and *Fanciulla del West*), to be produced under Grevillius at the end of 1960.

Live, Radio and Film Recordings

A few words should also be devoted to a survey of the numerous recordings which are direct documents from JB's stage, radio and film career, and which are collected in Section 1:B of this phonography. This section shows how many of these recordings have been issued, but still more are circulated among collectors as tape copies. With the exception of the Carnegie Hall recordings already mentioned, the live recordings were not originally made for commercial publication. However, material from some Swedish concerts and recitals was issued on the RCA label, beginning in 1965, and many releases of live recordings have since the end of the 1950s been made by small companies or interested individuals, among which JB's friend E.J. Smith deserves special mention.

Most of the live recordings were a result of JB's association with the radio companies, either directly, when he was engaged by those companies for concerts or recitals, or indirectly, when other performances in which he took part were broadcast. Though JB's HMV recording career and his opera career both had a remarkably early start, his radio career began even earlier; he participated in a "variety entertainment" broadcast before he was accepted as a pupil at the conservatory. In the late thirties, he had reached a position as one of the most popular voices on the Swedish radio, a position which he would keep until his death. Not surprisingly, his first preserved live recording is a fragment from one of the more than thirty Stockholm Royal Opera performances during the thirties in which he sang and which were broadcast, at least in part (Section 1:B and its appendix testify of the cooperation between the Swedish Radio and the Royal Opera during this period). Of the 130 recordings in Section 1:B, one third are broadcasts by (or transcriptions for) the Swedish Radio. They cover most of JB's career since 1934, but there is a large gap in the late forties. At that time, JB was all the more active on radio in the US, and in all, more than fifty American broadcasts have survived, most of them radio concerts. These begin with JB's American debut as a tenor in 1937 and belong mainly to five series of programmes: *General Motors Concerts* (1937), *Ford Sunday Evening Hour* (1938-40, 1945-46), *Voice of Firestone* (1945-46, 1950-52), *Telephone Hour* (1948-51) and *Standard Hour* (1949, 1951). Valuable documents of JB's singing on the American opera stage are especially found among his eleven Metropolitan Saturday matinee broadcasts.

Among the live recordings which were not broadcast, the series of nine recordings from Gröna Lund outdoor recitals in Stockholm (1950-51, 1956-60) may deserve a special mention. Only a small part of the JB recordings are audiovisual documents from film or television. The only motion picture in which he took the lead part, *Fram för framgång*, deserves to be mentioned first among these. Five American TV concerts are known to have been preserved as AV recordings, including three *Voice of Firestone* programmes.

Unfortunately, the only JB opera performance which was telecast, *Don Carlo* at the 1950 Met opening night, does not seem to exist as an AV recording.

The Repertoire and What Is Left of It

During the nine seasons when JB remained at the Royal Opera in Stockholm, he appeared in 53 opera and operetta roles (39 of which were principal roles); he also sang with the company in two large sacred works. After his permanent Swedish contract expired in the summer of 1939, he added only Des Grieux in *Manon Lescaut* (1949) and *Don Carlo* (1950) to his stage repertoire, which thus totally comprised no fewer than 55 roles. However, his regular repertoire as an established world artist was much smaller. After the summer of 1939, he sang only sixteen of his roles on the stage, and in four of these sixteen operas, he appeared only once: *Fanal* and *Traviata* in the autumn of 1939, *Madama Butterfly* (the first act only) in 1945, all in Stockholm; *Fidelio* (in English) in 1948 at an abridged American concert performance. The remaining twelve operas, which JB sang many times at various opera houses, are listed below in order according to the total number of performances which I have found: *La bohème* (115), *Faust* (70), *Il trovatore* (67), *Rigoletto* (56), *Tosca* (51), *Roméo et Juliette* (44), *Un ballo in maschera* (38), *Aida* (32), *Cavalleria rusticana* (31), *Manon Lescaut* (25), *Pagliacci* (20), *Don Carlo* (16).

Complete recordings exist of all but two of the sixteen JB opera roles enumerated above (and of his performances in *Messa da Requiem* and *Missa Solemnis*). He recorded nine of these operas commercially (and with two exceptions, *Madama Butterfly* and *Aida*, they also exist in one or more complete live versions); the tenth opera role which he recorded, Calaf in *Turandot*, he never sang on stage. Five of the operas in JB's repertoire exist only as live recordings of varying technical quality: *Traviata, Ballo in maschera, Don Carlo* and the two French ones, *Roméo et Juliette* and *Faust*; a fragment from a *Fanal* performance has also been preserved.

An analysis of JB's recorded repertoire of songs, arias etc. shows that the total number of different songs and separately performed excerpts from larger works, recorded live or/and in the studio, is about 210; about forty of them were only recorded live. One fourth of the total number are popular songs in Swedish which were recorded by JB in his youth but hardly performed by him outside the recording studio. The rest of the material may be divided into three categories of approximately equal size: one group is made up by opera arias and duets, one by lieder and Scandinavian art songs, and one mainly by more or less popular songs in English, Italian or Swedish which were sung in public or recorded by JB as a mature artist.

Available programmes and reviews make it possible to give a more comprehensive picture of JB's concert repertoire by supplementing twenty-nine arias and songs which were probably never recorded and which are therefore not found in the Composer Index (items sung only in conservatory students' concerts are not included; items marked by an asterisk were only performed before 1939, as far as I know):
Hugo Alfvén, Lindagull; - Alfred Berg, Aftonsång [performed as late as 1957, this song also seems to have been JB's most popular solo number when he still sang together with his brothers]; - Harry Danielsson, Melodi; - Ernesto de Curtis, Canta pe' me; - Jean-Baptiste Faure, Crucifix* (?); - Ossip Gabrilovich, Goodbye; - Erik Gustaf Geijer, Afton-

klockan*, Natthimlen, Vallgossens visa*; - Edvard Grieg, Våren; - Joseph Haydn, Mit Würd' und Hoheit angetan* (*Die Schöpfung*); - Eugen Hildach, Lenz; - Frank La Forge, Hills; - Franz Liszt, *Eine Faust-Sinfonie* (tenor solo); - Jules Massenet, Pourquoi me réveiller (*Werther*); - Felix Mendelssohn, If with all your hearts* (*Elijah*), Then, then, shall the righteous* (*Elijah*); - Wolfgang Amadeus Mozart, Abendempfindung, Dalla sua pace (*Don Giovanni*); - Wilhelm Peterson-Berger, Ditt namn jag hade skrivit; - Jean Sibelius, Den första kyssen, Jubal* [this song first performed in public by JB, New York 1938]; - August Söderman, Längtan; - Charles G. Spross, Will o' the Wisp; - Per Ulrik Stenhammar, Omvänden Eder I avfälliga barn*; - Richard Strauss, Heimliche Aufforderung; - Vilhelm Svedbom, Sten Sture; - Richard Wagner, Mit Gewitter und Sturm (*Der fliegende Holländer*); - Ivar Widéen, Serenad ("Tallarnas barr"); - Hugo Wolf, Fussreise.

The Recorded Legacy: A Quantitative Summary

Not surprisingly, the material from live performances and broadcasts shows to be much larger than that which was recorded in the gramophone studio. Section 1:A demonstrates that JB made 243 studio recordings for the Columbia, HMV, RCA and Decca companies, 230 of which have now been issued. Twelve of these numbers represent complete operas and one the *Messa da Requiem*. This should be compared to the fact that in Section 1:B are included about 400 preserved, individually performed songs, arias, duets and scenes (derived from 81 different concerts and other music recordings, films, etc.), as well as material from 37 live opera performances (24 of them complete or almost so) and two complete oratorios. Thus, JB's recorded legacy, as it is known today, consists of more than 650 items of varying length and includes at least 36 complete (or almost complete) opera and 3 oratorio recordings. To this should be added 10 transcriptions of speech only.

Explanations and Commentaries on the Disposition of the Phonography

Section 1:A, the first part of the chronological list, comprises studio recordings arranged by commercial record companies. Each song, aria or duet recorded at one session, or complete opera recorded at a series of sessions, has been given a number from 1 to 244 (followed by A or B when different takes of the recordings were issued). This means that 78 rpm. recordings which were repeated on a later date, are listed under different numbers for the two recordings, even if the same matrix numbers were also used for the repeats. Matrix or serial numbers of the recordings are found below the title in the left-hand margin. All known take numbers are listed after the matrix numbers, and such information has been verified by checking the recording ledgers and/or the discs themselves. If the recording ledgers show more than one take, the issued take numbers are bold. Information about unissued takes which are known to be preserved is given in the notes (inserted after Section 1:A). (The Swedish EMI company does not possess any matrices of JB recordings but it is not clear whether unissued takes may in some cases still be kept by the British mother company.)

Section 1:B comprises all other recordings, *proved to still exist*. A performance which may or may not exist in recorded form is listed in the following Appendix. (This rule was not strictly followed in the first edition of this work, and some performances have therefore now been transferred to the Appendix; see the Key to Index Numbers for details.) This subsection contains concerts, recitals, opera performances, films, radio and television recordings, etc., mainly live recordings. Each recording is given a four-digit number, from 3401 to 6004, with the items sung sub-numbered by letters. The numbering is not continuous, but the first two figures indicate the recording year, the last two the chronological order within that year (for example, 4302c = the third song from the second listed performance in 1943).

If a certain recording of a performance may be regarded as "original" (e.g. being the archive copy the broadcasting company), available information about its location and archive number is given in the right-hand margin under the first paragraph of the listing. A few numbers for Sw. Radio copies of other rare material (e.g. from the Björling family collection) have also been listed there. (The Swedish Broadcasting Corporation, Stockholm - Sveriges Radio AB - is here often referred to as "Sw. Radio". In Swedish, the company was originally called AB Radiotjänst and 1979-1992 Sveriges Riksradio AB [Swedish National Radio Co.].) In the Sw. Radio Programme Archive, tape copies of an important part of the material listed in Section 1:B are preserved. Sw. Radio numbers indicate the original storage medium: L-B = acetate discs; S = steel tape; other tape prefixes generally refer to modern soundtape. Acetate discs which have been transferred to tape are no longer preserved in the archive. Valuable Sw. Radio recordings were earlier also transferred to metal masters and these are now stored as duplicates at the ALB; this applies to Nos. 3401, 4201, 4401 & 5204a,b.

Concerts and recitals where only a part of JB's programme is known to be preserved are listed in their entirety, but with missing items preceded by a question-mark, if it seems possible that they may still appear, otherwise with the missing items enumerated in a concluding note only (items not performed by JB are left out). When operatic performances were only fragmentarily recorded, the total length in minutes of all preserved material is given, but only excerpts where JB sings are listed in detail.

The Appendix to Section 1:B comprises: (1) all known JB broadcasts, from which no material is yet known to have survived; (2) non-broadcast performances, recordings of which are rumoured but not proved to exist. This list may be helpful in the search for further surviving recordings. Performances in the Appendix are continuously numbered from A01 to A81.

Dates in Section 1 indicate the *recording* day(s), if known. The dates given for complete opera recordings specify only the sessions at which JB is known to have been present, where this is possible. Broadcasts were live, unless otherwise noted. For radio transcriptions, the date of the first broadcast is also given. Exact dating is especially problematic for many early Swedish HMV recordings, and information from Swedish recording ledgers must sometimes be complemented or corrected by information from other sources; all such problems are discussed in the corresponding notes.

Orchestras always have their names given in English. Names of orchestras on the HMV 78 rpm. recordings are generally translated from the label. The conductor's name (or Christian name) has been added from the ledgers when missing on the labels. For exceptions (primarily the indication of the Royal Orch. according to the ledgers), see the notes.

The following translations are used for the larger Swedish orchestras:
Band of the Royal Svea Life Guards = Kungliga Svea Livgardes musikkår, Stockholm
Gothenburg Symphony Orch. = Göteborgs Symfoniker
Malmö Concert Hall Foundation Orch. = Malmö konserthusstiftelses orkester (presently called Malmö symfoniorkester)
Royal Orch. = Kungliga Hovkapellet (the orchestra of the Royal Opera)
Stockholm Band of the Swedish Army = Arméns musikkår i Stockholm
Stockholm Concert Association Orch. = Konsertföreningens orkester, Stockholm (from 1957 renamed Stockholms filharmoniska orkester)
Stockholm Philharmonic Orch. = Stockholms filharmoniska orkester (presently called Kungliga Filharmoniska orkestern i Stockholm)
Stockholm Radio Orch. = Stockholms radioorkester (1937-1948; consisted of members from the Concert Association Orch.)
Swedish Radio Orch. = Radioorkestern, Stockholm (existed 1925-1937, consisting of members from other orchestras, and 1948-1967 as the Sw. Broadcasting Corp.'s own main orchestra (presently called Radiosymfonikerna)
Swedish Radio Symphony Orch. = Radiotjänsts symfoniorkester, Stockholm (1937-1948 name for the whole Concert Association Orch. when playing under radio contract; after 1948 for that part of it which was earlier called "Stockholms radioorkester")

Where information about the orchestrations or the size of the orchestra has been available from EMI or RCA documents, it is added in the corresponding notes. Such information shows that the size of the orchestra accompanying JB on his recordings for the X series varied considerably (the orchestra was probably much enlarged when recordings for the international market began in 1936). The "Nils Grevillius' Orch." or "Nils Grevillius & his orch." does not indicate a regular orchestra. Grevillius stated (*Jussi Björling: En minnesbok*, p. 71) that to start with, his recordings with JB were made with an orchestra "which I had put together especially for this purpose, and which was therefore called the 'Nils Grevillius' Orch.', but the musicians were almost without exception drawn from the Royal Orch. and the Stockholm Concert Association Orch., later practically always from the Royal Orch.".

Titles are first listed in the original language. If they were sung in translation (or with an independent text in another language), this version is added in brackets after the abbreviation for the language used (Swedish, Danish, Norwegian, English, German, Italian, French or Latin) which always follows the title in the original language. Operatic titles are generally given by quoting the first line of the (recitative and) aria, but original label titles, when variations occur, are supplemented.

Opera recordings have the soloists arranged by pitch (soprano, mezzosoprano, contralto, tenor, baritone, bass), with the voice types separated by semicolons. The distribution of separately issued excerpts from larger recordings is shown by means of a detailed breakdown of the opera and a sub-numbering system. In this connection, excerpts in which JB did not sing have been disregarded.

Issues of recordings are in Section 1 grouped by types of disc (78, 45, 33 1/3 rpm., CD) or tape (open reel = OR, sound cassette = MC, cartridge = 8T, video cassette = VC). Transcription discs (only occuring in Section 1:B, and then always of American origin, with speed 33 1/3 rpm., size 14"/40 cm. and bearing matrix numbers only) are separated from other 33 1/3 rpm. discs and preceded by the abbreviation "Tr". For commercial recordings, discs or tape issues of the same type (45, 33 1/3 rpm., cassette, etc.) with identical contents are grouped together, separated from other issues by "//". These groups are arranged chronologically according to the earliest issue in each group, which issue (or the mono version of it) is preceded by "[1]". The record numbers for issues with identical contents appear in alphabetical order by label, country (for international labels) and release date. HMV's international 78 rpm. DA/DB series and records in the Scandinavian X series which were listed in the international catalogue are put before the corresponding local issues without indication of country. Internationally distributed CD issues are generally listed under the country of the mother company (Germany for BMG/RCA in Europe, Britain for EMI, etc.). "Germany" stands for West Germany prior to 1990. Labels are written in italics, and not repeated when they appear more than once in the same group. When the label is repeated as number prefix, the latter is omitted if no country indication comes between.

Section 2 gives a comprehensive survey of disc and tape numbers, arranged by labels in alphanumerical order (pure numbers first, prefixes of figures and of letters following). As a rule, the numbers are written as they occur in their most complete form on labels or sleeves, but some details are written in a standardized way (e.g., hyphens between letter prefixes and numbers are generally left out, and set numbers of the type "... 6711/2" are written "6711/12" (*two* last figures indicated)). Price suffixes are generally left out when two or more suffixes, intended for different markets, are printed on the same issue. Sleeve titles are given in the language(s) used.

The intention has been to treat each label separately, but it may sometimes be difficult to differentiate between a label and a series. Series titles are indicated either in the heading above a group of records or in brackets after the sleeve title. "His Master's Voice" in various languages is regarded as one label. Traditional EMI Labels (like HMV, Odeon, Columbia, etc.) are regarded as separate labels even if "EMI" is dominating the logotype; the label used for EMI CDs worldwide (EMI text only but Angel logo) is regarded as EMI label. Victrola and Red/Gold Seal are listed under RCA. The Victor / RCA Victor / RCA label is listed as Victor (abbreviated "Vic.") for 78 rpm. records only, otherwise as RCA. Details about the JB recordings contained in a coupling, issued under more than one number, are as a rule specified only for the earliest (mono) issue of any type. Parallel stereo issues, reissues and issues in other countries are referred for contents to this original issue. Tape versions of a record refer for contents to the earliest corresponding issue on 33 1/3 rpm. disc (or CD); CDs with simultaneously issued LP versions refer to the latter for contents.

Stereo recordings, issued in stereo, are indicated by "*" after the record number (all information refers to JB recordings on the issue only). The asterisk is followed by a question-mark, if the information is uncertain, or by "p" (partly), if there are also JB recordings in mono or electronic stereo on the same issue. The following two symbols, "(*)" and "*(*)" appear only in Section 2. The former indicates mono recordings stated to give stereo effect (electronically reprocessed) and the latter is used for issues which are also stated to be in stereo, but where some of the items were originally recorded in stereo, others in mono. One should keep in mind, however, that many CD (and corresponding LP/MC) issues of original mono recordings, which were digitally retransferred, also give stereo effect, though this is not noted on the issue (e.g., this is valid for most RCA JB CDs).

Release dates (year and month when available) have been obtained from various sources and may not always be exact. Some I have received directly from the issuing companies, others have been taken from numerical catalogues or monthly supplements. As far as possible, all issues have been dated at least approximately, for example: a.57 = before (or at the latest in) 1957; p.52 = after 1952; c.61-12 = about December, 1961. For many Teldec issues, copyright dates are given as approximations. In the release date column, a question-mark (?) is used when the release date is not known, a hyphen (-) when the recording was not issued in the respective country.

About 1650 disc and tape numbers are included in Section 2 of the phonography (set numbers composed of two or more individual record numbers being regarded as one number): about 850 are LPs while tapes number about 240, 78s and 45s about 200 each and CDs about 175. Since many records have two parallel numbers and/or have separate numbers for albums and individual discs, the actual number of issues is smaller.

The Indexes refer to Section 1:A and 1:B only, not to the Appendix to Section 1:B (with a few exceptions for programme titles in the Title Index) or to the Chronological Table.

The Composer Index (Section 3:A) arranges the recorded music by composers and titles. Each title of a song, aria, duet, etc., is given (a) in the original language, (b) if this language is a Scandinavian one, also in an English translation; (c) in the language used by JB. For songs with separate titles, also the first line of the text in the used language is indicated (followed by three full stops at the end). The year when an opera or operetta was first performed, names of text authors, years of birth and death for the composers and their nationality are also included in the information.

Numbers in brackets refer to live recordings which have not been located and may or may not exist, or to studio recordings assumed to have been destroyed. A number in italics means that the recording in question was not accompanied by orchestra (generally by piano).

The Title Index (Section 3:B) contains (1) names of operas, operettas and oratorios, and titles of separately performed arias, duets, ensembles and songs - both in the original language and the language used; (2) some well-known operatic excerpts which were not performed separately by JB and are therefore not found in the Composer Index, only in the opera break-downs in Section 1; (3) common English titles, especially for Scandinavian songs; (4) names of radio and television programmes, opera companies, motion pictures, recital and concert hall locations; (5) such categories as films and interviews. If the composer's name is known, the Composer Index should be directly used. The Title Index does not give direct reference to numbers for opera, operetta and oratorio recordings, which have to be sought through the Composer Index, but it gives direct reference to songs, the composers of which may often not be known by the user.

The alphabetical arrangement used in the indexes means that the letters *å* (pronounced like *a* in "call"), *ä* (pronounced like *a* in "hat"), *ö* (pronounced like *i* in "thirst") and *ü* are treated like *a*, *o* and *u*.

Columbia
SVENSKA RECORDS
Dessa artister skola glädja alla svenskar
10 tum, $1.00.
E4546 ALLMOGEVALS / LILLA LISA — Calle Sjöquist, baryton.
Skratta med den storartade Calle Sjöquist och han skall skratta med eder, så att ni nästan kiknar af skratt. Denne utomordentlige baryton sjunger dessa två sånger på ett så anturligt och trefligt sätt, att det är en sann fröjd att höra honom. Skaffa detta record och bjud edra vänner på något storartadt.
E4547 SOMMARGLÄDJE / BARNDOMSHEMMET — Olle, Jussi och Gösta Björling.
Dessa nya exklusiva Columbia-artister äro tre små svenska gossar, endast sex, sju och nio år gamla, men de ha länge utgjort samtalsämnet i den svenska kolonien och äro nu stadda på turné genom landet och roa sin publik öfverallt där de fara fram. De sjunga populära sånger med förundransvärd samsjungning och med berömvärdt resultat. Hör detta record hos er handlande i dag.
Här är edert tillfälle att dansa och höra William Oscar
E4537 SVENSKA PARADMARSCHEN / SVENSK BYVALS — Thavius orkester.
E4538 VÖGGNLJED / O, GUD, HVARS LAND — Wm. Oscar, violinsolo och orkester.
4483 SOLNEDGÅNG I SVERIGE / EKO FRÅN SKANDINAVIEN — Columbia skandinaviska orkester.
Begär den nya katalogen öfver internationella records.
Columbia Records ljuda bäst på Columbia Grafonola. Pris $32.50 upp till $2,100.
Hvarje Columbiahandlare i U. S. och Canada skall med nöje spela hvilket som helst af dessa records för er kostnadsfritt. Han skall äfven ge eder en katalog öfver Columbia records med svensk musik. Fråga honom därom.
När ni köper records, begär
Columbia Records coh nämn numret
Se efter handelsmärket noten på hvarje record.
Columbia Grafonola
COLUMBIA GRAPHOPHONE COMPANY

The first advertisment for a Björling record, **Columbia** *E 4547 (***Svea***, May 19, 1920). The Björling brothers are introduced with the following words: "These new, exclusive Columbia artists are three little Swedish boys, only six, seven and nine years old (!), but they have for a long time been a topic of conversation in the Swedish colony and are now touring the country, entertaining their audience in all places where they appear. They sing popular songs with admirable coordination and laudable result. Listen to this record at your dealer today."*

Section 1: Chronological List of Recordings

A. Studio Recordings for Record Companies

1920, February [or earlier; see note for Nos. 1-6]. New York, Columbia studio. "Juvenile trio" with brothers Olle & Gösta Björling (boy sopranos) & reed-organ.

1
Der Gottesacker [Sw: O, hur stilla] (Beneken)
85780-1

[78] *Col.* (US) E 4768
[33] *SR* SRLP 1354/55
[CD] *Bluebell* ABCD 016

2
I himmelen [Nor] (trad.)
85781-1

[78] *Col.* (US) E 4691
[33] *SR* SRLP 1354/55
[CD] *Bluebell* ABCD 016

3
O Lamm Gottes unschuldig [Sw: Guds rena lamm oskyldig] (trad.)
85782-1

[78] *Col.* (US) E 4691
[33] *SR* SRLP 1354/55
[CD] *Bluebell* ABCD 016

1920, February [or earlier (see note), but probably one or more days after Nos. 1-3]. New York, Columbia studio. "Juvenile trio" with brothers Olle & Gösta Björling (boy sopranos), accompanied by violin & piano (4-5) or by reed-organ (6).

4
Sommarglädje [Sw] (trad.) [Misspelled on orig. label: Sommar Glädge]
85798-1,-**2**

[78] *Col.* (US) E 4547 // *Radiotjänst* PR 5189
[33] *Odeon* (Sw) PMCS 308 // *Unique* UORC 377 // *SR* SRLP 1354/55 // *Legendary* LR 138

5
On the Banks of the Wabash, Far Away [Sw: Barndomshemmet] (Dresser)
85799-**1**,-**2** [Take 2, see note for Nos. 1-6]

[78] *Col.* (US) E 4547
[33] *Unique* UORC 377 // *ANNA* 1006 // *SR* SRLP 1354/55
[CD] *Bluebell* ABCD 016

*The **Columbia** "flag" label, used for the recordings of the Björling' boys from 1923 (blue, red and white on green background*

6
Psalm No. IV [Sw] (Wennerberg)
85800-1

[78] *Col.* (US) E 4768
[33] *Rococo* 5201 // *Unique* UORC 377 // *SR* SRLP 1354/55
[CD] *Bluebell* ABCD 016 // *Gala* GL 315

1929, September 4. Stockholm, Concert Hall, Attic Auditorium. With orch., cond. Hjalmar Meissner. [Recordings destroyed; see note]

7
For You Alone [Sw: För dig allén] (Geehl)
BE 1892-1

(Not issued. Compare No. 12)

8
Mattinata [Sw] (Leoncavallo)
BE 1893-1

(Not issued. Compare No. 17)

1929, December 18. Stockholm, Concert Hall, Attic Auditorium. With Nils Grevillius & his orch.

9
Torna a Surriento [Sw: Gondolsång] (E. de Curtis)
BE 2118-1,-**2**

[78] *HMV* (Sw) X 3376 // *HMV* (Sw) X 7536
[33] *Rococo* 5237 // *HMV* (GB) [1]RLS 715, (Sw) 7C 153-06518/20M = *WRC* (Au) R 05223/25, (NZ) WE 26451/53 // *Unique* UORC 377
[CD] *Legato* LCD 103-1
[MC] *WRC* (Au) C 05223/25

10
I drömmen du är mig nära [Sw] (Sjögren)
BE 2119-1,-**2**

[78] *HMV* (Sw) [1]X 3377 = *Vic.* (US) 26-1093 // *HMV* (Sw) X 7536
[33] *Rococo* 5341 // *Rubini* GV 21 // *HMV* (GB) [1]RLS 715, (Sw) 7C 153-06518/20M = *WRC* (Au) R 05223/25, (NZ) WE 26451/53 // *ANNA* 1006 // *Dacapo* [1]1C 147-03354/55M, 1C 137 1033543M
[MC] *WRC* (Au) C 05223/25

11
Vita rosor [Sw] (Körling)
BE 2120-**1**,-2

[78] *HMV* (Sw) [1]X 3377 = *Vic.* (US) 26-1093

[33] *Rococo* 5341 // *Rubini* GV 21 // *HMV* (GB) [1]RLS 715, (Sw) 7C 153-06518/20M = *WRC* (Au) R 05223/25, (NZ) WE 26451/53 // *ANNA* 1006

[MC] *WRC* (Au) C 05223/25

12
For You Alone [Sw: För dig allén] (Geehl)
BE 2121-1,-**2**

[78] *HMV* (Sw) X 3376

[33] *HMV* (Sw) [1]SGLP 507 = *MFP* (Sw) MFP 5571 = *Odeon* (Sw) PMES 507, (US) SGLP 507 // *Rococo* 5237 // *Excel.* 1286 001-18 // *HMV* (GB) [1]RLS 715, (Sw) 7C 153-06518/20M = *WRC* (Au) R 05223/25, (NZ) WE 26451/53

[MC] *Odeon* (US) MCPF 6032 // *WRC* (Au) C 05223/25

[8T] *Odeon* (US) 8PF 6032

1930, May 12. Stockholm, Concert Hall, Attic Auditorium. With orch., cond. Nils Grevillius.

13
Ah! Sweet Mystery of Life [Sw: Liv, du är ej längre en mystär] (Herbert: *Naughty Marietta*)
BE 2444-1,-**2**

[78] *HMV* (Sw) X 3466

[33] *Rococo* 5201 // *ANNA* 1006 // *HMV* (Sw) 1359931

14
I de lyse nætter [Sw: Sommarnatt] (Schrader)
BE 2445-1,-**2**

[78] *HMV* (Sw) X 3466

[33] *Rococo* 5341 // *ANNA* 1006 // *HMV* (Sw) 1359931

1930, September 29. Stockholm, Concert Hall, Small Auditorium (?). With orch., cond. Nils Grevillius.

15
Ah! lève-toi, soleil! [Sw: Höj dig, du klara sol] (Gounod: *Roméo et Juliette*) [On orig. label title is written "Höj dig, min sköna sol", but it is sung as indicated above]
BT 5206-1,-**2**

[78] *HMV* (Sw) X 3628

[33] *Rubini* GV 21 // *HMV* (GB) [1]RLS 715, (Sw) 7C 153-06518/20M = *WRC* (Au) R 05223/25, (NZ) WE 26451/53 // *ANNA* 1006 // *Dacapo* [1]1C 147-03354/55M, 1C 137 1033543M

[MC] *WRC* (Au) C 05223/25

16

Questa o quella [Sw: O, I kvinnor] (Verdi: *Rigoletto*) [Orig. label: Hertigens aria]
BT 5207-1,-**2**

[78] *HMV* (Sw) X 3628

[33] *Golden Age* EJS 337 // *Rococo* 5231 // *Rubini* GV 21 // *HMV* (GB) [1]RLS 715, (Sw) 7C 153-06518/20M = *WRC* (Au) R 05223/25, (NZ) WE 6451/53 // *ANNA* 1006 // *Dacapo* [1]1C 147-03354/55M, 1C 137 1033543M

[CD] *Nimbus* NI 7835

[MC] *WRC* (Au) C 05223/25 // *Nimbus* NC 7835

17

Mattinata [Sw] (Leoncavallo)
BT 5208-1,-**2**

[78] *HMV* (Sw) X 3622

[33] *HMV* (Sw) [1]SGLP 507 = *MFP* (Sw) MFP 5571 = *Odeon* (Sw) PMES 507, (US) SGLP 507 // *Rococo* 5237 // *Excel.* 1286 001-18

[MC] *Odeon* (US) MCPF 6032

[8T] *Odeon* (US) 8PF 6032

18

När jag för mig själv i mörka skogen går [Sw] (Peterson-Berger)
BT 5209-1,-**2**

[78] *HMV* (Sw) X 3675

[33] *HMV* (Sw) [1]SCLP 1008 = *Odeon* (Sw) PMES 551 // *Rococo* 5341 // *HMV* (Sw) [1]7C 153-35445/46M = *Odeon* (US) 7C 153-35445/46M // *HMV* (Sw) PRO 3034

[CD] *EMI* (Sw) CDC 7 61075 2

[MC] *Odeon* (US) MCPF 6031 // *HMV* (Sw) 7C 253-35445/46M

[8T] *Odeon* (US) 8PF 6031

19

Bland skogens höga furustammar [Sw] (Peterson-Berger)
BT 5210-1,-**2**

[78] *HMV* (Sw) X 3675

[33] *HMV* (Sw) [1]SCLP 1008 = *Odeon* (Sw) PMES 551 // *Rococo* 5341 // *HMV* (Sw) [1]7C 153-35445/46M = *Odeon* (US) 7C 153-35445/46M // *HMV* (Sw) PRO 3034

[CD] *EMI* (Sw) CDC 7 61075 2

[MC] *Odeon* (US) MCPF 6031 // *HMV* (Sw) 7C 253-35445/46M

[8T] *Odeon* (US) 8PF 6031

1930, October 8. Stockholm, Concert Hall. With orch., cond. Nils Grevillius.

20
Serenata [Sw] (Toselli)
BT 5266-**1**,-2

[78] *HMV* (Sw) X 3556
[33] *HMV* (Sw) [1]SCLP 1008 = *Odeon* (Sw) PMES 551 // *HMV* (Sw) [1]7C 153-35445/46M = *Odeon* (US) 7C 153-35445/46M // *HMV* (GB) [1]RLS 715, (Sw) 7C 153-06518/20M = *WRC* (Au) R 05223/25, (NZ) WE 26451/53 // *Dacapo* [1]1C 147-03354/55M, 1C 137 1033543M // *HMV* (Sw) PRO 3034 // *HMV* (Sw) 7C 061-35731M // *HMV* (Au) [1]OXLP 7660 = *WRC* (Au) R 11409
[CD] *EMI* (Sw) CDC 7 61075 2
[MC] *Odeon* (US) MCPF 6031 // *HMV* (Sw) 7C 253-35445/46M // *WRC* (Au) C 05223/25 // *HMV* (Sw) 7C 261-35731M // *HMV* (Au) TC-OXCP 7660
[8T] *Odeon* (US) 8PF 6031

21
To-day [Sw: I dag] (Arthur)
BT 5267-1,-**2**
[78] *HMV* (Sw) X 3556 // *Vic.* (US) 26-1099
[33] *Rococo* 5341 // *HMV* (GB) [1]RLS 715, (Sw) 7C 153-06518/20M = *WRC* (Au) R 05223/25, (NZ) WE 26451/53 // *Unique* UORC 377
[MC] *WRC* (Au) C 05223/25

22
Salut d'amour [Sw: Violer] (Elgar)
BT 5268-**1**,-2

[78] *HMV* (Sw) X 3622
[33] *Angel* (Ch) 3ACX 47530, (Ur) UAL 12513 = *HMV* (GB,Au) [1]HQM 1190, (GB,SA) HLM 7038, (SA) JALP 29 = *Odeon* (US) PHQM 1190 = *Sera.* (US) 60168
[MC] *HMV* (SA) L4HLM 7038 = *Sera.* (US) [1]4XG 60168

1931, February 11. Stockholm, Concert Hall, Small Auditorium (?). With Nils Grevillius' orch.

23
Tantis serenad [Sw] (trad.)
0T 130-1,-**2**

[78] *HMV* X 3702
[33] *HMV* (Sw) [1]SCLP 1008 = *Odeon* (Sw) PMES 551 // *Rococo* 5341 // *Rubini* GV 21 // *HMV* (Sw) [1]7C 153-35445/46M = *Odeon* (US) 7C 153-35445/46M // *HMV* (Sw) PRO 3034 // *HMV* (Sw) 7C 061-35731M

[CD] *EMI* (Sw) CDC 7 61075 2

[MC] *Odeon* (US) MCPF 6031 // *HMV* (Sw) 7C 253-35445/46M // *HMV* (Sw) 7C 261-35731M

[8T] *Odeon* (US) 8PF 6031

24

Carmela [Sw] (G. de Curtis)

0T 131-1,-**2**

[78] *HMV* X 3702

[33] *HMV* (Sw) [1]SCLP 1008 = *Odeon* (Sw) PMES 551 // *Rococo* 5341 // *Rubini* GV 21 // *HMV* (Sw) [1]7C 153-35445/46M = *Odeon* (US) 7C 153-35445/46M // *HMV* (Sw) PRO 3034

[CD] *EMI* (Sw) CDC 7 61075 2

[MC] *Odeon* (US) MCPF 6031 // *HMV* (Sw) 7C 253-35445/46M

[8T] *Odeon* (US) 8PF 6031

25

Love Me and the World Is Mine [Sw: Bliv min, så är världen min] (Ball)

0T 132-**1**,-2

[78] *HMV* (Sw) X 3724

[33] *HMV* (Sw) [1]SCLP 1008 = *Odeon* (Sw) PMES 551 // *HMV* (Sw) [1]7C 153-35445/46M = *Odeon* (US) 7C 153-35445/46M // *HMV* (Sw) PRO 3034

[MC] *Odeon* (US) MCPF 6031 // *HMV* (Sw) 7C 253-35445/46M

[8T] *Odeon* (US) 8PF 6031

1931, February 13. Stockholm, Concert Hall, Small Auditorium (?). With Hanns Bingang & his orch.

26

Du Veilchen vom Montmartre [Sw: Du går som en liten prinsessa] (Kálmán: *Das Veilchen vom Montmartre*)

0T 144-1,-**2**,-3? [Take 3 is listed in documents from British EMI only]

[78] *HMV* (Sw) X 3683

[33] *Rococo* 5231 // *HMV* (GB) [1]RLS 715, (Sw) 7C 153-06518/20M = *WRC* (Au) R 05223/25, (NZ) WE 26451/53 // *Unique* UORC 377 // *Dacapo* [1]1C 147-03354/55M, 1C 137 1033543M

[MC] *WRC* (Au) C 05223/25

27

The Sunshine of Your Smile [Sw: Säg mig godnatt] (Ray)

0T 145-1,-**2**

[78] *HMV* (Sw) X 3724

[33] *HMV* (Sw) [1]SCLP 1008 = *Odeon* (Sw) PMES 551 // *Rococo* 5201 // *HMV* (Sw) [1]7C 153-35445/46M = *Odeon* (US) 7C 153-35445/46M // *HMV* (Sw) PRO 3034
[MC] *Odeon* (US) MCPF 6031 // *HMV* (Sw) 7C 253-35445/46M
[8T] *Odeon* (US) 8PF 6031

28
The Desert Song [Sw: Från öknen det brusar] (Romberg: *The Desert Song*)
0T 146-**1**,-2

[78] *HMV* (Sw) X 3683
[33] *HMV* (Sw) [1]SGLP 507 = *MFP* (Sw) MFP 5571 = *Odeon* (Sw) PMES 507, (US) SGLP 507 // *Rococo* 5231
[MC] *Odeon* (US) MCPF 6032
[8T] *Odeon* (US) 8PF 6032

1931, September 18. Stockholm, Concert Hall, Small Auditorium. With Nils Grevillius' orch.

29
I lyckans tempelgård [Sw] (Åström)
0T 499-1,-**2**

[78] *HMV* (Sw) X 3829
[33] *Rococo* 5231 // *HMV* (Sw) 1359931

30
O, milda sång [Sw] (Törnquist)
0T 500-**1**,-2

[78] *HMV* (Sw) X 3829
[33] *Rococo* 5231 // *HMV* (Sw) 1359931

1931, September 19. Stockholm, Concert Hall, Small Auditorium. With Fred Winter (pseud. of Sten Njurling) & his orch. (vocal refrain: JB).

31
När rosorna vissna och dö [Sw] (Borganoff; pseud. of Njurling)
0T 505-**1**,-2

[78] *HMV* (Sw) X 3826
[33] *Bluebell* BELL 132

1932, January 7. Stockholm, Concert Hall, Small Auditorium (?). With Nils Grevillius' orch.

32
Varför älskar jag? [Sw] (trad.)
0T 512-1,-2,-**3**

[78] *HMV* (Sw) X 3928
[33] *Rococo* 5237 // *HMV* (Sw) 1359931

33
Min sommarmelodi [Sw] (Bickvor; pseud. of Bick)
0T 513-**1**,-2

[78] *HMV* (Sw) X 3928
[33] *Rococo* 5237 // *HMV* (Sw) 1359931

1932, January 11. Stockholm, Concert Hall, Small Auditorium (?). With Nils Grevillius' orch.

34
Dein ist mein ganzes Herz [Sw: Du är min hela värld] (Lehár: *Das Land des Lächelns*)
0T 529-**1**,-2

[78] *HMV* X 3885
[45] *HMV* (Sw) 7EBS 10
[33] *Rococo* 5201 // *Excel.* 1286 001-18 // *HMV* (Sw) [1]4E 153-34532/33M = *Odeon* (US) 4E 153-34532/33M // *Unique* UORC 377 // *ANNA* 1006 // *HMV* (Sw) PRO 3034 // *HMV* (Sw) 7C 061-35731M // *HMV* (Fi) 7691751
[CD] *Legato* LCD 103-1 // *EMI* (Sw) CDC 7 61075 2
[MC] *HMV* (Sw) 4E 278-51007M // *HMV* (Sw) 7C 261-35731M // *HMV* (Fi) 7691754

35
Von Apfelblüten einen Kranz [Sw: Av äppelblommor jag binder en krans] (Lehár: *Das Land des Lächelns*)
0T 530-**1**,-2

[78] *HMV* X 3885
[45] *HMV* (Sw) 7EBS 10
[33] *Rococo* 5201 // *Excel.* 1286 001-18 // *HMV* (Sw) [1]4E 153-34532/33M = *Odeon* (US) 4E 153-34532/33M // *Unique* UORC 377 // *HMV* (Sw) PRO 3034
[CD] *EMI* (Sw) CDC 7 61075 2
[MC] *HMV* (Sw) 4E 278-51007M

1932, January 12. Stockholm, Concert Hall, Small Auditorium (?). With Fred Winter (pseud. of Sten Njurling) & his orch. (vocal refrain: JB, under pseud. "Erik Odde").

36
Det är något som binder mitt hjärta vid dig [Sw] (Sylvain; pseud. of Hansson)
0T 540-1,-**2**

[78] *HMV* (Sw) X 3880
[33] *Bluebell* BELL 132

1932, January 13. Stockholm, Concert Hall, Small Auditorium (?). With Nils Grevillius' orch.

37
Du traumschöne Perle der Südsee [Sw: En skimrande pärla i havet] (Abraham: *Die Blume von Hawaii*)
0T 542-**1**,-2

[78] *HMV* (Sw) X 3879
[33] *Rococo* 5237 // *HMV* (Sw) 1359931

38
Kann nicht küssen ohne Liebe [Sw: Kyssar utan kärlek] (Abraham: *Die Blume von Hawaii*)
0T 543-**1**,-2

[78] *HMV* (Sw) X 3879
[33] *Rococo* 5237 // *HMV* (Sw) 1359931

1932, January 14. Stockholm, Concert Hall, Small Auditorium (?). With Fred Winter (pseud. of Sten Njurling) & his orch. (vocal refrain: JB, under pseud. "Erik Odde").

39
Bagdad [Sw] (Lindberg)
0T 554-1,-**2**

[78] *HMV* (Sw) X 3882
[33] *Rococo* 5237 // *Bluebell* BELL 132

1932, August 8. Stockholm, Fenixpalatset, Odeon studio (?). With Hanns Bingang & his orch.

40
Es führt kein andrer Weg zur Seligkeit [Sw: Den enda väg, som för till salighet] (Heymann)
0PA 28-1,-2

(Not issued; see note. Compare No. 44)

41
Slut dina ögon [Sw] (Ammandt; pseud. of Ahlberg)
0PA 29-1,-2

(Not issued; see note. Compare No. 45)

1932, August 10. Stockholm, Fenixpalatset, Odeon studio (?). With Hanns Bingang & his orch. (vocal refrain: JB, under pseud. "Erik Odde").

42
Varje litet ord av kärlek [Sw] (Carsten; pseud. of Nordlander)
0PA 30-1,-**2**

[78] *HMV* (Sw) X 3992
[33] *Rococo* 5237 // *Bluebell* BELL 132

43
Aj, aj, aj du [Sw] (Sahlberg)
0PA 31-1,-**2**

[78] *HMV* (Sw) X 3992
[33] *Rococo* 5237 // *Bluebell* BELL 132

1932, August 10 (?) [see note]. Stockholm, Fenixpalatset, Odeon studio (?). With piano.

44
Es führt kein andrer Weg zur Seligkeit [Sw: Den enda väg, som för till salighet] (Heymann)
0PA 32-1

(Test record; not issued. Compare No. 40)

1932, September 9 (?) [see note]. Copenhagen. With Jens Warny & his orch.

45
Slut dina ögon [Sw] (Ammandt; pseud. of Ahlberg)
0PF 46-1,-**2**

[78] *HMV* X 3993
[33] *HMV* (Sw) [1]SGLP 507 = *MFP* (Sw) MFP 5571 = *Odeon* (Sw) PMES 507, (US) SGLP 507 // *Rococo* 5231 // *Excel.* 1286 001-18
[MC] *Odeon* (US) MCPF 6032
[8T] *Odeon* (US) 8PF 6032

46
Heut' nacht hab' ich geträumt von dir [Sw: Jag drömmer varje natt om dig] (Kálmán: *Das Veilchen vom Montmartre*)
0PF 47-1,-**2**

[78] *HMV* X 3993 // *Vic.* (US) 26-1111
[45] *RCA* (US) 43-1111
[33] *Rococo* 5201 // *HMV* (Sw) [1]SGLP 507 = *MFP* (Sw) MFP 5571 = *Odeon* (Sw) PMES 507, (US) SGLP 507 // *Excel.* 1286 001-18 // *HMV* (GB) [1]RLS 715, (Sw) 7C 153-06518/20M = *WRC* (Au) R 05223/25, (NZ) WE 26451/53 // *Dacapo* [1]1C 147-03354/55M, 1C 137 1033543M
[MC] *Odeon* (US) MCPF 6032 // *WRC* (Au) C 05223/25
[8T] *Odeon* (US) 8PF 6032

1932, September (or October 1?) [see note]. Stockholm, Fenixpalatset, Odeon studio. With Håkan von Eichwald & his orch. (vocal refrain: JB, under pseud. "Erik Odde").

47
Warum? [Sw: Varför?] (Lesso-Valerio; pseud. of Plessow)
0PA 45-1,-**2**

[78] *HMV* (Sw) X 4011
[33] *Rococo* 5237 // *Bluebell* BELL 132

1932, November 24. Stockholm, Fenixpalatset, Odeon studio (?). With Hanns Bingang & his orch. (vocal refrain: JB, under pseud. "Erik Odde").

48
Irgendwo auf der Welt [Sw: Någonstans på vår jord] (Heymann)
0PA 85-1,-**2**

[78] *HMV* (Sw) X 4036
[33] *Rococo* 5237 // *Bluebell* BELL 132

1933, February 2 (?) [see note]. Stockholm, Concert Hall, Attic Auditorium (?). With Folke Andersson's orch. (vocal refrain: JB, under pseud. "Erik Odde").

49
Läppar som le så röda [Sw] (Baumann)
0PA 97-**1**,-2

[78] *HMV* (Sw) X 4095
[33] *Rococo* 5237 // *Bluebell* BELL 132

1933, March [Nos. 50-51 at the latest on the 12?; see note]. Stockholm, Concert Hall, Attic Auditorium (?). With Nils Grevillius' orch.

50
Mélancolique tombe le soir [Sw: Fylld av vemod sänker sig natten] (Laparra: *L'illustre Fregona*) [Orig. label: Serenad ur 'Den fagra Fregona']
0PA 122-1,-**2**

[78] *HMV* X 4108
[33] *Rococo* R 31 // *Eterna* 8 20 829 // *HMV* (GB) [1]RLS 715, (Sw) 7C 153- 06518/20M = *WRC* (Au) R 05223/25, (NZ) WE 26451/53 // *ANNA* 1006 // *Dacapo* [1]1C 147-03354/55M, 1C 137 1033543M
[CD] *Nimbus* NI 7835
[MC] *WRC* (Au) C 05223/25 // *Nimbus* NC 7835

51
Vladimir's Cavatina: Medlenno den' ugasal [Sw: Dagen gick långsamt till ro] (Borodin: *Knyaz* [*Prince*] *Igor*)
0PA 123-**1**,-**2**,-3

A (Take 1)

[78] *HMV* X 4108 v.1
[CD] *Bluebell* ABCD 016 // *EMI* (GB) CDH 7 64707 2

B (Take 2)

[78] *HMV* X 4108 v.2
[33] *Rococo* R 31 // *HMV* (Sw) [1]SGLP 507 = *MFP* (Sw) MFP 5571 = *Odeon* (Sw) PMES 507, (US) SGLP 507 // *Eterna* 8 20 829 // *Excel.* 1286 001-18 // *HMV* (Sw) [1]7C 153-35445/46M = *Odeon* (US) 7C 153-35445/46M // *HMV* (GB) [1]RLS 715, (Sw) 7C 153-06518/20M = *WRC* (Au) R 05223/25, (NZ) WE 26451/53 // *HMV* (Sw) PRO 3034 // *Dacapo* [1]1C 147-03354/55M, 1C 137 1033543M
[CD] *EMI* (Sw) CDC 7 61075 2 // *Nimbus* NI 7835
[MC] *Odeon* (US) MCPF 6032 // *HMV* (Sw) 7C 253-35445/46M // *WRC* (Au) C 05223/25 // *Nimbus* NC 7835
[8T] *Odeon* (US) 8PF 6032

52
Bachanal [Sw] (Dahl)
0PA 125-1,-**2**

[78] *HMV* (Sw) X 4121 (Not issued; see note. Compare No. 57)
[CD] *Bluebell* ABCD 016

53
Brinnande gula flod [Sw] (Nyblom)
0PA 126-**1**,-2

[78] *HMV* (Sw) X 4121 (Not issued; see note. Compare No. 58)
[CD] *Bluebell* ABCD 016

1933, April (11?). Stockholm, Concert Hall, Attic Auditorium (?). With Nils Grevillius' orch.

54
Tangoflickan [Sw] (K.O.W.A.; pseud. of Almroth)
0PA 127-1,-2

(Not issued; see note. Compare No. 59)

55
Ochi chernye [Sw: Svarta ögon] (trad.)
0PA 128-**1**,-2

[78] *HMV* (Sw) X 4128
[33] *Rococo* 5201 // *ANNA* 1005 // *HMV* (Sw) 1359931

56
(Test record, contents not known; see note)
0PA 131-1

1933, June (1?). Stockholm, Concert Hall, Attic Auditorium (?). With orch., cond. Hjalmar Meissner.

57
Bachanal [Sw] (Dahl)
0PA 140-**1**,-2

[78] *HMV* (Sw) X 4127 // *Vic.* (US) 26-1099
[33] *Rococo* 5231 // *HMV* (Sw) 1359931

58
Brinnande gula flod [Sw] (Nyblom)
0PA 141-**1**,-2

[78] *HMV* (Sw) X 4127
[33] *Rococo* 5201

59
Tangoflickan [Sw] (K.O.W.A.; pseud. of Almroth)
0PA 142-**1**,-2

[78] *HMV* (Sw) X 4128
[33] *Rococo* 5231 // *ANNA* 1005

1933, August (10?). Stockholm, Concert Hall, Attic Auditorium (?). With Gösta Säfbom & his soloist orch. (vocal refrain: JB, under pseud. "Erik Odde").

60
Alt hvad der er dejligt [Sw: Allting som är vackert, minner mig om dig] (Tognarelli)
0PA 148-1,-**2**

[78] *HMV* (Sw) X 4133
[33] *Rococo* 5231 // *Bluebell* BELL 132

61
Kanske att vi på samma drömmar bär [Sw] (Tilling)
0PA 149-1,-**2** [See note]

[78] *HMV* (Sw) X 4134
[33] *Rococo* 5231 // *Bluebell* BELL 132

62
Sommerens melodi [Sw: Sommarens melodi är som poesi] (Reidarson)
0PA 150-1,-**2**

[78] *HMV* (Sw) X 4133
[33] *Rococo* 5231 // *Bluebell* BELL 132

1933, September 13. Stockholm, Concert Hall, Attic Auditorium (?). With Nils Grevillius' orch.

63
Min längtan är du [Sw] (Bode)
0PA 172-1,-**2**

[78] *HMV* (Sw) X 4176
[33] *Unique* UORC 377 // *ANNA* 1006 // *HMV* (Sw) 1359931

64
Klovnens tango [Sw: Klownens tango] (Handberg-Jørgensen)
0PA 173-1,-**2**

[78] *HMV* (Sw) X 4176
[33] *Rococo* 5237 // *Unique* UORC 377 // *ANNA* 1006 // *HMV* (Sw) 1359931

1933, October 10. Stockholm, Concert Hall, Attic Auditorium (?). With Nils Grevillius' orch.

65
Ninon [Sw] (Jurmann & Kaper)
0PA 180-**1**,-2

[78] *HMV* (Sw) X 4179
[33] *Rococo* 5201 // *HMV* (Sw) 1359931

66
Gitarren klinger [Sw: Gitarren klingar] (Gyldmark)
0PA 181-1,-**2**

[78] *HMV* (Sw) X 4179
[33] *Rococo* 5201 // *Unique* UORC 377 // *ANNA* 1006 // *HMV* (Sw) 1359931

1933, October 10. Stockholm, Concert Hall, Attic Auditorium (?). With HMV Special Orch., cond. Sune Waldimir (pseud. of Engström) (vocal refrain: JB, under pseud. "Erik Odde").

67
Dina blåa ögon lova mer, än dina röda läppar ger [Sw] (Sylvain; pseud. of Hansson)
0PA 182-1,-**2**

[78] *HMV* (Sw) X 4192
[33] *Rococo* 5231 // *Bluebell* BELL 132

68
Kärlekens sång [Sw] (Le Beau; pseud. of Henrikson)
0PA 183-1,-**2**

[78] *HMV* (Sw) X 4196
[33] *Rococo* 5231 // *Bluebell* BELL 132

Filmsäsongen står nu i sitt högsta flor. Glädjande nog kunna de svenska tonfilmerna numera segerrikt konkurrera med de bästa utländska. Fyra nya svenska tonfilmer komma att lanceras inom den närmaste tiden och naturligtvis har »Husbondens Röst» spelat in de bästa schlagerna ur dem. *Jussi Björlings* »SÄG, ATT DU EVIGT HÅLLER MIG KÄR» ur »Två man om en änka» och *Karin Juels* sång i »DET ÄR MIN CHARME» ur »Inled mig i frestelse», äro **veritabla praktnummer.**

Filmmusik

"Inled mig i frestelse"

H. M. V. Specialorkester

DET ÄR MIN CHARME. Slow-fox av Winter. **Sång av Karin Juel** .... X 4196

KÄRLEKENS SÅNG. Vals av Alice le Beau. Sång av Erik Odde ....

"Falska Greta"

Hanns Bingang och hans orkester

NI ÄR ENSAM, JAG ÄR ENSAM, MEN TILLSAMMANS BLI VI TVÅ. Tango av Wehle. **Sång av Johnny Bode** .... X 4178

DU SVARTA ZIGENARE. Tango av Karel Vacek. Sång av Johnny Bode ....

"Två man om en änka"

Jussi Björling, Tenor

SÄG, ATT DU EVIGT HÅLLER MIG KÄR, av Sylvain. Text av Åke Söderblom .... • X 4204

VAR DET EN DRÖM, av Jacques Armand. Text av Axel Berggren .... •

Nea Hedberg

"En stilla flirt"

H. M. V. Specialorkester

DINA BLÅA ÖGON LOVA MER ÄN DINA RÖDA LÄPPAR GER. Tango av Sylvain. **Sång av Erik Odde** .... X 4192

EN STILLA FLIRT. Sångvals av Sylvain. **Sång av Nea Hedberg** ....

Jussi Björling and Erik Odde listed together under the heading "Film Music" in the swedish HMV supplement for Christmas 1993

1933, October 25. Stockholm, Concert Hall, Attic Auditorium (?). With orch., cond. Sune Waldimir (pseud. of Engström).

69
Säg, att du evigt håller mig kär [Sw] (Sylvain; pseud. of Hansson)
0PA 191-1,-**2**

[78] *HMV* (Sw) X 4204
[33] *Rococo* 5201 // *HMV* (Sw) [1]SGLP 507 = *MFP* (Sw) MFP 5571 = *Odeon* (Sw) PMES 507, (US) SGLP 507
[MC] *Odeon* (US) MCPF 6032
[8T] *Odeon* (US) 8PF 6032

70
Var det en dröm [Sw] (Armand; pseud. of Thiel)
0PA 192-**1**,-**2** [For difference between takes, see note]

A (Take 1)

[78] *HMV* (Sw) X 4204 v.1

B (Take 2)

[78] *HMV* (Sw) X 4204 v.2
[33] *Rococo* 5201 // *Unique* UORC 377
[CD] *Bluebell* ABCD 016

1933, November 13. Stockholm, Concert Hall, Attic Auditorium (?). With Nils Grevillius' orch.

71
Recondita armonia [Sw: Det sköna står att finna] (Puccini: *Tosca*)
0PA 194-**1**,-2

[78] *HMV* (Sw) X 4205
[33] *HMV* (Sw) [1]SCLP 1008 = *Odeon* (Sw) PMES 551 // *Rococo* R 31 // *Eterna* 8 20 829 // *HMV* (GB) [1]RLS 715, (Sw) 7C 153-06518/20M = *WRC* (Au) R 05223/25, (NZ) WE 26451/53
[CD] *Nimbus* NI 7835
[MC] *Odeon* (US) MCPF 6031 // *WRC* (Au) C 05223/25 // *Nimbus* NC 7835
[8T] *Odeon* (US) 8PF 6031

72
E lucevan le stelle [Sw: Jag minns stjärnorna lyste] (Puccini: *Tosca*) [Orig. label: Sången till livet]
0PA 195-**1**,-2

[78] *HMV* (Sw) X 4205
[33] *HMV* (Sw) [1]SCLP 1008 = *Odeon* (Sw) PMES 551 // *Rococo* R 31 // *Eterna* 8 20 829 // *HMV* (GB) [1]RLS 715, (Sw) 7C 153-06518/20M = *WRC* (Au) R 05223/25, (NZ) WE 26451/53
[CD] *Nimbus* NI 7835
[MC] *Odeon* (US) MCPF 6031 // *WRC* (Au) C 05223/25 // *Nimbus* NC 7835
[8T] *Odeon* (US) 8PF 6031

1933, December 20. Stockholm, Concert Hall, Attic Auditorium (?). With Nils Grevillius' orch.

73
La donna è mobile [Sw: Ack, som ett fjun så lätt] (Verdi: *Rigoletto*)
0PA 213-1,-**2**

[78] *HMV* (Sw) X 4220
[33] *HMV* (Sw) [1]SCLP 1008 = *Odeon* (Sw) PMES 551 // *Rococo* R 31 // *Eterna* 8 20 829 // *HMV* (GB) [1]RLS 715, (Sw) 7C 153-06518/20M = *WRC* (Au) R 05223/25, (NZ) WE 26451/53 // *Dacapo* [1]1C 147- 03354/55M, 1C 137 1033543M
[CD] *Nimbus* NI 7835
[MC] *Odeon* (US) MCPF 6031 // *WRC* (Au) C 05223/25 // *Nimbus* NC 7835
[8T] *Odeon* (US) 8PF 6031

74
Recitar!...Vesti la giubba [Sw: Spela komedi!...Pudra ditt anlet] (Leoncavallo: *Pagliacci*) [Orig. label: Skratta Pajazzo]
0PA 214-**1**,-2

[78] *HMV* (Sw) X 4220
[33] *HMV* (Sw) [1]SCLP 1008 = *Odeon* (Sw) PMES 551 // *Rococo* R 31 // *Eterna* 8 20 829 // *HMV* (GB) [1]RLS 715, (Sw) 7C 153-06518/20M = *WRC* (Au) R 05223/25, (NZ) WE 26451/53 // *Dacapo* [1]1C 147-03354/55M, 1C 137 1033543M
[CD] *Nimbus* NI 7835
[MC] *Odeon* (US) MCPF 6031 // *WRC* (Au) C 05223/25 // *Nimbus* NC 7835
[8T] *Odeon* (US) 8PF 6031

1934, March 3. Stockholm. With Nils Grevillius' orch.

75
Di quella pira [Sw: Skyhögt mot himlen] (Verdi: *Il trovatore*) [Orig. label: Strettan ur 'Trubaduren']
0PA 235-1,-**2**

[78] *HMV* (Sw) X 4265
[33] *HMV* (Sw) [1]SCLP 1008 = *Odeon* (Sw) PMES 551 // *Rococo* R 31 // *Eterna* 8 20 829 // *TAP* T 333

[CD] *Nimbus* NI 7835
[MC] *Odeon* (US) MCPF 6031 // *Nimbus* NC 7835
[8T] *Odeon* (US) 8PF 6031

76
O Lola [Sw] (Mascagni: *Cavalleria rusticana*) [Orig. label: Siciliana ur 'På Sicilien']
0PA 236-**1**,-2 [Take 2 missing, probably by mistake, in recording ledgers]

[78] *HMV* (Sw) X 4265
[33] *HMV* (Sw) [1]SCLP 1008 = *Odeon* (Sw) PMES 551 // *Rococo* R 31 // *Golden Age* EJS 337 // *Eterna* 8 20 829 // *MDP* 026
[CD] *Nimbus* NI 7835
[MC] *Odeon* (US) MCPF 6031 // *Nimbus* NC 7835
[8T] *Odeon* (US) 8PF 6031

1935, March 4. Stockholm. With Nils Grevillius' orch.

77
I männer över lag och rätt [Sw] (Atterberg: *Fanal*)
0SB 99-**1**,-2

[78] *HMV* (Sw) X 4436
[33] *Rococo* R 31 // *HMV* (Sw) [1]SGLP 507 = *MFP* (Sw) MFP 5571 = *Odeon* (Sw) PMES 507, (US) SGLP 507 // *Eterna* 8 20 829 // *HMV* (Sw) [1]7C 153-35445/46M = *Odeon* (US) 7C 153-35445/46M // *HMV* (Sw) PRO 3034
[CD] *Nimbus* NI 7835
[MC] *Odeon* (US) MCPF 6032 // *HMV* (Sw) 7C 253-35445/46M // *Nimbus* NC 7835
[8T] *Odeon* (US) 8PF 6032

78
Ch'ella mi creda [Sw: Låt henne tro] (Puccini: *La fanciulla del West*)
0SB 100-**1**,-2

[78] *HMV* (Sw) X 4436
[33] *HMV* (Sw) [1]SCLP 1008 = *Odeon* (Sw) PMES 551 // *Rococo* R 31 // *Eterna* 8 20 829
[CD] *Nimbus* NI 7835
[MC] *Odeon* (US) MCPF 6031 // *Nimbus* NC 7835
[8T] *Odeon* (US) 8PF 6031

1935, May 1. Stockholm. With Sune Waldimir's orch. (Waldimir = pseud. of Engström).

79
Bryllupsvalsen [Sw: Bröllopsvalsen] (Christgau)
0SB 126-**1**,-2

[78] *HMV* (Sw) X 4449
[33] *Rococo* 5231 // *Unique* UORC 377 // *HMV* (Sw) 1359931

80
Lilla prinsessa [Sw] (Enders)
0SB 127-1,-**2**

[78] *HMV* (Sw) X 4449
[33] *Rococo* 5231 // *ANNA* 1005
[CD] *Bluebell* ABCD 016

1936, October 7. Stockholm. With Nils Grevillius' orch.

81
Tonerna [Sw] (Sjöberg)
0SB 402-1,-**2** [Test pressing of Take 1 exists; see note]

[78] *HMV* [1]X 4716, (Fi) TG 128
[45] *HMV* (Sw) 7EBS 1
[33] *Angel* (Ch) 3ACX 47365, (J) HA 5032, AB 7123, (US) COLH 149 = *Cap.* (US) [1]G 7247 = *HMV* (Au) OALP 1857, (GB) ALP 1857, (NZ) MALP 1857 = *WRC* (Au) 3199, (NZ) CO 566 // *Odeon* (Sw) PMCS 308 // *HMV* (Sw) [1]4E 153-34532/33M = *Odeon* (US) 4E 153-34532/33M // *Rubini* GV 21 // *HMV* (GB) [1]RLS 715, (Sw) 7C 153-06518/20M = *WRC* (Au) R 05223/25, (NZ) WE 26451/53 // *HMV* (Sw) PRO 3034 // *Dacapo* [1]1C 147-03354/55M, 1C 137 1033543M // *Col.* (Sw) SPPH 016 // *HMV* (Sw) 7C 061-35731M // *HMV* (Sw) PRO 3053 // *HMV* (Au) [1]OXLP 7660 = *WRC* (Au) R 11409 // *Musik* LPFG 001 // *HMV* (Fi) 7691751
[CD] *EMI* (Sw) CDC 7 61075 2 // *Nimbus* NI 7842
[MC] *HMV* (Sw) 4E 278-51007M // *WRC* (Au) C 05223/25 // *HMV* (Sw) 7C 261-35731M // *HMV* (Au) TC-OXCP 7660 // *HMV* (Fi) 7691754

82
Ack Värmeland, du sköna [Sw] (trad.)
0SB 403-1,-**2**

[78] *HMV* [1]X 4720, (Nor) AL 2324 = *Vic.* (US) V 24110 // *Vic.* (US) [1]26-1097, 26-1105
[45] *RCA* (US) [1]53-5004, 43-1105 // *HMV* (Sw) 7EBS 1
[33] *Angel* (Ch) 3ACX 47365, (J) HA 5032, AB 7123, (US) COLH 149 = *Cap.* (US) [1]G 7247 = *HMV* (Au) OALP 1857, (GB) ALP 1857, (NZ) MALP 1857 = *WRC* (Au) 3199, (NZ) CO 566 // *Odeon* (Sw) PMCS 303 // *Odeon* (Sw) PMES 560 // *Odeon* (Sw) 4E 154-34398/99M // *HMV* (Sw) [1]4E 153-34532/33M = *Odeon* (US) 4E 153-34532/33M // *Marcato* 75316 // *Rubini* GV 21 // *Col.* (G) 1C 052-30174 // Col. (Sw) 4E 056-35326 // *HMV* (GB) [1]RLS 715, (Sw) 7C 153-06518/20M = *WRC* (Au) R 05223/25, (NZ) WE 26451/53 // *EMI* (Sw) 7C 138-35580/81 // *HMV* (Sw) PRO 3034 // *Dacapo* [1]1C 147-03354/55M, 1C 137 1033543M // *HMV* (Sw) 7C 061-35731M // *HMV* (Fi) 7691751

[CD] *EMI* (Sw) CDC 7 61075 2 // *Memoir* CDMOIR 409 // *Nimbus* NI 7835 // *Memoir* CDMCS 111

[MC] *EMI* (Sw) 1362764 = *Odeon* (Sw) [1]4E 254-34402, 7C 254-34206 // *EMI* (Sw) 1362734 = *Odeon* (Sw) [1]4E 254-34403M, 7C 254-34205M // *HMV* (Sw) 4E 278-51007M // *Emidisc* (Sw) 4E 278-51009M // *Col.* (G) 1C 228-30174 // *Col.* (Sw) [1]4E 246-35326M = *EMI* (Sw) 1362744 // *WRC* (Au) C 05223/25 // *HMV* (Sw) 7C 261-35731M // *HMV* (Fi) 7691754 // *Memoir* CMOIR 409 // *Nimbus* NC 7835

83
Allt under himmelens fäste [Sw] (trad.)
OSB 404-**1**,-2

[78] *HMV* [1]X 4720, (Nor) AL 2324 = *Vic.* (US) V 24110 // *Vic.* (US) 26-1095

[45] *RCA* (US) 53-5003 // *HMV* (Sw) 7EBS 11

[33] *Rococo* 5231 // *HMV* (Sw) [1]4E 153-34532/33M = *Odeon* (US) 4E 153- 34532/33M // *HMV* (GB) [1]RLS 715, (Sw) 7C 153-06518/20M = *WRC* (Au) R 05223/25, (NZ) WE 26451/53 // *HMV* (Sw) PRO 3034 // *Dacapo* [1]1C 147-03354/55M, 1C 137 1033543M

[CD] *EMI* (Sw) CDC 7 61075 2 // *Nimbus* NI 7835

[MC] *HMV* (Sw) 4E 278-51007M // *WRC* (Au) C 05223/25 // *Sv.Favoriter* SFMC 1057 // *Nimbus* NC 7835

1936, October 8 [see note]. Stockholm. With Nils Grevillius' orch.

84
I de lyse nætter [Sw: Sommarnatt] (Schrader)
OSB 409-1,-**2**

[78] *HMV* [1]X 4716, (Fi) TG 128 // *Vic.* (US) 26-1095

[45] *RCA* (US) 53-5003 // *HMV* (Sw) 7EBS 11

[33] *HMV* (Sw) [1]4E 153-34532/33M = *Odeon* (US) 4E 153-34532/33M // *Rubini* GV 21 // *HMV* (GB) [1]RLS 715, (Sw) 7C 153-06518/20M = *WRC* (Au) R 05223/25, (NZ) WE 26451/53 // *HMV* (Sw) PRO 3034 // *Dacapo* [1]1C 147-03354/55M, 1C 137 1033543M // *HMV* (Sw) 7C 061-35731M // *Odeon* (Sw) 7C 062-35947M // *Musik* LPFG 001 // *HMV* (Fi) 7691751 (?)

[CD] *EMI* (Sw) CDC 7 61075 2

[MC] *HMV* (Sw) 4E 278-51007M // *WRC* (Au) C 05223/25 // *HMV* (Sw) 7C 261-35731M // *Odeon* (Sw) 1359474 // *HMV* (Fi) 7691754 (?)

85
Song of India: Ne shchest almazov [Sw: I söderns hav] (Rimsky-Korsakov: *Sadko*) [Orig. label: Chanson hindoue]
OSB 410-**1**,-2

[78] *HMV* [1]X 4723, (Au) EC 60

[33] *HMV* (Sw) [1]SGLP 507 = *MFP* (Sw) MFP 5571 = *Odeon* (Sw) PMES 507, (US) SGLP 507 // *Rococo* 5237 // *Excel.* 1286 001-18 // *HMV* (Sw) [1]7C 153-35445/46M

= *Odeon* (US) 7C 153-35445/46M // *HMV* (Sw) PRO 3034 // *HMV* (Au) [1]OXLP 7660 = *WRC* (Au) R 11409

[CD] *EMI* (Sw) CDC 7 61075 2 // *Nimbus* NI 7835

[MC] *Odeon* (US) MCPF 6032 // *HMV* (Sw) 7C 253-35445/46M // *HMV* (Au) TC-OXCP 7660 // *Nimbus* NC 7835

[8T] *Odeon* (US) 8PF 6032

86

Ay, ay, ay [Sw] (Pérez-Freire)
0SB 411-1,-**2**

[78] *HMV* [1]X 4723, (Au) EC 60

[33] *Rococo* R 31 // *HMV* (Sw) [1]SGLP 507 = *MFP* (Sw) MFP 5571 = *Odeon* (Sw) PMES 507, (US) SGLP 507 // *Eterna* 8 20 829 // *HMV* (Sw) [1]7C 153-35445/46M = *Odeon* (US) 7C 153-35445/46M // *HMV* (Sw) PRO 3034 // *HMV* (Au) [1]OXLP 7660 = *WRC* (Au) R 11409

[MC] *Odeon* (US) MCPF 6032 // *HMV* (Sw) 7C 253-35445/46M // *HMV* (Au) TC-OXCP 7660

[8T] *Odeon* (US) 8PF 6032

1936, December 1 & 3 [see note]. Stockholm, Concert Hall, Small Auditorium. With orch., cond. Nils Grevillius.

87

Che gelida manina [It] (Puccini: *La bohème*)
2SB 439-1,-**2**

[78] *Elec.* DB 3049 = *HMV* [1]DB 3049, (Nor) DBN 3049 = *Vic.* (J) RL 31, ND 434, (US,Ca) 12039 // *Vic.* (US) M 633 // *HMV* DB 5393 // *Vic.* (US) MO 1275

[45] *HMV* (Au) 7PO 239, (GB) 7P 239, (It) [1]7RQ 3128, (NL) 7PH 1013 // *HMV* (Au) 7ERO 5196, (GB) [1]7ER 5196, (It) 7ERQ 251 // *HMV* (Fr) ROVL 9040

[33] *Angel* (Ar) LPC 12083, 6083, (Ch) 3ACX 47190, (J) HA 5085, AB 7134, (US) COLH 148 = *Cap.* (US) G 7239 = *HMV* (Au) OALP 1620, OELP 9673, (Fr) FALP 629, (GB) [1]ALP 1620, (It) QALP 10266, (NL) XLPH 1002, (NZ) MALP 1620, (SA) JALP 1620 = *Voix Ill.* 50018 // *Elec.* E 70412 // *HMV* (NL) GHLP 1027 // *HMV* (Au) OALP 7534, (It) [1]QALP 10402 = *Odeon* (It) QALP 10402, 3C 061-00739M // *Dacapo* [1]1C 177-(147-)00947/48M, 1C 137 1009473M = *HMV* (Sw) 7C 137-00947/48M // *HMV* (Sw) [4]4E 153-34532/33M = *Odeon* (US) 4E 153-34532/33M // *HMV* (NL) 5C 045-01715M // *HMV* (GB) [1]RLS 715, (Sw) 7C 153-06518/20M = *WRC* (Au) R 05223/25, (NZ) WE 26451/53 // *HMV* (Au) OXLP 7633 // *HMV* (Sw) PRO 3034 // *HMV* (Sw) [1]SPPH 030, 7C 061-35822 // *HMV* (Sw) 7C 061-35731M // *MET* 110 // *Angel* (J) GR 70085 // *HMV* (Fr) 7540161

[CD] *MET* 110CD // *EMI* (GB) CDC 7 61053 2 // *Pro Arte* CDD 489 // *EMI* (Fr) CDC 7 54016 2 // *Tring* TFP 013 // *Award* AWCD 29115 // *Axis* 7017672 // *Nimbus* NI 7835

[MC] *HMV* (It) [1]CV 5003 = *Odeon* (It) MC 5003 // *HMV* (Sw) 4E 278-51007M // *HMV* (Sw) 7C 237-00948M // *WRC* (Au) C 05223/25 // *HMV* (Sw) 7C 261-35731M // *HMV* (Sw) 7C 261-35822 // *MET* 110C // *HMV* (Fr) 7540164 // *Nimbus* NC 7835

88
Se quel guerrier...Celeste Aida [It] (Verdi: *Aida*)
2SB 440-1,-**2**

[78] *Elec.* DB 3049 = [1]HMV *DB 3049*, (Nor) DBN 3049 = *Vic.* (J) RL 31, ND 434, (US,Ca) 12039 // *Vic.* (US) MO 1275
[45] *RCA* (US,G) ERA 209 // *HMV* (Au) 7PO 239, (GB) 7P 239, (It) [1]7RQ 3128, (NL) 7PH 1013
[33] *RCA* (US,G) LM 1801 // *Angel* (Ar) LPC 12193, (Br) 3CBX 328, (Ch) 3ACX 47341, (J) HA 5031, AB 7127, (US) COLH 150 = *Cap.* (US) [1]G 7248 = *HMV* (Au) OALP 1841, (GB) ALP 1841, (It) QALP 10319, (NL) XLPH 20010, 5C 045-(047-)00191M, (NZ) MALP 1841, (SA) JALP 1841 = *WRC* (Au) 3145 // *Dacapo* [1]1C 177-(147-)00947/48M, 1C 137 1009473M = *HMV* (Sw) 7C 137-00947/48M // *HMV* (Sw) [1]4E 153-34532/33M = *Odeon* (US) 4E 153-34532/33M // *EMI* (SA) EMGJ 6004 // *Sera.* (US) 60219 // *Elec.* 29601-2 // *Col.* (A) Parnass 62528 = *Parnass* [1]62528 // *HMV* (GB) [1]RLS 715, (Sw) 7C 153-06518/20M = *WRC* (Au) R 05223/25, (NZ) WE 26451/53 // *HMV* (Au) OXLP 7633 // *HMV* (Sw) PRO 3034 // *HMV* (Sw) [1]SPPH 030, 7C 061-35822 // *Fame* (SA) FAME 20 // *Angel* (J) GR 70085 // *HMV* (Fi) 7691751
[CD] *EMI* (GB) CDC 7 61053 2 // *Award* AWCD 29115 // *Axis* 7017672 // *Nimbus* NI 7835
[MC] *HMV* (Sw) 4E 278-51007M // *EMI* (SA) L4EMGJ 6004 // *HMV* (Sw) 7C 237-00948M // *WRC* (Au) C 05223/25 // *Sera.* (US) 4XG 60219 // *HMV* (Sw) 7C 261-35822 // *Fame* (SA) L4FAME 20 // *HMV* (Fi) 7691754 // *Nimbus* NC 7835
[8T] *EMI* (SA) L8EMGJ 6004

1936, December 3 [see note]. Stockholm, Concert Hall, Small Auditorium. With Nils Grevillius & his orch.

89
La donna è mobile [It] (Verdi: *Rigoletto*)
0SB 441-1,-**2**,-3

[78] *Elec.* DA 1548 = *HMV* [1]DA 1548, (Ir) IR 420, (Nor) DAN 1548 = *Vic.* (J) JE 100, (US) 4372 // *Vic.* (J) HL 54
[45] *Angel* (Br) TCB 13 = *HMV* (GB) [1]7ER 5087, (It) 7ERQ 229
[33] *Angel* (Ar) LPC 12193, (Br) 3CBX 328, (Ch) 3ACX 47341, (J) HA 5031, AB 7127, (US) COLH 150 = *Cap.* (US) [1]G 7248 = *HMV* (Au) OALP 1841, (GB) ALP 1841, (It) QALP 10319, (NL) XLPH 20010, 5C 045-(047-)00191M, (NZ) MALP 1841, (SA) JALP 1841 = *WRC* (Au) 3145 // *Dacapo* [1]1C 177-(147-)00947/48M, 1C 137 1009473M = *HMV* (Sw) 7C 137-00947/48M // *HMV* (Sw) [1]4E 153-34532/33M = *Odeon* (US) 4E 153-34532/33M // *Sera.* (US) 60219 // *Sel.Read.Dig.* 3C 147-52402/10 // *HMV* (GB) [1]RLS 715, (Sw) 7C 153-06518/20M

= *WRC* (Au) R 05223/25, (NZ) WE 26451/53 // *HMV* (Au) OXLP 7633 // *HMV* (Sw) PRO 3034 // *HMV* (Sw) 7C 061-35731M // *MET* 110 // *Angel* (J) GR 70085 // *HMV* (Fi) 7691751

[CD] *MET* 110CD // *Axis* 7017672 // *Testament* SBT 1005 // *Nimbus* NI 7842 // *EMI* (GB) CDH 7 64707 2

[MC] *HMV* (Sw) 4E 278-51007M // *HMV* (Sw) 7C 237-00947M // *WRC* (Au) C 05223/25 // *Sera.* (US) 4XG 60219 // *HMV* (Sw) 7C 261-35731M // *MET* 110C // *HMV* (Fi) 7691754

90
Recondita armonia [It] (Puccini: *Tosca*)
OSB 442-1,-**2**

[78] *Elec.* DA 1548 = *HMV* [1]DA 1548, (Ir) IR 420, (Nor) DAN 1548 = *Vic.* (J) JE 100, (US) 4372 // *Vic.* (J) NF 4128

[45] *Angel* (Br) TCB 13 = *HMV* (GB) [1]7ER 5087, (It) 7ERQ 229

[33] *Angel* (Ar) LPC 12193, (Br) 3CBX 328, (Ch) 3ACX 47341, (J) HA 5031, AB 7127, (US) COLH 150 = *Cap.* (US) [1]G 7248 = *HMV* (Au) OALP 1841, (GB) ALP 1841, (It) QALP 10319, (NL) XLPH 20010, 5C 045-(047-)00191M, (NZ) MALP 1841, (SA) JALP 1841 = *WRC* (Au) 3145 // Angel (Br) 3BBX 28 // *Sera.* (US) 60219 // *HMV* (Au) [1]OXLP 7586 = *WRC* (Au) R 03176 // *HMV* (Sw) [1]7C 153-35445/46M = *Odeon* (US) 7C 153-35445/46M // *HMV* (Sw) PRO 3034 // *HMV* (Sw) 7C 061-3573lM // *MET* 110 // *WRC* (Au) R 13509 // *Angel* (J) GR 70085 // *EMI* (Sw) EMISP 127 // *BBC* REH 715

[CD] *MET* 110CD // *EMI* (GB) CDH 7 61053 2 // *BBC* CD 715 // *Laser* LAS 4777 // *Memoir* (Br) RGE 342.8010, (GB) [1]CDMOIR 405 // *Award* AWCD 29115 // *Axis* 7017672 // *Nimbus* NI 7842

[MC] *WRC* (Au) C 03176 // *HMV* (Sw) 7C 253-35445/46M // *Sera.* (US) 4XG 60219 // *HMV* (Sw) 7C 261-35731M // *MET* 110C // *BBC* ZCF 715 // *Laser* LASC 4777 // *Memoir* CMOIR 405

1937, January 26. Stockholm. With Nils Grevillius & his orch.

91
Sverige [Sw] (Stenhammar: *Ett folk*)
OSB 471-**1**,-2

[78] *HMV* [1]X 4777 = *Vic.* (US) V 24111 // *Vic.* (US) [1]26-1097, 26-1105

[45] *RCA* (US) [1]53-5004, 43-1105 // *HMV* (Sw) 7EBS 1

[33] *Angel* (Ch) 3ACX 47365, (J) HA 5032, AB 7123, (US) COLH 149 = *Cap.* (US) [1]G 7247 = *HMV* (Au) OALP 1857, (GB) ALP 1857, (NZ) MALP 1857 = *WRC* (Au) 3199, (NZ) CO 566 // *Odeon* (Sw) PMCS 308 // *Odeon* (Sw) 4E 154-34398/99M // *HMV* (Sw) [1]4E 153-34532/33M = *Odeon* (US) 4E 153-34532/33M // *Rubini* GV 21 // *EMI* (Sw) 7C 138-35580/81 // *HMV* (Sw) PRO 3034 // *HMV* (Sw) 7C 061-35731M // *Col.* (Sw) SPPH 061

[CD] *EMI* (Sw) CDC 7 61075 2 // *EMI* (Sw) CMCD 6061
[MC] *HMV* (Sw) 4E 278-51007M // *Emidisc* (Sw) 4E 278-51009M // *HMV* (Sw) 7C 261-35731M // *Col.* (Sw) TC-SPPH 061

92
Land, du välsignade [Sw] (Althén)
OSB 472-1,-**2**

[78] *HMV* [1]X 4777 = *Vic.* (US) V 24111 // *Vic.* (US) 26-1098
[45] *HMV* (Sw) 7EBS 1
[33] *Angel* (Ch) 3ACX 47365, (J) HA 5032, AB 7123, (US) COLH 149 = *Cap.* (US) [1]G 7247 = *HMV* (Au) OALP 1857, (GB) ALP 1857, (NZ) MALP 1857 = *WRC* (Au) 3199, (NZ) CO 566 // *Odeon* (Sw) PMCS 308 // *HMV* (Sw) [1]4E 153-34532/33M = *Odeon* (US) 4E 153-34532/33M // *Rubini* GV 21 // *Odeon* (Sw) 4E 054-34633M // *HMV* (Sw) PRO 3034 // *HMV* (Sw) [1]7C 061-35731M = *Odeon* (Sw) 7C 138-35818/20 // *Odeon* (Sw) 7C 158-35912/13 // *EMI* (Sw) 2600833 // *Musik* LPFG 001 // *HMV* (Fi) 7691751
[CD] *EMI* (Sw) CDC 7 61075 2
[MC] *HMV* (Sw) 4E 278-51007M // *HMV* (Sw) 7C 261-35731M // *EMI* (Sw) 1362774 = *Odeon* (Sw) [1]7C 458-35914 // *HMV* (Fi) 7691754

1937, April 22. Stockholm. With Nils Grevillius & his orch.

93
Dreams of Long Ago [Sw: Ungdomsdrömmar] (Caruso)
OSB 538-**1**,-2,-3

[78] *HMV* X 4832
[45] *HMV* (Sw) 7EBS 11
[33] *Excel.* 1286 001-18 // *HMV* (Sw) [1]4E 153-34532/33M = *Odeon* (US) 4E 153-34532/33M // *Rococo* 5341 // *HMV* (GB) [1]RLS 715, (Sw) 7C 153-06518/20M = *WRC* (Au) R 05223/25, (NZ) WE 26451/53 // *Unique* UORC 377 // *ANNA* 1006 // *HMV* (Sw) PRO 3034 // *Dacapo* [1]1C 147-03354/55M, 1C 137 1033543M
[MC] *HMV* (Sw) 4E 278-51007M // *WRC* (Au) C 05223/25

94
Sjung din hela längtan ut [Sw] (Widestedt) [Orig. label: Sjung din hela längtan]
OSB 539-1,-**2**

[78] *HMV* X 4832
[45] *HMV* (Sw) 7EBS 11
[33] *Rococo* 5201 // *Excel.* 1286 001-18 // *HMV* (Sw) [1]4E 153-34532/33M = *Odeon* (US) 4E 153-34532/33M // *Unique* UORC 377 // *ANNA* 1006 // *HMV* (Sw) PRO 3034
[MC] *HMV* (Sw) 4E 278-51007M

1937, September 3. Stockholm, Concert Hall, Small Auditorium. With orch. [see note], cond. Nils Grevillius.

95
Cielo e mar! [It] (Ponchielli: *La Gioconda*)
2SB 570-1,-**2** [Test pressing of Take 1 exists; see note]

[78] *HMV* [1]DB 3302 = *Vic.* (J) RL 42, (US) 12150 // *HMV* DB 5393
[45] *HMV* (GB) [1]7ER 5207, (It) 7ERQ 258
[33] *Angel* (Ar) LPC 12083, 6083, (Ch) 3ACX 47190, (J) HA 5085, AB 7134, (US) COLH 148, Cap. (US) G 7239 = *HMV* (Au) OALP 1620, OELP 9673, (Fr) FALP 629, (GB) [1]ALP 1620, (It) QALP 10266, (NL) XLPH 1002, (NZ) MALP 1620, (SA) JALP 1620 = *Voix Ill.* 50018 // *Dacapo* [1]1C 177-(147-)00947/48M, 1C 137 1009473M = *HMV* (Sw) 7C 137-00947/48M // *HMV* (Sw) [1]4E 153-34532/33M = *Odeon* (US) 4E 153-34532/33M // *Sera.* (US) 60219 // *HMV* (NL) 5C 045-01715M // *HMV* (Sw) PRO 3034 // *Angel* (J) GR 70085
[CD] *MET* 207CD // *Testament* SBT 1005 // *Axis* 7017672 // *Nimbus* NI 7835 // *EMI* (GB) CDH 7 64707 2
[MC] *HMV* (Sw) 4E 278-51007M // *HMV* (Sw) 7C 237-00948M // *Sera.* (US) 4XG 60219 // *MET* 207C // *Nimbus* NC 7835

96
Ch'ella mi creda [It] (Puccini: *La fanciulla del West*)
0SB 571-1,-**2**

[78] *Elec.* DA 1584 = [1]HMV *DA 1584*, (Nor) DAN 1584 = *Vic.* (J) JE 176, (US) 4408
[45] *Angel* (Br) TCB 13 = *HMV* (GB) [1]7ER 5087, (It) 7ERQ 229
[33] *HMV* (It) QALP 10305 // *Angel* (Ch) 3ACX 47530, (Ur) UAL 12513 = *HMV* (GB,Au) [1]HQM 1190, (GB,SA) HLM 7038, (SA) JALP 29 = *Odeon* (US) PHQM 1190 = *Sera.* (US) 60168 // *Dacapo* [1]1C 177-(147-)00947/48M, 1C 137 1009473M = *HMV* (Sw) 7C 137-00947/48M // *HMV* (NL) 5C 045-01715M // *HMV* (Au) OXLP 7633 // *HMV* (GB) [1]RLS 715, (Sw) 7C 153-06518/20M = *WRC* (Au) 05223/25, (NZ) WE 26451/53 // *ABC* 836 642-1
[CD] *EMI* (GB) CDH 7 61053 2 // *ABC* 836 642-2 // *Award* AWCD 29115 // *Axis* 7017672 // *Memoir* CDMOIR 412 // *Nimbus* NI 7842
[MC] *HMV* (Sw) 7C 237-00948M // *WRC* (Au) C 05223/25 // *HMV* (SA) L4HLM 7038 = *Sera.* (US) [1]4XG 60168 // *ABC* 836 642-4 // *Memoir* CMOIR 412

97
For You Alone [Eng] (Geehl)
0SB 572-1,-**2**

[78] *HMV* DA 1594
[45] *HMV* (Au) 7PO 330, (GB) [1]7P 330
[33] *Angel* (Ch) 3ACX 47365, (J) HA 5032, AB 7123, (US) COLH 149 = *Cap.* (US) [1]G 7247 = *HMV* (Au) OALP 1857, (GB) ALP 1857, (NZ) MALP 1857 = *WRC* (Au) 3199, (NZ) CO 566 // *HMV* (Sw) [1]7C 153-35445/46M = *Odeon* (US) 7C

153-35445/46M // *HMV* (GB) [1]RLS 715, (Sw) 7C 153-06518/20M = *WRC* (Au) R 05223/25, (NZ) WE 26451/53 // *HMV* (Sw) PRO 3034 // *Dacapo* [1]1C 147-03354/55M, 1C 137 1033543M

[MC] *HMV* (Sw) 7C 253-35445/46M // *WRC* (Au) C 05223/25

1937, September 4. Stockholm, Concert Hall, Small Auditorium. With orch. [see note], cond. Nils Grevillius.

98

Pays merveilleux...Ô paradis [It: Mi batte il cor...O paradiso] (Meyerbeer: *L'africaine*)
2SB 573-1,-**2**

[78] *HMV* [1]DB 3302 = *Vic.* (J) RL 42, (US) 12150

[45] *HMV* (Au) 7ERO 5193, (GB) [1]7ER 5193

[33] *Angel* (Ar) LPC 12083, 6083, (Ch) 3ACX 47190, (J) HA 5085, AB 7134, (US) COLH 148 = *Cap.* (US) G 7239 = *HMV* (Au) OALP 1620, OELP 9673, (Fr) FALP 629, (GB) [1]ALP 1620, (It) QALP 10266, (NL) XLPH 1002, (NZ) MALP 1620, (SA) JALP 1620 = *Voix Ill.* 50018 // *Elec.* E 70412 // *HMV* (NL) GHLP 1027 // *Dacapo* [1]1C 177-(147-)00947/48M, 1C 137 1009473M = *HMV* (Sw) 7C 137-00947/48M // *HMV* (GB,Au,SA) [1]HLM 7004, (NL) 5C 047-01266M = *Sera.* (US) 60206 = *WRC* (Au) R 10132 // *Sera.* (US) 60219 // *HMV* (NL) 5C 045-01715M // *Marcato* 34399-6

[CD] *EMI* (GB) CDH 7 61053 2 // *Laser* LAS 4777 // *Memoir* CDMOIR 409 // *Award* AWCD 29115 // *Axis* 701762 // *Nimbus* NI 7835

[MC] *HMV* (Sw) 7C 237-00947M // *HMV* (GB) TC-HLM 7004, (SA) L4HLM 7004 // *Sera.* (US) 4XG 60219 // *Marcato* 33332-8 // *Laser* LASC 4777 // *Memoir* CMOIR 409 // *Nimbus* NC 7835

99

E lucevan le stelle [It] (Puccini: *Tosca*)
0SB 574-1,-**2**

[78] *Elec.* DA 1584 = *HMV* [1]DA 1584, (Nor) DAN 1584 = *Vic.* (J) JE 176, (US) 4408 // *Vic.* (J) NF 4128

[45] *Angel* (Br) TCB 13 = *HMV* (GB) [1]7ER 5087, (It) 7ERQ 229

[33] *Angel* (Ar) LPC 12193, (Br) 3CBX 328, (Ch) 3ACX 47341, (J) HA 5031, AB 7127, (US) COLH 150, Cap. (US) [1]G 7248 = *HMV* (Au) OALP 1841, (GB) ALP 1841, (It) QALP 10319, (NL) XLPH 20010, 5C 045-(047-)00191M, (NZ) MALP 1841, (SA) JALP 1841 = *WRC* (Au) 3145 // *Angel* (Br) 3BBX 28 // *Dacapo* [1]1C 177-(147-)00947/48M, 1C 137 1009473M = *HMV* (Sw) 7C 137-00947/48M // *Sera.* (US) 60219 // *HMV* (Au) OXLP 7586 = *WRC* (Au) R 03176 // *HMV* (Sw) [1]7C 153-35445/46M = *Odeon* (US) 7C 153-35445/46M // *HMV* (Sw) PRO 3034 // *HMV* (Sw) [1]SPPH 030, 7C 061-35822 // *HMV* (Sw) 7C 061-35731M // *MET* 110 // *Angel* (J) GR 70085 // *HMV* (Fi) 7691751

[CD] *MET* 110CD // *EMI* (GB) CDH 7 61053 2 // *Award* AWCD 29115 // *Axis* 7017672 // *Nimbus* NI 7842
[MC] *WRC* (Au) C 03176 // *HMV* (Sw) 7C 253-35445/46M // *HMV* (Sw) 7C 237-00948M // *Sera.* (US) 4XG 60219 // *HMV* (Sw) 7C 261-35731M // *HMV* (Sw) 7C 261-35822 // *MET* 110C // *HMV* (Fi) 7691754

100
Only a Rose [Eng] (Friml: *The Vagabond King*)
0SB 575-**1**,-2

[78] *HMV* DA 1607
[33] *HMV* (GB) [1]RLS 715, (Sw) 7C 153-06518/20M = *WRC* (Au) R 05223/25, (NZ) WE 26451/53 // *Dacapo* [1]1C 147-03354/55M, 1C 137 1033543M
[MC] *WRC* (Au) C 05223/25

1937, September 5. Stockholm, Concert Hall, Small Auditorium. With orch. [see note], cond. Nils Grevillius.

101
'O sole mio [It] (di Capua)
0SB 576-1,-**2**

[78] *Elec.* DA 1582 = *HMV* [1]DA 1582, (Ir) IR 409, (Nor) DAN 1582 = *Vic.* (J) JE 149, (US) 4379 // *HMV* DA 1607
[45] *Angel* (Br) TCB 02 = *HMV* (Au) 7EBO 6030, (GB) 7EB 6030, 7ER 5189, (It) 7EPQ 607, (NZ) 7EBM 6030, 7ERM 5189, (Sw) [1]7EBS 13
[33] *Angel* (Ch) 3ACX 47365, (J) HA 5032, AB 7123, (US) COLH 149 = *Cap.* (US) [1]G 7247 = *HMV* (Au) OALP 1857, (GB) ALP 1857, (NZ) MALP 1857 = *WRC* (Au) 3199, (NZ) CO 566 // *Angel* (Br) 3BBX 21 // *Dacapo* [1]1C 177-(147-) 00947/48M, 1C 137 1009473M = *HMV* (Sw) 7C 137-00947/48M // *HMV* (Sw) [1]7C 153-35445/46M = *Odeon* (US) 7C 153-35445/46M // *HMV* (GB) [1]RLS 715, (Sw) 7C 153-06518/20M = *WRC* (Au) R 05223/25, (NZ) WE 26451/53 // *HMV* (Sw) PRO 3034 // *HMV* (Sw) 7C 061-35731M // *HMV* (Au) OXLP 7660 = *WRC* (Au) R 11409 // *HMV* (Fi) 7691751
[CD] *Conifer* TQ 305 // *Memoir* CDMOIR 409
[MC] *HMV* (Sw) 7C 253-35445/46M // *HMV* (Sw) 7C 237-00948M // *WRC* (Au) C 05223/25 // *HMV* (Sw) 7C 261-35731M // *HMV* (Au) TC-OXCP 7660 // *HMV* (Fi) 7691754 // *Conifer* TQC 305 // *Memoir* CMOIR 409

102
Ideale [It] (Tosti)
0SB 577-1,-**2**

[78] *Elec.* DA 1582 = *HMV* [1]*DA 1582*, (Ir) IR 409, (Nor) DAN 1582 = *Vic.* (J) JE 149, (US) 4379 // *HMV* DA 1594 // *Vic.* (J) HL 47 // *Vic.* (J) NF 4220
[45] *Angel* (Br) TCB 02 = *HMV* (Au) 7EBO 6030, (GB) 7EB 6030, 7ER 5189, (It) 7EPQ 607, (NZ) 7EBM 6030, 7ERM 5189, (Sw) [1]7EBS 13

[33] *Angel* (Ch) 3ACX 47365, (J) HA 5032, AB 7123, (US) COLH 149 = *Cap.* (US) [1]G 7247 = *HMV* (Au) OALP 1857, (GB) ALP 1857, (NZ) MALP 1857 = *WRC* (Au) 3199, (NZ) CO 566 // *Dacapo* [1]1C 177-(147-)00947/48M, 1C 137 1009473M = *HMV* (Sw) 7C 137-00947/48M // *HMV* (Sw) [1]7C 153-35445/46M = *Odeon* (US) 7C 153-35445/46M // *HMV* (GB) [1]RLS 715, (Sw) 7C 153-06518/20M = *WRC* (Au) R 05223/25, (NZ) WE 26451/53 // *HMV* (Sw) PRO 3034 // *EMI* (Au) [1]SCA 034 = *WRC* (Au) R 08064 // *HMV* (Au) [1]OXLP 7660 = *WRC* (Au) R 11409

[CD] *Memoir* CDMOIR 409 // *Nimbus* NI 7842 // *EMI* (GB) CDH 7 64707 2

[MC] *HMV* (Sw) 7C 253-35445/46M // *HMV* (Sw) 7C 237-00948M // *WRC* (Au) C 05223/25 // *WRC* (Au) C 08064 // *HMV* (Au) TC-OXCP 7660 // *Memoir* CMOIR 409

[1937, November. London. For discussion of planned but cancelled recordings, see note for No. 102X.]

1938, April 28. Stockholm, Concert Hall, Attic Auditorium. With Nils Grevillius & his orch.

103
Wer uns getraut? [Sw: Vem oss har vigt?] (J. Strauss: *Der Zigeunerbaron*). With Hjördis Schymberg (sop.).
0SB 741-1,-2,(-3)

(Not issued; see note. Compare No. 106)

104
Sjung om studentens lyckliga dag [Sw] (Prince Gustaf). With double male quartet.
0SB 742-1,-**2** [For Take 1TS, see note]

[78] *HMV* X 6235 // *HMV* (Dk) X 7255 // *Vic.* (US) 26-1111

[45] *RCA* (US) 43-1111 // *HMV* (Dk) 45X 8433

[33] *Odeon* (Sw) PMCS 308 // *Rococo* 5341 // *Rubini* GV 21 // *Unique* UORC 377 // *HMV* (Sw) 1359931

105
Ich hab' kein Geld, bin vogelfrei [Sw: Nu är jag pank och fågelfri] (Millöcker: *Der Bettelstudent*)
0SB 743-1,-2

(Not issued; see note. Compare No. 107)

1938, May 30. Stockholm, Concert Hall, Small Auditorium. With Nils Grevillius & his orch.

106

Wer uns getraut? [Sw: Vem oss har vigt?] (J. Strauss: *Der Zigeunerbaron*) [Orig. label: Duett ur 'Zigenarbaronen']. With Hjördis Schymberg (sop.).
0SB 741-3,-**4**,-**5**

A (Take 4)

[78] (Not issued)
[CD] *Bluebell* ABCD 016

B (Take 5)

[78] *HMV* X 6146
[33] *Rococo* 5201 // *HMV* (Sw) [1]SGLP 507 = *MFP* (Sw) MFP 5571 = *Odeon* (Sw) PMES 507, (US) SGLP 507 // *HMV* (Sw) [1]7C 153-35445/46M = *Odeon* (US) 7C 153-35445/46M // *HMV* (GB) [1]RLS 715, (Sw) 7C 153-06518/20M = *WRC* (Au) R 05223/25, (NZ) WE 26451/53 // *HMV* (Sw) PRO 3034 // *Dacapo* [1]1C 147-03354/55M, 1C 137 1033543M // *HMV* (Au) [1]OXLP 7639 = *WRC* (Au) R 06137 // *HMV* (Fi) 7691751
[CD] *EMI* (Sw) CDC 7 61075 2 // *Nimbus* NI 7842
[MC] *Odeon* (US) MCPF 6032 // *HMV* (Sw) 7C 253-35445/46M // *WRC* (Au) C 05223/25 // *WRC* (Au) C 06137 // *HMV* (Fi) 7691754
[8T] *Odeon* (US) 8PF 6032

107

Ich hab' kein Geld, bin vogelfrei [Sw: Nu är jag pank och fågelfri] (Millöcker: *Der Bettelstudent*)
0SB 743-**3**,-**4**

A (Take 3)

[78] (Not issued)
[CD] *Bluebell* ABCD 016

B (Take 4)

[78] *HMV* [1]X 6090, (Au) EC 214, (Fi) TG 129, (Nor) AL 3096
[45] *HMV* (Sw) 7EBS 10
[33] *Rococo* 5201 // *Odeon* (G) O 83343 // *HMV* (Sw) [1]4E 153-34532/33M = *Odeon* (US) 4E 153-34532/33M // *HMV* (GB) [1]RLS 715, (Sw) 7C 153-06518/20M = *WRC* (Au) R 05223/25, (NZ) WE 26451/53 // *HMV* (Sw) PRO 3034 // *Dacapo* [1]1C 147-03354/55M, 1C 137 1033543M // *HMV* (Au) [1]OXLP 7639 = *WRC* (Au) R 06137 // *HMV* (Sw) 7C 061-35731M // *HMV* (Fi) 7691751
[CD] *EMI* (Sw) CDC 7 61075 2 // *Memoir* CDMOIR 409 // *Nimbus* NI 7842

[MC] *HMV* (Sw) 4E 278-51007M // *WRC* (Au) C 05223/25 // *WRC* (Au) C 06137 // *HMV* (Sw) 7C 261-35731M // *Col.* (Sw) TC-SPPH 036 // *HMV* (Fi) 7691754 // *Memoir* CMOIR 409

108
Nämner du Sverige [Sw] (Wide; pseud. of Widestedt)
0SB 753-1,-**2** [Test pressing of Take 1 exists. For discussion of Take 1TS, see note]

[78] *HMV* X 6235 // *Vic.* (US) 26-1098
[33] *HMV* (Sw) [1]SCLP 1008 = *Odeon* (Sw) PMES 551 // *Rococo* 5341 // *Rubini* GV 21 // *HMV* (Sw) [1]7C 153-35445/46M = *Odeon* (US) 7C 153-35445/46M // *ANNA* 1006 // *HMV* (Sw) PRO 3034 // *Dacapo* [1]1C 147-03354/55M, 1C 137 033543M
[CD] *EMI* (Sw) CDC 7 61075 2
[MC] *Odeon* (US) MCPF 6031 // *HMV* (Sw) 7C 253-35445/46M
[8T] *Odeon* (US) 8PF 6031

109
(Test record; contents not given in recording ledger)
0SB 754-1

1938, May 31. Stockholm, Concert Hall, Small Auditorium. With Nils Grevillius & his orch.

110
Au mont Ida trois déesses [Sw: Uti en skog på berget Ida] (Offenbach: *La belle Hélène*) [Orig. label: Paris' entrésång ur 'Den sköna Helena']
0SB 755-**1**,-**2**

A (Take 1)

[78] *HMV* [1]X 6090, (Au) EC 214, (Fi) TG 129, (Nor) AL 3096
[45] *HMV* (Sw) 7EBS 10
[33] *Rococo* 5201 // *Odeon* (Sw) PMCS 308 // *HMV* (Sw) [1]4E 153-34532/33M = *Odeon* (US) 4E 153-34532/33M // *Rubini* GV 21 // *HMV* (Au) [1]OXLP 7617 = *WRC* (Au) R 03668 // *HMV* (GB) [1]RLS 715, (Sw) 7C 153-06518/20M = *WRC* (Au) R 05223/25, (NZ) WE 26451/53 // *Club "99"* CL 110 // *HMV* (Sw) PRO 3034 // *Dacapo* [1]1C 147-03354/55M, 1C 137 1033543M // *Accord* ACC 1500 17 // *HMV* (Sw) 7C 061-35731M // *WRC* (Au) R 13509 // *HMV* (Au) [1]OXLP 7660 = *WRC* (Au) R 11409 // *HMV* (GB) [1]EX 29 0169 3 = *Sera.* (US) IM 1643
[CD] *Legendary* LR-CD 1004 // *EMI* (Sw) CDC 7 61075 2 // *Club "99"* CL 511/12 // *Nimbus* NI 7842 // *EMI* (GB) CDH 7 64707 2
[MC] *HMV* (Sw) 4E 278-51007M // *WRC* (Au) C 05223/25 // *WRC* (Au) C 03668 // *HMV* (Sw) 7C 261-35731M // *HMV* (Au) TC-OXCP 7660

B (Take 2)

[78] (Not issued)
[33] *OASI* 660
[CD] *Bluebell* ABCD 016 // *OASI* 7006

111
Soll ich reden...Ich setz' den Fall [Sw: Skall jag tala...Antag det fall] (Millöcker: *Der Bettelstudent*) [Orig. label: Duett ur 'Tiggarstudenten']. With Hjördis Schymberg (sop.).
0SB 756-1,-**2**

[78] *HMV* X 6146
[33] *Rococo* 5201 // *HMV* (Sw) [1]SGLP 507 = *MFP* (Sw) MFP 5571 = *Odeon* (Sw) PMES 507, (US) SGLP 507 // *HMV* (Sw) [1]7C 153-35445/46M = *Odeon* (US) 7C 153-35445/46M // *HMV* (GB) [1]RLS 715, (Sw) 7C 153-06518/20M = *WRC* (Au) R 05223/25, (NZ) WE 26451/53 // *HMV* (Sw) PRO 3034 // *Dacapo* [1]1C 147 03354/55M, 1C 137 1033543M
[CD] *EMI* (Sw) CDC 7 61075 2
[MC] *Odeon* (US) MCPF 6032 // *HMV* (Sw) 7C 253-35445/46M // *WRC* (Au) C 05223/25
[8T] *Odeon* (US) 8PF 6032

1938, August 10. Stockholm, Concert Hall, Small Auditorium. With orch., cond. Nils Grevillius.

112
Instant charmant...En fermant les yeux [Fr] (Massenet: *Manon*)
2SB 779-1,-**2**

[78] *Elec.* DB 3603 = *HMV* [1]DB 3603, (Ir) IRX 91, (Nor) DBN 3603 = *Vic.* (J) JD 1513, ND 139, (US,Ca) 12635
[45] *HMV* (Au) 7ERO 5193, (GB) [1]7ER 5193 = *HMV* (Fr) ROVL 9016 = *Pl.Mus.* 7ERF 17.121 // *HMV* (It) 7ERQ 255
[33] *Angel* (Ar) LPC 12083, 6083, (Ch) 3ACX 47190, (J) HA 5085, AB 7134, (US) COLH 148 = *Cap.* (US) G 7239 = *HMV* (Au) OALP 1620, OELP 9673, (Fr) FALP 629, (GB) [1]ALP 1620, (It) QALP 10266, (NL) XLPH 1002, (NZ) MALP 1620, (SA) JALP 1620 = *Voix Ill.* 50018 // *Dacapo* [1]1C 177-(147-)00947/48M, 1C 137 1009473M = *HMV* (Sw) 7C 137-00947/48M // *Sera.* (US) 60219 // *HMV* (NL) 5C 045-01715M // *Bongiovanni* GB 1035/36
[CD] *Axis* 7017672 // *Nimbus* NI 7835 // *EMI* (GB) CDH 7 64707 2
[MC] *HMV* (Sw) 7C 237-00947M // *Sera.* (US) 4XG 60219 // *Nimbus* NC 7835

113
La fleur que tu m'avais jetée [Fr] (Bizet: *Carmen*)
2SB 780-**1**,-2

[78] *Elec.* DB 3603 = *HMV* [1]DB 3603, (Ir) IRX 91, (Nor) DBN 3603 = *Vic.* (J) JD

1513, ND 139, (US,Ca) 12635 // *Vic.* (US) MO 1275
[45] *HMV* (GB) [1]7P 261, (SA) 7PJ 736 // *HMV* (Au) 7ERO 5193, (GB) [1]7ER 5193
[33] *Angel* (Ar) LPC 12083, 6083, (Ch) 3ACX 47190, (J) HA 5085, AB 7134, (US) COLH 148 = *Cap.* (US) G 7239 = *HMV* (Au) OALP 1620, OELP 9673, (Fr) FALP 629, (GB) [1]ALP 1620, (It) QALP 10266, (NL) XLPH 1002, (NZ) MALP 1620, (SA) JALP 1620 = *Voix Ill.* 50018 // *Elec.* E 70412 // *HMV* (NL) GHLP 1027 // *Dacapo* [1]1C 177-(147-)00947/48M, 1C 137 1009473M = *HMV* (Sw) 7C 137-00947/48M // *Sera.* (US) 60219 // *HMV* (NL) 5C 045-01715M // *ANNA* 1045 // *Sera.*(?)(J) EAC 60178/82 // *HMV* (Au) OXLP 7633 // *EMI* (Sw) EMISP 127
[CD] *Axis* 7017672 // *Nimbus* NI 7842 // *EMI* (GB) 7 64707 2
[MC] *HMV* (Sw) 7C 237-00947M // *Sera.* (US) 4XG 60219

1938, October 12. Stockholm, Concert Hall, Small Auditorium. With orch., cond. Nils Grevillius.

114
Cujus animam [Lat] (Rossini: *Stabat mater*)
2SB 823-**1**,-2,(-**3**) [For difference between takes, see note]

A (Take 1)

[78] *Elec.* DB 3665 = *HMV* [1]DB 3665 v.1
[33] *ANNA* 1006
[CD] *Bluebell* ABCD 016

B (Take 3)

[78] *HMV* [1]DB 3665 v.2, (Ir) IRX 74 (?) = *Vic.* (US) 13588
[45] *RCA* (B) 65.519
[33] *Rococo* R 31 // *Eterna* 8 20 829 // *Angel* (Ch) 3ACX 47530, (Ur) UAL 12513 = *HMV* (GB,Au) [1]HQM 1190, (GB,SA) HLM 7038, (SA) JALP 29 = *Odeon* (US) PHQM 1190 = *Sera.* (US) 60168 // *Dacapo* [1]1C 177-(147-)00947/48M, 1C 137 1009473M = *HMV* (Sw) 7C 137-00947/48M // *HMV* (NL) 5C 045-01715M // *HMV* (Au) OXLP 7633
[CD] *EMI* (GB) CDH 7 61053 2 // *Award* AWCD 29115 // *Axis* 7017672 // *Nimbus* NI 7835
[MC] *HMV* (Sw) 7C 237-00947M // *HMV* (SA) L4HLM 7038 = *Sera.* (US) [1]4XG 60168 // *Nimbus* NC 7835

115
Ingemisco [Lat] (Verdi: *Messa da Requiem*)
2SB 824-**1**,-2

[78] *Elec.* DB 3665 = *HMV* [1]DB 3665, (Ir) IRX 74 = *Vic.* (US) 13588
[45] *RCA* (B) 65.519
[33] *Rococo* R 31 // *Eterna* 8 20 829 // *Angel* (Ch) 3ACX 47530, (Ur) UAL 12513 = *HMV* (GB,Au) [1]HQM 1190, (GB,SA) HLM 7038, (SA) JALP 29 = *Odeon* (US)

PHQM 1190 = *Sera.* (US) 60168 // *Dacapo* [1]1C 177-(147-)00947/48M, 1C 137 1009473M = *HMV* (Sw) 7C 137-00947/48M // *HMV* (NL) 5C 045-01715M // *HMV* (Au) OXLP 7633

[CD] *Memoir* CDMOIR 411 // *Nimbus* NI 7835 // *EMI* (GB) CDH 7 64707 2

[MC] *HMV* (Sw) 7C 237-00947M // *HMV* (SA) L4HLM 7038 = *Sera.* (US) [1]4XG 60168 // *Memoir* CMOIR 411 // *Nimbus* NC 7835

116

Ah sì, ben mio [It] (Verdi: *Il trovatore*)
0SB 825-1,-2,-**3** [Test pressing of Take 2 exists; see note]

[78] (Not issued)

[33] *OASI* 660

[CD] *Bluebell* ABCD 016 // *OASI* 7006

117

Di quella pira (Verdi: *Il trovatore*)
0SB 826-**1**,-2 [See note]

[78] (Not issued)

[CD] *Bluebell* ABCD 016

1939, July 14. Stockholm, Concert Hall, Small Auditorium. With orch., cond. Nils Grevillius.

118

Ach, so fromm [It: M'apparì tutt'amor] (Flotow: *Martha*)
2SB 983-1,-2,-**3**

[78] *HMV* [1]DB 3887, (Ir) IRX 64 = *Vic.* (US,Ca) 13790 // *Vic.* (US) MO 1275

[33] *Angel* (Ch) 3ACX 47530, (Ur) UAL 12513 = *HMV* (GB,Au) [1]HQM 1190, (GB,SA) HLM 7038, (SA) JALP 29 = *Odeon* (US) PHQM 1190 = *Sera.* (US) 60168 // *Dacapo* [1]1C 177-(147-)00947/48M, 1C 137 1009473M = *HMV* (Sw) 7C 137-00947/48M

[CD] *EMI* (GB) CDH 7 61053 2 // *Award* AWCD 29115 // *Axis* 7017672 // *Nimbus* NI 7842

[MC] *HMV* (Sw) 7C 237-00947M // *HMV* (SA) L4HLM 7038 = *Sera.* (US) [1]4XG 6016

119

Salut! demeure chaste et pure [Fr] (Gounod: *Faust*)
2SB 984-1,-2,-**3**

[78] *HMV* [1]DB 3887, (Ir) IRX 64 = *Vic.* (US,Ca) 13790 // *Vic.* (US) MO 1275

[45] *Pl.Mus.* 7ERF 17.109

[33] *Angel* (Ar) LPC 12193, (Br) 3CBX 328, (Ch) 3ACX 47341, (J) HA 5031, AB 7127, (US) COLH 150 = *Cap.* (US) [1]G 7248 = *HMV* (Au) OALP 1841, (GB) ALP 1841, (It) QALP 10319, (NL) XLPH 20010, 5C 045-(047-)00191M, (NZ)

MALP 1841, (SA) JALP 1841 = *WRC* (Au) 3145 // *Dacapo* [1]1C 177-(147-)00947/48M, 1C 137 1009473M = *HMV* (Sw) 7C 137-00947/48M // *HMV* (Sw) [1]4E 153-34532/33M = *Odeon* (US) 4E 153-34532/33M // *Sera.* (US) 60219 // *HMV* (GB) [1]RLS 715, (Sw) 7C 153-06518/20M = *WRC* (Au) R 05223/25, (NZ) WE 26451/53 // *HMV* (Au) OXLP 7633 // *HMV* (Sw) PRO 3034 // *HMV* (Sw) [1]SPPH 030, 7C 061-35822 // *MET* 110

[CD] *MET* 110CD // *EMI* (GB) CDH 7 61053 2 // *Victorie* 290 222 // *Memoir* CDMOIR 409 // *Nimbus* NI 7842

[MC] *HMV* (Sw) 4E 278-51007M // *HMV* (Sw) 7C 237-00947M // *WRC* (Au) C 05223/25 // *Sera.* (US) 4XG 60219 // *HMV* (Sw) 7C 261-35822 // *MET* 110C // *Memoir* CMOIR 409

1939, July 15. Stockholm, Concert Hall, Small Auditorium. With orch., cond. Nils Grevillius.

120
Ah sì, ben mio [It] (Verdi: *Il trovatore*)
0SB 825-4,-**5**

[78] *Elec.* DA 1701 = *HMV* [1]DA 1701 = *Vic.* (US) 2136

[33] *HMV* (GB) CSLP 500/04 = *RCA* (US) [1]LCT 6701 // *Rococo* R 31 // *Col.* (G) [1]C 91296 = *Odeon* (US) C 91296 // *Eterna* 8 20 829 // *Angel* (Ch) 3ACX 47530, (UR) UAL 12513 = *HMV* (GB,Au) [1]HQM 1190, (GB,SA) HLM 7038, (SA) JALP 29 = *Odeon* (US) PHQM 1190 = *Sera.* (US) 60168 // *Dacapo* [1]1C 177-(147-)00947/48M, 1C 137 1009473M = *HMV* (Sw) 7C 137-00947/48M // *HMV* (NL) 5C 045-01715M // *HMV* (GB) [1]RLS 715, (Sw) 7C 153-06518/20M = *WRC* (Au) R 05223/25, (NZ) WE 26451/53 // *HMV* (Au) OXLP 7633 // *MET* 110

[CD] *MET* 110CD // *EMI* (GB) CDH 7 61053 2 // *Award* AWCD 29115 // *Nimbus* NI 7835

[MC] *HMV* (Sw) 7C 237-00947M // *WRC* (Au) C 05223/25 // *HMV* (SA) L4HLM 7038 = *Sera.* (US) [1]4XG 60168 // *MET* 110C // *Nimbus* NC 7835

121
Di quella pira [It] (Verdi: *Il trovatore*)
0SB 826-3,-4,-5 (0EA 8086-**1**) [For transfer from 0SB to 0EA, see note]

[78] *Elec.* DA 1701 = *HMV* [1]DA 1701 = *Vic.* (US) 2136

[33] *Angel* (Ar) LPC 12193, (Br) 3CBX 328, (Ch) 3ACX 47341, (J) HA 5031, AB 7127, (US) COLH 150 = *Cap.* (US) [1]G 7248 = *HMV* (Au) OALP 1841, (GB) ALP 1841, (It) QALP 10319, (NL) XLPH 20010, 5C 045-(047-)00191M, (NZ) MALP 1841, (SA) JALP 1841 = *WRC* (Au) 3145 // *Odeon* (Sw) PMCS 308 // *Dacapo* [1]1C 177-(147-)00947/48M, 1C 137 1009473M = *HMV* (Sw) 7C 137-00947/48M // *HMV* (Sw) [1]4E 153-34532/33M = *Odeon* (US) 4E 153-34532/33M // *Sera.* (US) 60219 // *Col.* (A) Parnass 62528 = *Parnass* [1]62528 // *HMV* (Au) OXLP 7633 // *HMV* (GB) [1]RLS 715, (Sw) 7C 153-06518/20M = *WRC* (Au) R 05223/25, (NZ) WE 26451/53 // *HMV* (Sw) PRO 3034 // MET 110 // *HMV* (Fr) 2910753

[CD] *MET* 110CD // *Bongiovanni* GB 1051-2 // *Axis* 7017672 // *Nimbus* NI 7835 // *EMI* (GB) CDH 7 64707 2
[MC] *HMV* (Sw) 4E 278-51007M // *HMV* (Sw) 7C 237-00947M // *WRC* (Au) C 05223/25 // *Sera.* (US) 4XG 60219 // *MET* 110C // *Nimbus* NC 7835

1939, July 15. Stockholm, Concert Hall, Small Auditorium. With Harry Ebert, piano.

122
Morgen [Ger] (R. Strauss)
0SB 985-1,-2,-**3**

[78] *HMV* [1]DA 1704, (Au) EC 89
[33] *Angel* (Ch) 3ACX 47530, (Ur) UAL 12513 = *HMV* (GB,Au) [1]HQM 1190, (GB,SA) HLM 7038, (SA) JALP 29 = *Odeon* (US) PHQM 1190 = *Sera.* (US) 60168 // *HMV* (Au) [1]OXLP 7660 = *WRC* (Au) R 11409
[CD] *EMI* (GB) CDH 7 64707 2
[MC] *HMV* (SA) L4HLM 7038 = *Sera.* (US) [1]4XG 60168 // *HMV* (Au) TC-OXCP 7660

123
Cäcilie [Ger] (R. Strauss)
0SB 986-1,-2,-**3**

[78] *HMV* [1]DA 1704, (Au) EC 89
[33] *Angel* (Ch) 3ACX 47350, (Ur) UAL 12513 = *HMV* (GB,Au) [1]HQM 1190, (GB,SA) HLM 7038, (SA) JALP 29 = *Odeon* (US) PHQM 1190 = *Sera.* (US) 60168
[CD] *Nimbus* NI 7842
[MC] *HMV* (SA) L4HLM 7038 = *Sera.* (US) [1]4XG 60168

124
Adelaide [Ger] (Beethoven)
0SB 987-1,-**2**,-3 + 988-1,-**2**,-3 [Take 3, see note]

[78] *HMV* DA 1705 = *Vic.* (US) 2195
[33] *Angel* (Ch) 3ACX 47530, (Ur) UAL 12513 = *HMV* (GB,Au) [1]HQM 1190, (GB,SA) HLM 7038, (SA) JALP 29 = *Odeon* (US) PHQM 1190 = *Sera.* (US) 60168 // *HMV* (Au) [1]OXLP 7660 = *WRC* (Au) R 11409
[CD] *Nimbus* NI 7812 // *Nimbus* NI 7842 // *EMI* (GB) CDH 7 64707 2
[MC] *HMV* (SA) L4HLM 7038 = *Sera.* (US) [1]4XG 60168 // *HMV* (Au) TC-OXCP 7660 // *Nimbus* NC 7812

1940, January 30. New York, Manhattan Center, Victor Studio 2. With Harry Ebert, piano.

125
An Sylvia [Ger] (Schubert)
CS 046742-1 [issued by HMV as 2A 046742-1]

[78] *HMV* DB 5759, (Au) ED 87 = *Vic.* (US) [1]12725
[33] *ANNA* 1017 // *Bluebell* BELL 187
[CD] *Nimbus* NI 7842 // *Bluebell* ABCD 050

126
Ständchen [Ger] (Schubert)
CS 046743-1 [issued by HMV as 2A 046743-1]

[78] *HMV* DB 5759, (Au) ED 87 = *Vic.* (US) [1]12725 // *Vic.* (J) RL 76
[33] *ANNA* 1017 // *Bluebell* BELL 187
[CD] *Nimbus* NI 7842 // *Bluebell* ABCD 050

127
An die Leier [Ger] (Schubert)
CS 046744-1 [issued by HMV as 2A 046744-1]

[78] *HMV* DB 5787 = *Vic.* (US) [1]12831
[33] *ANNA* 1017 // *Bluebell* BELL 187
[CD] *Nimbus* NI 7842 // *Bluebell* ABCD 050

128
Die böse Farbe [Ger] (Schubert)
BS 046745-1

[78] (Not issued)
[33] *Voce* 88
[CD] *Bluebell* ABCD 050

129
Frühlingsglaube [Ger] (Schubert)
BS 046746-1

[78] (Not issued)
[33] *Voce* 88
[CD] *Bluebell* ABCD 050

130
Wandrers Nachtlied [Ger] (Schubert)
BS 046747-1

[78] (Not issued)
[33] *Voce* 88

131
Svarta rosor [Sw] (Sibelius)
BS 046748-1(A) [Issued by HMV as 0A 046748-1]

[78] *HMV* DA 1797 (not issued), (Au) EC 117 = *Vic.* (US) [1]4531
[33] *ANNA* 1006 // *Bluebell* BELL 187
[CD] *Nimbus* NI 7842 // *Bluebell* ABCD 050

1940, March 1. New York, Manhattan Center, Victor Studio 2. With Harry Ebert, piano.

132
Ich möchte schweben [Ger] (Sjögren)
BS 047735-1

[78] (Not issued)
[CD] *Bluebell* ABCD 050

133
Säv, säv, susa [Sw] (Sibelius)
BS 047736-1 [Issued by HMV as 0A 047736-1]

[78] *HMV* DA 1797 (not issued), (Au) EC 117 = *Vic.* (US) [1]4531
[33] *ANNA* 1006 // *Bluebell* BELL 187
[CD] *Nimbus* NI 7842 // *Bluebell* ABCD 050

134
Skogen sover [Sw] (Alfvén)
CS 047737-1 (part 1) [Issued by HMV as part of 2A 047737]

[78] *HMV* DB 5787 = *Vic.* (US) [1]12831
[33] *ANNA* 1017 // *Bluebell* BELL 187
[CD] *Nimbus* NI 7842 // *Bluebell* ABCD 050

135
Morgon [Sw] (Eklöf)
CS 047737-1 (part 2) [Issued by HMV as part of 2A 047737]

[78] *HMV* DB 5787 = *Vic.* (US) [1]12831
[33] *ANNA* 1017 // *Bluebell* BELL 187
[CD] *Nimbus* NI 7842 // *Bluebell* ABCD 050

136
Wandrers Nachtlied [Ger] (Schubert)
BS 046747-2(A)

[78] (Not issued)
[CD] *Bluebell* ABCD 050

1941, June 16. Stockholm, Concert Hall, Small Auditorium. With orch., cond. Nils Grevillius.

137
Di' tu se fedele [It] (Verdi: *Un ballo in maschera*)
OSB 2032-1,-2,-3 [Test pressing of Take 3 exists; see note]

[78] *HMV* DA 1818 (Not issued; compare No. 148)

138
Questa o quella [It] (Verdi: *Rigoletto*)
OSB 2033-1,-2,-3(?) [Test pressing of "Take 3" exists; see note]

[78] *HMV* DA 1818 (not issued)
[33] *HMV* (GB) [1]RLS 715, (Sw) 7C 153-06518/20M = *WRC* (Au) R 05223/25, (NZ) WE 26451/53
[MC] *WRC* (Au) C 05223/25

1941, June 17. Stockholm, Concert Hall, Small Auditorium. With Hjördis Schymberg (sop.) & orch., cond. Nils Grevillius.

139
O soave fanciulla [It] (Puccini: *La bohème*)
2SB 2034-**1**,-**2**

A (Take 1)

[78] *HMV* DB 6119 v.1, (Au) ED 375, (Ir) IRX 87, (Sw) [1]DB 6000 = *Vic.* (US) 11-8440
[45] *HMV* (NL) 7OPH 1004
[33] *Angel* (Ar) LPC 12193, (Br) 3CBX 328, (Ch) 3ACX 47341, (J) HA 5031, AB 7127, (US) COLH 150 = *Cap.* (US) [1]G 7248 = *HMV* (Au) OALP 1841, (GB) ALP 1841, (It) QALP 10319, (NL) XLPH 20010, 5C 045-(047-)00191M, (NZ) MALP 1841, (SA) JALP 1841 = *WRC* (Au) 3145 // *HMV* (Au) [1]OXLP 7617 = *WRC* (Au) R 03668 // *HMV* (Sw) [1]7C 153-35445/46M = *Odeon* (US) 7C 153-35445/46M // *HMV* (Sw) PRO 3034 // *WRC* (Au) R 13509 // *HMV* (Sw) 7C 037-35918M // *HMV* (Fi) 7691751 // *EMI* (Sw) EMISP 127
[CD] *EMI* (GB) CDH 7 61053 2 v.2 // *Axis* 7017672 // *Nimbus* NI 7842
[MC] *HMV* (Sw) 7C 253-35445/46M // *WRC* (Au) C 03668 // *HMV* (Fi) 7691754

B (Take 2)

[78] *HMV* DB 6119 v.2

140
È il sol dell'anima [It] (Verdi: *Rigoletto*)
2SB 2035-**1**,-**2** [For difference between takes, see note]

A (Take 1)

[78] *HMV* DB 6119 v.1, (Au) ED 375, (Ir) IRX 87, (Sw) DB [1]6000 v.l = *Vic.* (US) 11-8440

[45] *HMV* (NL) 7OPH 1004

[33] *Angel* (Ch) 3ACX 47530, (Ur) UAL 12513 = *HMV* (GB,Au) [1]HQM 1190, (GB,SA) HLM 7038, (SA) JALP 29 = *Odeon* (US) PHQM 1190 = *Sera.* (US) 60168 // *Dacapo* [1]1C 177-(147-)00947/48M, 1C 137 1009473M = *HMV* (Sw) 7C 137-00947/48M // *HMV* (Sw) 7C 037-35918M

[CD] *Nimbus* NI 7842 // *EMI* (GB) CDH 7 64707 2

[MC] *HMV* (Sw) 7C 237-00947M // *HMV* (SA) L4HLM 7038 = *Sera.* (US) [1]4XG 60168

B (Take 2)

[78] *HMV* (Sw) DB 6000 v.2 // *HMV* DB 6119 v.2

[CD] *Bluebell* ABCD 016

1944, March 27-30 [see note]. Stockholm, Concert Hall, Small Auditorium. With orch., cond. Nils Grevillius.

141
Come un bel dì di maggio [It] (Giordano: *Andrea Chénier*)
0SB 2397-1,-**2** [Test pressing of Take 1 exists; see note]

[78] *HMV* [1]DA 1836, (Nor) DAN 1836 // *Vic.* (US) 10-1323

[33] *Angel* (Ar) LPC 12193, (Br) 3CBX 328, (Ch) 3ACX 47341, (J) HA 5031, AB 7127, (US) COLH 150 = *Cap.* (US) [1]G 7248 = *HMV* (Au) OALP 1841, (GB) ALP 1841, (It) QALP 10319, (NL) XLPH 20010, 5C 045-(047-)00191M, (NZ) MALP 1841, (SA) JALP 1841 = *WRC* (Au) 3145 // *Rococo* R 31 // *Eterna* 8 20829 // *Sera.* (US) IB 6058 // *Dacapo* [1]1C 177-(147-)00947/48M, 1C 137 1009473M = *HMV* (Sw) 7C 137-00947/48M // *Golden Age* EJS 530 // *HMV* (Sw) [1]7C 153-35445/46M = *Odeon* (US) 7C 153-35445/46M // *HMV* (GB) [1]RLS 715, (Sw) 7C 153-06518/20M = *WRC* (Au) R 05223/25, (NZ) WE 26451/53 // *HMV* (Au) OXLP 7633 // *HMV* (Sw) PRO 3034 // *Angel* (J) GR 70085

[CD] *EMI* (GB) CDH 7 64707 2

[MC] *HMV* (Sw) 7C 253-35445/46M // *HMV* (Sw) 7C 237-00948M // *WRC* (Au) C 05223/25

142
Amor ti vieta [It] (Giordano: *Fedora*)
0SB 2398-1,-**2** [Test pressing of Take 1 exists; see note]

[78] *HMV* [1]DA 1836, (Nor) DAN 1836

[33] *Angel* (Ar) LPC 12193, (Br) 3CBX 328, (Ch) 3ACX 47341, (J) HA 5031, AB 7127, (US) COLH 150 = *Cap.* (US) [1]G 7248 = *HMV* (Au) OALP 1841, (GB) ALP 1841, (It) QALP 10319, (NL) XLPH 20010, 5C 045-(047-)00191M, (NZ) MALP 1841, (SA) JALP 1841 = *WRC* (Au) 3145 // *Rococo* R 31 // *Odeon* (Sw) PMCS 308 // *HMV* (It) QALP 5340 = *Odeon* (It) 3C 061-00740M // *Eterna* 8 20 829 // *Sera.* (US) IB 6058 // *Dacapo* [1]1C 177-(147-)00947/48M, 1C 137 1009473M = *HMV* (Sw) 7C 137-00947/48M // *HMV* (Sw) [1]7C 153-35445/46M = *Odeon* (US) 7C 153-35445/46M // *HMV* (GB) [1]RLS 715, (Sw) 7C 153-06518/20M = *WRC* (Au) R 05223/25, (NZ) WE 26451/53 // *HMV* (Au) OXLP 7633 // *HMV* (Sw) PRO 3034

[CD] *EMI* (GB) CDH 7 61053 2

[MC] *HMV* (Sw) 7C 253-35445/46M // *HMV* (Sw) 7C 237-00948M // *WRC* (Au) C 05223/25

143

Nessun dorma! [It] (Puccini: *Turandot*)
0SB 2399-1,-**2**

[78] *Elec.* DA 1841 = *HMV* [1]DA 1841, (Au) EC 143, (Ir) IR 370, (Nor) DAN 1841 // *Vic.* (US,Br) 10-1200

[45] *RCA* (US) 49-0621 // *Elec.* 7RW 131 = *HMV* (GB) [1]7R 106, 7P 208, (It) 7RQ 3007, (NL) 7PH 1011, (SA) 7PJ 713 // *RCA* (US,G) ERA 245 // *Angel* (Br) TCB 26 // *HMV* (GB) [1]7ER 5207, (It) 7ERQ 258 // *HMV* (Fr) ROVL 9040

[33] *HMV* (GB) CSLP 500/04 = *RCA* (US) [1]LCT 6701 // *Angel* (Ar) LPC 12083, 6083, (Ch) 3ACX 47190, (J) HA 5085, AB 7134, (US) COLH 148 = *Cap.* (US) G 7239 = *HMV* (Au) OALP 1620, OELP 9673, (Fr) FALP 629, (GB) [1]ALP 1620, (It) QALP 10266, (NL) XLPH 1002, (NZ) MALP 1620, (SA) JALP 1620 = *Voix Ill.* 50018 // *Elec.* E 70412 // *Angel* (Br) 3BBX 21 // *HMV* (NL) GHLP 1027 // *Dacapo* [1]1C 177-(147-)00947/48M, 1C 137 1009473M = *HMV* (Sw) 7C 137-00947/48M // *HMV* (Sw) [1]4E 153-34532/33M = *Odeon* (US) 4E 153-34532/33M // *HMV* (GB,Au,SA) [1]HLM 7004, (NL) 5C 047-01266M = *Sera.* (US) 60206 = *WRC* (Au) R 10132 // *EMI* (SA) EMCJ 6001 // *Sera.* (US) 60219 // *HMV* (NL) 5C 045-01715M // *HMV* (GB) [1]RLS 715, (Sw) 7C 153-06518/20M = *WRC* (Au) R 05223/25, (NZ) WE 26451/53 // *HMV* (Au) OXLP 7633 // *HMV* (Sw) PRO 3034 // *HMV* (Sw) 7C 061-35731M // *Fame* (SA) FAME 13 // *Angel* (J) GR 70085 // *HMV* (Fi) 7691751 // *EMI* (Sw) EMISP 127

[CD] *EMI* (GB) CDH 7 61053 2 // *Opera Now* // *Award* AWCD 29115 // *Axis* 7017672

[MC] *HMV* (Sw) 4E 278-51007M // *EMI* (SA) L4EMCJ 6001 // *HMV* (Sw) 7C 237-00948M // *WRC* (Au) C 05223/25 // *HMV* (GB) [1]TC-HLM 7004, (SA) L4HLM 7004 // *Sera.* (US) 4XG 60219 // *HMV* (Sw) 7C 261-35731M // *Fame* (SA) L4FAME 13 // *HMV* (Fi) 7691754

144

Recitar!...Vesti la giubba [It] (Leoncavallo: *Pagliacci*)
2SB 2400-1,-**2**

[78] *HMV* [1]DB 6163, (Au) ED 1239 = *Vic.* (US) 11-9387

[45] *HMV* (GB) [1]7ER 5207, (It) 7ERQ 258

[33] *Angel* (Ar) LPC 12083, 6083, (Ch) 3ACX 47190, (J) HA 5085, AB 7134, (US) COLH 148 = *Cap.* (US) G 7239 = *HMV* (Au) OALP 1620, OELP 9673, (Fr) FALP 629, (GB) [1]ALP 1620, (It) QALP 10266, (NL) XLPH 1002, (NZ) MALP 1620, (SA) JALP 1620 = *Voix Ill.* 50018 // *Elec.* E 70412 // *HMV* (NL) GHLP 1027 // *Dacapo* [1]1C 177-(147-)00947/48M, 1C 137 1009473M = *HMV* (Sw) 7C 137-00947/48M // *HMV* (Sw) [1]4E 153-34532/33M = *Odeon* (Sw) 4E 153-34532/33M // *EMI* (SA) EMGJ 6004 // *HMV* (GB) [1]RLS 715, (Sw) 7C 153-06518/20M = *WRC* (Au) R 05223/25, (NZ) WE 26451/53 // *HMV* (Sw) PRO 3034 // *Fame* (SA) FAME 20 // *HMV* (Fi) 7691751

[CD] *EMI* (GB) CDH 7 61053 2 // *Axis* 7017672 // *Bongiovanni* GB 1071-2

[MC] *HMV* (Sw) 4E 278-51007M // *EMI* (SA) L4EMGJ 6004 // *HMV* (Sw) 7C 237-00948M // *WRC* (Au) C 052237/25 // *Fame* (SA) L4FAME 20 // *HMV* (Fi) 7691754 // *Utbildningsradion* 26-92299-1

[8T] *EMI* (SA) L8EMGJ 6004

145

Questa o quella [It] (Verdi: *Rigoletto*)

0SB 2401-1,-**2**

[78] *HMV* [1]DA 1837, (Au) EC 207, (Ir) IR 369, (Nor) DAN 1837 // *Vic.* (US,Br) 10-1200 // *Vic.* (US) DM 1474

[45] *RCA* (US) 49-0621 // *RCA* (US) WDM 1474 // *HMV* (Fr) 7RF 115 // *HMV* (GB) [1]7P 261, (SA) 7PJ 736 // *HMV* (GB) [1]7ER 5207, (It) 7ERQ 258 // *RCA* (Au) 26019, (GB) RCX 7114, (US,G) [1]ERA 134

[33] *Angel* (Ar) LPC 12083, 6083, (Ch) 3ACX 47190, (J) HA 5085, AB 7134, (US) COLH 148 = *Cap.* (US) G 7239 = *HMV* (Au) OALP 1620, OELP 9673, (Fr) FALP 629, (GB) [1]ALP 1620, (It) QALP 10266, (NL) XLPH 1002, (NZ) MALP 1620, (SA) JALP 1620 = *Voix Ill.* 50018 // *Dacapo* [1]1C 177-(147-)00947/48M, 1C 137 1009473M = *HMV* (Sw) 7C 137-00947/48M // *HMV* (Sw) [1]4E 153-34532/33M = *Odeon* (US) 4E 153-34532/33M // *EMI* (SA) EMGJ 6004 // *Sera.* (US) 60219 // *HMV* (NL) 5C 045-01715M // *HMV* (Sw) PRO 3034 // *HMV* (Sw) 7C 061-35731M // *MET* 110 // *Fame* (SA) FAME 19 // *EMI* (Sw) EMISP 127

[CD] *MET* 110CD // *Axis* 7017672 // *EMI* (GB) CDH 7 64707 2

[MC] *HMV* (Sw) 4E 278-51007M // *EMI* (SA) L4EMGJ 6004 // *HMV* (Sw) 7C 237-00947M // *Sera.* (US) 4XG 60219 // *HMV* (Sw) 7C 261-35731M // *MET* 110C // *Fame* (SA) L4FAME 19

[8T] *EMI* (SA) L8EMGJ 6004

146

Mattinata [It] (Leoncavallo)

0SB 2402-1,-**2**

[78] *Elec.* DA 1841 = *HMV* [1]DA 1841, (Au) EC 143, (Ir) IR 370, (Nor) DAN 1841

[45] *Elec.* 7RW 131 = *HMV* (GB) [1]7R 106, 7P 208, (It) 7RQ 3007, (NL) 7PH 1011, (SA) 7PJ 713 // *Angel* (Br) TCB 02 = *HMV* (Au) 7EBO 6030, (GB) 7EB 6030, 7ER 5189, (It) 7EPQ 607, (NZ) 7EBM 6030, 7ERM 5189, (Sw) [1]7EBS 13

[33] *Angel* (Ch) 3ACX 47365, (J) HA 5032, AB 7123, (US) COLH 149 = *Cap.* (US) [1]G 7247 = *HMV* (Au) OALP 1857, (GB) ALP 1857, (NZ) MALP 1857 = *WRC*

(Au) 3199, (NZ) CO 566 // *Angel* (Br) 3BBX 21 // *Odeon* (Sw) PMCS 308 // *Sera.* (US) IB 6058 // *Dacapo* [1]1C 177-(147-)00947/48M, 1C 137 1009473M = *HMV* (Sw) 7C 137-00947/48M // *HMV* (Sw) [1]7C 153-35445/46M = *Odeon* (US) 7C 153-35445/46M // *HMV* (GB) [1]RLS 715, (Sw) 7C 153-06518/20M = *WRC* (Au) R 05223/25, (NZ) WE 26451/53 // *HMV* (Sw) PRO 3034 // *HMV* (Sw) 7C 061-35731M // *HMV* (Au) [1]OXLP 7660 = *WRC* (Au) R 11409

[CD] *EMI* (GB) CDH 7 64707 2

[MC] *HMV* (Sw) 7C 253-35445/46M // *HMV* (Sw) 7C 237-00948M // *WRC* (Au) C 05223/25 // *HMV* (Sw) 7C 261-35731M // *HMV* (Au) TC-OXCP 7660

147
Mamma!...Quel vino [It] (Mascagni: *Cavalleria rusticana*)
2SB 2403-**1**,-**2** [For difference between takes, see note]

A (Take 1)

[78] *HMV* DB 6163 v.1

[33] *Angel* (Ar) LPC 12193, (Br) 3CBX 328, (Ch) 3ACX 47341, (J) HA 5031, AB 7127, (US) COLH 150 = *Cap.* (US) [1]G 7248 = *HMV* (Au) OALP 1841, (GB) ALP 1841, (It) QALP 10319, (NL) XLPH 20010, 5C 045-(047-)00191M, (NZ) MALP 1841, (SA) JALP 1841 = *WRC* (Au) 3145 // *Sera.* (US) IB 6058 // *Dacapo* [1]1C 177-(147-)00947/48M, 1C 137 1009473M = *HMV* (Sw) 7C 137-00947/48M // *HMV* (Sw) [1]7C 153-35445/46M = *Odeon* (US) 7C 153-3545/46M // *HMV* (GB) [1]RLS 715, (Sw) 7C 153-06518/20M = *WRC* (Au) R 05223/25, (NZ) WE 26451/53 // *HMV* (Au) OXLP 7633 // *HMV* (Sw) PRO 3034 // *Angel* (J) GR 70085

[CD] *Axis* 7017672 // *EMI* (GB) CDH 7 64707 2

[MC] *HMV* (Sw) 7C 253-35445/46M // *HMV* (Sw) 7C 237-00948M // *WRC* (Au) C 05223/25

B (Take 2)

[78] *HMV* [1]DB 6163 v.2, (Au) ED 1239 = *Vic.* (US) 11-9387 // *V-Disc* 623 // *Vic.* (US) MO 1275

[33] *ANNA* 1017 // *MET* 110 // *Enharmonic* 82-004

[CD] *MET* 110CD // *Bluebell* ABCD 016 // *Nickson* NN 1003

[MC] *MET* 110C

148
Di' tu se fedele [It] (Verdi: *Un ballo in maschera*)
0SB 2404-1,-**2** [Test pressing of Take 1 exists; see note]

[78] *HMV* [1]DA 1837, (Au) EC 207, (Ir) IR 369 // *Vic.* (US) 10-1323

[45] *HMV* (Fr) 7RF 115

[33] *Rococo* R 31 // *Eterna* 8 20 829 // *Angel* (Ch) 3ACX 47530, (Ur) UAL 12513 = *HMV* (GB,Au) [1]HQM 1190, (GB,SA) HLM 7038, (SA) JALP 29 = *Odeon* (US) PHQM 1190 = *Sera.* (US) 60168 // *Dacapo* [1]1C 177-(147-)00947/48M, 1C 137 1009473M = *HMV* (Sw) 7C 137-00947/48M // *HMV* (NL) 5C 045-01715M // *HMV* (Au) OXLP 7633 // *MET* 110

[CD] *MET* 110CD // *EMI* (GB) CDH 7 61053 2
[MC] *HMV* (Sw) 7C 237-00947M // *HMV* (SA) L4HLM 7038 = *Sera.* (US) [1]4XG 60168 // *MET* 110C

1944, April 5. Stockholm, Concert Hall, Small Auditorium. With orch., cond. Sune Waldimir (pseud. of Engström).

149
Bön i ofredstid [Sw] (Nordqvist)
0SB 2409-**1**,-2

[78] *HMV* (Sw) X 7077
[33] *Unique* UORC 377 // *Bluebell* BELL 187

150
Bisp Thomas' frihetssång [Sw] (Nordqvist)
0SB 2410-**1**,-2

[78] *HMV* (Sw) X 7077
[33] *Unique* UORC 377 // *Bluebell* BELL 187

1945, September 6. Stockholm, Concert Hall, Small Auditorium. With Royal Orch., cond. Nils Grevillius.

151
Ah! lève-toi, soleil [Fr] (Gounod: *Roméo et Juliette*)
2SB 2535-**1**,-**2**

A (Take 1)

[78] (Not issued)
[33] *OASI* 660
[CD] *Bluebell* ABCD 016 // *OASI* 7006

B (Take 2)

[78] *HMV* DB 6249 = *Vic.* (US) 12-0527
[45] *Pl.Mus.* 7ERF 17.109
[33] *Angel* (Ar) LPC 12193, (Br) 3CBX 328, (Ch) 3ACX 47341, (J) HA 5031, AB 7127, (US) COLH 150 = *Cap.* (US) [1]G 7248 = *HMV* (Au) OALP 1841, (GB) ALP 1841, (It) QALP 10319, (NL) XLPH 20010, 5C 045-(047-)00191M, (NZ) MALP 1841, (SA) JALP 1841 = *WRC* (Au) 3145 // *Dacapo* [1]1C 177-(147-)00947/48M, 1C 137 1009473M = *HMV* (Sw) 7C 137-00947/48M // *HMV* (Sw) [1]4E 153-34532/33M = *Odeon* (US) 4E 153-34532/33M // *Sera.* (US) 60219 // *HMV* (GB) [1]RLS 715, (Sw) 7C 153-06518/20M = *WRC* (Au) R 05223/25, (NZ) WE 26451/53 // *HMV* (Au) OXLP 7633 // *HMV* (Sw) PRO 3034 // *MET* 110 //

EMI (Sw) EMISP 127 // *EMI* (GB) [1]EX 7 69741 1 = *Sera.* (US) IH 6150

[CD] *MET* 110CD // *EMI* (GB) CHS 7 69741 2 // *Award* AWCD 29115 // *Axis* 7017672 // *EMI* (GB) CDH 7 64707 2

[MC] *HMV* (Sw) 4E 278-51007M // *HMV* (Sw) 7C 237-00947M // *WRC* (Au) C 05223/25 // *Sera.* (US) 4XG 60219 // *MET* 110C

152
Je suis seul!...Ah! fuyez, douce image [Fr] (Massenet: *Manon*)
2SB 2536-**1**,-2

[78] *HMV* [1]DB 6249 = *Vic.* (US) 12-0527

[45] *HMV* (Au) 7ERO 5196, (GB) [1]7ER 5196, (It) 7ERQ 251 // *HMV* (Fr) ROVL 9016 // *Pl.Mus.* 7ERF 17.121

[33] *Angel* (Ar) LPC 12083, 6083, (Ch) 3ACX 47190, (J) HA 5085, AB 7134, (US) COLH 148 = *Cap.* (US) G 7239 = *HMV* (Au) OALP 1620, OELP 9673, (Fr) FALP 629, (GB) [1]ALP 1620, (It) QALP 10266, (NL) XLPH 1002, (NZ) MALP 1620, (SA) JALP 1620 = *Voix Ill.* 50018 // *Elec.* E 70412 // *HMV* (NL) GHLP 1027 // *Dacapo* [1]1C 177-(147-)00947/48M, 1C 137 1009473M = *HMV* (Sw) 7C 137-00947/48M // *Sera.* (US) 60219 // *HMV* (NL) 5C 045-01715M

[CD] *EMI* (GB) CDH 7 61053 2

[MC] *HMV* (Sw) 7C 237-00947M // *Sera.* (US) 4XG 60219

1945, September 7 (?) [see note]. Stockholm, Concert Hall, Small Auditorium. With Royal Orch., cond. Nils Grevillius.

153
Una furtiva lagrima [It] (Donizetti: *L'elisir d'amore*)
2SB 2537-1,-**2** [See note]

[78] *HMV* [1]DB 6714, *Vic.* (US) 12-3086

[45] *RCA* (US) 49-3086 // *RCA* (US,G) ERA 245 // *RCA* (B) 75.543 // *HMV* (Au) 7ERO 5193, (GB) [1]7ER 5193

[33] *Angel* (Ar) LPC 12083, 6083, (Ch) 3ACX 47190, (J) HA 5085, AB 7134, (US) COLH 148, Cap. (US) G 7239 = *HMV* (Au) OALP 1620, OELP 9673, (Fr) FALP 629, (GB) [1]ALP 1620, (It) QALP 10266, (NL) XLPH 1002, (NZ) MALP 1620, (SA) JALP 1620 = *Voix Ill.* 50018 // *Elec.* E 70412 // *Dacapo* [1]1C 177-(147-) 00947/48M, 1C 137 1009473M = *HMV* (Sw) 7C 137-00947/48M // *Sera.* (US) 60219 // *HMV* (NL) 5C 045-01715M // *Angel* (J) GR 70085 // *EMI* (Sw) EMISP 127

[CD] *EMI* (GB) CDH 7 61053 2 // *Parlophone* (GB) CDP 7 91916 2 // *Axis* 7017672

[MC] *HMV* (Sw) 7C 237-00948M // *Sera.* (US) 4XG 60219

154
Je crois entendre encore [Fr] (Bizet: *Les pêcheurs de perles*)
2SB 2538-1,-2 [It is not known which take was used for these issues]

[78] (Not issued)

[33] *HMV* (GB) [1]RLS 715, (Sw) 7C 153-06518/20M = *WRC* (Au) R 05223/25, (NZ) WE 26451/53 // *Dacapo* [1]1C 147-03354/55M, 1C 137 1033543M

[CD] *EMI* (GB) CDH 7 64707 2

[MC] *WRC* (Au) C 05223/25

1947, November 27. Stockholm, Concert Hall, Small Auditorium. With Stockholm Concert Association Orch., cond. Nils Grevillius.

155
V molchan'i nochi taynoy [Eng: In the Silence of Night] (Rachmaninov)
0SB 2880-1,-**2**

[78] *HMV* DA 1890

[33] *Angel* (Ch) 3ACX 47365, (J) HA 5032, AB 7123, (US) COLH 149 = *Cap.* (US) [1]G 7247 = *HMV* (Au) OALP 1857, (GB) ALP 1857, (NZ) MALP 1857 = *WRC* (Au) 3199, (NZ) CO 566 // *HMV* (Sw) [1]7C 153-35445/46M = *Odeon* (US) 7C 153-35445/46M // *HMV* (GB) [1]RLS 715, (Sw) 7C 153-06518/20M = *WRC* (Au) R 05223/25, (NZ) WE 26451/53 // *HMV* (Sw) PRO 3034 // *Dacapo* [1]1C 147-03354/55M, 1C 137 1033543M

[CD] *EMI* (GB) CDH 7 64707 2

[MC] *HMV* (Sw) 7C 253-35445/46M // *WRC* (Au) C 05223/25

156
Siren' [Eng: Lilacs] (Rachmaninov)
0SB 2881-**1**,-2

[78] *HMV* DA 1890

[33] *Angel* (Ch) 3ACX 47365, (J) HA 5032, AB 7123, (US) COLH 149 = *Cap.* (US) [1]G 7247 = *HMV* (Au) OALP 1857, (GB) ALP 1857, (NZ) MALP 1857 = *WRC* (Au) 3199, (NZ) CO 566 // *HMV* (Sw) [1]7C 153-35445/46M = *Odeon* (US) 7C 153-35445/46M // *HMV* (GB) [1]RLS 715, (Sw) 7C 153-06518/20M = *WRC* (Au) R 05223/25, (NZ) WE 26451/53 // *HMV* (Sw) PRO 3034 // *Dacapo* [1]1C 147-03354/55M, 1C 137 1033543M

[CD] *EMI* (GB) CDH 7 64707 2

[MC] *HMV* (Sw) 7C 253-35445/46M // *WRC* (Au) C 05223/25

157
È la solita storia [It] (Cilea: *L'arlesiana*)
2SB 2882-**1**,-2

[78] *HMV* [1]DB 6714 = *Vic.* (US) 12-3086

[45] *RCA* (US) 49-3086 // *RCA* (Au) 26019, (GB) RCX 7114, (US,G) [1]ERA 134

[33] *Angel* (Ar) LPC 12083, 6083, (Ch) 3ACX 47190, (J) HA 5085, AB 7134, (US) COLH 148 = *Cap.* (US) G 7239 = *HMV* (Au) OALP 1620, OELP 9673, (Fr) FALP 629, (GB) [1]ALP 1620, (It) QALP 10266, (NL) XLPH 1002, (NZ) MALP 1620, (SA) JALP 1620 = *Voix Ill.* 50018 // *Elec.* E 70412 // *HMV* (NL) GHLP 1027 // *Sera.* (US) IB 6058 // *HMV* (Sw) [1]4E 153-34532/33M = *Odeon* (US) 4E

153-34532/33M // *HMV* (GB) [1]RLS 715, (Sw) 7C 153-06518/20M = *WRC* (Au) R 05223/25, (NZ) WE 26451/53 // *HMV* (Sw) PRO 3034 // *Dacapo* [1]1C 147-03354/55M, 1C 137 1033543M

[CD] *EMI* (GB) CDH 7 61053 2

[MC] *HMV* (Sw) 4E 278-51007M // *WRC* (Au) C 05223/25

158
Una furtiva lagrima [It] (Donizetti: *L'elisir d'amore*)
2SB 2537-3

(Not issued; see note for Nos. 153 & 158)

1948, September 7. Stockholm, Concert Hall, Small Auditorium. With Royal Orch., cond. Nils Grevillius.

159
Jeanie with the Light Brown Hair [Eng] (Foster)
0SB 2926-**1**,-**2**

A (Take 1)

[78] (Not issued)

[CD] *Bluebell* ABCD 016

B (Take 2)

[78] *HMV* [1]DA 1902, (Ir) IR 340, (Nor) DAN 1902

[45] *HMV* (Au) 7PO 330, (GB) 7P 330

[33] *Angel* (Ch) 3ACX 47365, (J) HA 5032, AB 7123, (US) COLH 149 = *Cap.* (US) [1]G 7247 = *HMV* (Au) OALP 1857, (GB) ALP 1857, (NZ) MALP 1857 = *WRC* (Au) 3199, (NZ) CO 566 // *HMV* (Sw) [1]7C 153-35445/46M, Odeon (US) 7C 153-35445/46M // *HMV* (GB) [1]RLS 715, (Sw) 7C 153-06518/20M = *WRC* (Au) R 05223/25, (NZ) WE 26451/53 // *HMV* (Sw) PRO 3034 // *Dacapo* [1]1C 147-03354/55M, 1C 137 1033543M // *EMI* (Au) [1]SCA 016, (GB) NTS 208, (SA) CEY 247 = *WRC* (Au) R 05957 // *HMV* (Au) [1]OXLP 7660 = *WRC* (Au) R 11409

[CD] *Evasound* EMD 021

[MC] *EMI* (Au) [1]TC-SCA 016, (GB) TC-NTS 208, (SA) L4CEY 247 // *HMV* (Sw) 7C 253-35445/46M // *WRC* (Au) C 05223/25 // *WRC* (Au) C 05957 // *HMV* (Au) TC-OXCP 7660 // *Vogue* VM 23C // *Evasound* EMC 021

160
Because [Eng] (d'Hardelot; pseud. of Rhodes)
0SB 2927-**1**,-**2**

A (Take 1)

[78] (Not issued)

[CD] *Bluebell* ABCD 016

B (Take 2)

[78] *HMV* [1]DA 1902, (Ir) IR 340, (Nor) DAN 1902
[45] *Angel* (Br) TCB 02 = *HMV* (Au) 7EBO 6030, (GB) 7EB 6030, 7ER 5189, (It) 7EPQ 607, (NZ) 7EBM 6030, 7ERM 5189, (Sw) [1]7EBS 13
[33] *Angel* (Ch) 3ACX 47365, (J) HA 5032, AB 7123, (US) COLH 149 = *Cap.* (US) [1]G 7247 = *HMV* (Au) OALP 1857, (GB) ALP 1857, (NZ) MALP 1857 = *WRC* (Au) 3199, (NZ) CO 566 // *EMI* (SA) EMGJ 6006 // *HMV* (Sw) [1]7C 153-35445/46M = *Odeon* (US) 7C 153-35445/46M // *HMV* (GB) [1]RLS 715, (Sw) 7C 153-06518/20M = *WRC* (Au) R 05223/25, (NZ) WE 26451/53 // *HMV* (Sw) PRO 3034 // *Dacapo* [1]1C 147-03354/55M, 1C 137 1033543M // *HMV* (Au) [1]OXLP 7660 = *WRC* (Au) R 11409 // *Fame* (SA) FAME 22
[MC] *EMI* (SA) L4EMGJ 6006 // *HMV* (Sw) 7C 253-35445/46M // *WRC* (Au) C 05223/25 // *HMV* (Au) TC-OXCP 7660 // *Fame* (SA) L4FAME 22

1948, September 15. Stockholm, Concert Hall, Small Auditorium. With Royal Orch., cond. Nils Grevillius.

161
Donna non vidi mai [It] (Puccini: *Manon Lescaut*)
0SB 2936-**1**,-**2**

A (Take 1)

[78] (Not issued)
[CD] *Bluebell* ABCD 016

B (Take 2)

[78] *Elec.* DA 1908 = *HMV* [1]DA 1908, *Vic.* (J) SF 19, (US) 10-1477
[45] *RCA* (US) 49-0475 // *HMV* (GB) 7ER 5025 = *RCA* (Au?, US?) 26044, (B) 95.250, (Br) 585-0005, (It) A72R 0086, (J) EP 3046, (Sp) 3-26004, (US,G) [1]ERA 109 // *HMV* (Au) 7ERO 5196, (GB) [1]7ER 5196, (It) 7ERQ 251
[33] *Angel* (Ar) LPC 12083, 6083, (Ch) 3ACX 47190, (J) HA 5085, AB 7134, (US) COLH 148 = *Cap.* (US) G 7239 = *HMV* (Au) OALP 1620, OELP 9673, (Fr) FALP 629, (GB) [1]ALP 1620, (It) QALP 10266, (NL) XLPH 1002, (NZ) MALP 1620, (SA) JALP 1620 = *Voix Ill.* 50018 // *Elec.* E 70412 // *HMV* (NL) GHLP 1027 // *Odeon* (Sw) PMCS 308 // *Sera.* (US) IB 6058 // *Dacapo* [1]1C 177-(147-) 00947/48M, 1C 137 1009473M = *HMV* (Sw) 7C 137-00947/48M // *HMV* (NL) 5C 045-01715M // *HMV* (GB) [1]RLS 715, (Sw) 7C 153-06518/20M = *WRC* (Au) R 05223/25, (NZ) WE 26451/53 // *Angel* (J) GR 70085 // *MET* 50
[CD] *EMI* (GB) CDH 7 64707 2
[MC] *HMV* (Sw) 7C 237-00948M // *WRC* (Au) C 05223/25 // *MET* 50C

162
O Lola [It] (Mascagni: *Cavalleria rusticana*)
0SB 2937-**1**,-**2**

A (Take 1)

[78] *Elec.* DA 1908 = *HMV* [1]DA 1908 = *Vic.* (J) SF 19, (US) 10-1477
[45] *RCA* (US) 49-0475 // *RCA* (US) WDM 1565 // *HMV* (GB) 7ER 5025 = *RCA* (Au?,US?) 26044, (B) 95.250, (Br) 585-0005, (It) A72R 0086, (J) EP 3046, (Sp) 3-26004, (US,G) [1]ERA 109 // *RCA* (G) ERA 9511 // *RCA* (G) (4)47-9155 // *HMV* (Au) 7ERO 5196, (GB) [1]7ER 5196, (It) 7ERQ 251
[33] *RCA* (Br) BRL 100, (G) LM 1160-C, (US) [1]LM 1160 // *Angel* (Ar) LPC 12083, 6083, (Ch) 3ACX 47190, (J) HA 5085, AB 7134, (US) COLH 148 = Cap. (US) G 7239 = *HMV* (Au) OALP 1620, OELP 9673, (Fr) FALP 629, (GB) [1]ALP 1620, (It) QALP 10266, (NL) XLPH 1002, (NZ) MALP 1620, (SA) JALP 1620 = *Voix Ill.* 50018 // *Elec.* E 70412 // *HMV* (NL) GHLP 1027 // *Sera.* (US) IB 6058 // *HMV* (Sw) [1]4E 153-34532/33M = *Odeon* (US) 4E 153-34532/33M // *HMV* (GB) [1]RLS 715, (Sw) 7C 153-06518/20M = *WRC* (Au) R 05223/25, (NZ) WE 26451/53 // *HMV* (Sw) PRO 3034 // *Dacapo* [1]1C 147-03354/55M, 1C 137 1033543M // *MET* 110 // *Angel* (J) GR 70085
[CD] *MET* 110CD // *Verona* 28030/31 // *EMI* (GB) 7 64707 2
[MC] *HMV* (Sw) 4E 278-51007M // *WRC* (Au) C 05223/25 // *MET* 110C

B (Take 2)

[78] (Not issued)
[CD] *Bluebell* ABCD 016

1949, August 10. Stockholm, Concert Hall, Small Auditorium. With Anna-Lisa Björling (sop.) & Stockholm Concert Association Orch., cond. Nils Grevillius.

163
Ange adorable [Fr] (Gounod: *Roméo et Juliette*)
2SB 3069-1,-**2**

[78] (Not issued)
[CD] *Bluebell* ABCD 016

164
O soave fanciulla [It] (Puccini: *La bohème*)
2SB 3070-**1**,-2

[78] (Not issued)
[33] *HMV* (GB) [1]RLS 715, (Sw) 7C 153-06518/20M = *WRC* (Au) R 05223/25, (NZ) WE 26451/53 // *Dacapo* [1]1C 147-03354/55M, 1C 137 1033543M
[CD] *EMI* (GB) CDH 7 61053 2 v.1 // *EMI* (GB) CDH 7 64707 2
[MC] *WRC* (Au) C 05223/25

1949, August 11. Stockholm, Concert Hall, Small Auditorium. With Stockholm Concert Association Orch., cond. Nils Grevillius.

165
L'alba separa dalla luce l'ombra [It] (Tosti)
0SB 3071-1,-**2**

[78] *HMV* ^{1}DA 1931, (Ir) IR 344, (Nor) DAN 1931
[33] *Rococo* R 31 // *Angel* (Ch) 3ACX 47530, (Ur) UAL 12513 = *HMV* (GB,Au) ^{1}HQM 1190, (GB,SA) HLM 7038, (SA) JALP 29 = *Odeon* (US) PHQM 1190 = *Sera.* (US) 60168 // *Dacapo* ^{1}1C 147-03354/55M, 1C 137 1033543M // *HMV* (Au) ^{1}OXLP 7660 = *WRC* (Au) R 11409
[MC] *HMV* (SA) L4HLM 7038 = *Sera.* (US) ^{1}4XG 60168 // *HMV* (Au) TC-OXCP 7660

166
Berceuse: Cachés dans cet asile [Eng: Concealed in this retreat] (Godard: *Jocelyn*)
0SB 3072-1,-**2** [Test pressing of Take 1 exists; see note]

[78] *HMV* ^{1}DA 1931, (Ir) IR 349, (Nor) DAN 1931
[45] *RCA* (B) 75.542
[33] *Angel* (Ch) 3ACX 47530, (Ur) UAL 12513 = *HMV* (GB,Au) ^{1}HQM 1190, (GB,SA) HLM 7038, (SA) JALP 29 = *Odeon* (US) PHQM 1190 = *Sera.* (US) 60168 // *Dacapo* ^{1}1C 147-03354/55M, 1C 137 1033543M // *HMV* (Au) OXLP 7650 // *HMV* (Au) ^{1}OXLP 7660 = *WRC* (Au) R 11409
[MC] *HMV* (SA) L4HLM 7038 = *Sera.* (US) ^{1}4XG 60168 // *HMV* (Au) TC-OXCP 7660

1950, September 12. Stockholm, Royal Academy of Music (?). With Sw. Radio Orch., cond. Nils Grevillius.

167
E lucevan le stelle [It] (Puccini: *Tosca*)
0SB 3314 [See note]

[78] (Not issued)
[33] *HMV* (GB) ^{1}RLS 715, (Sw) 7C 153-06518/20M = *WRC* (Au) R 05223/25, (NZ) WE 26451/53 // *Dacapo* ^{1}1C 147-03354/55M, 1C 137 1033543M
[MC] *WRC* (Au) C 05223/25

168
Recondita armonia [It] (Puccini: *Tosca*)
0SB 3315 [See note]

[78] (Not issued)
[33] *HMV* (GB) ^{1}RLS 715, (Sw) 7C 153-06518/20M = *WRC* (Au) R 05223/25, (NZ) WE 26451/53 // *Dacapo* ^{1}1C 147-03354/55M, 1C 137 1033543M
[MC] *WRC* (Au) C 05223/25

1950, September 19. Stockholm, Royal Academy of Music (?). With Sw. Radio Orch., cond. Nils Grevillius.

169
La fleur que tu m'avais jetée [Fr] (Bizet: *Carmen*)
2SB 3318-1 [See note]

[78] (Not issued)
[45] *RCA* (US) WDM 1546 // *RCA* (B) 65.505 // *RCA* (Fr) FVA 630.259
[33] *Elec.* WBLP 1055 = *HMV* (GB) BLP 1055 = *RCA* (US) [1]LM 105 // *RCA* (Au) L 16098, (Fr) A 630.255, (G) LM 1841-C v.1, (NZ) RSL 3519, (US) [1]LM 1841 // *RCA* (Fr) 630.383/84 // *Melodiya* D 21793/94 (?) // *RCA* (GB) SER 5704/06 // *RCA* (J) RVC 7531/35 // *RCA* (G) RL 43077 EF
[MC] *RCA* (G) RK 43077 CF

170
Mamma!...Quel vino [It] (Mascagni: *Cavalleria rusticana*)
2SB 3319-1 [See note. For difference between this recording & No. 147, see also note for that number]

[78] (Not issued)
[45] *RCA* (US) WDM 1546 // *RCA* (US) WDM 1565 // *RCA* (B) 65.504, (Fr) FVA 630.255 // *RCA* (G) (4)47-9150 // *RCA* (G) 447-9366
[33] *Elec.* WBLP 1055 = *HMV* (GB) BLP 1055 = *RCA* (US) [1]LM 105 // *RCA* (Br) BRL 100, (G) LM 1160-C, (US) [1]LM 1160 // *RCA* (Au) L 16098, (Fr) A 630.255, (G) LM 1841-C v.1, (NZ) RSL 3519, (US) [1]LM 1841 // *RCA* (Fr) 630.383/84 // *RCA* (G) LM 1841-C v.2 // *Melodiya* D 00019605/06 (?) // *Melodiya* D 21793/94 (?) // *RCA* (GB) SER 5704/06 // *RCA* (It) VL 42436 // *RCA* (G) RL 43077 EF
[MC] *RCA* (G) RK 43077 CF

1950, November 30. New York, Manhattan Center, RCA Victor studio. With Robert Merrill (bar.), Emil Markow (bass) & RCA Victor Orch. & Chorus, cond. Renato Cellini. [See note]

171
Io l'ho perduta...Qual pallor!...Dio, che nell'alma infondere [It] (Verdi: *Don Carlo*)
E0-RC-1946-1 (A) + E0-RC-1947-1 (A)

Complete:

[78] *HMV* DB 21622
[45] *RCA* (US) WDM 1495 // *RCA* (US) WDM 7007 // *RCA* (US) ERB 7027
[33] *RCA* (US) LM 1128 // Elec. WBLP 1053 = *HMV* (GB) BLP 1053 = *RCA* (Br) BRL 3031, (G) LM 9844-E, (US) [1]LM 7007 // *RCA* (US) LRM 7027 // *RCA* (G) LM 2736-C, (GB) RB 6585, RL 43243, RCALP 3043, GL 84889, (US,Au) [1]LM 2736, (US) AGM1-4889 // *RCA* (Fr) 430.731 // *RCA* (G) KR 11014/1-2 (26.48016 DP) // *RCA* (GB) SER 5704/06 // *RCA* (J) RVC 7531/35 // *RCA* (G) RL 43077 EF

// *MET* 110 // *RCA* (G) GL 87799
[CD] *MET* 110CD // *RCA* (G) GD 87799, (US) [1]7799-2-RG
[OR] *RCA* (US) TR3-5035
[MC] *RCA* (G) RK 43077 CF // *RCA* (Ca) AGK1-4889, (GB) [1]RK 43243, RCAK 3043, GK 84889 // *MET* 110C // *RCA* (G) GK 87799, (US) [1]7799-4-RG

Excerpts:
a1. Io l'ho perduta... a2. Qual pallor!...Dio, che nell'alma infondere... a3. Giuriamo insiem.

(a1-2) [CD] *Tring* TFP 013
(a2-3) [33] *RCA* (US) [1]LM 6171, AGM3-4805 // *RCA* (It) LM 20129
[MC] *RCA* (US) AGK3-4805

1951, January 3. New York, Manhattan Center, RCA Victor studio. With Robert Merrill (bar.) & RCA Victor Orch., cond. Renato Cellini.

172
O mostruosa colpa...Sì, pel ciel marmoreo giuro [It] (Verdi: *Otello*)
E1-RC-2104-1(A),-2(A) [For difference between takes, see note]

A (Take 1)

[78] *Elec.* DB 21426 = *HMV* [1]DB 21426
[33] *RCA* (Au) LB 16193, (SA) 30190/91, (US) [1]LM 6061 // *RCA* (GB) RB 16089 // *RCA* (G) GL 87799
[CD] *RCA* (G) GD 87799, (US) [1]7799-2-RG // *RCA* (GB) RD 49524 // *Tring* TFP 013
[MC] *RCA* (G) GK 87799, [1]7799-4-RG

B (Take 2)

[78] (Not issued?)
[45] *RCA* (US) WDM 7007 // *RCA* (US) ERB 7027
[33] Elec. WBLP 1053 = *HMV* (GB) BLP 1053 = *RCA* (Br) BRL 3031, (G) LM 9844-E, (US) [1]LM 7007 // *RCA* (US) LRM 7027 // *RCA* (G) LM 2736-C, (GB) RB 6585, RL 43243, RCALP 3043, GL 84889, (US,Au) [1]LM 2736, (US) AGM1-4889 // *RCA* (G) KR 11014/1-2 (26.48016 DP) // *RCA* (GB) SER 5704/06 // *RCA* (J) RVC 7531/35 // *RCA* (G) RL 43077 EF // *OASI* 660
[CD] *OASI* 7006
[OR] *RCA* (US) TR3-5035
[MC] *RCA* (G) RK 43077 CF // *RCA* (Ca) AGK1-4889, (GB) [1]RK 43243, RCAK 3043, GK 84889

173
In un coupè...O Mimì, tu più non torni [It] (Puccini: *La bohème*)
E1-RC-2105-1(A)

[78] *Elec.* DB 21311 = *HMV* [1]DB 21311

[45] *RCA* (B) 65.517= *Elec.* 7RW 110 = *HMV* (Au) 7RO 105, (GB) [1]7R 124, (It) 7RQ 3008 = *RCA* (G) (4)47-9133, (GB) RB 9271 // *RCA* (US) WDM 7007 // *RCA* (Au) 26019, (GB) RCX 7114, (US,G) [1]ERA 134

[33] *Elec.* WBLP 1053 = *HMV* (GB) BLP 1053 = *RCA* (Br) BRL 3031, (G) LM 9844-E, (US) [1]LM 7007 // *RCA* (G) LM 2736-C, (GB) RB 6585, RL 43243, RCALP 3043, GL 84889, (US,Au) [1]LM 2736, (US) AGM1-4889 // *RCA* (G) KR 11014/1-2 (26.48016 DP) // *RCA* (GB) SER 5704/06 // *RCA* (J) RVC 7531/35 // *RCA* (G) RL 43077 EF // *RCA* (G) GL 87799

[CD] *MET* 501CD // *RCA* (G) GD 87799, (US) [1]7799-2-RG // *RCA* (GB) RD 49524

[OR] *RCA* (US) TR3-5035

[MC] (G) RK 43077 CF // *RCA* (Ca) AGK1-4889, (GB) [1]RK 43243, RCAK 3043, GK 84889 // *MET* 501C // *RCA* (G) GK 87799, (US) [1]7799-4-RG

174
Solenne in quest'ora [It] (Verdi: *La forza del destino*)
E1-RC-2106-1(A)

[78] Elec. DB 21311 = *HMV* [1]DB 21311

[45] *RCA* (US) WDM 7007 // *RCA* (US) ERB 7027

[33] *Elec.* WBLP 1053 = *HMV* (GB) BLP 1053 = *RCA* (Br) BRL 3031, (G) LM 9844-E, (US) [1]LM 7007 // *RCA* (US) LRM 7027 // *RCA* (G) LM 2736-C, (G) RB 6585, RL 43243, RCALP 3043, GL 84889, (US,Au) [1]LM 2736, (US) AGM1-4889 // *RCA* (G) KR 11014/1-2 (26.48016 DP) // *RCA* (GB) SER 5704/06 // *RCA* (J) RVC 7531/35 // *RCA* (GB) PL 42146 // *RCA* (G) RL 43077 EF // *RCA* (G) GL 87799

[CD] *RCA* (G) GD 87799, (US) [1]7799-2-RG // *RCA* (GB) RD 49524 // *Tring* TFP 013

[OR] *RCA* (US) TR3-5035

[MC] *RCA* (G) RK 43077 CF // *RCA* (Ca) AGK1-4889, (GB) [1]RK 43243, RCAK 3043, GK 84889 // *RCA* (G) GK 87799, (US) [1]7799-4-RG

175
Au fond du temple saint [Fr] (Bizet: *Les pêcheurs de perles*)
E1-RC-2107-1(A)

[78] *Elec.* DB 21426 = *HMV* [1]DB 21426

[45] *RCA* (US) WDM 7007 // *Elec.* 7RW 110 = *HMV* (Au) 7RO 105, (GB) [1]7R 124, (It) 7RQ 3008 = *RCA* (B) 65.517, (G) (4)47-9133, (GB) RB 9271 // *RCA* (B) 75.532 // *RCA* (G) ERA 9513 // *RCA* (Au) 26019, (GB) RCX 7114, (US,G) [1]ERA 134 // *CCGC* PR 900

[33] *Elec.* WBLP 1053 = *HMV* (GB) BLP 1053 = *RCA* (Br) BRL 3031, (G) LM 9844-E, (US) [1]LM 7007 // *RCA* (G) LM 2736-C, (GB) RB 6585, RL 43243, RCALP 3043, GL 84889, (US,Au) [1]LM 2736, (US) AGM1-4889 // *RCA* (G) KR 11014/1-2 (26.48016 DP) // *RCA* (GB) SER 5704/06 // *K-tel* (Au) NA 468 // *RCA* (J) RVC 7531/35 // *Impact* IMA 011 = *RCA* (Au) [1]SP 185 = *WRC* (Au) R 10033 // *RCA* (G) RL 43077 EF // *RCA* (G) GL 87799 // *Eva* 304 391

[CD] *RCA* (G) GD 87799, (US) [1]7799-2-RG // *RCA* (GB) RD 49524 // *Tring* TFP 013 // *Laser* LAS 4777 // *Eva* 354 391 // *RCA* (US) 09026-61440-2

[OR] *RCA* (US) TR3-5035

[MC] *RCA* (G) RK 43077 CF // *RCA* (Ca) AGK1-4889, (GB) [1]RK 43243, RCAK 3043, GK 84889 // *RCA* (Au) [1]SPK 185 = *WRC* (Au) C 10033 // *RCA* (G) GK 87799, (US) [1]7799-4-RG // *Vogue* VM 23C // *Laser* LASC 4777 // *Eva* 504 391 // *RCA* (US) 09026-61440-4

1951, January 13. New York, Manhattan Center, RCA Victor studio. With RCA Victor Orch., cond. Renato Cellini.

176
Che gelida manina [It] (Puccini: *La bohème*)
E1-RC-2124-1(A)

[78] *HMV* [1]DB 21602, (Ir) IRX 77
[45] *RCA* WDM 1546 // *HMV* (GB) 7R 173 = *RCA* (US,G) [1]447-0808 // *RCA* (B) 65.511 // *RCA* (Fr) FVA 630.259 // *RCA* (US,G) ERA 245 // *RCA* (G) ERA 9511 // *RCA* (G) [1]ERA 9515, ERA 9548
[33] *Elec.* WBLP 1055 = *HMV* (GB) BLP 1055 = *RCA* (US) [1]LM 105 // *RCA* (Au) L 16098, (Fr) A 630.255, (G) LM 1841-C v.1, (NZ) RSL 3519, (US) [1]LM 1841 // *RCA* (Fr) 630.383/84 // *RCA* (G) LM 1841-C v.2 // *RCA* (Au) L 16301, (GB) RB 16268, (US) [1]LM 2574 // *Melodiya* D 21793/94 (?) // *RCA* (G) KR 11014/1-2 (26.48016 DP) // RCA (GB) SER 5704/06 // *RCA* (J) RVC 7531/35 // *RCA* (It) VL 42436 // *RCA* (G) RL 43077 EF
[CD] *RCA* (G) RD 85934, GD 85277, (US) [1]5934-2-RC
[MC] *RCA* (G) RK 43077 CF

177
Se quel guerrier io fossi...Celeste Aida [It] (Verdi: *Aida*)
E1-RC-2125-1(A)

[78] *Elec.* DB 21563 = *HMV* [1]DB 21563, (Ir) IRX 62 = *Vic.* (Br) 886-5031
[45] *HMV* (GB) 7R 160
[33] *ANNA* 1017 // *Bluebell* BELL 187

178
Cielo e mar! [It] (Ponchielli: *La Gioconda*)
E1-RC-2126-1(A)

[78] *Elec.* DB 21563 = *HMV* [1]DB 21563, (Ir) IRX 62 = *Vic.* (Br) 886-5031
[45] *HMV* (GB) 7R 160
[33] *ANNA* 1017 // *Bluebell* BELL 187

1951, March 9. New York, Manhattan Center, RCA Victor studio. With RCA Victor Orch., cond. Renato Cellini.

179
Pays merveilleux...Ô paradis [It: Mi batte il cor...O paradiso] (Meyerbeer: *L'africaine*)
E1-RC-3150-1(A)

[78] *HMV* [1]DB 21621 = *Vic.* (Ar) 66-6143 // *Vic.* (J) SD 199
[45] *RCA* (US) WDM 1546 // *RCA* (US,G) 447-0809 // *RCA* (Au) 26012 // *HMV* (GB) 7ER 5025 = *RCA* (Au?,US?) 26044, (B) 95.250, (Br) 585-005, (It) A72R 0086, (J) EP 3046, (Sp) 3-26004, (US,G) [1]ERA 109 // *RCA* (B) 65.511 // *RCA* (B) 75.537 // *RCA* (G) ERA 9511 // *RCA* (G) (4)47-9155 // *RCA* (J) ES 8510
[33] *Elec.* WBLP 1055 = *HMV* (GB) BLP 1055 = *RCA* (US) [1]LM 105 // *RCA* (Au) L 16098, (Fr) A 630.255, (G) LM 1841-C v.l, (NZ) RSL 3519, (US) [1]LM 1841 // *RCA* (Fr) 630.383/84 // *RCA* (G) LM 1841-C v.2 // *RCA* (Au) L 16352, (G) [1]HR 212, (GB) RB 6515, (SA) 30231, (US) LM 2631 // *RCA* (GB) SER 5704/06 // *RCA* (J) RVC 7531/35 // *RCA* (It) VL 42436 // *RCA* (G) RL 43077 EF
[MC] *RCA* (G) RK 43077 CF

180
Salut! demeure chaste et pure [Fr] (Gounod: *Faust*)
E1-RC-3151-1(A)

[78] *HMV* DB 21621 = *Vic.* (Ar) 66-6143
[45] *RCA* (US) WDM 1546 // *RCA* (US) WDM 1626 // *RCA* (US,G) 447-0809 // *RCA* (B) 65.505 // *RCA* (Fr) FVA 630.259 // *RCA* (G) (4)47-9157
[33] *Elec.* WBLP 1055 = *HMV* (GB) BLP 1055 = *RCA* (US) [1]LM 105 // *RCA* (Br) BRL 57, (SA) 30066, (US) [1]LM 1202 // RCA (Au) L 16098, (Fr) A 630.255, (G) LM 1841-C v.l, (NZ) RSL 3519, (US) [1]LM 1841 // *RCA* (Fr) 630.383/84 // *RCA* (G) LM 1841-C v.2 // *RCA* (Fr) 530.268 // *RCA* (Fr) 630.826, (It) [1]LM 20083 // *Melodiya* D 21793/94 (?) // *RCA* (GB) SER 5704/06 // *RCA* (J) RVC 7531/35 // *RCA* (G) RL 43077 EF // *MET* 404
[CD] *RCA* (G) RD 85934, GD 85277, (US) [1]5934-2-RC
[MC] *RCA* (G) RK 43077 CF // *MET* 404C

181
Recitar!...Vesti la giubba [It] (Leoncavallo: *Pagliacci*)
El-RC-3152-l(A),-2(A) [For difference between takes, see note]

[78] *HMV* [1]DB 21602, (Ir) IRX 77 // *Vic.* (J) SD 199
[45] *RCA* (US) WDM 1546 // *HMV* (GB) 7ER 5025 = *RCA* (Au?, US?) 26044, (B) 95.250, (Br) 585-005, (It) A72R 0086, (J) EP 3046, (Sp) 3-26004, (US,G) [1]ERA 109 // *RCA* (B) 65.504, (Fr) FVA 630.255 // *RCA* (B) 75.534 // *HMV* (GB) 7R 173 = *RCA* (US,G) [1]447-0808 // *HMV* (Sp) 7ERL 1307 // *RCA* (G) ERA 9511 // *RCA* (G) ERA 9516 // *RCA* (G) ERA 9574
[33] *Elec.* WBLP 1055 = *HMV* (GB) BLP 1055 = *RCA* (US) [1]LM 105 // *RCA* (Au) L 16098, (Fr) A 630.255, (G) LM 1841-C v.l, (NZ) RSL 3519, (US) [1]LM 1841 // *RCA* (Fr) 630.383/84 // *RCA* (G) LM 1841-C v.2 // *RCA* (GB) SER 5704/06 // *RCA* (J) RVC 7531/35 // *RCA* (It) VL 42436 // *RCA* (G) RL 43077 EF
[CD] *RCA* (G) RD 85934, GD 85277, (US) [1]5934-2-RC

[OR]	*RCA* (US) TR3-5035
[MC]	*RCA* (G) RK 43077 CF

1952, February 22 & March 6,7,11,13,14,16,30. New York, Manhattan Center, RCA Victor studio. With RCA Victor Orch. & Robert Shaw Chorale, cond. Renato Cellini. Producer: Richard Mohr.

182
Il trovatore (Verdi), sung in It. by Zinka Milanov (Leonora), Margaret Roggero (Ines); Fedora Barbieri (Azucena); JB (Manrico), Paul Franke (Ruiz), Nathaniel Sprinzena (Messenger); Leonard Warren (Di Luna); Nicola Moscona (Ferrando), George Cehanovsky (Gypsy).
[Orig. LP matrix (LM 6008): E2-RP-4107/10]

Complete:

[45]	*RCA* (US) WDM 6008
[33, 4 sides]	*Elec.* WALP 1112/13 = *HMV* (GB) ALP 1112/13, ALP 1832/33, (SA) JALP 1112/13 = *RCA* (Au) LB 16012, (Fr) A 630.361/62, (G) LM 6008/1-2, VIC 6008/1-2 (26.35003 DM,DP), (It) B12R 0023/24, KV 6008, MCV 536, VL 43536, VLS 00699, (J) RGC 1106/07, (US,Ar,Sp) [1]LM 6008, (US,Au) AVM2-0699
[33, 6 sides]	*Melodiya* D 033317/22
[CD]	*RCA* (G) [1]GD 86643, (US) 6643-2-RG
[OR]	*HMV* (GB) HTA 9/10
[MC]	*RCA* (It) [1]VKS 00699, (US) CLK2-5377

Excerpts:

(Act 1)	a. Deserto sulla terra;
(Act 2)	b. Stride la vampa [through "L'arcana parola ognor"]; c1. Mal reggendo... c2. Inoltra il piè...Perigliarti ancor languente;
(Act 3)	d1. Di qual tetra luce... d2. Amor! sublime amore... d3. Ah sì, ben mio... d4. Manrico?... d5. Di quella pira;
(Act 4)	e. Miserere...Ah! che la morte ognora; f1. Se m'ami ancor... f2. Sì, la stanchezza...Ai nostri monti... f3. Che! non m'inganno!

(a1,c1,d2-5)	[33]	*RCA* (J) RVC 7531/35
(a,d1-3,d5)	[33]	*RCA* (G) LM 2736-C, (GB) RB 6585, RL 43243, RCALP 3043, GL 84889, (US,Au) [1]LM 2736, (US) AGM1-4889 // *RCA* (GB) SER 5704/06 // *RCA* (G) RL 43077 EF
	[OR]	*RCA* (US) TR3-5035
	[MC]	*RCA* (G) RK 43077 CF // *RCA* (Ca) AGK1-4889, (GB) [1]RK 43243, RCAK 3043, GK 84889
(b,c1)	[45]	*RCA* (US,G) [1]ERA 113, (US?) 26072
(c,d3-5,e,f2-3)	[CD]	*RCA* (G) GD 60191, (US) [1]60191-2-RG
	[MC]	*RCA* (G) GK 60191, (US) [1]60191-4-RG
(c1,d3-5,e,f1-2)	[33]	*HMV* (GB) ALP 1391 = *RCA* (Fr) 630.344, (G) LM 1827-B,-C,

		(SA) 30061, (Sp) 3L 16174 (?), (US) [1]LM 1827
	[OR]	*RCA* (US) DC 34
(d2-3)	[33]	*RCA* (It) [1]TRL1-7055, VLS 45510
	[MC]	*RCA* (It) VKS 45510
(d3-5)	[33]	*RCA* (It) VL 42436
(d3,d5)	[45]	*RCA* (B) 65.506 // *RCA* (Au) 26012
(d5)	[45]	*RCA* (US) ERB 7027 // *RCA* (B) 75.534 // *RCA* (G) 447-9156
	[33]	*RCA* (US) LRM 7027 // *RCA* (Br) BRL 173, (NL) DVLB 16480, (US) [1]LM 1847 // *RCA* (Br) 105.4004
(e,f2)	[45]	*RCA* (B) [1]65.510, (G) (4)47-9149
(e)	[33]	*RCA* (Fr) 530.269
(e, abridged)	[45]	*RCA* (G) [1]ERA 9515, ERA 9548
(f2)	[45]	*RCA* (US,G) [1]ERA 112, (US?) 26071
(f3)	[CD]	*MET* 509CD
	[MC]	*MET* 509C

1952, April 11. New York, Manhattan Center, RCA Victor studio. With Frederick Schauwecker, piano.

183
En svane [Nor] (Grieg)
E2-RC-0776-1(A)

[78] *HMV* DB 21620
[45] *RCA* (Sp) 3-26068, (US,G?) [1]ERA 141, (US?,Au?) 26045
[33] Elec. WALP 1187 = *HMV* (GB) ALP 1187 = *RCA* (Au) L 17007, (SA) 30019, (US) [1]LM 1771

184
Ein Traum [Nor: En drøm] (Grieg)
E2-RC-0777-1(A)

[78] *HMV* DB 21620 [Other matrix number used; see note]
[45] *RCA* (Sp) 3-26068, (US,G?) [1]ERA 141, (US?,Au?) 26045
[33] *Elec.* WALP 1187 = *HMV* (GB) ALP 1187 = *RCA* (Au) L 17007, (SA) 30019, (US) [1]LM 1771 // *RCA* (Br) LMB 500, (US,G) [1]LM 1802

185
Die Mainacht [Ger] (Brahms)
E2-RC-0778-1(A)

[78] *HMV* DB 21620 v.1 [Record mislabelled; see note]
[33] *Elec.* WALP 1187 = *HMV* (GB) ALP 1187 = *RCA* (Au) L 17007, (SA) 30019, (US) [1]LM 1771 // *RCA* (J) RVC 7531/35

186
Ständchen [Ger] (R. Strauss)
E2-RC-0779-1 (A)

[78] *HMV* DB 21620 v.2
[33] *Elec.* WALP 1187 = *HMV* (GB) ALP 1187 = *RCA* (Au) L 17007, (SA) 30019, (US) [1]LM 1771 // *RCA* (J) RVC 7531/35

187
Morgen [Ger] (R. Strauss)
E2-RC-0780-1 (A)

[78] (Not issued)
[45] *RCA* (Sp) 3-26068, (US,G?) [1]ERA 141, (US?,Au?) 26045
[33] *Elec.* WALP 1187 = *HMV* (GB) ALP 1187 = *RCA* (Au) L 17007, (SA) 30019, (US) [1]LM 1771 // *RCA* (J) RVC 7531/35

188
Tonerna [Sw] (Sjöberg)
E2-RC-0781-1(A) [Issued by HMV as 0EA 18071-1A]

[78] *HMV* DA 2068
[45] *HMV* (GB) 7ERC 1
[33] *Elec.* WALP 1187 = *HMV* (GB) ALP 1187 = *RCA* (Au) L 17007, (SA) 30019, (US) [1]LM 1771
[CD] *MET* 210CD
[MC] *MET* 210C

189
Die Allmacht [Ger] (Schubert)
E2-RC-0782-1 (A)

[78] (Not issued)
[45] *HMV* (GB) 7ERC 2
[33] *Elec.* WALP 1187 = *HMV* (GB) ALP 1187 = *RCA* (Au) L 17007, (SA) 30019, (US) [1]LM 1771 // *RCA* (J) RVC 7531/35

190
Wandrers Nachtlied [Ger] (Schubert)
E2-RC-0783-1 (A)

[78] (Not issued)
[45] *HMV* (GB) 7ERC 2
[33] *Elec.* WALP 1187 = *HMV* (GB) ALP 1187 = *RCA* (Au) L 17007, (SA) 30019, (US) [1]LM 1771 // *RCA* (J) RVC 7531/35

191
Svarta rosor [Sw] (Sibelius)
E2-RC-0784-1(A) [Issued by *HMV* as 0EA 18074-1A]

[78] *HMV* DA 2068
[45] *HMV* (GB) 7ERC 1 // *RCA* (Sp) 3-26068, (US,G?) [1]ERA 141, (US?,Au?) 26045
[33] *Elec.* WALP 1187 = *HMV* (GB) ALP 1187 = *RCA* (Au) L 17007, (SA) 30019, (US) [1]LM 1771

192
Es muss ein Wunderbares sein [Ger] (Liszt)
E2-RC-0785-1 (A)

[78] (Not issued)
[45] *HMV* (GB) 7ERC 1
[33] *Elec.* WALP 1187 = *HMV* (GB) ALP 1187 = *RCA* (Au) L 17007, (SA) 30019, (USA) [1]LM 1771 // *RCA* (J) RVC 7531/35

193
Verborgenheit [Ger] (Wolf)
E2-RC-0786-1 (A)

[78] (Not issued)
[45] *HMV* (GB) 7ERC 1 // *RCA* (Sp) 3-25068, (US,G?) [1]ERA 141, (US?,Au?) 26045
[33] *Elec.* WALP 1187 = *HMV* (GB) ALP 1187 = *RCA* (Au) L 17007, (SA) 30019, (US) [1]LM 1771 // *RCA* (J) RVC 7531/35

194
Siren' [Eng: Lilacs] (Rachmaninov)
E2-RC-0787-1(A)

[78] (Not issued)
[33] *Elec.* WALP 1187 = *HMV* (GB) ALP 1187 = *RCA* (Au) L 17007, (SA) 30019, (US) [1]LM 1771 // *RCA* (J) RVC 7531/35

195
Ideale [It] (Tosti)
E2-RC-0788-1(A)

[78] (Not issued)
[33] *Elec.* WALP 1187 = *HMV* (GB) ALP 1187 = *RCA* (Au) L 17007, (SA) 30019, (US) [1]LM 1771

196
Ständchen [Ger] (Schubert)
E2-RC-0789-1(A)

[78] *HMV* [1]DB 21593 = *Vic.* (Ar) 66-6105
[33] *Elec.* WALP 1187 = *HMV* (GB) ALP 1187 = *RCA* (Au) L 17007, (SA) 30019, (US) [1]LM 1771 // *RCA* (J) RVC 7531/35

197
Die böse Farbe [Ger] (Schubert)
E2-RC-0790-1(A)

[78] (Not issued)
[45] *HMV* (GB) 7ERC 2
[33] *Elec.* WALP 1187 = *HMV* (GB) ALP 1187 = *RCA* (Au) L 17007, (SA) 30019, (US) [1]LM 1771 // *RCA* (J) RVC 7531/35

198
Die Forelle [Ger] (Schubert)
E2-RC-0791-1(A)

[78] *HMV* [1]DB 21593 = *Vic.* (Ar) 66-6105
[33] *Elec.* WALP 1187 = *HMV* (GB) ALP 1187 = *RCA* (Au) L 17007, (SA) 30019, (US) [1]LM 1771 // *RCA* (J) RVC 7531/35

1952, November 21. London, HMV studio. With Ivor Newton, piano. [See note]

199
Sylvia [Eng] (Speaks)
0EA 16909-1(A)

[78] *Angel* (Ar) 292708 = *Col.* (Ar) 292708 = *HMV* [1]DA 2039, (Au) EC 221
[33] *Angel* (Ch) 3ACX 47530, (Ur) UAL 12513 = *HMV* (GB,Au) [1]HQM 1190, (GB,SA) HLM 7038, (SA) JALP 29 = *Odeon* (US) PHQM 1190 = *Sera.* (US) 60168 // *Dacapo* [1]1C 147-03354/55M, 1C 137 1033543M
[MC] *HMV* (SA) L4HLM 7038 = *Sera.* (US) [1]4XG 60168

200
Tonerna [Eng: I Bless Ev'ry Hour] (Sjöberg)
0EA 16914-1(A),-2(A)

[78] *HMV* [1]DA 2025, (Au) EC 198
[33] *Angel* (Ch) 3ACX 47530, (Ur) UAL 12513 = *HMV* (GB,Au) [1]HQM 1190, (GB,SA) HLM 7038, (SA) JALP 29 = *Odeon* (US) PHQM 1190 = *Sera.* (US) 60168
[MC] *HMV* (SA) L4HLM 7038 = *Sera.* (US) [1]4XG 60168

201
A Spirit Flower [Eng] (Campbell-Tipton)
0EA 16915-1(A)

[78] *Angel* (Ar) 292708, Col. (Ar) 292708 = *HMV* [1]DA 2039, (Au) EC 221
[33] *Angel* (Ch) 3ACX 47530, (Ur) UAL 12513 = *HMV* (GB,Au) [1]HQM 1190, (GB,SA) HLM 7038, (SA) JALP 29 = *Odeon* (US) PHQM 1190 = *Sera.* (US) 60168 // *Dacapo* [1]1C 147-03354/55M, 1C 137 1033543M

[MC] *HMV* (SA) L4HLM 7038 = *Sera.* (US) [1]4XG 60168

202
Ah, Love, but a Day [Eng] (Beach)
0EA 16916-1(A)

[78] *HMV* [1]DA 2025, (Au) EC 198
[33] *Angel* (Ch) 3ACX 47530, (Ur) UAL 12513 = *HMV* (GB,Au) [1]HQM 1190, (GB,SA) HLM 7038, (SA) JALP 29 = *Odeon* (US) PHQM 1190 = *Sera.* (US) 60168 // *Dacapo* [1]1C 147-03354/55M, 1C 137 1033543M
[MC] *HMV* (SA) 4HLM 7038 = *Sera.* (US) [1]4XG 60168

1953, January 7,13,18,27,29 & February 1. New York, Manhattan Center, RCA Victor studio. With RCA Victor Orch. & Robert Shaw Chorale, cond. Renato Cellini. Producer: Richard Mohr.

203
Cavalleria rusticana (Mascagni), sung in It. by Zinka Milanov (Santuzza); Carol Smith (Lola); Margaret Roggero (Lucia); JB (Turiddu); Robert Merrill (Alfio).
[Orig. LP matrix (LM 6106): E3-RP-5114/16]

Complete:

[45] *RCA* (US) WDM 6106
[33] *Elec.* WALP 1126/28 = *HMV* (Au) OALP 1126/28, (Fr) FALP 301/03, (GB) ALP 1126/28, (It) QALP 10050/52, (SA) JALP 1126/28, (Sp) LALP 262/64 = *RCA* (US) [1]LM 6106 // *RCA* (G) LM 6046/1-2, (US) [1]LM 6046 // *RCA* (Fr) 630.383/84 // *Opus* 9112 0821/22 = *RCA* (GB) VICS 6044, (It) MCV 534, VL 43534, VLS 43534, (US,Au) [1]VIC 6044
[CD] *RCA* (G) GD 86510, (US) [1]6510-2-RG
[MC] *RCA* (It) RK 6046 // *RCA* (It) VKS 43534

Excerpts:
a. O Lola; b1. Tu qui, Santuzza?... b2. Ah! lo vedi; c1. A casa... c2. Intanto amici, qua...Viva il vino; d1. Compar Alfio... d2. Mamma!...Quel vino.

(a,b,c2,d2)	[33]	*RCA* (J) RVC 7531/35 // *RCA* (NL) AVL 10987
(a,b2,d2)	[33]	*HMV* (GB) ALP 1481, (It) QALP 10212, (NZ) MALP 1481 = *RCA* (US) [1]LM 1828
(a,d)	[45]	*RCA* (It) [1]A72R 0090, ERA 50-090
(a)	[45]	*RCA* (Au) 26012 // *HMV* (GB) 7ER 5063, (It) [1]7ERQ 141 // *HMV* (It) 7ERQ 167
	[33]	*RCA* (Au) L 16174, (Br) BRL 253, (G) LM 2269-C, (GB) RB 16149, (SA) 30095, (Sp) 3L 16282, (US) [1]LM 2269, AGM1-4806 // *Melodiya (Akkord)* D 007487/88 // *RCA* (G) KR 11014/1-2 (26.48016 DP) // *RCA* (GB) SER 5704/06 // *RCA* (G) RL 43077 EF // *RCA* (G) GL 85277, (US) [1]AGM1-5277

	[CD]	*RCA* (G) RD 85934, GD 85277, (US) [1]5934-2-RC
	[OR]	*RCA* (US) TR3-5035
	[MC]	*RCA* (G) RK 43077 CF // *RCA* (US) AGMK-4806 // *RCA* (G) GK 85277, (US) [1]AGK1-5277
(b1,d2)	[33]	*Sel.Read.Dig.* RDS 13D
	[CD]	*Sel.Read.Dig.* RDCD 101
(b)	[CD]	*MET* 512CD
	[MC]	*MET* 512C
(c,d)	[45]	*HMV* (GB) 7ER 5079, (It) [1]7ERQ 143
(d2)	[45]	*RCA* (Sp) 3B 26035, (US) [1]ERB 38

1953, January 10,11,15,19,29. New York, Manhattan Center, RCA Victor studio. With RCA Victor Orch., Robert Shaw Chorale & Columbus Boychoir, cond. Renato Cellini. Producer: Richard Mohr.

204

Pagliacci (Leoncavallo), sung in It. by Victoria de los Angeles (Nedda); JB (Canio), Paul Franke (Beppe), Richard Wright (Peasant); Leonard Warren (Tonio), Robert Merrill (Silvio), George Cehanovsky (Peasant).

[Orig. LP matrix (LM 6106): E3-RP-5117/19]

Complete:

[45]	*RCA* (US) WDM 6106
[33]	*Elec.* WALP 1126/28 = *HMV* (Au) OALP 1126/28, (Fr) FALP 301/03, (GB) ALP 1126/28, (It) QALP 10050/52, (SA) JALP 1126/28, (Sp) LALP 262/64 = *RCA* (US) [1]LM 6106 // *RCA* (US) LM 6045 // *RCA* (Fr) 630.577/78, (G) LM 6084/1-2, (SA) B 30216, (US) [1]LM 6084 // *Sera.* (US) IB 6058 // *WRC* (Au) TE 241/42
[CD]	*EMI* (GB) CDC 7 49503 2

Excerpts:

(Act 1)	a1. Recitar!... a2. Vesti la giubba;
(Act 2)	b1. Attenti! Pagliaccio... b2. Coraggio...No! Pagliaccio non son [to end of opera].

(a,b)	[45]	*RCA* (Sp) 3B 26035, (US) [1]ERB 38
	[33]	*HMV* (GB) ALP 1481, (It) QALP 10212, (NZ) MALP 1481 = *RCA* (US) [1]LM 1828 // *RCA* (It) LM 20039
(a)	[45]	*RCA* (US,G) ERA 209 // *HMV* (GB) [1]7ER 5055, (It) 7ERQ 136 // *RCA* (G) (4)47-9150
	[33]	*RCA* (US,G) LM 1801
(a2)	[33]	*Magnavox*
(b2)	[45]	*HMV* (GB) [1]7ER 5062, (It) 7ERQ 140

1953, September 30. Stockholm, Royal Academy of Music. With orch., cond. Bertil Bokstedt.

205

Till havs [Sw] (Nordqvist)
0SB 3843-1S

[78] *HMV* [1]X 7947 = *Vic.* (US) 26-1123

[45] *RCA* (US) 43-1123 // *HMV* (Sw) 7EBS 3

[33] *Angel* (Ch) 3ACX 47365, (J) HA 5032, AB 7123, (US) COLH 149 = Cap. (US) [1]G 7247 = *HMV* (Au) OALP 1857, (GB) ALP 1857, (NZ) MALP 1857 = *WRC* (Au) 3199, (NZ) CO 566 // *Odeon* (Sw) PMCS 308 // *HMV* (Sw) [1]4E 153-34532/33M = *Odeon* (US) 4E 153-34532/33M // *HMV* (Sw) PRO 3034 // *HMV* (Sw) 7C 061-35731M // *Musik* LPFG 001

[CD] *EMI* (Sw) CDC 7 61075 2

[MC] *HMV* (Sw) 4E 278-51007M // *HMV* (Sw) 7C 261-35731M

206

Sången till havet [Sw] (Salén)
0SB 3844-1S

[78] *HMV* (Sw) [1]X 7964, *Vic.* (US) 26-1122

[45] *RCA* (US) 43-1122 // *HMV* (Sw) 7EBS 3

[33] *Angel* (Ch) 3ACX 47365, (J) HA 5032, AB 7123, (US) COLH 149 = *Cap.* (US) [1]G 7247 = *HMV* (Au) OALP 1857, (GB) ALP 1857, (NZ) MALP 1857 = *WRC* (Au) 3199, (NZ) CO 566 // *HMV* (Sw) [1]4E 153-34532/33M, *Odeon* (US) 4E 153-34532/33M // *HMV* (Sw) PRO 3034

[CD] *EMI* (Sw) CDC 7 61075 2

[MC] *HMV* (Sw) 4E 278-51007M

207

Visa kring slånblom och månskära [Sw] (Salén)
0SB 3845-1S

[78] *HMV* (Sw) [1]X 7964 = *Vic.* (US) 26-1122

[45] *RCA* (US) 43-1122 // *HMV* (Sw) 7EBS 3

[33] *Angel* (Ch) 3ACX 47365, (J) HA 5032, AB 7123, (US) COLH 149 = *Cap.* (US) [1]G 7247 = *HMV* (Au) OALP 1857, (GB) ALP 1857, (NZ) MALP 1857 = *WRC* (Au) 3199, (NZ) CO 566 // *Odeon* (Sw) PMCS 308 // *HMV* (Sw) [1]4E 153-34532/33M = *Odeon* (US) 4E 153-34532/33M // *Rococo* 5341 // *HMV* (Sw) PRO 3034

[CD] *EMI* (Sw) CDC 7 61075 2

[MC] *HMV* (Sw) 4E 278-51007M

208

Jungfrun under lind [Sw] (Peterson-Berger)
0SB 3846-1S

[78] *HMV* [1]X 7947 = *Vic.* (US) 26-1123

[45] *RCA* (US) 43-1123 // *HMV* (Sw) 7EBS 3

[33] *Angel* (Ch) 3ACX 47365, (J) HA 5032, AB 7123, (US) COLH 149 = *Cap.* (US)

	[1]G 7247 = *HMV* (Au) OALP 1857, (GB) ALP 1857, (NZ) MALP 1857 = *WRC* (Au) 3199, (NZ) CO 566 // *HMV* (Sw) [1]4E 153-34532/33M = *Odeon* (US) 4E 153-34532/33M // *HMV* (Sw) PRO 3034 // *HMV* (Sw) 7C 061-35731M
[CD]	*EMI* (Sw) CDC 7 61075 2
[MC]	*HMV* (Sw) 4E 278-51007M // *HMV* (Sw) 7C 261-35731M // *Sv.Favoriter* SFMC 1063

1954, July 11-13,15-17. Rome, Opera House. With Rome Opera House Orch. & Chorus, cond. Jonel Perlea. Producer: Richard Mohr.

209

Manon Lescaut (Puccini), sung in It. by Licia Albanese (Manon); Anna Maria Rota (Singer); JB (Des Grieux), Mario Carlin (Edmondo, Dancing Master, Lamplighter); Robert Merrill (Lescaut); Franco Calabrese (Geronte, Sergeant), Enrico Campi (Innkeeper, Sea Captain).
[Orig. LP matrix (LM 6116): F2-RP-0625/30]

Complete:

[33, 6 sides]	*Elec.* WALP 1326/28 = *HMV* (GB) ALP 1326/28 = *RCA* (It) C12R 0164/66, (Sp) 3LC 16269, (US,Ca,Ch) [1]LM 6116
[33, 4 sides]	*RCA* (G) VIC 6027/1-2 (26.48002 DM,DP), (It) KV 6110, MCV 544, VL 43544, VLS 43544, (US,Au,GB) [1]VIC 6027
[CD]	*RCA* (G) [1]GD 60573, (US) 60573-2-RG
MC]	*RCA* (It) [1]VKS 43544, (US) 60573-4-RG

Excerpts:

(Act 1)	a. Ma se vi talenta...Tra voi, belle; b1. Cortese damigella... b2. Donna non vidi mai; c. Vedete? Io son fedele;
(Act 2)	d. Oh, sarò la più bella [through "Dolcissimo soffrir"]; e. Ah! Manon, mi tradisce;
(Act 3)	f1. Rosetta! Eh! che aria!... f2. Presto! In fila!... f3. Ah! guai a chi... f4. No! no! pazzo son!;
(Act 4)	g. Vedi, vedi, son io che piango.

(a,b2,f2-4)	[33]	*MET* 110
	[CD]	*MET* 110CD
	[MC]	*MET* 110C
(b,c,d,f,g)	[33]	*RCA* (G) LM 2059-C, (GB) RB 16078, (SA) 30058, (US,Ca) [1]LM 2059
(b2,d)	[33]	*RCA* (J) RVC 7531/35
(b2,e,f2-4)	[33]	*RCA* (GB) SER 5704/06 // *RCA* (G) RL 43077 EF
	[OR]	*RCA* (US) TR3-5035
	[MC]	*RCA* (G) RK 43077 CF
(b2,f3-4)	[33]	*RCA* (It) VL 42436
(b2)	[33]	*RCA* (Au) L 16174, (Br) BRL 253, (G) LM 2269-C, (GB) RB 16149, (SA) 30095, (Sp) 3L 16282, (US) [1]LM 2269, AGM1-4806 // *Melodiya (Akkord)* D 007487/88 // *RCA* (Au) L 16352,

(G) [1]HR 212, (GB) RB 6515, (SA) 30231, (US) LM 2631 // *Melodiya* D 00019605/06 // *Melodiya* D 21793/94 (?) // *RCA* (Au) VICS 1672, (US,GB) [1]VICS 1672(e) // *RCA* (G) GL 85277, (US) [1]AGM1-5277

	[CD]	*RCA* (G) RD 85934, GD 85277, (US) [1]5934-2-RC
	[MC]	*RCA* (GB) MCK 570 // *RCA* (US) AGK1-4806 // *RCA* (G) GK 85277, (US) [1]AGK1-5277
	[8T]	*RCA* (US) V8S 1048
(d,e)	[45]	*RCA* (It) ERA 50-148
(d)	[33]	*RCA* (Au) L 16347, (G) HR 210, (GB) RB 6516, (US) [1]LM 2628 // *MET* 405 // *RCA* (G) GL 87799
	[CD]	*RCA* (G) GD 87799, (US) [1]7799-2-RG
	[MC]	*MET* 405C // *RCA* (G) GK 87799, (US) [1]7799-4-RG
(e,f2-4)	[33]	*RCA* (G) LM 2736-C, (GB) RB 6585, RL 43243, RCALP 3043, GL 84889, (US,Au) [1]LM 2736, (US) AGM1-4889
	[MC]	*RCA* (Ca) AGK1-4889, (GB) [1]RK 43243, RCAK 3043, GK 84889
(f2-4)	[33]	*RCA* (Br) BRL 182, (US) [1]SRL 12-14
(f3-4)	[33]	*RCA* (G,It) RL 85177, (US) [1]CRM8-5177
	[MC]	*RCA* (US) CRK8-5177

1955, July 2,6,8,9,11,13 [see note]. Rome, Opera House. With Rome Opera House Orch. & Chorus, cond. Jonel Perlea. Producer: Richard Mohr.

210

Aida (Verdi), sung in It. by Zinka Milanov (Aida); Fedora Barbieri (Amneris), Bruna Rizzoli (Priestess); JB (Radamès), Mario Carlin (Messenger); Leonard Warren (Amonasro); Boris Christoff (Ramfis), Plinio Clabassi (King).
[RCA serial Nos.: 2-F2-RH-4135/49,-51,-53/55; orig. LP matrix (LM 6122): F2-RP-5731/36]

Complete:

[33]	*HMV* (GB) ALP 1388/90 = *RCA* (Au) LC 16134, (Fr) A 630.373/75, 731.011/13, (G) LM 6122/1-3, VIC 6119/1-3 (26.35004 EA), VL 70190, (It) C12R 0175/77, KV 6103, MCV 533, VL 43533, VLS 43533, (J) RGC 1101/03, (SA) C 30014, (Sp) 3LC 16076, (US,Ch) [1]LM 6122, (US) VIC 6119
[CD]	*RCA* (G) GD 86652, (US) [1]6652-2-RG
[OR]	*RCA* (US) EC 42 + FC 41
[MC]	*RCA* (It) [1]VKS 43533, (US) ALK3-5380

Excerpts:

(Act 1)	a1. Se quel guerrier...Celeste Aida... a2. Quale insolita gioia...Dessa! Ei si turba; b. Su! del Nilo al sacro lido; c. Nume, custode e vindice;
(Act 2)	d1. Salvator della patria... d2. Gloria all'Egitto;
(Act 3)	e1. Pur ti riveggo... e2. Aida! Tu non m'ami... e3. Tu! Amonasro!;

(Act 4)	f. Già i sacerdoti adunansi; g1. La fatal pietra... g2. Morir! sì pura e bella!... g3. O terra addio.

(a,d,e1,f,g)	[33]	*RCA* (US) LM 6069
(a1,c,e,g2-3)	[33]	*RCA* (NL) AVL 10906
(a1,e,g)	[33]	*RCA* (Br) BRL 181, (Fr) 630.382, (G) LM 2046-C, (SA) 30065, (Sp) 3L 16153, (US) [1]SLP 19, LM 2046
(a1,e1,f,g)	[CD]	*RCA* (G) GD 60201, (US) [1]60201-2-RG
	[MC]	*RCA* (G) GK 60201, (US) [1]60201-4-RG
(a1,e3)	[33]	*RCA* (GB) SER 5704/06 // *RCA* (J) RVC 7531/35 // *RCA* (G) RL 43077 EF
	[OR]	*RCA* (US) TR3-5035
	[MC]	*RCA* (G) RK 43077 CF
(a1,g)	[45]	*RCA* (US) ERC 2046
(a1)	[45]	*RCA* (It) [1]A72R 0088, ERA 50-088 (?) // *RCA* (G) 447-9364
	[33]	*RCA* (Au) L 16174, (Br) BRL 253, (G) LM 2269-C, (GB) RB 16149, (SA) 30095, (Sp) 3L 16282, (US) [1]LM 2269, AGM1-4806 // *RCA* (Fr) 530.271 // *RCA* (It) LM 20075 // *RCA* (It) VL 42436 // *Impact* IMA 011 = *RCA* (Au) [1]SP 185 = *WRC* (Au) R 10033 // *RCA* (G) GL 85277, (US) [1]AGM1-5277
	[CD]	*RCA* (G) RD 85934, GD 85277, (US) [1]5934-2-RC
	[MC]	*RCA* (Au) [1]SPK 185 = *WRC* (Au) C 10033 // *RCA* (US) AGK1-4806 // *RCA* (G) GK 85277, (US) [1]AGK1-5277
(b)	[33]	*RCA* (Fr) 530.269
(d,f)	[33]	*RCA* (It) [1]LMD 60005, VL 42435
(d2)	[33]	*RCA* (It) TRL4-1173
(e1)	[33]	*RCA* (Au) L 16347, (G) HR 210, (GB) RB 6516, (US) [1]LM 2628
(e3)	[33]	*RCA* (G) LM 2736-C, (GB) RB 6585, RL 43243, RCALP 3043, GL 84889, (US,Au) [1]LM 2736, (US) AGM1-4889
	[MC]	*RCA* (Ca) AGK1-4889, (GB) [1]RK 43243, RCAK 3043, GK 84889
(g)	[33]	*RCA* (Au) LB 16193, (SA) 30190/91, (US) [1]LM 6061 // *RCA* (GB) RB 16089 // *RCA* (G) GL 87799
	[CD]	*RCA* (G) GD 87799, (US) [1]7799-2-RG
	[MC]	*RCA* (G) GK 87799, (US) [1]7799-4-RG
(g1-2)	[CD]	*Tring* TFP 013
(g3)	[33]	*RCA* (Fr) 430.367 (?)
(?)	[45]	*RCA* (Sp) 3-26114

1956, March 16,17,30 & April 1-3,5,6. New York, Manhattan Center, RCA Victor studio, With RCA Victor Symphony Orch., New York City Opera Chorus & Columbus Boychoir, cond. Thomas Beecham. Producer: Richard Mohr.

211

La bohème (Puccini), sung in It. by Victoria de los Angeles (Mimì), Lucine Amara (Musetta); JB (Rodolfo), William Nahr (Parpignol); Robert Merrill (Marcello), John

Reardon (Schaunard); Giorgio Tozzi (Colline), Fernando Corena (Benoit, Alcindoro), Thomas Powell (Customs Officer), George del Monte (Sergeant).
[RCA serial Nos.: G2-RB-2572/89; orig. LP matrix (LM 6042): G2-RP-3580/83. Mono two-track recording, later reprocessed for stereo effect; orig. stereo matrix (SLS 896): 2YEA 4961/64.]

Complete:

[33]	*Angel* (Ar) LPC 12243/44, 5675/76(?), 6001/02, (J) AB 9368/69, *HMV* (Au) OALP 1409/10, (Fr) FALP 554/55, 2905433, (GB) ALP 1409/10, SLS 896, (It) QALP 10171/72, 3C 153-00126/27, (NZ) MALP 1409/10, (SA) JALP 1409/10, (Sp) LALP 311/12, 1J 163-00126/27, (Sw) 7C 191-00126/27, *RCA* (US) [1]LM 6042, *Sera.* (J) EAC 30239/40, (US) IB 6000, SIB 6000, SIB 6099
[CD]	*EMI* (GB) CDS 7 47235 8 (CDCB 47235), (J) CC30 3583/84
[OR]	*HMV* (GB) HTA 34/35, *RCA* (US) [1]DC 45/46
[MC]	*HMV* (GB) [1]TC-SLS 896, (Sp) 1J 245-00126/27, *Sera.* (US) 4X2G 6099

Excerpts:

(Act 1)	a. Questo Mar Rosso...Nei cieli bigi; b1. Al quartiere latin... b2. Che gelida manina... b3. Sì. Mi chiamano Mimì... b4. O soave fanciulla... b5. V'aspettan gli amici;
(Act 2)	c. Chi guardi...Questa è Mimì; d. Quando me'n vo';
(Act 3)	e1. Entrate. - C'è Rodolfo?... e2. Addio. - Che! Vai?... e3. Donde lieta uscì... e4. Dunque è proprio...Addio, dolce svegliare...Quella gente che dirà?;
(Act 4)	f1. In un coupè... f2. O Mimì, tu più non torni; g1. Sono andati?... g2. Oh Dio! Mimì!... g3. Dorme? - Riposa [to end of opera].

(a)	[CD]	*MET* 501CD
	[MC]	*MET* 501C
(b,c,d,e1-3,f,g2-3)		
	[33]	*HMV* (GB) [1]ESD 7023, (Sw) 1031401
	[MC]	*HMV* (GB) [1]TC-ESD 7023, (Sw) 1031404
(b2-5,d,e,f,g)	[45]	*RCA* (US) ERC 2045
	[33]	*RCA* (US) [1]SLP 20, LM 2045
(b2-5,e,f2,g)	[33]	*HMV* (Au) OALP 1921, (GB) [1]ALP 1921, (NZ) MALP 1921, (SA) JALP 1921, *WRC* (Au) 3226, R 01933
(b2-5)	[45]	*HMV* (Au) 7ERO 5179, (GB) [1]7ER 5179
(b2)	[33]	*HMV* (NL) 5C 181-25204/05 // Sera.(?)(J) EAC 55101 // [See also note]
(b3)	[33]	*HMV* (GB) [1]SLS 5233, (Sp) 10C 165-078000/02
	[MC]	*HMV* (GB) TC-SLS 5233
(b4-5)	[33]	*RCA* (Au) LB 16193, (SA) 30190/91, (US) [1]LM 6061
(b4)	[33]	*RCA* (US) SRL 12-28
(e2-3,f)	[45]	*HMV* (GB) [1]7ER 5186, (NZ) 7ERM 5186, (Sp) 7ERL 1453
(e3-4)	[33]	*Sel.Read.Dig.* 3C 147-52050/55
(g)	[45]	*HMV* (GB) 7ER 5190

1956, June 16,18,20-22,25,26,28. Rome, Opera House. With Rome Opera House Orch. & Chorus, cond. Jonel Perlea. Producer: Richard Mohr. [See note]

212

Rigoletto (Verdi), sung in It. by Roberta Peters (Gilda); Silvana Celli (Giovanna), Lidia Grandi (Countess Ceprano), Santa Chissari (Page); Anna Maria Rota (Maddalena); JB (Duke), Tommaso Frascati (Borsa); Robert Merrill (Rigoletto), Vittorio Tatozzi (Monterone), Arturo La Porta (Marullo); Giorgio Tozzi (Sparafucile), Leonardo Monreale (Count Ceprano), Andrea Mineo (Usher).
[RCA serial Nos.: G2-RB-4228/29,-31/44; orig. LP matrix (LM 6051): G2-RP-7017/20]

Complete:

[33]	*RCA* (Au) LB 16239, (G) LM 6051/1-2, VIC 6005/1-2 (26.48001 DM,DP), (GB) RB 16031/32, (It) KV 6005, MCV 540, VL 43540, VLS 43540, (Sp) 3LB 16273, (US,Ch) [1]LM 6051, (US,Au,GB) VIC 6041
[CD]	*RCA* (G) [1]GD 60172, (US) 60172-2-RG
[MC]	*RCA* (G) GK 60172, (It) [1]VKS 43540, (US) 60172-4-RG

Excerpts:

(Act 1)	a1. Della mia bella... a2. Questa o quella; b. È il sol dell'anima;
(Act 2)	c. Ella mi fù rapita...Parmi veder le lagrime;
(Act 3)	d. La donna è mobile; e1. Un dì, se ben... e2. Bella figlia dell'amore.

(a,b,d,e2)	[33]	*RCA* (G) LM 9847-E
(a2,c,d,e)	[33]	*RCA* (GB) SER 5704/06 // *RCA* (J) RVC 7531/35 // *RCA* (G) RL 43077 EF
	[OR]	*RCA* (US) TR3-5035
	[MC]	*RCA* (G) RK 43077 CF
(a2,e)	[33]	*RCA* (G) LM 2736-C, (GB) RB 6585, RL 43243, RCALP 3043, GL 84889, (US,Au) [1]LM 2736, (US) AGM1-4889
	[MC]	*RCA* (Ca) AGK1-4889, (GB) [1]RK 43243, RCAK 3043, GK 84889
(c,d)	[33]	*RCA* (Au) L 16174, (Br) BRL 253, (G) LM 2269-C, (GB) RB 16149, (SA) 30095, (Sp) 3L 16282, (US) [1]LM 2269, AGM1-4806 // *RCA* (G) GL 85277, (US) [1]AGM1-5277
	[CD]	*RCA* (G) RD 85934, GD 85277, (US) [1]5934-2-RC
	[MC]	*RCA* (US) AGK1-4806 // *RCA* (G) GK 85277, (US) [1]AGK1-5277
(c)	[33]	*Melodiya (Akkord)* D 007487/88 // *RCA* (G) KR 11014/1-2 (26.48016 DP) // *RCA* (It) VL 42436
(d)	[45]	*RCA* (G) (4)47-9365
	[33]	*RCA* (Au) LB 16193, (SA) 30190/91, (US) [1]LM 6061 // *RCA* (It) TRL4-1173 // *Impact* IMA 011, *RCA* (Au) [1]SP 185, *WRC* (Au) R 10033
	[MC]	*RCA* (Au) [1]SPK 185, *WRC* (Au) C 10033

1957, January 22. Stockholm, Concert Hall, Large Auditorium. With Royal Orch., cond. Nils Grevillius.

213
Ach, so fromm [It: M'apparì tutt'amor] (Flotow: *Martha*)
6H2-RH-0005

[45] *RCA* (G) ERA 9509 // *RCA* (G) (4)47-9365
[33] *RCA* (G) LM 9800-D,-E // *RCA* (Au) L 16174, (Br) BRL 253, (G) LM 2269-C, (GB) RB 16149, (SA) 30095, (Sp) 3L 16282, (US) [1]LM 2269, AGM1-4806 // *Melodiya (Akkord)* D 007487/88 // *RCA* (GB) SER 5704/06 // *RCA* (J) RVC 7531/35 // *RCA* (It) VL 42436 // *RCA* (G) RL 43077 EF // *RCA* (G) GL 85277, (US) [1]AGM1-5277
[CD] *RCA* (G) RD 85934, GD 85277, (US) [1]5934-2-RC
[OR] *RCA* (US) TR3-5035
[MC] *RCA* (G) RK 43077 CF // *RCA* (US) AGK1-4806 // *RCA* (G) GK 85277, (US) [1]AGK1-5277

214
Kung Heimer och Aslög [Sw] (Söderman)
6H2-RH-0006

[45] *RCA* (Sw) ERAS 102
[33] *RCA* (G) LM 9800-D,-E // *RCA* (Au) L 16370, (Sw,US) [1]LM 9884 // *RCA* (GB) SER 5719, (Sw,Au) [1]LSC 9884 // *RCA* (J) RVC 7531/35
[CD] *Sw.Society* SCD 1010
[MC] *RCA* (Sw) RK 9884 // *Sw.Society* SSC 1010

215
Lensky's Aria: Kuda, kuda [Sw: Förbi, förbi] (Tchaikovsky: *Evgeny Onegin*)
6H2-RH-0007

[45] *RCA* (Sw) ERAS 102
[33] *RCA* (G) LM 9800-D,-E // *RCA* (Au) L 16174, (Br) BRL 253, (G) LM 2269-C, (GB) RB 16149, (SA) 30095, (Sp) 3L 16282, (US) [1]LM 2269, AGM1-4806 // *RCA* (J) RVC 7531/35 // *RCA* (G) GL 85277, (US) [1]AGM1-5277
[CD] *RCA* (G) RD 85934, GD 85277, (US) [1]5934-2-RC
[OR] *RCA* (US) TR3-5035
[MC] *RCA* (US) AGK1-4806 // *RCA* (G) GK 85277, (US) [1]AGK1-5277

1957, January 23. Stockholm, Concert Hall, Large Auditorium. With Royal Orch., cond. Nils Grevillius.

216
Una furtiva lagrima [It] (Donizetti: *L'elisir d'amore*)
6H2-RH-0008 [For difference between versions, see note]

A (Version 1)

[45] *RCA* (G) ERA 9509 // *RCA* (G) 447-9364
[33] *RCA* (G) LM 9800-D,-E // *RCA* (G) LM 9823-E // *Melodiya* D 21793/94(?)

B (Version 2)

[33] *RCA* (Au) L 16174, (Br) BRL 253, (G) LM 2269-C, (GB) RB 16149, (SA) 30095, (Sp) 3L 16282, (US) [1]LM 2269, AGM1-4806 // *RCA* (GB) SER 5704/06 // *RCA* (J) RVC 7531/35 // *RCA* (G) RL 43077 EF // *RCA* (G) GL 85277, (US) [1]AGM1-5277 // *Eva* 304 391
[CD] *RCA* (G) RD 85934, GD 85277, (US) [1]5934-2-RC // *Eva* 354 391
[OR] *RCA* (US) TR3-5035
[MC] *RCA* (G) RK 43077 CF // *RCA* (US) AGK1-4806 // *RCA* (G) GK 85277, (US) [1]AGK1-5277 // *Eva* 504 391

217
Come un bel dì di maggio [It] (Giordano: *Andrea Chénier*)
6H2-RH-0009

[45] *RCA* (G) ERA 9509 // *RCA* (G) 447-9156
[33] *RCA* (G) LM 9800-D,-E // *RCA* (G) LM 1841-C v.2 // *RCA* (Au) L 16174, (Br) BRL 253, (G) LM 2269-C, (GB) RB 16149, (SA) 30095, (Sp) 3L 16282, (US) [1]LM 2269, AGM1-4806 // *RCA* (GB) SER 5704/06 // *RCA* (J) RVC 7531/35 // *RCA* (It) VL 42436 // *RCA* (G) RL 43077 EF // *RCA* (G) GL 85277, (US) [1]AGM1-5277
[CD] *RCA* (G) RD 85934, GD 85277, (US) [1]5934-2-RC
[OR] *RCA* (US) TR3-5035
[MC] *RCA* (G) RK 43077 CF // *RCA* (US) AGK1-4806 // *RCA* (G) GK 85277, (US) [1]AGK1-5277

218
Vladimir's Cavatina: Medlenno den' ugasal [Sw: Dagen gick långsamt till ro] (Borodin: *Knyaz* [*Prince*] *Igor*)
6H2-RH-0010

[45] *RCA* (G) ERA 9509
[33] *RCA* (G) LM 9800-D,-E // *RCA* (Au) L 16174, (Br) BRL 253, (G) LM 2269-C, (GB) RB 16149, (SA) 30095, (Sp) 3L 16282, (US) [1]LM 2269, AGM1-4806 // *Melodiya (Akkord)* D 007487/88 // *RCA* (GB) SER 5704/06 // *RCA* (J) RVC 7531/35 // *RCA* (G) GL 85277, (US) [1]AGM1-5277
[CD] *RCA* (G) RD 85934, GD 85277, (US) [1]5934-2-RC
[OR] *RCA* (US) TR3-5035
[MC] *RCA* (US) AGK1-4806 // *RCA* (G) GK 5277, (US) [1]AGK1-5277

1957, July 2,4,6,8,14,16,18. Rome, Opera House. With Rome Opera House Orch. & Chorus, cond. Erich Leinsdorf. Producer: Richard Mohr.

219

Tosca (Puccini), sung in It. by Zinka Milanov (Tosca); Giovanni Bianchini (Shepherd); JB (Cavaradossi), Mario Carlin (Spoletta); Leonard Warren (Scarpia), Nestore Catalani (Sciarrone), Vincenzo Preziosa (Jailer); Fernando Corena (Sacristan), Leonardo Monreale (Angelotti).
[RCA serial Nos.: 2-H2-RB-2539,-41/52; orig. LP matrix: H2-RP-5372/75 (LM 6052), K2-RY-6777/81 (LSC 6052)]

Complete:

[33, 4 sides] *CML* 062/63* = *RCA* (Au) LB 16110, (Fr) 630.456/57, (G) LM 6052/1-2, LSC 6052/1-2*, VIC 6000/1-2, VICS 6000/1-2* (26.48009 DM,DP*), SMR 8008*, (GB) RB 16051/52, (It) KVS 6000*, MCV 535*, VL 43535*, VLS 43535*, (J) RGC 1036/37, (NZ) RSL 3551/52, (US) [1]LM 6052, VIC 6000, (US,GB,Sp) VICS 6000*, (US) AGL2-4514* = *Westm.* (Br) 630501001/02* // *Sel.Read.Dig.* RDP/T 1-2*
[33, 5 sides] *RCA* (US) LSC 6052*
[CD] *RCA* (GD 84514*, (US) [1]4514-2-RG*
[MC] *RCA* (G) [1]PVK2-9005* (24.48009 CT*), (It) VK 43535*, VKS 43535*, (US) AGK2-4514*, 4514-4-RG* = *Westm.* (Br) 630701016/17*

Excerpts:
(Act 1) a1. Che fai?... a2. Dammi i colori!... a3. Recondita armonia; b1. Gente la dentro!... b2. Angelotti!... b3. Mario! Mario!... b4. Tanto! - Tornalo a dir!...b5. Dai boschi...Ah! M'avvinci; c1. Or lasciami... c2. Come mi guarda fiso!... c3. Qual'occhio al mondo... c4. Mia gelosa!;
(Act 2) d. Ov'è Angelotti?; e. Floria! - Amore...Vittoria!;
(Act 3) f1. E lucevan le stelle... f2. Ah! Franchigia...Scarpia che cede?... f3. Il tuo sangue... f4. O dolci mani... f5. Senti, l'ora è vicina... f6. Amaro sol per te... f7. E non giungono... f8. Parlami ancor.

(a,b1-3,c3-4,f1-2,f4,f6,f8)
[33] *RCA* (G) LM 9811-C
(a,b3-5,c4,f1,f4-8)
[33] *RCA* (G) LSC 9811-B*
(a,b3-5,d,e,f) [CD] *RCA* (G) GD 60192*, (US) [1]60192-2-RG* = *Symphony* SYCD 6159*
[MC] *RCA* (G) GK 60192*, (US) [1]60192-4-RG*
(a2-3,b2-5,c3-4,f1,f4-6)
[8T] *RCA* (US) V8S 1022*
(a2-3,f1,f4) [33] *RCA* (G) GL 85277*, (US) [1]AGM1-5277*
[CD] *RCA* (G) RD 85934*, GD 85277*, (US) [1]5934-2-RC*
[MC] *RCA* (G) GK 85277*, (US) [1]AGK1-5277*
(a2-3,f1) [33] *RCA* (J) RVC 7531/35
[CD] *RCA* (GB) GD 89788*
[MC] *RCA* (G) GK 89788*
(a2-3,f4) [33] *RCA* (Au) L 16305, (G) LM 2570-C, LSC 2570-B*, (GB) VICS 1740*, (J) SHP 2103*, (SA) 30209, (US) [1]LM 2570, LSC 2570 // *RCA* (G) KR 11014/1-2* (26.48016 DP*)

(a3,f1)	[45]	*RCA* (G) [1]ERA 9791, ESC 9791* // *RCA* (G) 447-9363 // *RCA* (J) SX 8536*
	[33]	*RCA* (G) VIP 2* (26.41213 AF*), (US,Au) [1]LSC 5003* // *RCA* (Au) VICS 1672*, (US,GB) [1]VICS 1672(e)*
	[MC]	*RCA* (US) RK 1195* // *RCA* (G) MCK 570*
	[8T]	*RCA* (US) R8S 1195* // *RCA* (US) V8S 1048*
(a)	[CD]	*MET* 516CD*
	[MC]	*MET* 516C*
(a2-3)	[33]	*K-West* KNEWLP 602*
	[CD]	*K-West* KNEWCD 602*
	[MC]	*K-West* KNEWMC 602*
(a3)	[45]	*RCA* (G) [1]RCX 206, SRC 7042*
	[33]	*RCA* (It) LRC 51-007
	[OR]	*RCA* (US) TR3-5005*
	[8T]	*RCA* (US) R8S 5044*
(b3c)	[33]	*RCA* (G) GL 87799*
	[CD]	*RCA* (G) GD 87799*, (US) [1]7799-2-RG*
	[MC]	*RCA* (G) GK 87799*, (US) [1]7799-4-RG*
(b3-4,c)	[CD]	*Tring* TFP 013*
(c2-4,f1)	[33]	*Read.Dig.* (Au,GB) RD4-67-1/6* // *Read.Dig.* (GB) RDM 2678+RDS 6671/77*
(f1)	[45]	*RCA* (G) ERA 6052 // *RCA* (J) ES 8510
	[33]	*RCA* (Au) LB 16193, (SA) 30190/91, (US) [1]LM 6061 // *RCA* (Au) L 16174, (Br) BRL 253, (G) LM 2269-C, (GB) RB 16149, (SA) 30095, (Sp) 3L 16282, (US) [1]LM 2269, AGM1-4806 // *RCA* (Au) L 16237, (G) LM 2391-C, LSC 2391-B*, (SA) 30126, (US) [1]LM 2391, LSC 2391* // *RCA* (GB) SER 5704/06 // *Valitut Palat* VPS 1041/48* // *RCA* (It) VL 42436 // *RCA* (G) RL 43077 EF // *K-West* KNEWLP 601*
	[CD]	*K-West* KNEWCD 601*
	[OR]	*RCA* (US) FTC 2039* // *RCA* (US) TR3-5035
	[MC]	*RCA* (G) RK 43077 CF // *RCA* (US) AGK1-4806 // *K-West* KNEWMC 601*

1957, September 1-7. Florence, Teatro Comunale. With orch. & (in 220 only) chorus of Maggio Musicale Fiorentino, cond. Alberto Erede. Producer: James Walker.

220

Cavalleria rusticana (Mascagni), sung in It. by Renata Tebaldi (Santuzza); Lucia Dani (Lola); Rina Corsi (Lucia); JB (Turiddu); Ettore Bastianini (Alfio).
[Orig. LP matrix: J2-RP-3022/24 (LM 6059), J2-RY 3026/28 (LSC 6059)]

Complete:

[33, 3 sides]	*Ace Diam.* (GB,Sp) GOS 634/35* = *Decca* (G) 6.35317 DX* = *London* (J) SLA 7004/05*, (US) OSA 12101* = *RCA* (Au) LB 16157, (G) LM

	6059/1-2, LSC 6059/1-2*, (GB) RB 16081/82, SB 2021/22*, (J) SHP 2010/11*, (SA) B 30194, (US) [1]LM 6059, LSC 6059*
[33, 4 sides?]	*RCA* (Fr) [1]630.559/60, 640.521/22*
[CD]	*Decca* (GB) [1]425 985-2* = *London* (US) 425 985-2*
[OR]	*London* (US) K 490250*
[MC]	*London* (US) D 31250*

Excerpts:
a. O Lola; b1. Tu qui, Santuzza?... b2. Ah! lo vedi; c. Intanto, amici, qua...Viva il vino spumeggiante; d1. Compar Alfio... d2. Mamma!...Quel vino.

(a,b,cd)	[MC]	*Decca* 424 040-4*
(a,b1,c,d)	[33]	*RCA* (Fr) 630.503, (G) LM 2243-C, LSC 2243-B*, (SA) 30086, (US) [1]LM 2243, LSC 2243*
(b,c,d2)	[33]	*Decca* (GB) GRV 4* = *London* (Br) 0417823-1* = *Rich.* (US,Ca) [1]SR 33254*
	[CD]	*Decca* (GB) [1]421 316-2* = *London* (J) POCL 2449*
	[OR]	*London* (US) SRO 33254-A*
	[MC]	*Decca* (GB) [1]KGRC 4*, 421 316-4* = *London* (US) 414 085-4*
(b1,d2)	[33]	*Sel.Read.Dig.* (It) RDS 13D*
(b1)	[45]	*RCA* (G) ERA 6059-1
(b2)	[33]	*RCA* (US) [1]LM 6138, LSC 6138* // *RCA* (Fr) 430.367 (?) // *RCA* (It) LM 20039 // *RCA* (Au) LB 16348, SLB 16348*, (US) [1]LM 6097, LSC 6097* // *RCA* (GB) [1]RB 6543, SB 6543*
(c)	[45]	*RCA* (GB) [1]RCX 150, SRC 7027*
	[33]	*RCA* (Au) L 16305, (G) LM 2570-C, LSC 2570-B*, (GB) VICS 1740*, (J) SHP 2103*, (SA) 30209, (US) [1]LM 2570, LSC 2570* // *RCA* (G) KR 11014/1-2* (26.48016 DP*)
(d)	[33]	*Decca* (Au) SXLA 7515* = *London* (US) [1]OS 26207*
	[OR]	*London* (US) L 90184*
	[MC]	*London* (US) [1]M 31184*, 414 356-4*
	[8T]	*London* (US) M 69184*
(d2)	[33]	*RCA* (It) LM 20076 // *Classics* 50-5552*

221
Cielo e mar! [It] (Ponchielli: *La Gioconda*)
[Orig. LP matrix: part 1 of J2-RP-3025 (=LM); of J2-RY-3029 (=LSC)]

[45]	*RCA* (GB) [1]RCX 206, SRC 7042*
[33]	*Ace Diam.* (GB,Sp) GOS 634/35* = *Decca* (G) 6.35317 DX* = *London* (J) SLA 7004/05*, (US) OSA 12101* = *RCA* (Au) LB 16157, (G) LM 6059/1-2, LSC 6059/1-2*, (GB) RB 16081/82, SB 2021/22*, (J) SHP 2010/11*, (SA) B 30194, (US) [1]LM 6059, LSC 6059* // *RCA* (Au) L 16305, (G) LM 2570-C, LSC 2570-B*, (GB) VICS 1740*, (J) SHP 2103*, (SA) 30209, (US) [1]LM 2570, LSC 2570* // *RCA* (It) LMD 67002 // *Ace Diam.* (GB) GOSB 636/38* // *Decca* (GB) GRV 4* = *London* (Br) 0417823-1* = *Rich.* (US,Ca) [1]SR 33254* // *Decca* (G) 6.48138 DX*
[CD]	*Decca* (GB) [1]421 316-2* = *London* (J) POCL 2449* // *Decca* (GB) 433 066-2* //

Decca (GB) 436 463-2*

[OR] *RCA* (US) TR3-5005* // *London* (US) K 490250* // *London* (US) SRO 33254-A*

[MC] *London* (US) D 31250* // *Ace Diam.* (GB) K2C7* // *Decca* (GB) [1]KGRC 4*, 421 316-4* = *London* (US) 414 085-4* // *Decca* (GB) 433 066-4* // *Decca* (GB) 436 463-4*

[8T] *RCA* (US) R8S 5044*

222

Ch'ella mi creda [It] (Puccini: *La fanciulla del West*)

[Orig. LP matrix: part 2 of J2-RP-3025 (=LM); of J2-RY-3029 (=LSC)]

[45] *RCA* (It) ERA 50-151 (?) // *RCA* (It) [1]NC 0060, NSC 0060* // *RCA* (GB) [1]RCX 155, SRC 7031* // *RCA* (G) [1]ERA 9791, ESC 9791*

[33] *Ace Diam.* (GB,Sp) GOS 634/35* = *Decca* (G) 6.35317 DX* = *London* (J) SLA 7004/05*, (US) OSA 12101* = *RCA* (Au) LB 16157, (G) LM 6059/1-2, LSC 6059/1-2*, (G) RB 16081/82, SB 2021/22*, (J) SHP 2010/11*, (SA) B 30194, (US) [1]LM 6059, LSC 6059* // *RCA* (US) LSC 6052* // *RCA* (Au) L 16305, (G) LM 2570-C, LSC 2570-B*, (GB) VICS 1740*, (J) SHP 2103*, (SA) 30209, (US) [1]LM 2570, LSC 2570* // *RCA* (It) LRC 51-007 // *RCA* (It) LMD 67002 // *Ace Diam.* (GB) GOSC 666/68* // *Decca* (G) 6.35311 DX* // *Decca* (Au) DTS 533/34*, (GB) [1]DPA 533/34*, (It) OCSI 14/15* // *Decca* (GB) GRV 4* = *London* (Br) 0417823-1* = *Rich.* (US,Ca) [1]SR 33254* // *Sel.Read.Dig.* RDIS 212-1/8* // *Decca* (GB) [1]SPA 574*, 417 686-1*

[CD] *Decca* (GB) [1]417 686-2*, 433 636-2* = *London* (US) 417 686-2* // *Decca* (GB) [1]421 316-2* = *London* (J) POCL 2449* // *Decca* (GB) 433 069-2* // *Decca* (GB) 433 755-2*

[OR] *London* (US) K 490250* // *London* (US) SRO 33254-A*

[MC] *London* (US) D 31250* // *Decca* (Au) TC-DTS 533/34*, (GB) [1]KDPC 533/34* // *Decca* (GB) [1]KGRC 4*, 421 316-4* = *London* (US) 414 085-4* // *Decca* (GB) 410 217-4* // *Decca* (GB) [1]KCSP 574*, 417 686-4*, 433 636-4* // *Decca* (GB) 417 173-4* // *Decca* (GB) 433 069-4*

223

Amor ti vieta [It] (Giordano: *Fedora*)

[Orig. LP matrix: part 3 of J2-RP-3025 (=LM); of J2-RY-3029 (=LSC)]

[45] *RCA* (It) [1]NC 0061, NSC 0061* // *RCA* (GB) [1]RCX 155, SRC 7031*

[33] *Ace Diam.* (GB,Sp) GOS 634/35*, *Decca* (G) 6.35317 DX*, *London* (J) SLA 7004/05*, (US) OSA 12101*, *RCA* (Au) LB 16157, (G) LM 6059/1-2, LSC 6059/1-2*, (G) RB 16081/82, SB 2021/22*, (J) SHP 2010/11*, (SA) B 30194, (US) [1]LM 6059, LSC 6059* // *RCA* (Au) L 16225, (Fr) 630.537, 830.501, (G) LM 2372-C, (GB) RB 16198, (US,Sp) [1]LM 2372 // *RCA* (Au) L 16305, (G) LM 2570-C, LSC 2570-B*, (GB) VICS 1740*, (J) SHP 2103*, (SA) 30209, (US) [1]LM 2570, LSC 2570* // *RCA* (It) LRC 51-007 // *RCA* (It) LMD 67002 // *Read.Dig.* (Br) BMI 1966, BMIS 1966* = *Sel.Read.Dig.* [1]BMI 1/10 // *Decca* (GB) GRV 4* = *London* (Br) 0417823-1* = *Rich.* (US,Ca) [1]SR 33254* // *Sel.Read.Dig.* RDIS 212-1/8*

[CD] *Decca* (GB) [1]421 018-2* = *London* (US) 421 018-2* // *Decca* (GB) [1]421 316-2*

= *London* (J) POCL 2449* // *Decca* (GB) [1]421 869-2* = *London* (US) 421 869-2* // *Award* AWCD 29115* // *Decca* (GB) 433 064-2* // *Decca* (GB) 433 755-2* // *Decca* (GB) 436 300-2*

[OR] *London* (US) K 490250* // *London* (US) SRO 33254-A*

[MC] *London* (US) D 31250* // *Decca* (GB) [1]KGRC 4*, 421 316-4* = *London* (US) 414 085-4* // *Decca* (GB) 417 534-4* // *Decca* (GB) 421 018-4* // *Decca* (GB) 433 064-4* // *Decca* (GB) 436 300-4*

224
È la solita storia [It] (Cilea: *L'Arlesiana*)
[Orig. LP matrix: part 4 of J2-RP-3025 (=LM); of J2-RP-3029 (=LSC)]

[45] *RCA* (It) [1]NC 0061, NSC 0061* // *RCA* (GB) [1]RCX 155, SRC 7031*

[33] *Ace Diam.* (GB,Sp) GOS 634/35* = *Decca* (G) 6.35317 DX* = *London* (J) SLA 7004/05*, (US) OSA 12101* = *RCA* (Au) LB 16157, (G) LM 6059/1-2, LSC 6059/1-2*, (GB) RB 16081/82, SB 2021/22*, (J) SHP 2010/11*, (SA) B 30194, (US) [1]LM 6059, LSC 6059* // *RCA* (Au) L 16305, (G) LM 2570-C, LSC 2570-B*, (GB) VICS 1740*, (J) SHP 2103*, (SA) 30209, (US) [1]LM 2570, LSC 2570* // *RCA* (It) LRC 51-007 // *RCA* (It) LMD 67002 // *Melodiya* D 21793/94 (?) // *RCA* (G) KR 11014/1-2* (26.48016 DP*) // *Decca* (GB) GRV 4*, *London* (Br) 0417823-1* = *Rich.* (US,Ca) [1]SR 33254*

[CD] *Decca* (GB) [1]421 316-2* = *London* (J) POCL 2449* // *Decca* (GB) [1]421 869-2* = *London* (US) 421 869-2* // *Award* AWCD 29115* // *Decca* (GB) 433 069-2* // *Decca* (GB) 436 463-2*

[OR] *London* (US) K 490250* // *London* (US) SRO 33254-A*

[MC] *London* (US) D 31250* // *Decca* (GB) [1]KGRC 4*, 421 316-4* = *London* (US) 414 085-4* // *Decca* (GB) 417 534-4* // *Decca* (GB) 433 069-4* // *Decca* (GB) 436 463-4*

225
Di' tu se fedele [It] (Verdi: *Un ballo in maschera*)
[Orig. LP matrix: part 5 of J2-RP-3025 (=LM); of J2-RP-3029 (=LSC)]

[45] *RCA* (GB) [1]RCX 155, SRC 7031*

[33] *Ace Diam.* (GB,Sp) GOS 634/35* = *Decca* (G) 6.35317 DX* = *London* (J) SLA 7004/05*, (US) OSA 12101* = *RCA* (Au) LB 16157, (G) LM 6059/1-2, LSC 6059/1-2*, (GB) RB 16081/82, SB 2021/22*, (J) SHP 2010/11*, (SA) B 30194, (US) [1]LM 6059, LSC 6059* // *RCA* (Au) L 16305, (G) LM 2570-C, LSC 2570-B*, (GB) VICS 1740*, (J) SHP 2103*, (SA) 30209, (US) [1]LM 2570, LSC 2570* // *RCA* (It) LMD 67002 // *RCA* (Fr) 530.271 // *London* (US) OSA 1441* // *Decca* (GB) GRV 4* = *London* (Br) 0417823-1* = *Rich.* (US,Ca) [1]SR 33254*

[CD] *Decca* (GB) [1]421 316-2* = *London* (J) POCL 2449*

[OR] *RCA* (US) TR3-5042* // *London* (US) R 490219* // *London* (US) K 490250* // *London* (US) SRO 33254-A*

[MC] *London* (US) P 31219* // *London* (US) D 31250* // *Decca* (GB) [1]KGRC 4*, 421 316-4* = *London* (US) 414 085-4*

[8T] *RCA* (US) R8S 5053*

226
Tra voi, belle, brune e bionde [It] (Puccini: *Manon Lescaut*)
[Orig. LP matrix: part 6 of J2-RP-3025 (=LM); of J2-RP-3029 (=LSC)]

[45] *RCA* (It) [1]NC 0060, NSC 0060*
[33] *Ace Diam.* (GB,Sp) GOS 634/35* = *Decca* (G) 6.35317 DX* = *London* (J) SLA 7004/O5*, (US) OSA 12101* = *RCA* (Au) LB 16157, (G) LM 6059/1-2, LSC 6059/1-2*, (GB) RB 16081/82, SB 2021/22*, (J) SHP 2010/11*, (SA) B 30194, (US) [1]LM 6059, LSC 6059* // *RCA* (US) LSC 6052* // *RCA* (Au) L 16305, (G) LM 2570-C, LSC 2570-B*, (GB) VICS 1740*, (J) SHP 2103*, (SA) 30209, (US) [1]LM 2570, LSC 2570* // *RCA* (It) LRC 51-007 // *RCA* (It) LMD 67002 // *RCA* (G) KR 11014/1-2* (26.48016 DP*) // *Decca* (GB) GRV 4* = *London* (Br) 0417823-1* = *Rich.* (US,C) [1]SR 33254* // *Sel.Read.Dig.* RDIS 212-1/8*
[CD] *Decca* (GB) [1]421 316-2* = *London* (J) POCL 2449*
[OR] *London* (US) K 490250* // *London* SRO 33254-A*
[MC] *London* (US) D 31250* // *Decca* (GB) [1]KGRC 4*, 421 316-4* = *London* (US) 414 085-4*

1957, September 25. Stockholm, Europafilm Studio. With Royal Orch., cond. Nils Grevillius.

227
Tonerna [Sw] (Sjöberg)
6H2-RW-0085

[45] *RCA* (Sw) ERAS 87
[33] *RCA* (Au) L 16370, (Sw,US) [1]LM 9884 // *RCA* (GB) SER 5719, (Sw,Au) [1]LSC 9884 // *RCA* (J) RVC 7531/35
[CD] *Sw.Society* SCD 1010 // *Verona* 28030/31
[MC] *RCA* (Sw) RK 9884 // *Sw.Society* SSC 1010

228
Land, du välsignade [Sw] (Althén)
6H2-RW-0086

[45] *RCA* (Sw) ERAS 87
[33] *RCA* (Au) L 16370, (Sw,US) [1]LM 9884 // *RCA* (GB) SER 5719, (Sw,Au) [1]LSC 9884 // *RCA* (J) RVC 7531/35
[CD] *Sw.Society* SCD 1010 // *Verona* 28030/31
[MC] *RCA* (Sw) RK 9884 // *Sw.Society* SSC 1010

229
Sverige [Sw] (Stenhammar: *Ett folk*)
6H2-RW-0087

[45] *RCA* (Sw) ERAS 87
[33] *RCA* (Au) L 16370, (Sw,US) [1]LM 9884 // *RCA* (GB) SER 5719, (Sw,Au) [1]LSC

9884 // *RCA* (J) RVC 7531/35
[CD] *Sw.Society* SCD 1010 // *Verona* 28030/31
[MC] *RCA* (Sw) RK 9884 // *Sw.Society* SSC 1010

230
När jag för mig själv i mörka skogen går [Sw] (Peterson-Berger)
6H2-RW-0088 (part 1)

[45] *RCA* (Sw) ERAS 87
[33] *RCA* (Au) L 16370, (Sw,US) [1]LM 9884 // *RCA* (GB) SER 5719, (Sw,Au) [1]LSC 9884 // *RCA* (J) RVC 7531/35
[CD] *Sw.Society* SCD 1010
[MC] *RCA* (Sw) RK 9884 // *Sw.Society* SSC 1010

231
Bland skogens höga furustammar [Sw] (Peterson-Berger)
6H2-RW-0088 (part 2)

[45] *RCA* (Sw) ERAS 87
[33] *RCA* (Au) L 16370, (Sw,US) [1]LM 9884 // *RCA* (GB) SER 5719, (Sw,Au) [1]LSC 9884 // *RCA* (J) RVC 7531/35
[CD] *Sw.Society* SCD 1010 // *Verona* 28030/31
[MC] *RCA* (Sw) RK 9884 // *Sw.Society* SSC 1010

1959, February 8. Stockholm, Concert Hall, Large Auditorium. With Royal Orch., cond. Nils Grevillius. [Most songs recorded in stereo; see note]

232
Trollsjön [Sw] (Söderman)
KSAW-0120

[45] *RCA* (Sw) ERAS 113
[33] *RCA* (Au) L 16370, (Sw,US) [1]LM 9884
[CD] *Sw.Society* SCD 1010
[MC] *Sw.Society* SSC 1010

233
Die Ehre Gottes aus der Natur [Sw: Lovsång] (Beethoven)
KSAW-0121

[45] *RCA* (Sw) FRS 576
[33] *RCA* (Sw) VICS 1546
[CD] *Sw.Society* SCD 1010 // *Gala* GL 315
[MC] *Sw.Society* SSC 1010

234
Cantique de Noël [Sw: Julsång] (Adam)
KSAW-0122

[45] *RCA* (Sw) FRS 576
[33] *Vocal Rec.Coll.* VRCS 1962 // *RCA* (Sw) VICS 1546 // *Legendary* LR 136 // *Legendary* LR 138
[CD] *Sw.Society* SCD 1010 // *Bluebell* ABCD 3001 // *Gala* GL 315
[MC] *Bluebell* CELL 3001 // *Sw.Society* SSC 1010

235
Demanten på marssnön [Sw] (Sibelius)
KSAW-0123

[45] *RCA* (Sw) FRS 569
[33] (Au) L 16370, (Sw,US) [1]LM 9884 // *RCA* (GB) SER 5719, (Sw,Au) [1]LSC 9884 // *RCA* (J) RVC 7531/35*
[CD] *Sw.Society* SCD 1010* // *Gala* GL 315*
[MC] *RCA* (Sw) RK 9884* // *Sw.Society* SSC 1010*

236
Säv, säv, susa [Sw] (Sibelius)
KSAW-0124

[45] *RCA* (Sw) FRS 569
[33] *RCA* (Au) L 16370, (Sw,US) [1]LM 9884 // *RCA* (GB) SER 5719*, (Sw,Au) [1]LSC 9884* // *RCA* (J) RVC 7531/35*
[CD] *Sw.Society* SCD 1010* // *Gala* GL 315*
[MC] *RCA* (Sw) RK 9884* // *Sw.Society* SSC 1010*

237
Aftonstämning [Sw] (Körling)
KSAW-0125

[45] *RCA* (Sw) ERAS 113
[33] *RCA* (Au) L 16370, (Sw,US) [1]LM 9884 // *RCA* (GB) SER 5719*, (Sw,Au) [1]LSC 9884* // *RCA* (J) RVC 7531/35*
[CD] *Sw.Society* SCD 1010*
[MC] *RCA* (Sw) RK 9884* // *Sw.Society* SSC 1010*

238
Så tag mit hjerte [Dan] (Alfvén)
KSAW-0126

[45] *RCA* (Sw) ERAS 113
[33] *RCA* (Au) L 16370, (Sw,US) [1]LM 9884 // *RCA* (GB) SER 5719*, (Sw,Au) [1]LSC 9884* // *RCA* (J) RVC 7531/35*
[CD] *Sw.Society* SCD 1010*
[MC] *RCA* (Sw) RK 9884* // *Sw.Society* SSC 1010*

239
Jag längtar dig [Sw] (Alfvén)
KSAW-0127

[45] *RCA* (Sw) ERAS 113
[33] *RCA* (Au) L 16370, (Sw,US) [1]LM 9884 // *RCA* (GB) SER 5719*, (Sw,Au) [1]LSC 9884* // *RCA* (J) RVC 7531/35*
[CD] *Sw.Society* SCD 1010*
[MC] *RCA* (Sw) RK 9884* // *Sw.Society* SSC 1010*

1959, July 3,4,6-11. Rome, Opera House. With Rome Opera House Orch. & Chorus, cond. Erich Leinsdorf. Producer: Richard Mohr.

240
Turandot (Puccini), sung in It. by Birgit Nilsson (Turandot), Renata Tebaldi (Liù); Myriam Funari, Nelly Pucci, Anna di Stasio (Maids); JB (Calaf), Alessio de Paolis (Emperor), Piero de Palma (Pang), Tommaso Frascati (Pong), Adelio Zagonara (Prince of Persia); Mario Sereni (Ping), Leonardo Monreale (Mandarin); Giorgio Tozzi (Timur).
[RCA serial Nos.: 2-K2-RB-3329/33,-35/37; orig. LP matrix: K2-RP4225/30 (LM 6149), K2-RY-4231/36 (LSC 6149)]

Complete:

[33] *Melodiya* D 030 913/18*[?] = *Opus* 9112 1251/53* = *RCA* (Au) LC 16311, SLC 16311*, (Fr) 630.564/66, 640.660/62*, (G) LM 6149/1-3, LSC 6149/1-3*, 26.35116 EK*, (GB) RE 25020/22, SER 4520/22*, SER 5643/45*, (It) KVS 6114*, MCV 537*, VL 43537*, VLS 03970*, (J) SRA 2785/87*, (SA) C 30024, (US,Ca,Ch) [1]LM 6149, (US,Ar, Sp) LSC 6149*, (US) AGL3-3970*
[CD] *RCA* (G) RD 85932*, (US) [1]5932-2-RC*
[OR] *RCA* (US) FTC 8001*
[MC] [2 cassettes] *RCA* (It) RK 6149/1-2* // [3 cassettes] *RCA* (It) VK 43537*, VKS 03970*, (US) [1]ARK3-2537*, AGK3-3970*
[8T] *RCA* (It) R8S 6149/1-2*

Excerpts:
(Act 1) a. Popolo di Pekino!...Gira la cote; b1. Notte senza lumicino... b2. Non piangere, Liù... b3. Noi morrem... b4. Ah! per la ultima volta! [to end of act];
(Act 2) c1. In questa Reggia...No! no! Gli enigmi... c2. Nella cupa notte...Gelo che ti dà foco;
(Act 3) d1. Nessun dorma!... d2. Tu che guardi le stelle... d3. Eccolo il nome!; e1. Strappatelo il segreto!... e2. Tu che di gel...Ah! tu sei morta; f1. Principessa di morte!... f2. Questo, questo chiedevi [to end of opera].

(a,b,d,e2,f2) [33] *RCA* (G) [1]LM 9875-C, LSC 9875-B*
(b2-4,c,d1,e2,f) [33] *RCA* (GB) RB 16267, SB 2138*, (SA) 30170, (US) [1]LM 2539, LSC 2539*

	[OR]	*RCA* (US) FTC 2065*
(b2,b4,c2,d1,f)	[33]	*RCA* (G) [1]KD 9 (?), SKD 9* (?) // *RCA* (G) LSC 9964-B*
(b2,c1,e2)	[33]	*Sel.Read.Dig.* RDS 13D*
	[CD]	*Sel.Read.Dig.* RDCD 101*
(b2,c1)	[33]	*RCA* (GB) DPS 2004/1-2*, (US) [1]VCS 7061*
(b2,d1)	[45]	*RCA* (GB) [1]RCX 206, SRC 7042*
	[33]	*RCA* (Au) L 16305, (G) LM 2570-C, LSC 2570-B*, (GB) VICS 1740*, (J) SHP 2103*, (SA) 30209, (US) [1]LM 2570, LSC 2570* // *RCA* (G) KR 11014/1-2* (26.48016 DP*) // *RCA* (G) GL 85277*, (US) [1]AGM1-5277*
	[CD]	*RCA* (G) RD 85934*, GD 85277*, (US) [1]5934-2-RC*
	[MC]	*RCA* (G) GK 85277*, (US) [1]AGK1-5277*
(b2,e2)	[45]	*RCA* (It) [1]NC 0080, NSC 0080*
(b2-4)	[33]	*RCA* (G) GL 87799*
	[CD]	*RCA* (G) GD 87799*, (US) [1]7799-2-RG*
	[MC]	*RCA* (G) GK 87799*, (US) [1]7799-4-RG*
(b2)	[33]	*RCA* (It) LRC 51-007
(c1,d1)	[33]	*RCA* (G) LM 9872-C
(c1,e2)	[45]	*RCA* (G) ERA 6149
(c1)	[33]	*RCA* (It) LSC 20106* // *RCA* (It) TRL1-7011* // *RCA* (G) RL 42876 EF* // *RCA* (G,It) RL 85177*, (US) [1]CRM8-5177*
	[MC]	*RCA* (G) RK 42876 CF* // *RCA* (US) CRK8-5177*
(d1)	[45]	*RCA* (G) [1]ERA 9791, ESC 9791* // *RCA* (G) 447-9366
	[33]	*Melodiya* D 21793/94 (?) // *RCA* (It) LSC 20102* // *RCA* (G) VIP 2* (26.41213 AF*), (US,Au) [1]LSC 5003 // *RCA* (J) RVC 7531/35 // *RCA* (It) VL 42436 // *RCA* (G) BL 86587* // *K-West* KNEWLP 602*
	[CD]	*RCA* (G) BD 86587*, (US) [1]6587-2-RC* // RCA (GB) GD 89788* // *K-West* KNEWCD 602* // *RCA* (G) GD 60841*, (US) [1]60841-2-RG* // *RCA* (G) GD 60935*, (US) [1]09026-60935-2*
	[MC]	*RCA* (US) RK 1195* // *RCA* (G) BK 86587*, (US) [1]6587-4-RC* // *RCA* (G) GK 89788* // *K-West* KNEWMC 602* // *RCA* (G) GK 60841*, (US) [1]60841-4-RG* // *RCA* (G) GK 60935*, (US) [1]09026-60935-4*
	[8T]	*RCA* (US) R8S 1195*
	[VC]	*Virgin* VVD 546*
(e)	[45]	*RCA* (G) [1]ERA 9795, ESC 9795*
(e2)	[33]	*RCA* (It) LM 20076

1959, September 25-26 & October 11 [see note]. Rome, Opera House. With Rome Opera House Orch. & Chorus, cond. Gabriele Santini. Producer: Victor Olof.

241

Madama Butterfly (Puccini), sung in It. by Victoria de los Angeles (Butterfly), Silvia Bertona (Kate Pinkerton, Cousin), Nina de Courson (Aunt); Miriam Pirazzini (Suzuki), Vera Magrini (Mother); JB (Pinkerton), Piero de Palma (Goro), Paolo Caroli (Registrar); Mario Sereni (Sharpless), Arturo La Porta (Yamadori), Antonio Sacchetti (Commissioner);

Paolo Montarsolo (Bonze), Bonaldo Giaiotti (Yakuside).
[Orig. LP matrix: 2XBA 94/99 (ALP 1795/97), 2YBA 7/12 (ASD 373/75)]

Complete:

[33] *Angel* (Ar) LPC 12337/39, 5672/74*[?], 6877/79, (Br) 3CBX 322/24*, (Ch) SOA 539*, (J) AA 9603/05*[?], (US) CL 3604, SCL 3604* = *Cap.* (US) GCR 7232, SGCR 7232* = *CFP* (GB) CFPD 41 4446 3* = *Elec.* E 91076/78, STE 91076/78* = *HMV* (Au) OALP 1795/97, OASD 373/75*, (Fr) FALP 670/72, ASDF 177/79*, [1]ALP 1795/97, ASD 373/75*, SLS 5128*, (It) QALP 10293/95, ASDQ 5286/88*, (SA) ASDJ 373/75* = *Sera.* (J) EAC 30233/35*
[CD] *EMI* (GB) 7 63634 2* (CDMB 63634*)
[OR] *Angel* (US) ZC 3604*
[MC] *Angel* (US) 4X3S 3604* = *CFP* (GB) CFPD 41 4446 5* = *HMV* (GB) [1]TC-SLS 5128*

Excerpts:

(Act 1) a1. Dovunque al mondo... a2. Ed è bella la sposa?... Amore o grillo...Ancora un passo...Gran ventura; b1. Vieni, amor mio!... b2. Ieri son salita...O Kami!; c1. Che fai?... c2. Viene la sera... c3. Quest'obi pomposa... c4. Bimba dagli occhi [to end of act];
(Act 2) d1. Io so che alle sue pene... d2. Andate. Il tristo vero... d3. Addio, fiorito asil; e. Con onor muore [to end of opera].

(a,b,c2-4,d3,e) [33] *HMV* (Au) OALP 7521, OASD 7521*, (GB) [1]ALP 2060, ASD 609*, (NL) 5C 051-00243*, (NZ) MALP 2060, ASDM 609*
(a,b2,c3-4,d3,e)
[33] *Elec.* 1C 037-03071*
[MC] *Elec.* 1C 237-03071*
(a,c,d,e) [33] *HMV* (Fr) [1]2C 061-01502*, (NL) SXLPH 1510*
(a,c2-4,d3,e) [33] *HMV* (GB) [1]SXLP 30306* = *WRC* (Au) R 06662*
[MC] *HMV* (Au) TC-SMP 0046*, (GB) [1]TC-SXLP 30306* = *WRC* (Au) C 06662*
(a,c3-4,d3,e) [33] *Angel* (J) AA 8013*, (US) 35821, S 35821* = *Cap.* (US) [1]G 7233, SG 7233* = *HMV* (It) QALP 10321, ASDQ 5304* = *Sera.* (?)(J) EAC 30070*
[OR] *Angel* (US) [1]L 35821*, ZS 35821*
[MC] *Angel* (US) 4XS 35821*
[8T] *Angel* (US) 8XS 35821*
(a1,b2,c3-4,d2-3,e)
[33] *Elec.* [1]E 80789, SME (STE) 80789*
(Higlights, details not known)
[33] *HMV* (SA) [1]JALP 11, *Pl.Mus.* CVPM 130560*
(a1,d2-3) [33] *Odeon* (Sw) PMCS 308
(a) [33] *Elec.* 1C 049-30659*
[CD] *EMI* (G) 1 59909 2*
[MC] *Elec.* [1]1C 225-30659*, *EMI* (G) 1 59909 4*
(c2-4) [33] *Sel.Read.Dig.* 3C 147-52050/55*

(c3-4,e) [33] *Angel* (US) [1]BL 3683, SBL 3683*

(c4) [33] *Elec.* [1]SME 80994* = *Hör Zu* SHZE 184* // *Elec.* 1C 063-00372* // *CFP* (GB) CFP 41 4498 1* = *HMV* (Au) OASD 2382*, (GB) [1]ASD 2382*, (SA) ASDJ 2382*, (Sp) ASDL 977*, 1J 063-00372* = *WRC* (Au) R 04467* // *Elec.* 1C 187-30183/84*

[CD] *CFP* (GB) CD-CFP 9013* // *EMI* (GB) [1]CDZ 7 62520 2* = *HMV* (GB) 7 67630 2*

[MC] *CFP* (GB) CFP 41 4498 4* = *HMV* (GB) [1]TC-ASD 2382* = *WRC* (Au) C 04467* // *HMV* (GB) TC2-MOM 120 // *EMI* (GB) LZ 7 62520 4*

[8T] *HMV* (GB) 8X-ASD 2382*

(e) [33] *Sera.*(?)(J) EAC 40159* = *Sera.* (US) [1]S 60262* // *HMV* (Au) OALP 2274, OASD 2274*, (GB) [1]ALP 2274, ASD 2274*

[MC] *Sera.* (US) 4XG 60262*

1960, June 12,13,16,19 [see note]. Vienna, Sofiensaal. With Vienna Philharmonic Orch. & Chorus of Gesellschaft der Musikfreunde, cond. Fritz Reiner. Producer: Eric Smith.

242

Messa da Requiem (Verdi), sung in Lat. by Leontyne Price (sop.); Rosalind Elias (m.-sop.); JB (ten.); Giorgio Tozzi (bass).

[RCA serial Nos.: LFBP 8077/80 (mono), LFBY 8081/84 (stereo); orig. LP matrix: L2-RP-2518/21 (LD 6091), L2-RY-2522/25 (LDS 6091)]

Complete:

[33] *Ace Diam.* (GB,Sp) GOS 617/18* = *Decca* (Fr) 593.028*, (G) DK 11528/1-2*, 6.35137 DX*, 6.48169 DM*, (GB) DJB 2003* = *Franklin Mint* 13/14* = *London* (US) OSA 1294*, (US,Ca) JL 42004* = *Prestige Mus. Franklin* 13/14* = *RCA* (Fr) 630.597/98, 640.682/83*, (G) LM 6091/1-2, LSC 6091/1-2*, (GB) RE 25026/27, SER 4526/27*, (It) KVS 6011*, (J) SRA 3024/25*, (US,Ch) [1]LD 6091, (US) LDS 6091*

[CD] *Decca* (GB) [1]421 608-2* = *London* (J) 230E 1211/12*, (US) 421 608-2* // *Award* AWCD 28875*

[OR] *London* (US) K 90215* = *RCA* (US) [1]FTC 7001*

[MC] *Decca* (GB) KDJBC 2003* = *London* (US) [1]D 31215*, (US,Ca) JLS 42004* = *Franklin Mint* 13/14* = *Prestige Mus.Franklin* 13/14*

Excerpt: a. Ingemisco

(a) [33] *RCA* (Au) L 16305, (G) LM 2570-C, LSC 2570-B*, (GB) VICS 1740*, (J) SHP 2103*, (SA) 30209, (US) [1]LM 2570, LSC 2570* // *Decca* (GB) GRV 4* = *London* (Br) 0417823-1* = *Rich.* (US,Ca) [1]SR 33254*

[CD] *Decca* (GB) [1]421 316-2* = *London* (J) POCL 2449*

[OR] *London* (US) SRO 33254-A*
[MC] *Decca* (GB) [1]KGRC 4*, 421 316-4* = *London* (US) 414 085-4*

1960, June [around 16-19]. Vienna, Sofiensaal. With orch. [see note].

243
Dein ist mein ganzes Herz [Sw,Ger] (Lehár: *Das Land des Lächelns*)
[Orig. LP matrix: part 1 of ARL 4927-2D (MET 202); of ZAL 4927-5W (SET 202)]

[33] *Decca* (G) LXT 2023/25-C, SXL 20023/25-B*, SMA 25051-D/1-3*, 6.35107 EK*, (GB) [1]MET 201/03, SET 201/03*, D247D 3* = *Eterna* 8 25 517/19* = *London* (J) SLC 7028/30*, (US) A 4347, OSA 1319* = *Marcato* 73667* // *Eterna* [1]8 20 534 = *Marcato* LPD 011556-7* // *Decca* (GB) GRV 4* = *London* (Br) 0417823-1* = [1]*Rich.* SR 33254* // *Decca* (GB) 414 466-1*
[CD] *Decca* (GB) [1]421 046-2* = *London* (J) POCL 2278/79*, (US) 421 046-2* // *Decca* (GB) [1]421 316-2* = *London* (J) POCL 2449* // *Decca* (GB) 421 319-2*
[OR] *London* (US) R 90030* // *London* (US) SRO 33254-A*
[MC] *Decca* (G) [1]4.35107 MH*, (GB) K247K 32* // *London* (US) OSA5 1319* // *Decca* (GB) [1]KGRC 4*, 421 316-4* = *London* (US) 414 085-4* // *Decca* (GB) 414 466-4*

1960, July 10 (?). Rome, Accademia di Santa Cecilia. With Orch. of the Accademia di Santa Cecilia, cond. Georg Solti. Producer: John Culshaw.

244
Un ballo in maschera (Verdi) [Complete recording begun but cancelled; for details, see note]

Photo: Daniels/Röster i Radio

Jussi Björling at the radio concert on January 31, 1942 (No. ***4201****)*

Notes for Section 1:A

Nos. 1-6

The dates and places for the recordings made by David Björling's three eldest sons during their American tour with their father in 1919-21 cannot be established with certainty, as the original files of the Columbia "foreign" matrix series after 1916 seem to be lost (see P. Gronow, *Studies in Scandinavian-American Discography 2*, Helsinki 1977). However, the contemporary Swedish-American newspapers provide information about the Björling quartet's touring schedule and the release dates for the records which can be used for an approximate dating of the recordings. Under all circumstances, the recordings cannot have been made before October 28, 1919, when the family arrived in New York from Sweden (via Norway) and not later than April 1920, as the first record (E 4547) was advertised for the first time in the press on May 18.

Before more detailed conclusions about the recording dates can be drawn (matrix numbers suggest that there were two sessions with one or more days between), the possible recording places will have to be discussed. According to information from the Columbia Records Inc., quoted in JBRL (p. 67), "...at this time recording, save for 'folk' or 'race' recording, was done either at Bridgeport or in New York". There is no evidence that the quartet ever visited Bridgeport; but they spent a large part of the relevant period in New York. So, it seems very probable that the recordings were made there. However, this was contradicted by the only person known to have supplied first-hand information on the question, Mrs. Magnhild Lundquist-Palmgren (in 1920 still Miss Lundquist), who was the accompanist of the quartet at the beginning of 1920. In her contribution to *Jussi Björling: En minnesbok* (pp. 49-51), she states that she had accompanied the Björling family for three months (beginning with their two-week New England tour in January-February; her participation in that tour is confirmed by newspaper reports). In passing, referring to one of the records (probably E 4547), she remarked that "it was ... in the town of Providence that the record was made...". Providence was also mentioned by her as the recording place in a newspaper interview after the "Karusellen" programme on January 26, 1952 [cf. No. 5201].

The Björlings are known to have given two recitals in Providence, R.I., on January 24 and 25, 1920, with Miss Lundquist as their accompanist, and the family may have stayed in the town until they had to go to Pawtucket for their next recital on the 28. Miss Lundquist's remark probably refers to this visit. As the Columbia company did not make any regular recordings in Providence, and as they would hardly have sent people and heavy equipment there only to record a group which had just been in New York and could easily return to that city, it must be assumed that Mrs. Lundquist-Palmgren's memory about the recording place was wrong. Such an error may perhaps be more easily explained if the recordings had not yet been made when the New England tour began, but were prepared during the stay in Providence.

If the recordings were made in New York, which dates could then be possible? It seems unlikely that any recordings were made before the Björling quartet had made their first American public appearance at the Gustavus Adolphus Church on November 20. The family stayed in New York at least until December 27, when they gave a farewell recital before the tour through New England and the Western states began. They must have left the city before January 22, 1920, when the first recital outside New York was given at

Brockton, Mass. However, David Björling would soon be back in New York for a few days, as is confirmed by the following notice in the newspaper "Nordstjernan" for February 10: "Last Friday, the opera singer David Björling returned to New York for a short stay after a recital tour in the New England states, where he has given eleven different recitals in Swedish churches... Yesterday, Mr. Björling left for Jamestown, where recitals are already arranged. Later, the tour will go on to Chicago and possibly to the West Coast." Thus, some urgent business had caused David Björling to break off his tour and to return to New York for the weekend, arriving on the 6 and leaving again on the 9. Provided that Mrs. Lundquist-Palmgren was wrong about the recording place, it is possible that the recordings were a reason for the visit, especially as this may have been the last chance for making them in New York. The Björlings probably stayed in Jamestown until they went to Chicago (the last Jamestown recital took place on February 26 and they were already in Chicago on March 4). After the last Chicago recital on March 28, they continued westward. If the recordings were made at the beginning of February, JB was then almost exactly nine years old.

This discussion may be summed up as follows. The recordings were almost certainly made in New York. The most probable and latest possible period for the recordings is between February 6-9, 1920, but the possibility that they were made before January 22 cannot be excluded. There can only be guesses regarding the identity of the accompanists on the recordings. Mrs. Lundquist-Palmgren, as far as is known, did not actually state that she was present. It is difficult to see any reason for her to withhold such a fact in the "Minnesbok", and if she was wrong about the recording place, the possibility that she took part in the recordings seems even smaller. The names of two other accompanists of the quartet during this period are found in the reviews: professors O.T. Westlin (New York) and Samuel Thorstenberg (Jamestown). S. Stroff (*Guldstrupen*, 1981) stated that David Björling himself was the accompanist at the organ and the piano, but there is no evidence for this (the father regularly contributed to the recitals with solo singing).

The four copies of E 4547 inspected for this work have the matrix number 85799 completed by the following sequences impressed in the shellac: 1-28 (copy used for SR reissue), 1-C-5, 2-A-2 (two copies). As the first numeral indicates the take (the letter stands for the mother matrix from which stampers are processed, and the second numeral for the stamper used to press the copy), this should mean that two different takes of No. 5 (Barndomshemmet) were issued. However, it has been impossible to distinguish the two records from each other, so one and the same take seems to have been issued under different numbers. This may not be unique; in a work dealing with a later Columbia series (D. Mahony, *The Columbia 13/14000-D Series*, 2nd ed., Highland Park, N.J., 1969), W.C. Allen remarked that "in a few known cases, these early takes must be treated with caution, since copies with ostensibly different take numerals have turned out to be aurally identical". There seems to be no evidence that also Take 2 of 85800 was issued on E 4768, as was stated by Gronow (*Studies in Scandinavian-American Discography* 2, 1977).

Nos. 7-8
According to the recording ledgers, the matrices for these recordings were destroyed in March 1930.

Nos. 9-12
The orchestra was composed of 11 instruments: 3 1st vl, 2nd vl, vc, db, 2 cl, harp, pf, cel.

Nos 13-14
The orchestra was composed of 8 instruments: 3 1st vl, 2nd vl, va, vc, db, pf.

Nos. 15-19
The orchestra was composed of 18 instruments in Nos. 15 and 18-19: 2 1st vn, 2 2nd vn, 2 va, vc, db, fl, 2 cl, ob, 2 tpt, 2 ten trbn, tuba, harp; of 17 instruments in No. 16 (harp missing); of 13 instruments in No. 17 (brass missing).

Nos. 20-22
The orchestra was composed of 7 instruments: 2 1st vn, 2nd vn, va, vc, db, pf.

Nos. 23-25
The orchestra was composed of 7 instruments: 1st vn, 2 2nd vn, va, vc, db, pf.

Nos. 26-28
The original labels do not name the conductor (this was true also of several other early JB recordings). JBRL stated Grevillius as conductor instead of Bingang, and this error was repeated on LP issues and in discographies (including JBD). The recording date February 13 is taken from the Swedish recording ledgers. However, Bingang in his appointment-book indicated February 10 as the date when he was paid for the recordings. (A copy of Bingang's carefully kept appointment-book is preserved at Svenskt Visarkiv [The Swedish Centre for Folk Song and Folk Music Research (Jazz Department)], Stockholm; information from that book was obtained through B. Englund, ALB.) In almost all cases where Bingang's payment dates for his recordings can be compared to the corresponding recording dates in the ledgers of HMV and other recording companies, they prove identical, and Bingang's dates have therefore been used for some later recordings in this list where other information is lacking or doubtful [see note for Nos. 40-62]. Though it can be proved that the recording dates in the Swedish HMV ledgers are not always correct, the fact that the ledgers list different recordings for each of the days February 9 to February 13 makes it difficult to accept Bingang's date for Nos. 26-28. The conductor (who was also paid for the arrangements of Nos. 27 and 28 on February 6 and of No. 26 on February 9) may for instance have received an occasional payment in advance.

Nos. 29-30, 32-35, 37-38
The orchestra was composed of 5 instruments: 2 1st vn, vc, db, pf.

Nos. 40-62 (recording dates)
Neither the Swedish HMV recording ledgers, nor any documents found in the British EMI archive, nor the information cards for the Scandinavian X series (preserved at Nationaldiskoteket, Copenhagen, and examined by K. Liliedahl) give any exact dates for these recordings; only the months are noted in the ledgers. Nos. 40-43 and 48 are dated in Hanns Bingang's appointment-book [see note for Nos. 26-28], which is also referred to in a few other cases [see respective notes]. It has not been possible to find the sources for the exact dates which are given without reservation for all these recordings in JBRL. The fact that H. Rosenberg (one of the JBRL authors) stated that all his dates were taken from the Swedish HMV ledgers (Liliedahl, personal communication), makes the case still more dubious.

As long as the origin of the JBRL dates, which often differ from Bingang's, remains unexplained, these dates cannot generally be regarded as reliable. For the recordings in question which were not dated by Bingang, the JBRL dates are added in this list, in brackets, after the month, but only when the dating problems are not discussed further in the respective notes.

Nos. 40-48 (recording premises)
It is possible that the Odeon studio at Fenixpalatset, Stockholm (situated in Adolf Fredriks kyrkogata) was used for all Swedish HMV recordings from May up to December 1932. The ledgers indicate this studio for the first time in May. The recordings during the rest of 1932 were variously labeled as recorded either in the Odeon studio or just in Stockholm, but this may have been quite accidental, and there is no indication that any other studio was used during the period. However, No. 47 is the only of these recordings for which the ledgers actually confirm the recording premises.

Nos. 40-44
JBRL gives one date, August 10, for all these recordings. All Bingang's recordings on August 8 were cancelled on August 27 because of a defective machine. Nos. 40 and 41 were originally intended for X 3993. It seems probable that No. 44, which is not in Bingang's appointment-book, was recorded on the same day as No. 43. It cannot have been recorded later than September 2, when Bingang was paid for 0PA 33.

Nos. 45-46
The recording date September 9, which was given in JBRL, may be taken from the Danish recording ledgers. The fact that Bingang was paid for the orchestral arrangement of No. 46 on September 7 seems to confirm the given recording date.

No. 47
October 1 is the date given in JBRL.

Nos. 49-74 (recording premises)
The assumption that these recordings took place in the Attic Auditorium (Attiksalen) of the Concert Hall is founded primarily on the fact that the Skandinaviska Grammophon AB paid a lump sum for the right to use the auditorium during 1933. No dates are therefore given in the accounts. It should be noted that in his autobiography, JB named only the Concert Hall as premises for his early recordings. This indicates that the Odeon studio was not used for any longer period.

No. 49
Though the ledgers list this recording for January, it seems probable that the JBRL date February 2 is correct. According to Bingang, he was paid for 0PA 95 and 96 on that date, so 0PA 97 should not have been recorded earlier.

Nos. 50-53
The Swedish ledgers show that these recordings were probably made in March. The British ledgers give March 21 for 0PA 122-24 and April for 0PA 125-26 while JBRL has March 21 for all the recordings. However, Nos. 50-51 were probably not recorded later than on the 12. This is Bingang's date for 0PA 124, which was not a JB recording. For Nos. 52 and 53, the recording ledgers state (transl.): "This number was reported to Hayes as being

cancelled". X 4121 was pressed, at least in a small quantity. A "normal" copy (not a test pressing) exists in a private Swedish collection (L.-G. Frisk) and was used for the Bluebell issue.

No. 54
The recording ledgers have the note (transl.): "1 not good, 2 damaged 25.4.33".

No. 56
The contents of this recording are not given in the ledgers, and it may even be doubtful whether the original intention was to list it as a JB recording.

Nos. 60-62
These songs were winners of an all-Scandinavian competition for "the best summer tune" of each country.

No. 61
The two copies checked (one of them was used for the Bluebell reissue) have Take 2, which was marked "Best" in the recording ledgers, and also seems to be identical with the reissue on Rococo. JBRL shows Take 1 as issued, but this is most probably an error.

No. 70
The playing time for Take 1 is 3'07"; for Take 2, 3'00".

Nos. 79 & 80
These two songs were recorded on the occasion of the marriage of Princess Ingrid of Sweden to Crown Prince Frederik of Denmark on May 24, 1935.

No. 81
A test pressing of 0SB 402-1 is preserved in a private Swedish collection (H. Löwing).

Nos. 84-86
The date is given in JBRL but recording ledgers give October 7 for these recordings, too. As Nos. 81-86 were not recorded in succession, and the total number of recordings listed in the ledgers under October 7 is unusually large, the JBRL date is probably correct.

Nos. 87-90
The recording dates are given in the British HMV recording book and confirmed by the Concert Hall accounts. The Swedish recording ledgers give the date as December 4. According to a Swedish HMV supplement, JB's first recordings for the Red Label series were accompanied by an orchestra of 45 musicians, but according to a document from Hayes, the orchestra consisted of 42 instruments: 8 1st vn, 6 2nd vn, 3 va, 3 vc, 3 db, 2 fl, 2 ob, 2 cl, 2 bn, 4 hn, 2 tpt, 3 ten trbn, 1 timp, 1 harp.

Nos. 95-102
The Royal Orch. is given in JBRL, but neither the record labels nor the recording ledgers name the orchestra.

No. 95
A test pressing of 2SB 570-1 is preserved in an American collection.

No. 102X
In connection with JB's London debut Nov. 16, 1937 at Queen's Hall, the HMV company suggested to him to make recordings in London, which would have become his first as a tenor outside Scandinavia. According to a letter to JB from the HMV International Artistes' Department, dated Nov. 16, the company had "to-morrow ... reserved a studio at No. 3 Abbey Road to do a title with piano to couple with the one English song ... already recorded, 'For You Alone'". The song "My Dreams" (Tosti) was suggested for the recording and Ivor Newton had been engaged as accompanist. (The intention must have been to record also "For You Alone" again since JB's existing recording of that song was done with orchestra.) The company had further "reserved the Kingsway Hall for recording the following titles ... on Thursday afternoon [the 18] at 2.30: 'Ave Maria' (Percy Kahn); 'Ingemisco' - *Requiem* (Verdi); 'Una furtiva lagrima' - *Elisir d'amore* (if time permits)". The orchestrations for this session had been prepared. However, a letter of Nov. 19 from the same department to Skandinaviska Grammophon AB reports that both sessions had been cancelled: "Owing to a cold, Bjorling was unfortunately unable to record any titles for us and he leaves to-day for the United States". The company certainly regretted this, for in the letter to JB they had stressed: "We are very eager for you to record in London, so that we can compare the results with our work in Stockholm."

There were references to these cancelled recording sessions also in the Swedish press, though with discrepancies about details. A London report dated Nov. 16 states that before JB leaves Britain for the US (on the 19), he will "make two more records with piano accompaniment for HMV, including the two Sibelius songs which he performed this evening" [this refers to "Var det en dröm" and "Svarta rosor"]. After an interview on the 18, another journalist writes that "JB spent the afternoon in the HMV recording studio". This seems to confirm that the same morning, the singer still hoped to make the Kingsway Hall recordings as planned.

The belief that JB had actually made recordings in London in November 1937, must be the explanation for an error in the HMV advertisement in the December 1938 issue of *The Gramophone*, where it was stated regarding DB 3603 that JB "crossed from Sweden to make these superb recordings ... en route for the USA".

Before leaving the subject of early JB recordings in London, a statement in B. Hagman's biographical chapter in *Jussi Björling: En minnesbok* should be quoted: "In March [1937], he visits London for the first time but does not appear in public; however, he makes a record (arias from *La fanciulla del West* and *Tosca*)". The author can no longer identify the source of this information, and no other proof for such recordings or recording plans has been found. There is no mention of them in the British HMV correspondence. It might be added that JB spent most of March 1937 in Vienna. His last performance there took place on the 22 and he returned to Sweden on the 26.

Nos. 103-05 (orchestra)
The orchestra was composed of 13 instruments: 2 1st vn, 2 2nd vn, 2 va, db, fl, 2 cl, ten trb, drums, harp.

Nos. 103 & 105-07

Swedish recording ledgers list all five takes of 0SB 741 and all four takes of 0SB 743 for April 28. On the Hayes recording sheets for this date, only two takes are listed for each recording, and no entrance for the later takes has been found. However, the British information cards for 0SB 741 and 0SB 743 state that the issued takes (0SB 741-5 and 0SB 743-4) were recorded on May 30. It must therefore be assumed that, for some reason, two of the recordings from April 28 were repeated at the next session, though this was not noted in the ledgers. This is strongly supported by the otherwise unusually large number of takes made at the one and same session, and by the fact that the session of May 30 contains only one other recording. According to the Hayes recording book, a transfer of 0SB 741-1, made on May 26 (to pass the wear test) was also numbered 0SB 741-3.

Test pressings of 0SB 741-4 and 0SB 743-3 are preserved in the JB family collection and were used for the Bluebell issue.

Nos. 104 & 108

Both a Swedish and a British pressing of X 6235 with matrix numbers 0SB 742-1TS and 0SB 753-1TS have been found. As there seems to be no audible difference between Takes 2 and 1TS (= first transcription from the matrix), the transcriptions were probably made from Take 2 of each song. The reissue on *Unique* UORC 377 used 0SB 742-1TS; that on *ANNA* 1006 used 0SB 753-1TS.

No. 110

The original label adds the first line of the text as "I en skog...", but the indicated form of the word was sung.

A test pressing of Take 2 is preserved in the JB family collection and was used for the Bluebell issue.

Nos. 112-17

The recording ledgers indicate "Grevillius & his orch.".

No. 113

JBRL incorrectly listed Take 2 as issued and included under this date a number of issues which should be listed under No. 169.

No. 114

Take 3 is a transfer of Take 2; two such transfers were made at Hayes, one on November 9, 1938 (because the master shells were damaged in the factory) and the other on March 6, 1939 ("to replace shell destroyed in accordance with R.T.C. Minute No. 3425"). Differences between the two takes are subtle but clear. The playing time of Take 1 = 4'03", of Take 3 = 4'11". The musical clue is the high D-flat at the end: in Take 1 the attack is cautious and the note is constricted and tentatively held; in Take 3 the attack is secure, the note is open and is held seemingly without effort.

Nos. 116 & 117

The following remark is written in the Swedish recording ledgers (transl.): "Cancelled, will be repeated according to letter of Nov. 18, 1938". 0SB 825-3 and 0SB 826-1, respectively, were marked "Best". The Swedish ledgers list 0SB 825-3 both for this session and for the repeat of July 15, but the Hayes recording book for July 15 only mentions 0SB 825-4 and -5.

Test pressings of 0SB 825-2 and -3 and 826-1 are preserved in the JB family collection; tape copies in ALB, Stockholm. Two of them were used for the Bluebell issue.

Nos. 118-24 (dates)
At the top of the page, the Swedish recording ledgers give the dates July 14 and 15 for all of these recordings. The exact dates are given by the Hayes recording book.

Nos. 118 & 119
The orchestra was composed of 43 instruments: 8 1st vn, 8 2nd vn, 6 va, 4 vc, 4 db, 3 cl, 2 ob, 1 eng hn, 2 hn, 1 tpt, 2 ten trbn, 1 timp, drums.

The recording ledgers have the following remarks about 2SB 983-3 (transl.): "Bad, not approved by Mr. Björling", and about 2SB 984-3: "Not very good, but approved by Mr. Björling".

Nos. 120 & 121 (orchestra)
The orchestra was composed of 45 instruments: 8 1st vn, 8 2nd vn, 6 va, 4 vc, 4 db, 3 cl, 2 ob, 1 eng hn, 2 hn, 1 tpt, 2 ten trbn, 1 sax, 1 harp, 2 drums.

No. 121
For earlier takes, see No. 117. The Hayes recording book shows that a transfer of 0SB 826-1, made on Nov. 9, 1938 (because the master shell was damaged in the factory), was also numbered 0SB 826-3. In the Swedish recording ledgers, Takes 3 and 4 are marked "Good, for transfer" and the Hayes recording book confirms that 0EA 8086-1 and -2 were transferred on Aug. 15, 1939, "to combine records 0SB 826-4 and 0SB 826-3". (HMV had been able to undertake such combination transfers at least as early as 1927, and there is nothing to support the assumption made by J.W. Porter in JBD (p. 186) that 0EA 8086-1 did not actually combine two takes.)

Nos. 125-36
In Harry Ebert's contribution to *Jussi Björling: En minnesbok*, he gives a detailed description of his tour with JB from Europe to the US in October 1940. According to Ebert, they spent two days in New York before going to San Francisco. On the second of these days, which was probably October 10, Ebert claims they made the recordings which included "Adelaide", "Morgen" (Strauss) and "Morgon" (Eklöf). The RCA company does not know of any JB recordings in October, 1940, so it must be assumed that Ebert misdated these recordings and also confused them with the Swedish recordings in July 1939. JB's contract with Victor of January, 1940, comprised 12 selections only, a number which corresponds exactly to Nos. 125-36.

Nos. 137-40
For these recordings, 44 musicians were used during 4 hours, 5 musicians during 2 hours (according to recording invoices from Stockholm to Hayes).

"Grevillius & his orch." is indicated in the Swedish recording ledgers for Nos. 137 and 138. According to the ledgers and the label for the test pressing mentioned below, these recordings were planned to be issued as DA 2000, but the discography of the DA series in *Voices of the Past, vol. 6* gives the number DA 1818 instead. DA 2000 was actually used for a record issued in 1952 where Beniamino Gigli sang "Torna a Surriento" and "Addio a Napoli".

A test pressing of 0SB 2032-3 and 0SB 2033-3 (the latter an otherwise unknown take number) is preserved in a private Swedish collection (G. Söderwall). On the label, the unexplained date "5/9" (=Sept. 5, 1941?) is written. 0SB 2033-3 seems to be identical with the take issued on RLS 715.

The two takes of No. 140 are easily distinguished by listening to the last bars: the orchestra continues for less than a second longer than the singers in Take 1, but for a few seconds in Take 2.

Nos. 141-48 (dates)
According to the recording ledgers, all these recordings were made on the 27. The cards for the matrices at Hayes do not specify the dates. However, the recording bill from the Skandinaviska Grammophon AB to Hayes shows that the four days indicated were used for the recordings (altogether 8 hours with 39 musicians and 2 hours with 30 musicians).

Nos. 141-42
A test pressing of 0SB 2397-1 and 0SB 2398-1 is preserved in a private Swedish collection (G. Söderwall).

No. 147
The two takes are easily distinguished: the line "Ma prima voglio / che mi benedite" is sung as two phrases in Take 1, as one phrase in Take 2. In Take 1, the orchestra's last note is heard after the singer, while they stop almost simultaneously in Take 2. These two takes are distinguished from No. 170 by the pronunciation of the word "certo" in "...e certo oggi": "shairto" in No. 147, "chairto" in No. 170.

No. 148
A test pressing of 0SB 2404-1 is preserved in a private Swedish collection (L.-G. Frisk).

Nos. 151-54
At the top of the page, the Swedish recording ledgers give the dates September 6 and 7 for all these recordings. The indicated distribution of the recordings on the two dates is taken from JBRL. (It may well be based on information from Hayes. All British documents concerning these four recordings have not been checked for the present work.) The Royal Orch. is named in the Swedish ledgers only, not on the record labels. According to the recording invoice, 44 musicians were used.
A test pressing of 2SB 2535-1 is preserved in the JB family collection and was used for the issue on Bluebell.

Nos. 153 & 158
There must have been some misunderstanding between the Swedish and British HMV companies regarding the "Una furtiva lagrima" recording. All inspected copies of DB 6714 con-

tain 2SB 2537-2 (in spite of the fact that JBRL listed only Take 3 as issued), and have the Stockholm Concert Association Orch. printed on the label. However, according to the Swedish ledgers, this orchestra accompanied only Take 3, the repeat in 1947. The card for 2SB 2537 at Hayes lists the Concert Association Orch. for all takes, and gives recording dates different from those in the Swedish ledgers: Nov. 27, 1947, for Takes 1 and 2, and Dec. 18, 1947, for Take 3 (the latter date is also given for 0SB 2880-82). To add to the confusion, a handwritten note on the Swedish copy of the recording bill seems to indicate Nov. 5, 1947, as the recording date for 0SB 2880-82 and 2SB 2537. In another note of the same origin, the matrix for "Una furtiva lagrima" is described as having been kept in Sweden for two years, until the date just mentioned.

It is evident that 2SB 2537 was not sent to Hayes in 1945 (because a third take was decided upon, but could not be realized then?). Take 2 was noted to have been received at Hayes on Nov. 21, 1947 (thus before the recording date noted on the same card!). For some reason or other, the recording date for Take 3 in the Hayes files was given as the date for the two earlier takes; the date Dec. 18 remains unexplained. In any case, Dec. 18 is not a possible recording date, as JB was then in New York, and Nov. 5 is a most unlikely one, as he was suffering from lumbago at the time. According to a note on the Hayes card, Take 3, which seems to have been received at Hayes on Jan. 26, 1948, was "broken in transit, no good" and thus cannot have been issued.

Nos. 159-62

The Royal Orch. is named in the Swedish recording ledgers only, not on the original record labels.

Test pressings of 0SB 2926-1, 0SB 2927-1, 0SB 2936-1 and 0SB 2937-2 are preserved in the JB family collection and were used for the Bluebell issue.

Nos. 163 & 164

These recordings were originally not approved for issue by JB. A test pressing of 2SB 3069-2 is preserved in the JB family collection and was used for the Bluebell issue.

Nos. 165 & 166

The orchestral arrangements of these songs were made by Stig Rybrant.

A test pressing of 0SB 3072-1 was offered for auction in New York in 1970 (according to D. Hamilton in *ARSC Journal* XIV/4, pp. 98-99).

Nos. 167-70

The recording ledgers include a note "For RCA Victor" for these recordings. This means that Swedish HMV regarded them (contrary to Nos. 163-66) as made under the two-year contract with RCA Victor which JB signed at the beginning of 1949. The take numbers for 2SB 3318 and 3319 come from RCA record sheets, but their meaning is not clear. No information about take numbers is found in the Swedish ledgers or in documents from Hayes. It is also unclear whether the recordings were originally made on tape or not (if they were, this was the first time the new technique was used for JB recordings). A letter from Hayes to the Swedish company, dated July 25, 1950, refers to "a list of the repertoire which they (=RCA Victor) require re-recorded by Björling, provided that it can be done on tape", and adds "I understand ... that you are now able to record on tape". However, in a letter from Swedish HMV regarding these recordings, it is stated that the matrices were sent to England for transfer to tape. It is possible that at this time, both recording methods were used simultaneously.

The matrix numbers 0SB 3316 and 3317, in sequence between these sessions, were not used for JB recordings.

Test pressings of 0SB 3314-2 and 3315-2 are preserved in a private Swedish collection (T. Franzén).

Nos. 171-75
From now on, probably all recordings in Section 1:A were made on tape (this may also be valid for the preceding four numbers; see the respective note). Therefore, the take numbers in the recording ledgers do not tell how many times a recording had to be repeated, as was the case before. In a Swedish radio interview [No. 5103], JB discussed his duet recordings with Merrill and stated that the singers had to repeat No. 171 two or three times, No. 172 three times and No. 175 twice.

The orchestra which accompanied Nos. 172-75 consisted of 58 instruments: 16 vn, 6 va, 6 vc, 3 db, 3 fl, 2 ob, 2 cl, 1 bass cl, 4 bn, 4 hn, 1 tuba, 4 tpt, 3 trbn, 1 timp, 1 perc, 1 harp.

According to RCA archive sheets, E1-RC-2104-1R, a combination of both preserved takes of No. 172, was used for WDM 7007, LM 6061 and probably other microgroove issues. However, comparison with a test pressing of Take 2 in the JB family collection [tape copy in ALB, Stockholm], indicates that Take 2 was used for most microgroove issues. One of the differences between Take 1 on DB 21426 and the other issued take is the way Iago's phrase "...lo vidi in man di Cassio" is sung; the attack on "Cassio" is more forceful in Take 1, and on the following words "Ah! Mille vite...", the pitch of the performance seems to rise. It has not been possible to examine all issues, and the indicated distribution between the two takes must be regarded as preliminary.

No. 181
Take 1 appears on DB 21602, while RCA archive sheets mention Take 2 as being used for microgroove issues. However, there seems to be no audible difference between the versions.

No. 182
According to RCA recording pages, there was also a session on February 21, at which JB was not present.

Nos. 183 & 184
These songs were assigned different serial numbers (as indicated in the list), but appeared on the same side of DB 21620 with the same matrix number (E2-RC-0776-1A).

Nos. 199-202
These recordings were made on tape. The recording sheet proves that they were recorded on Nov. 21, not the 24 as has earlier been reported, and that the missing matrix numbers 0EA 16910/13 were not used for JB recordings. According to information from EMI Music

Archives, 0EA 16910/11 were probably not used at all and 0EA 16912/13 for recordings by The Kordites.

No. 203
According to RCA recording pages, there were also sessions on January 2, February 27 and March 8, at which JB was not present (in the note inserted by J.W. Porter in JBD, p. 186, it is stated that JB was present on January 2, but he sang in a *Rigoletto* performance in Stockholm on that day and left Stockholm on the 5).

No. 204
According to RCA recording pages, there were also sessions on January 6, February 27 and March 8, at which JB was not present.

Nos. 206-07
The orchestral arrangements of these songs were made by Herbert Sandberg.

No. 209
According to RCA recording pages, there were also sessions on July 14 and 18, at which JB was not present. LM 6116 gives Plinio Clabassi instead of Campi, but this was later changed.

No. 210
According to RCA recording pages, there were also sessions on July 4, 12, 15 and 18, at which JB was not present (in the note inserted by J.W. Porter in JBD, p. 187, it is stated that JB was present on July 18, but, as confirmed by Ann-Charlotte Björling's passport and by a Swedish newspaper notice, he arrived in Sweden on the 16).

No. 211
According to RCA recording pages, JB was present at all recording sessions.

In addition to the list of records issued, it should be noted that the first bars of No. 211a2 were also included on a one-sided 33 1/3 rpm. 7"/17 cm. disc without label or number, enclosed with a Swedish book: *Ett folk på marsch 1932-1946: En bokfilm* av Erik Lindorm [A People Marching 1932-1946: A Pictorial Survey by E.L.] (Stockholm, Bonniers, 1960).

No. 212
According to RCA recording pages, JB was present at all recording sessions except for one on June 14, at which only the orchestral prelude to act 1 was recorded. This refutes the statement by S. Stroff (*Guldstrupen*, 1981) that JB left Rome before the recording was finished and recorded his solo parts in Stockholm, to the pre-recorded orchestral accompaniment on tape. That statement has also been denied both by Richard Mohr, producer of the recording, and by JB's family. According to Ann-Charlotte Björling's passport, she and her father left for Rome on June 13 and returned to Stockholm on the 29.

No. 214
This song (like the other Swedish RCA recordings in January, 1957) was recorded in mono, but it was later electronically reprocessed for stereo effect.

No. 216
The two takes of this aria are clearly different. In version A, the final note is taken in a very soft pianissimo. No documents referring to the different versions have been found. Version A was used in the Russian film *Neokonchennaya pyesa dlya mekanicheskogo pianino* [Unfinished Piece for Player-Piano], directed by Nikita Mikhalkov (1977). It is not known for certain which version was issued on the Russian Melodiya label. Here that issue is assumed to have version A because that take was used in the film.

No. 219
According to RCA recording pages, there was also a session on July 12, at which JB was not present.

No. 223
It has been claimed that two takes of this recording have been issued (different takes on LM 2372 and LM/LSC 6059), but it is very difficult to detect any difference between them.

Nos. 227-31
These songs were recorded in mono, but later reprocessed for stereo effect. The orchestral arrangements for these recordings were all made by Herbert Sandberg.

It is known that during the Swedish RCA recording sessions (including also Nos. 213-18 and 232-39), JB rarely made more than one take (cf. note for No. 216), and it seems likely that no further unissued material has been preserved.

No. 230
This recording was also used for an arrangement "När jag för mig själv i mörka skogen går (Hommage à Jussi)" on the Swedish CD "Random Rhapsody" produced by P.A. Nilsson (*LJ* LJCD 5207), issued in 1993. There, JB's voice is mixed with acoustical instruments.

Nos. 232-39
These songs were recorded in stereo except Nos. 232-34 which were recorded in mono due to a defective machine. Nos. 233 and 234 were later electronically reprocessed for stereo effect, but for technical reasons, this was not possible for No. 232 ("Trollsjön" was therefore omitted in the stereo version of LM 9884, LSC 9884). The orchestral arrangements were made for No. 232 by Stig Rybrant, for Nos. 233-34 by Herbert Sandberg, for No. 235 by Leo Funtek and for No. 236 by Ivar Hellman.

No. 240
According to RCA recording pages, JB was present at all recording sessions.

No. 241
The dates indicated are those stated by EMI for the whole recording; it is not known whether JB was present at both September sessions. He had a heart attack during the recording, which was therefore finished a few weeks later than planned.

No. 242
It is not known whether JB was present at all the indicated recording sessions. There were also sessions on May 28, 30 & 31 & June 26, at which he cannot have been present.

According to Ann-Charlotte Björling's passport, she and her father stayed in Vienna June 10 - 21.

No. 243
This was JB's contribution to a gala sequence of a complete recording of J. Strauss' *Die Fledermaus*. The Decca recording pages do not give the date of JB's recording, nor do they name any conductor of the "scratch" orchestra which accompanied him. However, it was not von Karajan, the conductor of the *Fledermaus* recording, as stated in JBRL.

Ann-Charlotte Björling recollects that this recording was made towards the end of the *Requiem* period.

No. 244
This recording was begun by the Decca Record Co. on July 8 and was planned to go on until July 22 with Birgit Nilsson, Giulietta Simionato and Cornell MacNeil in other main roles (Nilsson has informed the author that she had not yet arrived when the recording was cancelled). The recording project and the events which lead to its cancellation have been described by the producer, John Culshaw, in *High Fidelity / Musical America*, June 1973 ("Fragments from an Unwritten Biography") and in his posthumously published autobiography *Putting the Record Straight* (1981). The article gives exact dates for all events, but is otherwise much less detailed than the book. The two accounts do not agree on all points. According to Culshaw (1973), JB took part in a rehearsal on July 8 and in the first session on July 10, when "we recorded a few passages before Bjoerling decided he wanted to go home". Culshaw's autobiography gives the impression that JB did not take part in any rehearsal, but states that he appeared at the first session "after about five minutes ... and demanded to sing one of his arias without any rehearsal at all; ... when his proposal was declined he shambled off". The recording was cancelled on July 12, according to Culshaw due to JB's failure to show up for rehearsals and his bad condition (JB himself left Rome on the 15th). JB's wife and daughter were both with him in Rome and confirm that his voice was in excellent condition, a fact fully corroborated by Cornell MacNeil in a recent interview with Andrew Farkas. They also confirmed that he was especially looking forward to recording Riccardo, one of his best roles and, incidentally, his favourite one. They - MacNeil included - do not accept Culshaw's description of the events and stress that though JB, who was well prepared, found Solti's demand for piano rehearsals unnecessary and though he could not share the conductor's opinion on important musical matters, especially the tempi in Riccardo's arias, he eventually agreed to change his interpretation of the role according to Solti's wishes, in order not to jeopardize the whole project. Under these circumstances, they mean that Solti and Culshaw must bear the main responsibility for the fact that an artistic conflict led to the cancellation of the recording (the project was later realized with Carlo Bergonzi as Riccardo). The events made JB very depressed; in Mrs. Björling's opinion, they might even have precipitated his early death.

There have been different rumours as to the extent of the material recorded by JB before the project was cancelled. For example, R. Gelatt stated in an article in *High Fidelity* (Nov. 1960) that the act 1 and 2 ensembles were taped, and Mrs. Björling believes that at least some solo of her husband in the first act was recorded. In the interview with Farkas referred to above, Cornell MacNeil maintained that the complete first act ensemble, "La rivedrà nell'estasi", had been recorded. According to Hans Boon, assistant to the manager of the Classical Division of London Records, "the portions of *Ballo in maschera* recorded by Mr. Bjoerling were not enough to fill up one record" (letter 1963 to Don Goldberg). On the other hand, the producer Culshaw could not recall that JB "recorded more than one note or two, if he recorded anything at all" (letter to the author of Sept. 18, 1975) and according to Christopher Raeburn of the Decca Co., "there were a few very short phrases of recitative recorded [by JB] and since they comprised about two bars, they were not worth preserving" (letter to the author). Thus, it is not known for certain whether any JB material from this unfinished recording exists. For further information on the subject, see the article "The Masked Ball Mystery" by Don Goldberg (*Opera News*, Jan. 19, 1991).

Jussi Björling

Den första svenskfödde sångare som vederfarits den äran att av vår internationella organisation uppflyttas i »stjärnklassen» (= skivor med röd etikett) är JUSSI BJÖRLING. Hans karriär synes därmed vara säkerställd, ty ingen operachef i världen, som hört hans nya storartade insjungningar, kommer att tveka ett ögonblick att erbjuda honom ett lysande engagemang. Den glansfulla ungdomliga stämman, den sydländska glöden i föredraget och höjdtonernas fenomenala styrka och skönhet; allt detta i förening motiverar fullt och fast att Jussi Björlings namn ställes i jämnbredd med de allra största inom världseliten.

För »Husbondens Röst» är det en tillfredsställelse att kunna konstatera att samtliga experter på musikens och sångens område, som varit i tillfälle höra de nya skivorna, enstämmigt förklara att inspelningen är av högsta klass och i alla avseenden utomordentligt lyckad.

Till det goda intrycket bidrager i hög grad det charmanta orkesterackompagnemanget av en 45 mans orkester under Hovkapellmästare Nils Grevillius konstnärliga ledning.

***Jussi Björling**, tenor*

LA DONNA È MOBILE, (Ack, som ett fjun så lätt) ur »Rigoletto», av Verdi ● RECONDITA ARMONIA, (Det sköna står att finna) ur »Tosca», av Puccini ●	DA 1548
CELESTE AIDA, FORMA DIVINA, (Ljuva Aida) ur »Aida», av Verdi ● CHE GELIDA MANINA, (Så kall Ni är om handen) ur »Bohême», av Puccini ●	DB 3049

Ovanstående insjungningar äro såsom synes gjorda på originalspråket.

*Presentation of Jussi Björling's first "Red Label" records in the swedish **HMV** supplement for March, 1937. Excerpts from the text: "The first swedish-born singer to whom our international organization has granted the honour of being transferred to the "star class" (= records with a red label) is JB. His career should now be guaranteed, for no opera manager whatsoever who has listened to his new splendid recordings will hesitate for a moment to offer him an excellent contratc. ... It is very pleasing to "His Master's Voice" to be able to state that all experts in the field of music and song who have had the opportunity to listen to the new records declare unanimously that the recording is first-rate and in all respects very successful."*

B. Live Recordings; Studio Recordings for Broadcasting Companies; Radio Interviews; Films

Items indicated by a question-mark have not been found and may or may not exist. Recordings are mono unless otherwise stated.

3401
1934, January 29. Stockholm, Royal Opera House. Parts of opera performance (from a broadcast of one act). With Royal Orch. & Royal Opera Chorus, cond. Nils Grevillius.
[Sw. Radio: L-B 306:1-2]

Fanal (Atterberg): act 3, excerpts [in all: 8 min. 40 sec.]. Sung in Sw. by Helga Görlin (Rosamund); JB (Martin Skarp), Gösta Bäckelin (Vassal); Joel Berglund (Jost), Leon Björker (Duke).

Preserved excerpt with JB:
Nu, bröder, ändas våra strider [finale]

[33] *Golden Age* EJS 347 // *HMV* (Sw) 7C 153-35350/58

3601
1936, February 16. Stockholm, Concert Hall, Small Auditorium (?). Parts of radio concert (operetta medley, broadcast without public). With Sw. Radio Orch. & Chorus, cond. Nils Grevillius.
[Sw. Radio: L-B 1369]

Från Strauss till Lehár [From Strauss to Lehár] (arr. Hruby): excerpts & fragments [in all: 16 min.]. Sung in Sw. by Hjördis Schymberg & Nella Valdi (sop.); JB (ten.); Gösta Kjellertz (bar.).

This was the second radio performance of Viktor Hruby's operetta medley [cf. Appendix, No. A31]. 1 1/2 hour long, the medley comprised over 70 tunes by 28 composers. The six preserved excerpts in which JB sings were taken from the following operettas and songs [further details, see Composer Index].

a-b. *Der Bettelstudent* (Millöcker): a. Dich nur lieb' ich so inniglich (Dig blott älskar jag). - b. Ach, er hat sie ja nur auf die Schulter geküsst (Ack, han gav henne blott uppå skuldran en kyss)
c. *Polenblut* (Nedbal): Alle Achtung, alle Achtung (Så betänksamt, så betänksamt)
d. *Die geschiedene Frau* (Fall): Kind, Du kannst tanzen wie meine Frau (Barn, du kan dansa såsom min fru)
e. *Rund um die Liebe* (Straus): Es gibt Dinge, die muss man vergessen (Det finns ting vilka äro för sköna)
f. *Die Csárdásfürstin* (Kálmán): Tanzen möcht' ich...Tausend kleine Engel singen (Dansa vill jag...Tusen röster hör jag sjunga)

3602
1936, June 7. Vienna, State Opera House. Parts of Wiener Festwochen opera performance (privately recorded on discs; see further below). With Vienna State Opera Orch. & Chorus, cond. Victor de Sabata. [Vienna State Opera Archive]

Aida (Verdi): excerpts & fragments [in all: 31 min.?]. Sung in Sw. by JB (Radamès); in Ger. by Maria Németh (Aida); Kerstin Thorborg (Amneris); Alexander Svéd (Amonasro); Nicola Zec (King).

Located excerpts & fragments with JB:

(Act 1)	a. Se quel guerrier...Celeste Aida (O, vore jag...Ljuva Aida);
(Act 3)	b1. Pur ti riveggo (Jag ser dig åter) through "Fuggir. Fuggire!"; b2. Va, va, t'attende all'ara Amneris (Geh, geh, es harret dein Amneris) through "...duce fia l'amor, fia l'amor"; b3. No, tu non sei colpevole (Nein, nein, du bist nicht schuldig) through "...la del tuo cor, del tuo...".

(a,b)	[33]	*HRE* 376-2
(a,b1-2)	[33]	*Golden Age* EJS 405 // *Belvedere* 76.23589
(a)	[33]	*Golden Age* EJS 337
(b1-2)	[33]	*MDP* 026

This recording, like 3701 & 3702, was made on gelatine or decelith discs by Hermann von May, engineer at the State Opera, with a microphone hanging over the stage. In 1933-1945, May transcribed many excerpts from live performances, originally with the permission of the opera director Clemens Krauss. The discs had a short playing time (about four minutes) and many of them were damaged by repeated playing; the preserved excerpts are therefore fragmentary and of varying technical quality. The list of located excerpts and fragments with JB is based on the Belvedere issue (where 3701 was not included) and on tapes sold in the US. It seems probable that the described excerpts and fragments may be all that was preserved from these performances with JB.

The dates stated for these Vienna performances are not always reliable (in JBRL, they had been misdated by confusing days and months). The listed *Aida* excerpts with JB must have been recorded on June 7, 1936, since this was his only performance in the role in Vienna, but at least the two ensemble scenes interpolated into this performance on American LPs and tapes (Act 1, "Su! Del Nilo al sacro lido" & Act 2, "Dunque tu sei?...Anch'io pugnai") must have been recorded on other dates; Radamès is there sung in German by other tenors (one of whom may perhaps be Kálmán Pataky). The total length of the excerpts on HRE 376-2 or available tape copies is 43 minutes; if these two ensemble scenes are excluded, the excerpts from this performance comprise 31 minutes only.

3701
1937, March 7. Vienna, State Opera House. Parts of opera performance (privately recorded on discs). With Vienna State Opera Orch. & Chorus, cond. Josef Krips.
[Vienna State Opera Archive]

Faust (Gounod): excerpts & fragments [in all: 26 min.]. Sung in Sw. by JB (Faust); in Ger. by Esther Réthy (Marguerite), Dora Komarek (Siebel); Alexander Svéd (Valentin); Alexander Kipnis (Méphistophélès).

Located excerpts & fragments with JB:

(Act 1) a. Eh bien! Puisque la mort...Salut! Ô mon dernier matin...Vains échos (Men vad? Om denna död...O hell, ljusnande morgon...Tomma eko); b1. Mais ce Dieu...Maudites soyez-vous (Denne Gud...Förbannad var och en) through "Me voici!"; b2. À moi les plaisirs (O skänk mig på nytt) through "Et que te donnerai-je en retour?"; b3. Et maintenant, maître (Von nun an soll, o Faust) to end of act;

(Act 2) c. Ne permettrez-vous pas...Ainsi que la brise légère (Min sköna fröken...Leichte Wölkchen sich erheben);

(Act 3) d1. Il se fait tard! (Es ist schon spät!) through "...ce mot sublime et doux"; d2. Éternelle! Éternelle! Ô nuit d'amour (Ingen ände! Måne som höjs) through [first] "Parle encore!"; e. Viens! Viens! - Marguerite! (Komm! Komm! - Margareta!) to end of act;

(Act 5) f. Quittons ce lieu sombre...Anges purs (Auf, rette ihr Leben...Engelchor) to end of opera.

(a-f)	[33]	*Golden Age* EJS 337 // *HRE* 214-2 // *HRE* 376-2

The date of this recording is beyond doubt, since it was JB's only Vienna performance of the opera (he was replaced in a scheduled performance on March 27). The time indicated above for the whole selection does not include the cavatina "Salut! demeure chaste et pure" which is inserted in its proper place in all the LP issues listed above, since it is an interpolation of 3903e. The excerpts may be slightly abridged on the LP records.

3702

1937, March 12. Vienna, State Opera House. Parts of opera performance (privately recorded on discs). With Vienna State Opera Orch. & Chorus, cond. Karl Alwin.

[Vienna State Opera Archive]

Pagliacci (Leoncavallo): excerpts & fragments [in all: 6 min. 30 sec.]. Sung in Sw. by JB (Canio); in Ger. by Margit Bokor (Nedda) & Friedrich Ginrod (Silvio).

Located excerpts:

(Act 1) a. A ventitre ore! A ventitre ore! (Kommen väl ihåg! Precis klockan elva!); b. Recitar!...Vesti la giubba (Spela komedi!...Pudra ditt anlet);

(Act 2) c1. No! Pagliaccio non son (Nej! Pajazzo är jag ej)... c2. Ebben! se mi giudichi (Nun wohl! Wenn du sagst) through "...e il nome del tuo ganzo".

(a-c)	[33]	*HRE* 376-2 // *Belvedere* 76.23596/97
(a-c1)	[CD]	*Legato* LCD 155-1
(b,c1)	[33]	*Golden Age* EJS 337
(b)	[33]	*MDP* 026

The date for this performance is confirmed by the Belvedere issue (in February, JB sang another *Pagliacci* performance in Vienna).

3703
1937, April 8. Stockholm, Concert Hall. *Parad för millionen* [A Parade for the Million], radio programme celebrating the sale of one million radio licenses (broadcast without public). With Sw. Radio Orch., cond. Nils Grevillius. [Sw. Radio: L-B+ 1880]

a. Morgon [Sw] (Eklöf)
b. Tonerna [Sw] (Sjöberg)
c. Land, du välsignade [Sw] (Althén)
d. O Lola [Sw] (Mascagni: *Cavalleria rusticana*)
e. Che gelida manina [Sw: Så kall ni är om handen] (Puccini: *La bohème*)

JB was heard on three different occasions during this long programme (2 hours 15 min.). Several of Sweden's most popular artists participated, among them Karin Juel, Sven-Olof Sandberg, Evert Taube and the Björlingkvartetten.

3704
1937, August 14 - November 10. Stockholm, Solna & Torö [for exact dates and places see below]. *Fram för framgång* [Head for Success], motion picture. Songs performed with SF [Svensk Filmindustri] Orch., cond. Nils Grevillius (in a,d-e) or without accompaniment (in b,c). [Sw. Film Institute]

a. La danza [Sw: Tarantella] (Rossini)
b. Hej dunkom, så länge vi levom [Sw] (trad.)
c. Bachanal [Sw] (Dahl]
d. Di' tu se fedele [Sw: O säg, när på skummande vågor] (Verdi: *Un ballo in maschera*)
e. Land, du välsignade (Althén)

(a,b) [33] *ANNA* 1069

Fram för framgång, the only film in which JB had a leading part, was produced by SF (Svensk Filmindustri AB) between August 3 and November 11, 1937, and released on February 7, 1938. In the same year, it was also shown in the US (in New York at the Forty-eighth Street Theatre; review in *The New York Times* Nov. 28). Though the film was generally well received by the Swedish critics (and JB given credit also as an actor), *Fram för framgång* does not seem to have been a success with the public. Excerpts from this film (and from 5302) were used for the Swedish Television programme *Jussi Björlings saga* [The Saga of JB], first telecast in 1977.

JB took part in the recording on the dates and at the places specified below. (The Kungsholmen studio was situated in central Stockholm, the other studios at "Filmstaden", Råsunda - a SF production centre in the Stockholm suburb of Solna. The Stockholm Tivoli, Gröna Lund, is an amusement park and Torö is an island in the Stockholm archipelago.) Aug. 14 & 16, Torö; Aug. 23, Kungsholmen studio; Aug. 26-27 & 29-30, Torö; Sept. 1-2, Kungsholmen studio; Sept. 5, Gröna Lund (scene with "Land, du välsignade"); Sept. 18, Kungsholmen studio (post-synchronization); Sept. 19 & 23, Gröna Lund; Sept. 26-27, Torö; Sept. 29, Small studio "Lasse's room"; Oct. 1, Gröna Lund; Oct. 2, 4 & 6, Small studio "Lasse's room" (scene with "Hej, dunkom" on the 4th); Oct. 7, Small studio "The radio studio" (scene with "La danza"); Oct. 12, Filmstaden & Stockholm (exterior scenes);

Oct. 14, Filmstaden "Street"; Oct. 18, Small studio "The Broadcasting House"; Nov. 2, Small studio (interior scenes) & Filmstaden (exterior scenes); Nov. 5, Large studio (back-projection); Nov. 10, Large projection room (postsynchronization).

It is now impossible to tell exactly how, when and in which order the song recordings were done, as the songs (here listed in the order in which they occur in the film) are not specified on the archive sheets from which the above dates are taken. It seems certain that playback technique was applied for the recordings with orchestra, and probably, it was used also for the unaccompanied song recordings. The orchestra took part in the sound recordings at Kungsholmen on Aug. 23 and Sept. 1 & 18, and in the Tivoli picture recording on Sept. 5. For Aug. 23, the archive cards indicate "music recording". For Sept. 1 & 18, they indicate "music and song" recordings; perhaps orchestral accompaniment may have been pre-recorded on the first date. There is no archive sheet for Sept. 2, but a special list of dates when JB was present states that he made song recordings on that day. In short, it seems probable that all song recordings were made between Aug. 23 and Sept. 18, but the possibility that the unaccompanied songs were recorded later cannot be excluded. Two persons who took part in the *Fram för framgång* production recall that JB also recorded "Till havs", but this recording was evidently rejected. Eric Bengtson was the chief conductor of the film music and present at all recordings with orchestra, but Grevillius conducted the orchestra when it accompanied JB's singing. Newspaper reports about the Gröna Lunds Tivoli session on Sept. 5, which was open to the public and combined with a concert, mention that the SF orchestra was then enlarged with members of the Royal Orchestra.

Direction & script: Gunnar Skoglund. Main roles: JB (Tore Nilsson), Åke Ohberg (Lasse Berg), Aino Taube (Monika Malm), Anders Boman (Pelle Mårtensson), Anders Henrikson ("Rövar'n"), Erik "Bullen" Berglund (Torman, editor-in-chief), Bror Bügler (Vadman, editor), Gösta Gustafson (Hallberg, photographer), Sven Björklund (A Pilot), Harry Roeck Hansen (Director of the Broadcasting Company), Gösta Cederlund (The Theatre Manager), Hugo Björne (The Police Commissioner).

Story: The author Lasse Berg receives a letter confirming that his play "The Fire" has been accepted by the National Theatre. He rushes out overjoyed. Outside the Broadcasting House, Berg runs into the singer Tore Nilsson. Nilsson is depressed; he has just for the seventh time in vain offered his services to the Radio. Berg encourages him and persuades him to go back in and call on the Director of the company. "Head for Success!" After having forced himself into a radio studio, where the Director is just presenting the educational programmes of the season to the schoolchildren, Nilsson demonstrates his talents by singing "La danza" on the air and disappears, chased by the police.
Lasse Berg visits the National Theatre. He interrupts a rehearsal when he finds that his manuscript has been revised and finally draws back his play in protest. This annoys the young actress Monika Malm who had been given the main role. She goes to see Berg at his home, where, also, Tore Nilsson has taken his refuge. Noting that none of the gentlemen can pay for the food which is delivered for dinner, she saves the situation and joins them at the table where Nilsson sings "Hej, dunkom".
The newspapers now write about two sensations: "The Singing X" who mysteriously appeared on the radio with a sensational voice and the young author who dared to withdraw his play from the National Theatre. The journalist Vadman, who is sent by Morgonbladet [The Morning News] to Berg's home for an interview, is delighted to also find "The Singing X" there. The newspaper arranges a hiding-place for him on an island in the Stockholm

archipelago. On his way in a motor-boat, Nilsson sings "Bachanal".
At the Broadcasting Company, Pelle Mårtensson decides to try to find "The Singing X", whose talent he has recognized, in spite of the fact that the Director is negative to the mysterious singer. Monika Malm also offers to help when Mårtensson happens to meet her at the Broadcasting House. She has succeeded in persuading the Director to accept "The Fire" for the Radio Theatre. Berg, who is unaware of this, has changed his attitude towards the National Theatre in order to save the main role for Malm with whom he has fallen in love. The theatre manager takes the play back, but in the discussion that follows it emerges that he wants to replace Malm.
Morgonbladet decides to exploit the story about "The Singing X" in a series of issues and finally to arrange his public debut at a Gröna Lund charity show. In the archipelago, the lonely Tore Nilsson happens to meet "Rövar'n" [The Robber] and is taken by him on an adventurous trip in a sailing-boat, where Nilsson sings "Di' tu se fedele". Malm and Mårtensson go to the archipelago in order to find Nilsson and engage him for a radio performance. Berg arrives in the Morgonbladet aeroplane, intending to take Nilsson back to Stockholm and the Gröna Lund show. He finds Malm and Mårtensson alone in the house and gets jealous. Back in Stockholm, Berg comes in an embarrassing situation when the National Theatre learns that "The Fire" has been announced as a radio play. Berg is thrown out of the theatre, but when the Director of the Broadcasting Company tells him about Malm's action for him, Berg understands that she loves him.
Mårtensson and Malm in their motor-boat succeed in finding Tore Nilsson and "Rövar'n" who have run aground. When they are returning with Nilsson, the Morgonbladet aeroplane appears with Berg onboard and Nilsson is flown back to Stockholm while Berg and Malm are happily reunited in the boat. Every measure is taken by Morgonbladet to boost the Gröna Lund show. On the evening before the show, Tore Nilsson is greeted at a dinner as a future great singer. The police suddenly intervene and declare that they have to arrest him for the incident at the Broadcasting House. However, the wrong person is taken and when Nilsson arrives at Gröna Lund, he is lifted to the top of a pylon from which he can sing "Land, du välsignade" in safety. The crowd gives him an enthusiastic ovation and cries for the name of "The Singing X" who has made his breakthrough. Introduced to the audience by Mårtensson, the couple who helped Tore Nilsson, Lasse Berg and Monika Malm, are also lifted to the top of the pylon, where they unite in a kiss.

3705
1937, October 3. Stockholm, radio studio. Transcription of JB's spoken greetings [in Eng.; 25 sec.] to the American public before his first American concert tour as a tenor - directed to Milton Cross, announcer for the General Motors Concerts. [Sw. Radio: L-B 2123]

This recording, which also contains a greeting by the German soprano Erna Sack, was intended for a shortwave broadcast during the night of October 4, but according to a note on the recording sheet, it was not transmitted.

3706
1937, November 11. Stockholm, SF Kungsholmen studio. Sound film recording for the motion picture *John Ericsson, segraren vid Hampton Roads* [John Ericsson, Victor of Hampton Roads]. With SF Orch., cond. Eric Bengtson. [Sw. Film Institute]

Ack Värmeland, du sköna [Sw] (trad.) [abridged]

This film, directed by Gustaf Edgren, was released in Sweden December 13, 1937, and had its American premiere in New York, May 1938. JB does not appear in the film. Only his singing voice is heard in the final scene, to remind the viewers of the Swedish-American inventor John Ericsson's native province, Värmland.

3707
1937, November 28. New York, Carnegie Hall. *General Motors Concert*: "Request Night", NBC radio concert. Announcer: Milton Cross. With Maria Jeritza (sop., in e) & General Motors Symphony Orch., cond. Erno Rapee.

a. Che gelida manina [It] (Puccini: *La bohème*)
b. La donna è mobile [It] (Verdi: *Rigoletto*)
c. Se quel guerrier...Celeste Aida [It] (Verdi: *Aida*)
d. Land, du välsignade [Sw] (Althén)
e. Bada, Santuzza, schiavo non sono...Ah, lo vedi [Sw: Jag är ej slav, förgäves du gråter...Å! där ser du] (Mascagni: *Cavalleria rusticana*) [Jeritza sings in It.]

(a-e)	[33]	*Golden Age* EJS 405
(a-d)	[33]	*ANNA* 1005
(a,c-e)	[33]	*MDP* 026
(a-c)	[33]	*ERR* 121-1
	[MC]	*ERR* ERRC 121
(e)	[33]	*Unique* UORC 350

This concert was JB's American debut as a tenor.

3708
1937, December 5. New York, Carnegie Hall. *General Motors Concert*: "Opera Night", NBC radio concert. Announcer: Milton Cross. With Grace Moore (sop., in d), Donald Dickson (bar., in c-d) & General Motors Symphony Orch., cond. Erno Rapee.
[Private Sw. coll.; Sw. Radio: L-B+ 23532]

a. Recondita armonia [It] (Puccini: *Tosca*)
b. Pays merveilleux...Ô paradis [It: Mi batte il cor...O paradiso] (Meyerbeer: *L'africaine*)
c. Solenne in quest'ora [It] (Verdi: *La forza del destino*)
d. Quittons ce lieu sombre...Anges purs [Fr; JB in Sw] (Gounod: *Faust*)

(a-d)	[CD]	*Legato* BIM 708-2
(c)	[33]	*ANNA* 1069

3901
1939, May 12. London, Royal Opera House (Covent Garden). Opera performance (probably preserved complete). With London Philharmonic Orch. & Chorus, cond. Vittorio Gui.

Il trovatore (Verdi), sung in It. by Gina Cigna (Leonora), Maria Huder (Ines); Gertrud Pålson-Wettergren (Azucena); JB (Manrico), Octave Dua (Ruiz), Giuseppe Zammit (Messenger); Mario Basiola (Di Luna); Corrado Zambelli (Ferrando), Leslie Horsman (Gypsy).

Located excerpts:

(Act 1)	a. Che più t'arresti [to end of act];
(Act 2)	b. Soli or siamo...Mal reggendo...Un momento può involarmi; c. Perché piangete? [to end of act];
(Act 3)	d. Quale d'armi fragor [to end of act];
(Act 4)	e. Siam giunti...Ah! che la morte ognora...Vivrà! Contende il giubilo; f. Che! non m'inganna [to end of opera].

(a-f) [33] *Golden Age* EJS 366 // *MDP* 004

The excerpts listed above [in all: 1 hour 18 min.] contain Manrico's whole part except for a few bars in act 2 and the duet with Azucena in act 4. Some of the excerpts are abridged on the EJS record, but this does not affect Manrico's role. The origin of the excerpts is not known for certain, but they are reported to come from a complete recording, copied from an original in the possession of Sir Thomas Beecham's family. According to a Beecham discography, published by the Sir Thomas Beecham Society in 1975, three operas conducted by him were recorded on film in the 1938/39 season and still exist. It may also be worth noting that experimental recordings of live performances were made by record companies at Covent Garden in 1936 and 1937, perhaps also in 1939.

The fact that JB's Covent Garden performance in the role on May 23 was broadcast live, makes it natural to wonder whether a transcription of this broadcast may erroneously have been given the earlier date (the broadcast is not preserved in the BBC archive). However, the broadcast was not complete as was originally intended. Acts 1 and 2 were heard on the Regional radio and act 4 on the National while act 3 (actually act 2 in this production) was replaced on the National radio by a debate on Palestine. Furthermore, both LP issues and available tape copies list Pålson-Wettergren and Basiola among the singers, and so far, there has been no reason to doubt that it is their voices that are actually heard on the recording, On May 23, however, they were replaced by Ebe Stignani and Armando Borgioli. It should be noted that one of the existing tape copies of this performance was stated to be derived from an off-the-air recording. According to a letter from an American collector to J.W. Porter, quoted in JBD, the copy in question is a dubbing from original discs, transcribed by a man named Mike Richter who "recorded the broadcast on his own equipment (transcription set-up) while living in England".

3902

1939, June 8. Hilversum (Netherlands), AVRO studio (AVRO = Algemeene Vereniging Radio Omroep [Public Radio Broadcasting Association]). Radio concert. With AVRO Hilversum Orch., cond. Frieder Weissmann.

[NOS (Dutch Broadcasting Foundation), Hilversum: EM-HM-1186]

a. Ingemisco [Lat] (Verdi: *Messa da Requiem*)
b. Pays merveilleux...Ô paradis [It: Mi batte il cor...O paradiso] (Meyerbeer: *L'africaine*)
c. La fleur que tu m'avais jetée [Fr] (Bizet: *Carmen*)

d. En fermant les yeux [Fr] (Massenet: *Manon*)
e. Salut! demeure chaste et pure [Sw: Var hälsad, dygdens kyska boning] (Gounod: *Faust*)
f. Che gelida manina [It] (Puccini: *La bohème*)

(a-f)	[33]	*ERR* 121-1 // *ANNA* 1005 // *Bluebell* BELL 163
	[CD]	*Bluebell* ABCD 006 // *Legato* LCD 103-1
	[MC]	*ERR* ERRC 121
(a-e)	[33]	*MDP* 026
(a,c,e,f)	[CD]	*Myto* 2MCD 89004
(a,e,f)	[33]	*Golden Age* EJS 279
	[CD]	*Verona* 27022
	[MC]	*Verona* 427022
(a)	[CD]	*Myto* 2MCD 90317 // *Myto* 1MCD 912.39
(b-e)	[33]	*Golden Age* EJS 337
(b,c)	[CD]	*Verona* 27068
(b)	[CD]	*Verona* 2700
(e)	[33]	*HRE* 214-2 // *HRE* 376-2
	[CD]	*Legato* BIM 708-2

3902e is interpolated into *Faust* excerpts from Vienna (3701) on EJS 337, HRE 214-2 and HRE 376-2.

3903
1939, August 6. Furuvik Park (near Gävle, Sweden). Part of open-air recital (privately recorded on an acetate disc). With Harry Ebert, piano. [Coll. A. Nyberg, Skutskär]

a. Jungfrun under lind [Sw] (Peterson-Berger)
b. Land, du välsignade [Sw] (Althén)

(b)	[33]	*Bluebell* BELL 187
	[CD]	*Legato* BIM 708-2

This recording was made by Anders Nyberg on home-built equipment and was approved by JB immediately after the recital. The recorded songs were the two last items on a programme which also contained arias from *Rigoletto*, *Tosca*, *Fanciulla del West*, *Gioconda* and *Carmen*, and four songs: Lenz; I drömmen du är mig nära; Tonerna; Mattinata. JB was also filmed by Anders Nyberg during this recital.

3904
1939, August 29. Stockholm, Royal Opera House. Complete opera performance (recorded by Sw. Broadcasting Corp.). First broadcasts: act 2 (= act 2, scene 1), Sept. 17, 1939; acts 3-4 (= act 2, scene 2 & act 3), Nov. 10, 1939; complete opera, April 15-17, 1975. With Royal Orch. & Royal Opera Chorus, cond. Herbert Sandberg.
[Sw. Radio: L-B+ 4014]

La traviata [Sw: *Den vilseförda*] (Verdi), sung in Sw. by Hjördis Schymberg (Violetta), Margit Sehlmark (Annina); Göta Allard (Flora); JB (Alfredo), Olle Strandberg (Gastone), Ryno Wallin (Giuseppe); Conny Molin (Germont), Georg Svensson (Baron Douphol);

Gösta Lindberg (Doctor Grenvil), Folke Jonsson (Marquis d'Obigny), Bertil Alstergård (Messenger).

Complete:	[33]	*Unique* UORC 269 // *SR* RMLP 1272/73
	[CD]	*Standing Room Only* SRO 832-2

Excerpts:

(Act 1)	a1. Libiamo; b. Un dì felice; c. Sempre libera;
(Act 2)	d. Lunge da lei...De' miei bollenti spiriti; e. Che fai? - Nulla. - Scrivevi?...Di Provenza il mar; f. Invitato a qui seguirmi [to end of act];
(Act 3)	g. Alfredo? Amato Alfredo!...Parigi, o cara [to end of opera].

(a-g)	[33]	*Golden Age* EJS 406
(a,b)	[33]	*HRE* 281-2

Traviata was played in four acts in Stockholm, while the original has three acts (as listed above). This was JB's last performance as Alfredo.

4001
1940, March 21. Stockholm, Royal Opera House. Part of opera performance (one act recorded by Sw. Broadcasting Corp.). First broadcast: May 7, 1940. With Royal Orch. & Royal Opera Chorus, cond. Nils Grevillius. [Sw. Radio: L-B+ 4141]

La bohème (Puccini): act 1, complete. Sung in Sw. by Hjördis Schymberg (Mimì); JB (Rodolfo); Sven Herdenberg (Marcello), Carl Richter (Schaunard); Leon Björker (Colline), Folke Cembraeus (Benoit).

Complete act: [33] *Golden Age* EJS 384 // *HRE* 281-2

Excerpts:
a1. Non sono in vena!...Che gelida manina... a2. Sì. Mi chiamano Mimì...Eh! Rodolfo!... a3. O soave fanciulla.

(a)	[33]	*Bluebell* BELL 198
	[CD]	*Bluebell* ABCD 013
(a1,a3)	[33]	*Rococo* 5304
(a1)	[CD]	*Legato* BIM 708-2

4002
1940, March 27. Stockholm, Royal Opera House. Complete opera performance (recorded by Sw. Broadcasting Corp.). First broadcasts: act 1, May 16, 1940; acts 2 & 5, August 14, 1977; acts 3-4, June 10, 1940. With Royal Orch. & Royal Opera Chorus, cond. Nils Grevillius. [Sw. Radio: L-B+ 4254]

Roméo et Juliette [Sw: *Romeo och Julia*] (Gounod), sung in Sw. by Hjördis Schymberg (Juliette), Benna Lemon-Brundin (Stéphano); Göta Allard (Gertrude); JB (Roméo), Simon Edwardsen (Tybalt), Folke Cembraeus (Benvolio); Olle Strandberg (Paris), Sven Herdenberg (Mercutio), Sven d'Ailly (Grégorio); Sigurd Björling (Capulet), Leon Björker (Friar Laurent), Folke Jonsson (Duke).

Complete: Not issued

Excerpts:

(Act 1) a. De grâce, demeurez!...Ange adorable;
(Act 2) b. Complete act; b1. L'amour!...Ah! lève-toi, soleil; b2. Ah! ne fuis pas encore;
(Act 4) c. Va! je t'ai pardonné...Nuit d'hyménée;
(Act 5) d1. C'est là!... d2. Salut! tombeau [to end of opera].

(a,b1,b2,c,d)	[33]	*Bluebell* BELL 198
	[CD]	*Bluebell* ABCD 013
(b,d2)	[33]	*HRE* 281-2 // *ANNA* 1045
(b1,d)	[CD]	*Legato* BIM 708-2

4003

1940, March 29. Stockholm, Royal Opera House. Part of opera performance (one act recorded by Sw. Broadcasting Corp.). First broadcast: April 23, 1940. With Royal Orch. & Royal Opera Chorus, cond. Kurt Bendix. [Sw. Radio: L-B+ 4255]

Aida (Verdi): act 1, complete [except prelude]. Sung in Sw. by Inez Köhler (Aida); Gertrud Pålson-Wettergren (Amneris); JB (Radamès), Georg Svensson (Messenger); Folke Jonsson (Ramfis).

Complete act: Not issued

Excerpt:

a. Dessa! Ei si turba

(a)	[33]	*ANNA* 1045

4004

1940, October 23. San Francisco, War Memorial Opera House. Part of opera performance (22 minutes were broadcast). With San Francisco Opera Orch., cond. Gennaro Papi.

Un ballo in maschera (Verdi): act 2, first part [through "Lo giuro, e sarà"]. Sung in It. by Elisabeth Rethberg (Amelia); JB (Riccardo); Richard Bonelli (Renato).

Complete broadcast:

[33] *Golden Age* EJS 168

Excerpts:

a1. Teco io sto...O qual soave brivido... a2. Chi giunge in questo soggiorno... a3. Amico, gelosa.

(a1-2)	[33]	*Op.Arch.* OPA 1051/52
(a1)	[33]	*Unique* UORC 350 // *ANNA* 1040/41 // *MDP* 034

The checked copies of this recording have several short breaks.

4005
1940, November 23. New York, Carnegie Hall. NBC radio concert, benefit for Alma Gluck Zimbalist Memorial of Roosevelt Hospital Development Fund. With NBC Symphony Orch. & Westminster Choir, cond. Arturo Toscanini.

Messa da Requiem (Verdi), sung in Lat. by Zinka Milanov (sop.); Bruna Castagna (cont.); JB (ten.); Nicola Moscona (bass).

Complete:	[33]	*ABC* 1001 // *ATS* 1005/06 // *Unique* UORC 229 // *ATS* THS 65031/32 // *Melodram* 006
	[CD]	*ATRA* 240 // *Melodram* MEL 38006 = *Palette* PAL 3004/06

4006
1940, December 8. Detroit, Masonic Temple Auditorium. *Ford Sunday Evening Hour*, ABC radio concert (only parts known to be preserved). With Ford Symphony Orch. [members of Detroit Symphony Orch.] & (in d) Chorus, cond. Eugene Ormandy.

?a. Che gelida manina [It] (Puccini: *La bohème*)
b. A Dream [Eng] (Bartlett)
c. La danza [Sw] (Rossini)
d. Funiculì, funiculà [It] (Denza)

(b-d)	[33]	*Legendary* LR 138
(d)	[33]	*Unique* UORC 254

There was another song at the end of this programme, "Lead On, O King Eternal" (Smart), but it was probably sung by the chorus, not by JB.

4007
1940, December 14. New York, Metropolitan Opera House. Complete opera performance (Saturday matinee, Texaco-Metropolitan broadcast). With Metropolitan Opera Orch. & Chorus, cond. Ettore Panizza.

Un ballo in maschera (Verdi), sung in It. by Zinka Milanov (Amelia), Stella Andreva (Oscar); Bruna Castagna (Ulrica); JB (Riccardo), John Carter (Judge), Lodovico Oliviero (Servant); Alexander Svéd (Renato); Arthur Kent (Silvano), Norman Cordon (Samuel), Nicola Moscona (Tom).

Complete:	[33]	*Golden Age* EJS 230 // *Rococo 1003* // *ERR* 109-3 // *Robin Hood* RHR 516-C // *MET* 8
	[CD]	*Myto* 2MCD 90317

Excerpt:
(Act 1) a. Di' tu se fedele.

(a)	[33]	*Rococo* 5304

4008

1940, December 28. New York, Carnegie Hall. NBC radio concert, benefit for the National Conference of Christians and Jews. With NBC Symphony Orch. & Westminster Choir, cond. Arturo Toscanini.

Missa Solemnis (Beethoven), sung in Lat. by Zinka Milanov (sop.); Bruna Castagna (cont.); JB (ten.); Alexander Kipnis (bass).

Complete:	[33]	*MR* 2000 // *ATS* 1023/24 // *Melodram* 006
	[CD]	*ATRA* CD 259 // *Melodram* MEL 38006 = *Palette* PAL 3004/06 // *AS disc* AS 307

4101

1941, January 11. New York, Metropolitan Opera House. Complete opera performance (Saturday matinee, Texaco-Metropolitan broadcast). With Metropolitan Opera Orch. & Chorus, cond. Ferruccio Calusio.

Il trovatore (Verdi), sung in It. by Norina Greco (Leonora), Maxine Stellman (Ines); Bruna Castagna (Azucena); JB (Manrico), Lodovico Oliviero (Ruiz); Francesco Valentino (Di Luna); Nicola Moscona (Ferrando), Arthur Kent (Gypsy).

Complete:	[33]	*Unique* UORC 115 // *Hist.Op.Perf.* HOPE 221 // *Cetra* LO 71 // *Robin Hood* RHR 509-B
	[CD]	*AS disc* AS 1110/11

Excerpts:

(Act 1)	a1. Deserto sulla terra... a2. Non m'inganno [to end of act];
(Act 2)	b1. Stride la vampa... b2. Non son tuo figlio... b3. Mal reggendo... b4. L'usato messo... b5. Perigliarti ancor...Un momento può involarmi;
(Act 3)	c1. Quale d'armi fragor...; c2. Di qual tetra luce... c3. Ah sì, ben mio... c4. Di quella pira;
(Act 4)	d. Miserere...Ah! che la morte ognora; e1. Madre, non dormi?...Ai nostri monti... e2. Che! non m'inganno! [to end of opera].

(a-e)	[33]	*Golden Age* EJS 207
(al,c3)	[33]	*Fabbri/ERI* V 30
(b2-3,c2-3,c4,e1)		
	[33]	*Rococo* 5304
(b2-5,c)	[CD]	*Myto* 2MCD 90317
(b5)	[33]	*Fabbri/ERI* V 21
(c)	[33]	*ERR* 121-1
	[MC]	*ERR* ERRC 121
(c3-4)	[33]	*Unique* UORC 350
(c3,c4)	[33]	*Golden Age* EJS 405

4102
1941, April 8. Stockholm, Concert Hall. *Honnör för lyssnarna!* [Salute to the Listeners!], radio programme celebrating the sale of one and a half million radio licenses (broadcast without public). With Hjördis Schymberg (sop., in c) & Stockholm Radio Orch., cond. Nils Grevillius. [Sw. Radio: L-B+ 3200]

a. Che gelida manina [It] (Puccini: *La bohème*)
b. La fleur que tu m'avais jetée [Fr] (Bizet: *Carmen*)
c. Ange adorable [Sw: Helgon, du ljuva] (Gounod: *Roméo et Juliette*)

(a,b)	[33]	*Bluebell* BELL 187
(c)	[33]	*SR* SRLP 1354/55

JB was heard on two occasions during this long programme (2 hours 30 min.), where many popular Swedish artists participated. Among the singers were Karin Juel, Alice Babs, Karl Gerhard, Sven-Olof Sandberg and Edvard Persson.

4201
1942, January 31. Stockholm, Concert Hall, Large Auditorium. Part of radio concert (broadcast without public). With Stockholm Radio Orch., cond. Sixten Ehrling. [Sw. Radio: L-B 2665]

a. En ballad om Lameks söner [Sw] (Rangström)
b. En ballad om Narren och Döden [Sw] (Rangström)
c. En ballad om god sömn [Sw] (Rangström)

(a-c)	[33]	*Golden Age* EJS 530 // *SR* SRLP 1354/55
	[CD]	*Bluebell* ABCD 050

JB also sang "O paradiso" and "Cielo e mar" in the first part of the concert, but no recording of these arias has been preserved in the radio archive. The concert presented the three Rangström ballads for the first time, with the composer present.

4301
1943, May 13. Stockholm, Royal Opera House. *För Europas barn* [For the Children of Europe], Radiotjänst [Sw. Broadcasting Corp.] festival soiree. With Royal Orch. & Royal Opera Chorus, cond. Nils Grevillius. [Sw. Radio: S 1990]

Roméo et Juliette (Gounod): act 2, complete. Sung in Sw. by Hjördis Schymberg (Juliette), Göta Allard (Gertrude); JB (Roméo).

Complete act: Not issued

Excerpt:
a. Ah! lève-toi, soleil.

(a)	[33]	*Unique* UORC 254 // *HRE* 281-2 // *MDP* 026

The soiree also included, among other things, scenes from *Così fan tutte* (Mozart) and *Zorina* (Sylvain), performed by artists from the R. Opera.

4302
1943, June 6. Stockholm, radio studio. *Sommarens kvart* [A Summer Quarter of an Hour], radio recital (broadcast without public). With Harry Ebert, piano.
[Sw. Radio: L-B 4657]

a. Morgon [Sw] (Eklöf)
b. När jag för mig själv i mörka skogen går [Sw] (Peterson-Berger)
c. Som stjärnorna på himmelen [Sw] (Peterson-Berger)
d. Bland skogens höga furustammar [Sw] (Peterson-Berger)
e. Land, du välsignade [Sw] (Althén)

(c)	[33]	*SR* SRLP 1354/55

This recital was intended to remind the listeners of Kungafonden [The Royal Foundation], which had recently been founded to help families with members that had either been killed or injured in emergency service.

4303
1943, July 10. Stockholm, Royal Academy of Music, Large Auditorium. *Sweden Calls America*, No. 13, concert transcription (without public) for Sw. Broadcasting Corp. Foreign Exchange Programme. With Stockholm Radio Orch., cond. Sixten Ehrling.
[Sw. Radio: L-B 4708:4, L-B 23541]

a. E lucevan le stelle [It] (Puccini: *Tosca*)
b. Tonerna (Sw] (Sjöberg)
c. Nessun dorma! [It] (Puccini: *Turandot*)

(a-c)	[Tr]	*US Office of War Inform.* 17-513
(a,b)	[33]	*MDP* 035
(a,c)	[33]	*Unique* UORC 350
(c)	[CD]	*Legato* LCD 103-1

This concert was the last programme in a series which was produced from April till July for the US. The programmes, all 15 minutes long and most of them containing music, were recorded on discs and sent to America to be broadcast once a week by about twenty radio stations in areas with a large Swedish population. It is not known when the programme was broadcast in America, but it may be assumed to have been sent in late July at the earliest. An unspecified excerpt from it was presented to Swedish radio listeners on July 27. No recording sheet has been preserved, and the recording date was established from an examination of accounts. According to Sven Wilson, head of the Foreign Division of the Sw. Broadcasting Co., who was in charge of the production and contributed on the programme with a greeting from Sweden to America, the concert was recorded at the Academy.
The original discs were found in the Sw. Radio archive as late as in the 1980s (L-B 4708:4). The other archive number refers to a tape copy of the U.S. transcription disc.

4401
1944, September 25. Stockholm, Royal Opera House. Parts of opera performance, for the benefit of the children of France (from broadcast of one act). With Royal Orch., cond. Nils Grevillius. [Sw. Radio: L-B+ 6089]

Faust (Gounod): act 3, excerpts [in all: 25 min. 15 sec.]. Sung in Fr. (JB throughout) & Sw. by Helga Görlin (Marguerite), Benna Lemon-Brundin (Siebel); Brita Ewert (Marthe); JB (Faust); Joel Berglund (Méphistophélès).

Preserved excerpts:
a. From beginning through "Salut! demeure chaste et pure" [cavatina incomplete: last 15 measures missing]; b. From "Je voudrais bien savoir" through beginning of "Prenez mon bras" [14 measures, ending with "Âme douce et pure"].

4402
1944, November 10. Stockholm, Concert Hall, Large Auditorium. Part of public radio concert, for the benefit of Stockholmsmusikernas humanitära orkesterfond [The Humanitarian Orchestra Foundation of the Stockholm Musicians]. With Sw. Radio Symphony Orch., cond. Tor Mann [Sw. Radio: L-B 6178]

a. Una furtiva lagrima [It] (Donizetti: *L'elisir d'amore*)
b. Mamma!...Quel vino [It] (Mascagni: *Cavalleria rusticana*)
c. Nessun dorma! [It] (Puccini: *Turandot*)

JB also sang three Swedish songs, "Jag längtar dig", "Skogen sover" and "Tristans död", in the first part of the concert, but no recording of them has been preserved in the Sw. Radio archive.

4501
1945, January 1. Stockholm, Concert Hall, Large Auditorium. *Radiotjänst 20 år* [Sw. Broadcasting Corp.'s 20th Anniversary], radio programme (broadcast without public). With Hjördis Schymberg (sop., in b) & Stockholm Radio Orch., cond. Tor Mann.
[Sw. Radio: L-B+ 6209]

a. Che gelida manina [It] (Puccini: *La bohème*)
b. O soave fanciulla [It] (Puccini: *La bohème*)
c. Mamma!...Quel vino [It] (Mascagni: *Cavalleria rusticana*)

JB was heard on two occasions during the long programme (2 hours 30 min.), where (as in 3703 and 4102) many of the most popular Swedish artists participated, among them Anders De Wahl, Karl Gerhard, Sigge Fürst and Carl-Axel Hallgren.

4502
1945, September 28. Stockholm, Concert Hall, Large Auditorium. Radio concert (broadcast without public). With Sw. Radio Symphony Orch., cond. Tor Mann.
[Sw. Radio: L-B+ 6451]

a. Je suis seul!...Ah! fuyez, douce image [Fr] (Massenet: *Manon*)
b. Élégie [Sw: Elegi] (Massenet)
c. Je crois entendre encore [Fr] (Bizet: *Les pêcheurs de perles*)
d. Una furtiva lagrima [It] (Donizetti: *L'elisir d'amore*)
e. È la solita storia [It] (Cilea: *L'arlesiana*)

(a-e)	[CD]	*Bluebell* ABCD 036
(a-c)	[33]	*ANNA* 1045
(a,c-e)	[33]	*Golden Age* EJS 530
(a,c)	[33]	*MDP* 026
(b,c)	[33]	*SR* SRLP 1354/55
(b)	[33]	*MDP* 035
	[CD]	*OASI* 7006
(c-e)	[CD]	*Legato* BIM 708-2

4503
1945, October 7. Detroit, Masonic Temple Auditorium. *Ford Sunday Evening Hour*, ABC radio concert (only parts known to be preserved). With Ford Symphony Orch., cond. Dimitri Mitropoulos.

?a. Che gelida manina [It] (Puccini: *La bohème*)
b. Zueignung [Ger] (R. Strauss)
c. Jeg elsker dig [Nor] (Grieg)
d. Mattinata [It] (Leoncavallo)

There was another song at the end of this programme, "Hymn to the City" (Storer), but it was probably not sung by JB. The only known transcription of 4503c is incomplete.

4504
1945, November 19. New York, Rockefeller Center, NBC studio. *Voice of Firestone*, NBC radio concert (only parts known to be preserved). With Firestone Orch., cond. Howard Barlow.

?a. If I Could Tell You [Eng] (Firestone)
b. An Sylvia [Eng: Who is Silvia] (Schubert)
c. Instant charmant...En fermant les yeux [Fr] (Massenet: *Manon*)
?d. Jeanie with the Light Brown Hair [Eng] (Foster)
e. Ach, so fromm [It: M'apparì tutt'amor] (Flotow: *Martha*)
?f. In My Garden [Eng] (Firestone)

(b)	[33]	*OASI* 660
	[CD]	*OASI* 7006

4505
1945, December 22. New York, Rockefeller Center, NBC studio. Transcription of Christmas programme with JB and his wife, intended for Sweden. Broadcast (shortwave): December 24, 1945. With Anna-Lisa Björling (sop., in a) & piano.
[JB family coll.; Sw. Radio: L-B+ 23534]

a. Stille Nacht, heilige Nacht [Sw: Stilla natt, heliga natt] (Gruber)
b. Cantique de Noël [Sw: Julsång] (Adam)

The songs were preceded by Mrs. Björling's spoken greetings. Original glass master disc broken: only second verse of "b" survives. [Label number: IS 4066 File 2877.] The JB family collection contains a transcription of the complete broadcast. "Cantique de Noël" was broadcast in Sweden Dec. 28 on the programme *På främmande breddgrader* [On Foreign Latitudes] where the song was preceded by a greeting from the Swedish minister in Washington, Herman Eriksson. This programme is also preserved in the Sw. Radio archive: L-B+ 6610.

4506
1945, December 29. New York, Metropolitan Opera House. Complete opera performance (Saturday matinee, Texaco-Metropolitan broadcast). With Metropolitan Opera Orch. & Chorus, cond. Cesare Sodero.

Rigoletto (Verdi), sung in It. by Bidú Sayão (Gilda); Thelma Altman (Giovanna, Page), Maxine Stellman (Countess Ceprano); Martha Lipton (Maddalena); JB (Duke), Richard Manning (Borsa); Leonard Warren (Rigoletto), William Hargrave (Monterone), George Cehanovsky (Marullo); Norman Cordon (Sparafucile), John Baker (Count Ceprano).

Complete:	[33]	*Op.Arch.* OPA 1019/20 // *Unique* UORC 176 // *Hist.Op.Perf.* HOPE 204
	[CD]	*Music & Arts* CD 636 // *Melodram* CDM 27079

Excerpts:

(Act 1)	a1. Della mia bella... a2. Questa o quella... a3. Partite? Crudele! [to end of act];
(Act 2)	b. Figlia! Mio padre!... È il sol dell'anima;
(Act 3)	c. Ella mi fù rapita!...Parmi veder le lagrime;
(Act 4)	d. La donna è mobile; e. Un dì, se ben...Bella figlia dell'amore [to end of opera].

(a-e)	[33]	*Golden Age* EJS 209
(a2,c,d)	[33]	*Estro Armonico* EA 020
(c)	[33]	*MDP* 035
	[CD]	*OASI* 7006
(d)	[33]	*Rococo* 5304 // *MDP* 026

4601
1946, January 13. Detroit, Masonic Temple Auditorium. *Ford Sunday Evening Hour,* ABC radio concert (only parts known to be preserved). With Ford Symphony Orch. [members of Detroit Symphony Orch.], cond. Eugene Ormandy.

a. Je suis seul!...Ah! fuyez, douce image [Fr] (Massenet: *Manon*)
b. Tonerna [Sw] (Sjöberg)
c. Ständchen [Ger] (R. Strauss)

?d. For You Alone [Eng] (Geehl)
e. Mamma!...Quel vino [It] (Mascagni: *Cavalleria rusticana*)

(a) [33] *Golden Age* EJS 252

There was another song at the end of this programme, "As with Gladness" (Kocher), but it was probably not sung by JB. The only known transcription of 4601c is incomplete.

4602
1946, January 21. New York, Rockefeller Center, NBC studio. *Voice of Firestone*, NBC radio concert (only parts known to be preserved). With Eleanor Steber (sop., in a,b,d,e) & Firestone Orch., cond. Howard Barlow.

?a. If I Could Tell You [Eng] (Firestone)
b. Will You Remember [Eng] (Romberg: *Maytime*)
?c. For You Alone [Eng] (Geehl)
d. Quel suon...Ah! che la morte ognora [It] (Verdi: *Il trovatore*)
?e. In My Garden [Eng] (Firestone)

(b,d)	[33]	*Golden Age* EJS 367 // *HRE* 214-2 // *Legendary* LR 141
	[CD]	*Legato* BIM 712-1
(b)	[33]	*Legendary* LR 138

4603
1946, March 25. New York, Rockefeller Center, NBC studio. *Voice of Firestone*, NBC radio concert. With Firestone Orch., cond. Howard Barlow. [Firestone Libr.]

a. If I Could Tell You [Eng] (Firestone)
b. Jeg elsker dig [Nor] (Grieg)
c. Cachés dans cet asile [Eng: Concealed in this retreat...Oh! wake not yet] (Godard: *Jocelyn*)
d. Because [Eng] (d'Hardelot, pseud. of Rhodes)
e. Neapolitan Love Song [Eng] (Herbert: *Princess Pat*)
f. In My Garden [Eng] (Firestone)

(b,c,e) [Tr] *US Dept. of State* 17-3553 / QND6-MM-9414

The excerpts on the transcription disc above are not dated, but according to the label, they were accompanied by Voorhees' orch. This would indicate that they were taken from a Telephone Hour broadcast. However, the contents of the disc correspond with the programme for this Firestone concert. Also, the fact that the matrix number of the disc is close to that of another disc known to have been made in 1946, strongly indicate that the record was mislabelled. As far as can be ascertained, two of the three songs have not been sung by JB on any Telephone Hour broadcast.

4604
1946, April 15. New York, Rockefeller Center, NBC studio. *Voice of Firestone*, NBC radio concert. With Firestone Orch. & (in c) Chorus, cond. Howard Barlow. [Firestone Libr.]

a. If I Could Tell You [Eng] (Firestone)
b. Repentir [Eng: O Divine Redeemer] (Gounod)
c. Sanctus [Lat] (Gounod: *Messe Solennelle à Sainte Cécile*)
d. Die Allmacht [Ger] (Schubert)
e. In My Garden [Eng] (Firestone)

(b,c)	[33]	*Rococo* 5329
(c)	[33]	*Golden Age* EJS 279

4605
1946, May 12. Detroit, Masonic Temple Auditorium. *Ford Sunday Evening Hour*, ABC radio concert (only parts known to be preserved). With Ford Symphony Orch. [members of Detroit Symphony Orch.], cond. Fritz Reiner.

?a. Salut! demeure chaste et pure [Fr] (Gounod: *Faust*)
b. Jungfrun under lind [Sw] (Peterson-Berger)
c. Land, du välsignade [Sw] (Althén)
d. Mother o'Mine [Eng] (Tours)

(b,c)	[33]	*Rococo* 5341
(d)	[33]	*ANNA* 1069

There was another song at the end of this programme, "Fairest Lord Jesus", but it was sung by the chorus and the audience, not by JB.

4606
1946, December 21. New York, Rockefeller Center, NBC studio. Transcription probably made for later shortwave broadcast to Sweden [compare 4505]. With piano.
[Private US coll.]

Cantique de Noël [Sw: Julsång] (Adam)

	[CD]	*Voce* 120CD

The original disc has only the following identification on the label: "Number: IS 5098 File 38140. Broadcast: X46-325, Dec. 21, 1946."

4701
1947, February 1. New York, Metropolitan Opera House. Complete opera performance (Saturday matinee, Texaco-Metropolitan broadcast). With Metropolitan Opera Orch. & Chorus, cond. Emil Cooper.

Roméo et Juliette (Gounod), sung in Fr. by Bidú Sayão (Juliette), Mimi Benzell (Stéphano); Claramae Turner (Gertrude); JB (Roméo), Thomas Hayward (Tybalt), Anthony Marlowe (Benvolio); George Cehanovsky (Paris), John Brownlee (Mercutio), Philip Kinsman (Grégorio); Kenneth Schon (Capulet), Nicola Moscona (Friar Laurent), William Hargrave (Duke).

Complete:	[33]	*Golden Age* EJS 154 // *MET* 11 // *RRE* AD 101/02
	[CD]	*Myto* 2MCD 89004 // *Rodolphe* RPV 32690/91

Excerpts:

(Act 1)	a1. Le nom de cette... a2. Ange adorable;
(Act 2)	b1. Ô nuit! sous tes ailes... b2. L'amour!...Ah! lève-toi, soleil... b3. Hélas! moi, le haïre; c. Ô nuit divine! [to end of act];
(Act 3)	d. Dieu que fis l'homme...Ô pur bonheur!;
(Act 4)	e. Va! je t'ai pardonné...Nuit d'hyménée!;
(Act 5)	f. C'est là! Salut! tombeau [to end of opera].

(a-f)	[33]	*ERR* 145-1
(a2,b2,c,e,f)	[33]	*Rococo* 5329
(a2)	[33]	*Op.Arch.* OPA 1008
(b2,c)	[CD]	*Verona* 28030/31
(b2)	[33]	*Unique* UORC 350

4702
1947, December 27. New York, Metropolitan Opera House. Complete opera performance (Saturday matinee, Texaco-Metropolitan broadcast). With Metropolitan Opera Orch. & Chorus, cond. Emil Cooper.

Il trovatore (Verdi), sung in It. by Stella Roman (Leonora), Inge Manski (Ines); Margaret Harshaw (Azucena); JB (Manrico), Lodovico Oliviero (Ruiz); Leonard Warren (Di Luna); Giacomo Vaghi (Ferrando), John Baker (Gypsy).

Complete: Not issued

Excerpts:

(Act 2)	a. Stride la vampa!...Soli or siamo...Mal reggendo...Perigliarti ancor languente;
(Act 3)	b. Ah sì, ben mio.

(a)	[CD]	*Verona* 27068
(b)	[33]	*MDP* 035
	[CD]	*OASI* 7006

4801
1948, March 15. New York, Rockefeller Center, NBC studio. *Telephone Hour*, NBC radio concert. With Bell Telephone Orch., cond. Donald Voorhees.

a. Mattinata [It] (Leoncavallo)
b. Siren' [Eng: Lilacs] (Rachmaninov)
c. Clorinda [Eng] (Morgan)
d. Je suis seul!...Ah! fuyez, douce image [Fr] (Massenet: *Manon*)

(a-c)	[78]	*V-Disc* 863
	[33]	*Golden Age* EJS 367 // *Rococo* 5341 // *Legendary* LR 138 // *Voce* 95 // *OASI* 660

	[CD]	*Legato* BIM 708-2 // *OASI* 7006
(a,d)	[33]	*Glendale* GL 8006
(a)	[CD]	*Verona* 27022
	[MC]	*Verona* 427022
(c)	[Tr]	*US Dept. of State* DS-1066
(d)	[33]	*Unique* UORC 350

4802
1948. September 26. Stockholm, Gustaf Vasa Church. Funeral ceremony for Count Folke Bernadotte (broadcast). With Royal Orch., cond. Nils Grevillius.
[Sw. Radio: L-B+ 9197]

Sverige [Sw] (Stenhammar: *Ett folk*)

Count Bernadotte, nephew of King Gustaf V and a personal friend of the Björling family, was assassinated on September 17 in Jerusalem by an Israeli extremist group called Lekhi, while working as a U.N. mediator in Palestine.

4803
1948, November 15. New York, Rockefeller Center, NBC studio. *Telephone Hour*, NBC radio concert. With Bell Telephone Orch., cond. Donald Voorhees.
[JB family coll.; Sw. Radio: L-B+ 23534]

a. Song of India: Ne shchest almazov [Eng: My heathen guests] (Rimsky-Korsakov: *Sadko*)
b. L'alba separa dalla luce l'ombra [It] (Tosti)
c. For You Alone [Eng] (Geehl)
d. La fleur que tu m'avais jetée [Fr] (Bizet: *Carmen*)

(a)	[33]	*Golden Age* EJS 367
(b-d)	[33]	*HRE* 214-2 // *Glendale* GL 8006
(b,c)	[CD]	*Legato* BIM 708-2
(c)	[33]	*Legendary* LR 138
(d)	[33]	*Unique* UORC 350

4804
1948, December 25. New York, Metropolitan Opera House. Complete opera performance (Saturday matinee, Texaco-Metropolitan broadcast). With Metropolitan Opera Orch. & Chorus, cond. Giuseppe Antonicelli.

La bohème (Puccini), sung in It. by Bidú Sayão (Mimì), Mimi Benzell (Musetta); JB (Rodolfo), Anthony Marlowe (Parpignol); Francesco Valentino (Marcello), George Cehanovsky (Schaunard); Nicola Moscona (Colline), Salvatore Baccaloni (Benoit, Alcindoro); Lawrence Davidson (Sergeant)

Complete:	[33]	*Unique* UORC 180 // *Robin Hood* RHR 515-B
	[CD]	*Myto* 2MCD 916.47

Excerpts:

(Act 1)	a1. Non sono in vena... a2. Che gelida manina... a3. Sì. Mi chiamano Mimì [to end of act];	
(Act 3)	b. Complete act;	
(Act 4)	c. In un coupè...O Mimì; d. Sono andati? [to end of opera].	

(a-d)	[33]	*Op.Arch.* OPA 1007
(a)	[33]	*Golden Age* EJS 405
(a2)	[33]	*ANNA* 1060

4901

1949, April 4. New York, Rockefeller Center, NBC studio. *Telephone Hour*, NBC radio concert. With Bell Telephone Orch., cond. Donald Voorhees.

a. Ständchen [Ger] (Schubert)
b. Neapolitan Love Song [Eng] (Herbert: *Princess Pat*)
c. Mamma!...Quel vino [It] (Mascagni: *Cavalleria rusticana*)

(a-c)	[Tr]	*US Dept. of State* DS-1066
	[33]	*HRE* 214-2
(a,b)	[33]	*Legendary* LR 138
(a)	[33]	*Glendale* GL 8006
(c)	[33]	*Golden Age* EJS 252
	[CD]	*Legato* BIM 708-2

4902

1949, April 11. New York, Carnegie Hall. *Sweden in Music*, benefit concert for the Swedish Seamen's Welfare Fund (broadcast by WNYC-FM, New York). With James W. Quillian, piano. [Sw. Radio: L-B+ 10225]

a. Trollsjön [Sw] (Söderman)
b. Skogen sover [Sw] (Alfvén)
c. I drömmen du är mig nära [Sw] (Sjögren)
d. Tristans död [Sw] (Rangström)
e. L'alba separa dalla luce l'ombra [It] (Tosti)
f. Jungfrun under lind [Sw] (Peterson-Berger)

(a-f)	[33]	*MDP* 026
(c,d,f)	[33]	*Golden Age* EJS 279

Other soloists on this programme were Joel Berglund and Karin Branzell, who sang with orchestra. The Sw. Radio tape copy of the recording was made from acetates, sent from the Swedish Consulate General in New York, while the MDP issue is reported on the sleeve to come from "a rare paper tape".

4903

1949, August 15. Stockholm, Bromma Airport, passenger waiting room. Interview [in Eng.; 2 min. 20 sec.] by Bill Arthur (recorded on wire) for Australian Broadcasting Commission (ABC). [Probably never broadcast by ABC, but used by a commercial radio

station in Sydney in 1950s for a programme called "World Famous Tenors".]
[ABC archive; Sw. Radio: B 57476]

Topics: JB's best recording; his favourite role; his fishing hobby; his family.

4904
1949, August 23. Los Angeles, Hollywood Bowl. *Symphonies Under the Stars*, open air concert (MBS [Mutual Broadcasting System] broadcast). With Anna-Lisa Björling (sop., in e-g) & Hollywood Bowl Symphony Orch., cond. Izler Solomon.

a. Frondi tenere...Ombra mai fù [It] (Handel: *Serse*)
b. Adelaide [Ger] (Beethoven)
c. Nessun dorma! [It] (Puccini: *Turandot*)
d. Che gelida manina [It] (Puccini: *La bohème*)
e. O soave fanciulla [It] (Puccini: *La bohème*)
f. Ange adorable [Fr] (Gounod: *Roméo et Juliette*)
g. Va! je t'ai pardonné...Nuit d'hymenée [Fr] (Gounod: *Roméo et Juliette*)

(a,g)	[33]	*ANNA* 1069
(a)	[MC]	*Demand* DPC 504
(b,c,f)	[33]	*MDP* 026
(b,d-f)	[33]	*ANNA* 1017 // *Voce* 95
(c,d)	[33]	*Unique* UORC 350
(f)	[33]	*ANNA* 1045

Mrs. Björling also sang "Sì. Mi chiamano Mimì" as a solo number.

4905
1949, September 25. San Francisco, War Memorial Opera House. Part of opera performance. With San Francisco Opera Orch., cond. Karl Kritz.

La bohème (Puccini): "O soave fanciulla". Sung in It. by Licia Albanese (Mimì) & JB (Rodolfo).

[Tr] *Salvation Army* RR 17175

4906
1949, October 23. San Francisco, War Memorial Opera House. *Standard Hour*, NBC radio concert. With Anna-Lisa Björling (sop., in b-c) & San Francisco Opera Orch., cond. Gaetano Merola. [Stanford Univ.]

a. Che gelida manina [It] (Puccini: *La bohème*)
b. O soave fanciulla [It] (Puccini: *La bohème*)
c. Va! je t'ai pardonné...Nuit d'hyménée [Fr] (Gounod: *Roméo et Juliette*)
d. Je suis seul!...Ah! fuyez, douce image [Fr] (Massenet: *Manon*)

(a,b,d)	[33]	*ANNA* 1069
	[MC]	*Demand* DPC 504
(b-d)	[CD]	*Myto* 1MCD 912.39

(c,d)	[33]	*Voce* 95
(c)	[33]	*Golden Age* EJS 252
(d)	[CD]	*Legato* BIM 708-2 // *Verona* 28030/31

Mrs. Björling also sang "Sì. Mi chiamano Mimì", "Je veux vivre" and "O mio babbino caro" as solo numbers.

4907

1949, November 7. New York, Rockefeller Center, NBC studio. *Telephone Hour*, NBC radio concert. With Bell Telephone Orch., cond. Donald Voorhees.

a. Jeanie with the Light Brown Hair [Eng] (Foster)
b. Ständchen [Ger] (R. Strauss)
c. Che gelida manina [It] (Puccini: *La bohème*)

(a-c)	[Tr]	*US Dept. of State* DS-1401/02
	[33]	*HRE* 214-2
(a,b)	[33]	*Golden Age* EJS 367
(a)	[33]	*Legendary* LR 138
(b)	[33]	*Glendale* GL 8006
(c)	[33]	*Golden Age* EJS 252
	[CD]	*Legato* BIM 708-2

4908

1949, December 10. New York, Metropolitan Opera House. Complete opera performance (Saturday matinee, Texaco-Metropolitan broadcast). With Metropolitan Opera Orch. & Chorus, cond. Giuseppe Antonicelli.

Manon Lescaut (Puccini), sung in It. by Dorothy Kirsten (Manon); Jean Madeira (Singer); JB (Des Grieux), Thomas Hayward (Edmondo), Alessio de Paolis (Dancing Master), Paul Franke (Lamplighter); Giuseppe Valdengo (Lescaut); Salvatore Baccaloni (Geronte), Clifford Harvuot (Sergeant), George Cehanovsky (Innkeeper), Osie Hawkins (Sea Captain).

Complete:	[33]	*Unique* UORC 207
	[CD]	*Myto* 2MCD 931.73

Excerpts:

(Act 1)	a. Tra voi, belle; b. Cortese damigella; c. Donna non vidi mai; d.Vedete? Io son fedele;
(Act 2)	e1. Tu, tu, amore?... e2. Ah! Manon, mi tradisce... e3. Un'altra volta [to end of act];
(Act 3)	f. Presto! In fila! [to end of act];
(Act 4)	g. Complete act.

(a-g)	[33]	*Golden Age* EJS 251
(c,e2,f)	[33]	*Rococo* 5304

5001
1950, March 6. New York, Rockefeller Center, NBC studio. *Voice of Firestone*, NBC radio & television concert. With Anna-Lisa Björling (sop., in a,d,e) & Firestone Orch., cond. Howard Barlow. [AV recording (Kinescope): Firestone Libr.]

a.	If I Could Tell You [Eng] (Firestone)
b.	Neapolitan Love Song [Eng] (Herbert: *Princess Pat*)
c.	Salut! demeure chaste et pure [Fr] (Gounod: *Faust*)
d.	O soave fanciulla [It] (Puccini: *La bohème*)
e.	In My Garden [Eng] (Firestone)

(a-e)	[vc]	*VAI* 69101
(a,e)	[33]	*ANNA* 1069
(c)	[33]	*Unique* UORC 350
(d)	[33]	*Golden Age* EJS 252

Mrs. Björling also sang "O mio babbino caro" as a solo number.

5002
1950, April 20 or 22. New Orleans, Municipal Auditorium. Complete opera performance (in-house recording). With New Orleans Opera House Assn. Orch. & Chorus, cond. Walter Herbert.

Un ballo in maschera (Verdi), sung in It. by Suzy Morris (Amelia), Audrey Schuh (Oscar); Martha Larrimore (Ulrica); JB (Riccardo), George Berger (Judge, Servant); Marko Rothmüller (Renato); Henri Feux (Silvano), Norman Treigle (Samuel), Jack Dabdoub (Tom).

Complete: Not issued

Excerpts:

(Act 1)	a1. Amici miei...La rivedrà nell'estasi... a2. Il cenno mio...Alla vita [to end of scene]; b1. Arrivo il primo!...Che v'agita così... b2. Or tu Sibilla...Di' tu se fedele... b3. Chi voi siate... b4. È scherzo od è follia;
(Act 2)	c1.Teco io sto...Ahimè! s'appressa alcun!... c2. Seguitemi;
(Act 3)	d. Forse la soglia attinse...Sì, rivederti; e. Ah! perché qui [to end of opera].

(a-e)	[CD]	*Legato* LCD 154-1
(a1,b2,b4,c1,d,e)	[33]	*Golden Age* EJS 468
(a)	[CD]	*Legato* BIM 708-2
(d)	[33]	*Golden Age* EJS 405

5003
1950, July 6. Stockholm, Gröna Lund, Tivoli. Part of open-air recital (privately recorded on acetate discs). With Harry Ebert, piano. [Private Sw. collection?]

a. Pays merveilleux...Ô paradis [It: Mi batte il cor...O paradiso] (Meyerbeer: *L'africaine*)
b. Die böse Farbe [Ger] (Schubert)
c. Ständchen [Ger] (R. Strauss)
d. L'alba separa dalla luce l'ombra [It] (Tosti)
e. Come un bel dì di maggio [It] (Giordano: *Andrea Chénier*)
f. O Colombina [Sw: O Colombin] (Leoncavallo: *Pagliacci*)

(a-f)	[33]	*Bluebell* BELL 116
(f)	[33]	*ANNA* 1064 // *OASI* 660
	[CD]	*OASI* 7006

The two last encores, "For You Alone" and "Sverige", were not preserved.

5004
1950, September 4. Virum (Denmark), "Flyv fugl flyv" (home of Knud Hegermann-Lindencrone at Furesøvej 115). Part of improvised performance at private party (recorded on tape). Without accompaniment. [Hegermann-Lindencrone coll., Virum]

a. Hej dunkom, så länge vi levom [Sw] (trad.)
b. Bachanal [Sw] (Dahl)
c. E voi, piuttosto [Sw: Och ni, långt hellre] (Leoncavallo: *Pagliacci*)

(c)	[33]	*OASI* 660
	[CD]	*OASI* 7006

The recording includes part of JB's speech of thanks. He also sang "Donna non vidi mai" on this occasion, but that recording was destroyed at his own request, while he approved the other items.

5005
1950, October 1. Berlin, Titania Palace. *Stars aus Europa*, RIAS-Berlin radio concert [RIAS = Rundfunk im amerikanischen Sektor]. With RIAS-Berlin Orch., cond. Kurt Gaebel. [RIAS: Bd. 40-932/V-VII]

a. E lucevan le stelle [It] (Puccini: *Tosca*)
b. La fleur que tu m'avais jetée [Fr] (Bizet: *Carmen*)
c. Mamma!...Quel vino [It] (Mascagni: *Cavalleria rusticana*)

(a-c)	[33]	*ANNA* 1069

The concert was also transmitted by foreign radio stations. Among the other artists who sang on this programme were Erich Kunz, Elsa Cavelti and Rita Streich.

5006
1950, October 23. New York, Rockefeller Center, NBC studio. *Telephone Hour*, NBC radio concert. With Bell Telephone Orch., cond. Donald Voorhees.

a. Pays merveilleux...Ô paradis [It: Mi batte il cor...O paradiso] (Meyerbeer: *L'africaine*)
b. V molchan'i nochi taynoy [Eng: In the Silence of Night] (Rachmaninov)
c. Zueignung [Ger] (R. Strauss)
d. Come un bel dì di maggio [It] (Giordano: *Andrea Chénier*)

(a,b,d)	[Tr]	*US Dept. of State* DS-2451
	[33]	*HRE* 214-2
(a,c,d)	[33]	*Golden Age* EJS 367
(a)	[33]	*Glendale* GL 8006
(b,c)	[33]	*Voce* 95
(d)	[33]	*Golden Age* EJS 337
	[CD]	*Legato* BIM 708-2

5007
1950, November 6. New York, Metropolitan Opera House. Complete opera performance (opening night telecast). With Metropolitan Opera Orch. & Chorus, cond. Fritz Stiedry.

Don Carlo (Verdi), sung in It. by Delia Rigal (Elisabetta), Anne Bollinger (Tebaldo), Lucine Amara (Voice); Fedora Barbieri (Eboli); JB (Don Carlo), Paul Franke (Count Lerma), Emery Darcy (Herald); Robert Merrill (Rodrigo); Cesare Siepi (Filippo II), Jerome Hines (Grand Inquisitor), Lubomir Vichegonov (Friar).

Only audio recordings of this telecast have been found, no AV recording. This recording has sometimes been confused with No. 5008 (e.g., the Myto *Don Carlo* issue is stated to be 5007). In No. 5007, on Rodrigo's "Signora! Per vostra Maestà" in act 1, an announcer breaks in with an excuse for trouble with the "video portion".

5008
1950, November 11. New York, Metropolitan Opera House. Complete opera performance (Saturday matinee, Texaco-Metropolitan broadcast). With Metropolitan Opera Orch. & Chorus, cond. Fritz Stiedry.

Don Carlo (Verdi), sung in It. [Cast same as in 5007.]

Complete:	[Tr]	*US Dept. of State* DS-2334/45
	[33]	*Unique* UORC 121 // *Magn.Ed.* ME 105-3
	[CD]	*Myto* 2MCD 911.35

Excerpts:

(Act 1)	a. Io l'ho perduta!; b. Io vengo a domandar;
(Act 2)	c. A mezza-notte; d. Sire! egli è tempo;
(Act 3)	e. Son io, mio Carlo [abbreviated];
(Act 4)	f. È dessa!...Un detto [to end of opera].

(a-f)	[33]	*Golden Age* EJS 208
(c)	[33]	*MET* 100

5009
1950, November 20. New York, Rockefeller Center, NBC studio. *Voice of Firestone*, NBC radio & television concert. With Firestone Orch. & (in d,e) Chorus, cond. Howard Barlow.
[AV recording (Kinescope): Firestone Libr.]

a. If I Could Tell You [Eng] (Firestone)
b. An Sylvia [Ger] (Schubert)
c. La fleur que tu m'avais jetée [Fr] (Bizet: *Carmen*)
d. Mattinata [It] (Leoncavallo)
e. Neapolitan Love Song [Eng] (Herbert: *Princess Pat*)
f. In My Garden [Eng] (Firestone)

(a-f)	[VC]	*VAI* 69111
(e)	[33]	*Legendary* LR 142-5

5010
1950, December 23. New York, Metropolitan Opera House. Complete opera performance (Saturday matinee, Texaco-Metropolitan broadcast). With Metropolitan Opera Orch. & Chorus, cond. Fausto Cleva.

Faust (Gounod), sung in Fr. by Dorothy Kirsten (Marguerite), Anne Bollinger (Siebel); Thelma Votipka (Marthe); JB (Faust); Frank Guarrera (Valentin), Lawrence Davidson (Wagner); Cesare Siepi (Méphistophélès).

Complete:	[33]	*Unique* UORC 110
	[CD]	*Myto* 2MCD 922.58

Excerpts:
(Act 1) a. Complete act;
(Act 2) b. Qu'as-tu donc?; c. Ne permettrez-vous pas;
(Act 3) d. Quel trouble...Salut! demeure; e. La fièvre de mes sens [abridged, but Faust's part complete]; f1. Il se fait tard... f2. Ô nuit d'amour!... f3. Tête folle!;
(Act 4) g. Que voulez-vous, messieurs?;
(Act 5) h. Mon coeur est pénétré.

(a-h)	[33]	*HRE* 210-1
(d)	[CD]	*Legato* BIM 708-2
(f)	[33]	*Golden Age* EJS 252
(f1-2)	[33]	*MET* 100
(f2)	[33]	*Rec.Coll.Club* 5

5101
1951, January 8. New York, Rockefeller Center, NBC studio. *Telephone Hour*, NBC radio concert. With Bell Telephone Orch., cond. Donald Voorhees.

a.	Instant charmant...En fermant les yeux [Fr] (Massenet: *Manon*)
b.	Jungfrun under lind [Sw] (Peterson-Berger)
c.	For You Alone [Eng] (Geehl)
d.	Donna non vidi mai [It] (Puccini: *Manon Lescaut*)

(a,d)	[33]	*HRE* 214-2
(a)	[33]	*Unique* UORC 350 // *Legendary* LR 137-2 // *Glendale* GL 8006
	[CD]	*Verona* 27022
	[MC]	*Verona* 427022
(a, aria only)	[33]	*Golden Age* EJS 252
(b-d)	[33]	*Golden Age* EJS 367
(b,d)	[Tr]	*US Dept. of State* DS-2451
(c)	[33]	*OASI* 660
	[CD]	*OASI* 7006
(d)	[33]	*Golden Age* EJS 337

5102
1951, March 12. New York, Carnegie Hall. *Telephone Hour*, NBC radio concert. With Bell Telephone Orch., cond. Donald Voorhees.

a.	Recitar!...Vesti la giubba [It] (Leoncavallo: *Pagliacci*)
b.	The Rose of Tralee [Eng] (Glover)
c.	Se quel guerrier...Celeste Aida [It] (Verdi: *Aida*)

(a-c)	[33]	*Golden Age* EJS 279
(a,c)	[33]	*HRE* 214-2
(c)	[33]	*Unique* UORC 350 // *Legendary* LR 137-2 // *Glendale* GL 8006

5103
1951, April 1 (?) [broadcast date; may have been recorded on one of the last days in March]. Stockholm, radio studio. Interview [in Sw.; 3 min. 40 sec.] by Per Lindfors (Sw. Broadcasting Corp. Music Department) for the radio programme *Musikkrönika* [Music Chronicle]. [Sw. Radio: L-B 13929]

Topic: The recent duet recordings with Robert Merrill in New York. [Cf. note for Nos. 171-75.]

5104
1951, April 17. Stockholm, Royal Academy of Music. Transcription of radio concert, pre-recorded without public. Broadcast: May 1, 1951 (privately recorded - see below). With Sw. Radio Orch., cond. Sten Frykberg. [Sw. Radio: B 57.503]

a.	Ingemisco [Lat] (Verdi: *Messa da Requiem*)
b.	Questa o quella [It] (Verdi: *Rigoletto*)
c.	Se quel guerrier io fossi...Celeste Aida [It] (Verdi: *Aida*)

d. Nessun dorma! [It] (Puccini: *Turandot*)
e. Che gelida manina [It] (Puccini: *La bohème*)

This concert was not originally preserved in the Sw. Radio archive, but a wire recording made by Mrs. Elin Dahlstrand, Stockholm, was in the 1980's given to the archive.

5105
1951, June 20. Helsinki, Yliopiston juhlasali (Universitetets solennitetssal) [University Auditorium]. Part of Sibelius Week radio symphony concert (privately recorded on tape, see below). With Finnish Radio Orch., cond. Nils-Eric Fougstedt[Coll. H. Christiernin]

a. Flickan kom ifrån sin älsklings möte [Sw] (Sibelius)
b. Säv, säv, susa [Sw] (Sibelius)
c. Var det en dröm [Sw] (Sibelius)
d. Svarta rosor [Sw] (Sibelius)

JB also sang a repeat of "Svarta rosor", which has not been preserved. The recording was made in a radio studio by the conductor Henrik Christiernin, then a free-lance member of the Finnish Radio staff. The original recording was restored in 1991, when "Var det en dröm" was rebroadcast Oct. 26 by the Finnish Radio on a Björling programme, the last in a series of eight.

5106
1951, July 5. Stockholm, Gröna Lund, Tivoli. Open-air recital (recorded by Gröna Lunds Tivoli AB; see note below). With Harry Ebert, piano.

a. Cielo e mar! [It] (Ponchielli: *La Gioconda*)
b. I drömmen du är mig nära [Sw] (Sjögren)
c. Ich möchte schweben [Ger] (Sjögren)
d. Nessun dorma! [It] (Puccini: *Turandot*)
e. Mamma!...Quel vino [It] (Mascagni: *Cavalleria rusticana*)
f. Sverige [Sw] (Stenhammar: *Ett folk*)
g. Mattinata [It] (Leoncavallo)

The original JB recordings in the Gröna Lunds Tivoli archive (Nos. 5106, 5107, 5604, 5704, 5803, 5905, 5907) were destroyed by fire January 4, 1993, but the whole material had been copied for releases on the Bluebell label and therefore still exists. It is possible that the two Gröna Lund recitals from 1951, which were preserved in the archive on tape, were originally recorded on acetate discs (like 5003).

5107
1951, August 10. Stockholm, Gröna Lund, Tivoli. Open-air recital (recorded by Gröna Lunds Tivoli AB). With Harry Ebert, piano.

a. La fleur que tu m'avais jetée [Fr] (Bizet: *Carmen*)
b. Tonerna [Sw] (Sjöberg)
c. Jungfrun under lind [Sw] (Peterson-Berger)
d. L'alba separa dalla luce l'ombra [It] (Tosti)
e. Come un bel dì di maggio [It] (Giordano: *Andrea Chénier*)

f. La donna è mobile [It] (Verdi: *Rigoletto*)
g. Morgon [Sw] (Eklöf)

5108
1951, September 30. San Francisco, War Memorial Opera House. *Standard Hour*, NBC radio concert. With Bidú Sayão (sop., in d-e) & San Francisco Opera Orch., cond. Gaetano Merola. [Stanford Univ.]

a. Cielo e mar! [It] (Ponchielli: *La Gioconda*)
b. L'alba separa dalla luce l'ombra [It] (Tosti)
c. E lucevan le stelle [It] (Puccini: *Tosca*)
d. Va! je t'ai pardonné...Nuit d'hyménée [Fr] (Gounod: *Roméo et Juliette*)
e. Ange adorable [Fr] (Gounod: *Roméo et Juliette*)

(a-c)	[33]	*Voce* 95
(a,b,d)	[33]	*Unique* UORC 340
(a,c)	[33]	*Golden Age* EJS 367
	[CD]	*Legato* BIM 708-2
(a,e)	[33]	*Unique* UORC 350
(a)	[CD]	*Verona* 28030/31
(d,e)	[CD]	*Voce* 119CD
(d)	[33]	*Op.Arch.* OPA 1036/37 // *MDP* 026 // *Glendale* GL 8006
(e)	[Tr]	*Salvation Army* CPM 16-1074

5109
1951, November 11. Los Angeles, CBS Hollywood radio studio. *Edgar Bergen - Charlie McCarthy Show*, CBS radio programme. With Anna-Lisa Björling (sop., in b) & Ray Noble and his orchestra.

a. Neapolitan Love Song [Eng] (Herbert: *Princess Pat*)
b. Ange adorable [Fr] (Gounod: *Roméo et Juliette*) [abridged]

(b)	[33]	*Golden Age* EJS 252

Jussi & Anna-Lisa Björling also took part in a comic dialogue with Bergen-McCarthy [3 min. 30 sec.].

5110
1951, November 19. New York, Rockefeller Center, NBC studio. *Voice of Firestone*, NBC radio & television concert. With Firestone Orch. & (in e) Chorus, cond. Howard Barlow. [AV recording (Kinescope): Firestone Libr.]

a. If I Could Tell You [Eng] (Firestone)
b. Ah, Love, but a Day [Eng] (Beach)
c. Ständchen [Ger] (R. Strauss)
d. Recitar!...Vesti la giubba [It] (Leoncavallo: *Pagliacci*)
e. Wilt heden nu treden [Eng: We Gather Together (Prayer of Thanksgiving)] (trad.)
f. In My Garden [Eng] (Firestone)

(a-f) [VC] *VAI* 69101
(b-e) [CD] *Verona* 27022
[MC] *Verona* 427022
(b,e) [33] *HRE* 214-2 [e is abridged on this record]
(b) [CD] *Legato* LCD 103-1
(c) [33] *MDP* 035 // *Voce* 95
[CD] *OASI* 7006
(d) [33] *Golden Age* EJS 252
(e) [33] *Golden Age* EJS 279 // *Legendary* LR 138

5111
1951, December 2. Los Angeles, CBS Hollywood radio studio. *Edgar Bergen - Charlie McCarthy Show*, CBS radio programme. With Anna-Lisa Björling (sop., in b) & Ray Noble and his orchestra.

a. L'alba separa dalla luce l'ombra [It] (Tosti)
b. Will You Remember [Eng] (Romberg: *Maytime*)

(b) [33] *Golden Age* EJS 252 // *MDP* 035
[CD] *OASI* 7006

5201
1952, January 25. Stockholm, Swedish Radio Studio 2 (at 8 Kungsgatan). Transcription made for *Karusellen* [The Merry-Go-Round], entertainment radio programme broadcast live on January 26. With Gösta & Olle Björling (ten.) & Stig Rybrant, piano.
[Sw. Radio: PR 5189 (matrix 4501 MA)]

Sommarglädje [Sw] (anonymous)

[78] *Radiotjänst* PR 5189
[33] *Unique* UORC 377 // *SR* SRLP 1354/55 // *Legendary* LR 138

This recording was pressed in a few copies on one side of an ordinary 78 rpm. record in the PR series, with a transfer of the same song recorded by the three brothers as children (No. 4) on the other side. The PR series was generally used for archive purposes only, but one copy of this record was made available to the public as the prize in a lottery [for further details about this unique release, see Section 2:A, note for *Radiotjänst* PR 5189]. In addition to this copy and a few copies in the Sw. Radio archive, PR 5189 is also preserved for instance in the JB family collection.

5202
1952, March 10. New York, Rockefeller Center, NBC studio. *Voice of Firestone*, NBC radio & television concert. With Firestone Orch. & (in b,e) Chorus, cond. Howard Barlow.
[Sound recording: Firestone Libr.]

a. If I Could Tell You [Eng] (Firestone)
b. Sylvia [Eng] (Speaks)
c. Nessun dorma! [It] (Puccini: *Turandot*)
d. L'alba separa dalla luce l'ombra [It] (Tosti)

e. Neapolitan Love Song [Eng] (Herbert: *Princess Pat*)
f. In My Garden [Eng] (Firestone)

(a-c)	[33]	*HRE* 214-2
(a,b,d,f)	[33]	*Legendary* LR 138
(b-e)	[CD]	*Verona* 27022
	[MC]	*Verona* 427022
(b,d,e)	[33]	*Golden Age* EJS 279
(b,e)	[CD]	*Legato* LCD 103-1
(c)	[33]	*Golden Age* EJS 252 // *Rococo* 5304 // *ANNA* 1017
(d,e)	[33]	*Rococo* 5341

Unlike JB's three other Firestone TV concerts, no AV recording of this one has been found.

5203
1952, May 25. Stockholm, Skansen. Part of open-air recital on "TCO Day" [TCO = The Central Organization of Salaried Employees in Sweden]. With Harry Ebert, piano.
[Sw. Radio: L-B 23519]

a. Pays merveilleux...Ô paradis [It: Mi batte il cor...O paradiso] (Meyerbeer: *L'africaine*) [Incomplete: last measures missing (after "s'arrivir")]
b. Ich hab' kein Geld, bin vogelfrei [Sw: Nu är jag pank och fågelfri] (Millöcker: *Der Bettelstudent*)
c. Cielo e mar! [It] (Ponchielli: *La Gioconda*) [Last measures incomplete]
d. Land, du välsignade [Sw] (Althén) [Incomplete: last four measures missing (after "skuggorna neder")]

These fragments from a Sw. Broadcasting Corp. recording were preserved by accident, labelled only as a Skansen recital from the 1950's. The recording has been almost certainly identified with this recital by comparing newspaper reviews of JB's many Skansen appearances. The complete programme and the original sequence of the items are not known.

5204
1952, October 3. Stockholm, Concert Hall, Large Auditorium. Transcription of radio concert, pre-recorded without public. First broadcast: (b-f only) December 25, 1952 - repeat of January 24, 1954, also transmitted to Denmark, Norway and Finland; (complete concert) September 7, 1980. With Sw. Radio Orch., cond. Sten Frykberg.
[Sw. Radio: B 26238]

a. In fernem Land [Sw: I fjärran land] (Wagner: *Lohengrin*)
b. Var det en dröm [Sw] (Sibelius) - [Short break in this recording]
c. Svarta rosor [Sw] (Sibelius)
d. Säv, säv, susa [Sw] (Sibelius)
e. Una furtiva lagrima [It] (Donizetti: *L'elisir d'amore*)
f. Mamma!...Quel vino [It] (Mascagni: *Cavalleria rusticana*)

(a)	[CD]	*Bluebell* ABCD 036
(b)	[33]	*SR* SRLP 1354/55

5301
1953, June 6. Stockholm, Stadion. *Svenska Flaggans Dag* [Swedish Flag Day], broadcast of open-air ceremony. With Band of the Royal Svea Life Guards, cond. Ille Gustafsson.
[Sw. Radio: A 53/3, L-B+ 19734]

a. Endräkt [Sw] (Alfvén)
b. Nämner du Sverige [Sw] (Wide)

(a)	[33]	*SR* SRLP 1354/55

5302
1953, September 27 or 28 (?). Stockholm, Oscar Theatre. Recording made (dubbing done a day or two later) for the motion picture *Resan till Dej* [The Journey to You], later renamed *En gång jag seglar i hamn* [Once I Will Sail into the Harbour]. With Royal Orch., cond. Sune Waldimir (pseud. for Engström). [Sw. Film Institute]

a. Celeste Aida [It] (Verdi: *Aida*) [Only last half of aria on soundtrack]
b. Till havs [Sw] (Nordqvist)

(b)	[33]	*ANNA* 1069 // *OASI* 660
	[CD]	*OASI* 7006

This film, directed by Stig Olin, was produced by Terraproduktion between September 23 and November 19, and released December 19, 1953. It was also shown on Swedish television in 1963. In the film, JB plays himself and he appears in a scene as a guest on a fictitious radio programme called *Familjelördag* [Family Saturday]. There he is received by the host of the programme, Sigge Fürst (a well-known entertainer who also plays himself).

5303
1953, end of November (?) [in period Nov. 17 - Dec. 17]. New York, Essex House Hotel (?). Interview [in Eng.; 11 min.] by Ruby Mercer, host of WNYC radio programme *Mr. & Mrs. Opera*. Partly rebroadcast [3 min. 25 sec. only] by Mercer, host of *Opera Time*, CBC Toronto, September 1960.

Topics: JB's first US visit in 1919-21; his father's and his brother Gösta's careers; his own musical training; his knowledge of foreign languages; the new Met *Faust* production; singing with Anna-Lisa; JB's family; his travelling plans; the planned *Ballo* with Toscanini; Christmas celebrations in Sweden; an operatic mishap in a *Bohème* finale; this year's singing activities; further plans for singing at the Met.

53xx
1953(?). Helsinki, B-Messuhalli (B-Mässhallen) [Exhibition Hall B]. Radio recital (privately recorded on tape). With piano.

a. In fernem Land [Sw: I fjärran land] (Wagner: *Lohengrin*) - [Short break in this recording]

b. En svane [Nor] (Grieg)
c. Ein Traum [Nor: En drøm] (Grieg)
d. Till havs [Sw] (Nordqvist) - [Short break in this recording]
e. Säv, säv, susa [Sw] (Sibelius)
f. Demanten på marssnön [Sw] (Sibelius)
g. L'alba separa dalla luce l'ombra [It] (Tosti)
h. Tonerna [Sw] (Sjöberg)
i. Mamma!...Quel vino [It] (Mascagni: *Cavalleria rusticana*)

A tape recording of this recital was in 1991 given to the Finnish Radio (YLE) by a private collector, who thinks he must have recorded it in 1953 or one of the following years. However, the performance is not identical with any of JB's known Finnish recitals, and neither YLE nor JB's Finnish agent, Fazer Artists' Management, has been able to date the performance. JB's Swedish agent, Konsertbolaget, received on March 3, 1953, a payment to him from Finland which may possibly be connected with this recital.

5401
1954, January 28. Milwaukee (Wisconsin), Pfister Hotel, room 622. Interview [in Eng.; 11'35"] by Jim Wallace (WFOX) after recital in Milwaukee on the preceding day. Broadcast: January 31, 1954. The interview also includes accompanist Frederick Schauwecker. [JB family coll.; Sw. Radio: L-B+ 23539]

Topics: JB's return from Europe; a touring singer's problems; JB's career, especially in Sweden during the war; advice to young singers.

5402
1954, June 4. Stockholm, Royal Opera House. Part of Stockholm Music Festival opera performance (one act was recorded by Sw. Broadcasting Corp.). Broadcast: June 5, 1954. With Royal Orch., cond. Lamberto Gardelli. [Coll. O. Söderholm; Sw. Radio: B 57486]

Rigoletto (Verdi): act 3, first part [through end of quartet]. Sung in It. by Hjördis Schymberg (Gilda); Bette (Wermine-)Björling (Maddalena), JB (Duke); Hugo Hasslo (Rigoletto), Sven-Erik Jacobsson (Sparafucile).

This recording was not originally preserved by the Sw. Broadcasting Corp. The present copy in the Swedish Radio archive was derived from the only known off-the-air recording, made on steel wire by Olle Söderholm, Västerås. There is a break in the quartet of about one second and a few other minor defects.

5403
1954, June 9. Bergen (Norway), Concert Palace. *Bergen International Festival Concert* (first part directly broadcast in Norway, larger part later broadcast in the US - recording incomplete?, see below). With Bergen Symphony Orch. (Musikselskabet Harmoniens orkester), cond. Carl Garaguly.

a. Frondi tenere...Ombra mai fù [It] (Handel: *Serse*)
b. Pietà, Signore [It] (Niedermeyer)
c. Ingemisco [Lat] (Verdi: *Messa da Requiem*)
d. Skogen sover [Sw] (Alfvén)

e.	Säv, säv, susa [Sw] (Sibelius)	
f.	En svane [Nor] (Grieg)	
?g.	Ein Traum [Nor: En drøm] (Grieg)	
h.	Jeg elsker dig [Nor] (Grieg)	

(a-f,h)	[33]	*MDP* 035 // *Bluebell* BELL 163
	[CD]	*Bluebell* ABCD 006 // *Verona* 27068
(a-c)	[33]	*ANNA* 1017
(a,b)	[33]	*Golden Age* EJS 279
	[CD]	*Legato* LCD 103-1
(c)	[33]	*Unique* UORC 350
	[CD]	*Legato* BIM 708-2
(f,h)	[33]	*Golden Age* EJS 367

The first part of the concert (through "Ingemisco") was directly broadcast by the Norwegian radio. The whole concert was recorded by James Fassett, CBS, and broadcast by him in the US on July 18, 1954 (probably except "En drøm", since the song is missing on all checked copies of this recording).

5404
1954, December 8. Stockholm, Royal Opera House. Complete opera performance (recorded by Sw. Broadcasting Corp.). First broadcast: August 30, 1955. With Royal Orch. & Royal Opera Chorus, cond. Kurt Bendix. [Sw. Radio: Ma 55/1039:1]

Cavalleria rusticana (Mascagni), sung in It. (JB throughout) & Sw. by Aase Nordmo-Løvberg (Santuzza); Bette (Wermine-)Björling (Lola), Margit Sehlmark (Lucia); JB (Turiddu); Georg Svedenbrant (Alfio).

Complete:	[33]	*Golden Age* EJS 346 [intermezzo not included]
	[CD]	*Legato* LCD 164-1 [intermezzo not included]

Excerpts:
a. Tu qui, Santuzza...Ah! lo vedi; b1. Comare Lola...Viva il vino spumeggiante... b2. Mamma!...Quel vino è generoso.

(a,b)	[CD]	*Bluebell* ABCD 028 // *Verona* 28030/31
(b2)	[CD]	*Legato* LCD 103-1

5405
1954, December 8. Stockholm, Royal Opera House. Complete opera performance (recorded by Sw. Broadcasting Corp.). First broadcast: February 17, 1955. With Royal Orch. & Royal Opera Chorus, cond. Lamberto Gardelli. [Sw. Radio: Ma 55/1039:2]

Pagliacci [Sw: *Pajazzo*] (Leoncavallo), sung in Sw. by Ruth Moberg (Nedda); JB (Canio), Arne Ohlson (Beppe); Erik Sundquist (Tonio), Carl-Axel Hallgren (Silvio).

Complete:	[33]	*Legendary* LR 137-2
	[CD]	*Legato* LCD 155-1

Excerpts:

(Act 1)	a. Un tal gioco; b. Recitar!...Vesti la giubba.	
(a,b)	[CD]	*Bluebell* ABCD 028
(b)	[33]	*ANNA* 1017

5406

1954, December 20. Stockholm, Södersjukhuset [The Söder Hospital]. *Pillerdosan* [The Pillbox], Programme No. 27. Recital, recorded for a Christmas programme produced by Sjukhusradion [Hospital Radio; a closed-circuit radio network for hospitals in the Stockholm area]. First broadcast: December 22, 1954. With Harry Ebert, piano.

[ALB, Stockholm: R88/104-05, (DAT) R89/0198:002,R89/0199:001]

a. In fernem Land [Sw: I fjärran land] (Wagner: *Lohengrin*)
b. När jag för mig själv i mörka skogen går [Sw] (Peterson-Berger)
c. Cantique de Noël [Sw: Julsång] (Adam)
d. Till havs [Sw] (Nordqvist)

(a)	[33]	*OASI* 660
	[CD]	*OASI* 7006

5501

1955, September 24. New York, Carnegie Hall. Recital (recorded by RCA for commercial publication). With Frederick Schauwecker, piano.

[RCA archive; (n-s) JB family coll., Sw. Radio: L-B+ 23538]

a. Adelaide [Ger] (Beethoven)
b. Frühlingsglaube [Ger] (Schubert)
c. Die Forelle [Ger] (Schubert)
d. Ständchen [Ger] (Schubert)
e. Die böse Farbe [Ger] (Schubert)
f. Traum durch die Dämmerung [Ger] (R. Strauss)
g. Cäcilie [Ger] (R. Strauss)
h. Ständchen [Ger] (Brahms)
i. Il mio tesoro [It] (Mozart: *Don Giovanni*)
j. Amor ti vieta [It] (Giordano: *Fedora*)
k. La fleur que tu m'avais jetée [Fr] (Bizet: *Carmen*)
l. Instant charmant...En fermant les yeux [Fr] (Massenet: *Manon*)
m. En svane [Nor] (Grieg)
n. Ein Traum [Nor: En drøm] (Grieg)
o. Demanten på marssnön [Sw] (Sibelius)
p. Säv, säv, susa [Sw] (Sibelius)
q. Svarta rosor [Sw] (Sibelius)
r. Tonerna [Sw] (Sjöberg)
s. Mamma!...Quel vino [It] (Mascagni: *Cavalleria rusticana*)
t. Ideale [It] (Tosti)
u. E lucevan le stelle [It] (Puccini: *Tosca*)
v. L'alba separa dalla luce l'ombra [It] (Tosti)
w. Jeanie with the Light Brown Hair [Eng] (Foster)

(a-l,t-w)	[33]	*RCA* (Au) L 16339, (Fr) 630.583, (G) LM 2003-C, SVA 1010, (GB) RB 16011, (J) RA 2203, (NL) GL 43194, (SA) 30035, (US) [1]LM 2003
(a,b,f-j,l,t,v,w)	[33]	*RCA* (J) RVC 7531/35
(a,c-e,h,t,v)	[33]	*RCA* (GB) SER 5704/06
(a-d)	[45]	*RCA* (G) ERA 9702
(c,d)	[45]	*RCA* (G) 447-9167
(i-l,t-v)	[33]	*RCA* (G) KR 11014/1-2 (26.48016 DP)
(i-l)	[45]	*RCA* (Sp) 3-26178
(i,j,l)	[CD]	*Legato* BIM 708-2
(i)	[45]	*RCA* (G) (4)47-9159
(t)	[33]	*RCA* (Au) L 16349, (G) HR 211, (US,Sp) [1]LM 2630

A master tape of the whole recital is presumed to exist in the RCA archive (matrix No. for LM 2003 is G2-RP-1848/49). On the acetate record in the JB family collection with most of the unissued items, "En drøm" is incomplete (first part missing).

5502
1955, December 14. New Orleans, Municipal Auditorium. Part of recital in New Orleans Community Concert Series (privately made in-house recording). With Frederick Schauwecker, piano.

a. Frondi tenere...Ombra mai fù [It] (Handel: *Serse*)
b. Frühlingsglaube [Ger] (Schubert)
c. Die Forelle [Ger] (Schubert)
d. Ständchen [Ger] (Schubert)
e. Traum durch die Dämmerung [Ger] (R. Strauss)
f. Zueignung [Ger] (R. Strauss)
g. Ein Traum [Nor: En drøm] (Grieg)
h. La fleur que tu m'avais jetée [Fr] (Bizet: *Carmen*)
i. Amor ti vieta [It] (Giordano: *Fedora*)
j. Siren' [Eng: Lilacs] (Rachmaninov)
k. V molchan'i nochi taynoy [Eng: In the Silence of Night] (Rachmaninov)
l. Demanten på marssnön [Sw] (Sibelius)
m. Svarta rosor [Sw] (Sibelius)
n. Tonerna [Sw] (Sjöberg)
o. Ideale [It] (Tosti)
p. L'alba separa dalla luce l'ombra [It] (Tosti)
q. Clorinda [Eng] (Morgan)
r. Come un bel dì di maggio [It] (Giordano: *Andrea Chénier*)

(a-r)	[33]	*Unique* UORC 376

Three encores were not recorded: "La donna è mobile", "E lucevan le stelle" and "Because".

5601
1956, January 30. New York, Rockefeller Center, NBC studio. *Producer's Showcase: Festival of Music*, NBC television concert (colour). Announcer: Charles Laughton. With Renata Tebaldi (sop.) & Metropolitan Opera Orch., cond. Max Rudolf.
[AV recording (black & white): Museum of Television & Radio, N.Y.: T81:0255]

a. O sventata, sventata...Che gelida manina...Sì. Mi chiamano Mimì [It] (Puccini: *La bohème*)
b. O soave fanciulla [It] (Puccini: *La bohème*)

(a,b)	[33]	*Golden Age* EJS 168 // *Rococo* 1003 // *Legendary* LR 137-2
(b)	[33]	*MDP* 026

5602
1956, March 31. New York, Metropolitan Opera House. Complete opera performance (Saturday matinee, Texaco-Metropolitan broadcast). With Metropolitan Opera Orch. & Chorus, cond. Dimitri Mitropoulos.

Manon Lescaut (Puccini), sung in It. by Licia Albanese (Manon); Rosalind Elias (Singer); JB (Des Grieux), Thomas Hayward (Edmondo), Alessio de Paolis (Dancing Master), James McCracken (Lamplighter); Frank Guarrera (Lescaut); Fernando Corena (Geronte), Calvin Marsh (Sergeant), George Cehanovsky (Innkeeper), Osie Hawkins (Sea Captain).

Complete:	[33]	*Morgan* 3MOR 5601 // *Fonit Cetra* DOC 9
	[CD]	*Melodram* CD 27502

Excerpts:
(Act 1) a1. L'amor? Questa tragedia... a2. Tra voi, belle... a3. Guardate, compagni... a4. Cortese damigella... a5. Donna non vidi mai; b. Vedete? Io son fedele;
(Act 2) c1. Oh, sarò la più bella!... c2. Affè, madamigella... c3. Ah! Manon, mi tradisce;
(Act 3) d1. Manon!... d2. Presto! In fila!...Ah! non v'avvicinate;
(Act 4) e. Sola, perduta, abbandonata...Fra le tue braccia [to end of opera].

(a,b,c,d,e)	[CD]	*Operaviva* OPV 017
(a1-2,a5,c3,d2)	[33]	*ANNA* 1005
(a2,a4-5,b,c1,d2)	[CD]	*Verona* 28030/31

5603
1956, April 4. New York, Metropolitan Opera House. Parts of opera performance (privately made in-house recording, probably taped from a [dressing-room?] monitor speaker). With Metropolitan Opera Orch. & Chorus, cond. Dimitri Mitropoulos.

Tosca (Puccini): excerpts from acts 1 & 2 [in all: 45 min.; see note below]. Sung in It. by Zinka Milanov (Tosca); JB (Cavaradossi), Alessio de Paolis (Spoletta); Walter Cassel (Scarpia), George Cehanovsky (Sciarrone); Gerhard Pechner (Sacristan), Clifford Harvuot (Angelotti).

Excerpt:
(Act 1) a. Dammi i colori!...Recondita armonia.

(a) [33] *HRE* 377-1

Acts 1 & 2 are complete except for a short break in act 1 (between Scarpia's "Un uom sospetto! Un vol..." and Tosca's "Ingannata? No, no, tradirmi egli non può") and for the beginning of act 2 (before Scarpia's "Per amor del suo Mario"). Thus, everything sung by JB in those two acts was preserved.

5604
1956, July 19. Stockholm, Gröna Lund, Tivoli. Open-air recital (recorded by Gröna Lunds Tivoli AB). With Harry Ebert, piano.

a. Se quel guerrier...Celeste Aida [It] (Verdi: *Aida*)
b. Ach, so fromm [It: M'apparì tutt'amor] (Flotow: *Martha*)
c. Ständchen [Ger] (R. Strauss)
d. Demanten på marssnön [Sw] (Sibelius)
e. Che gelida manina [It] (Puccini: *La bohème*)
f. La donna è mobile [It] (Verdi: *Rigoletto*)
g. Ich hab' kein Geld, bin vogelfrei [Sw: Nu är jag pank och fågelfri] (Millöcker: *Der Bettelstudent*)
h. Land, du välsignade [Sw] (Althén)

5605
1956, July 22. Furuvik Park (near Gävle, Sweden). Part of open-air recital (recording on colour film). With Harry Ebert, piano. [AV recording: Gävle Town Archives]

Ich hab' kein Geld, bin vogelfrei [Sw: Nu är jag pank och fågelfri]: verse 2 only?

The sequence must have been taken at the first of two recitals which JB gave at Furuvik on this day (at 16.00). It was shot at rather long range, and the synchronization is bad (sound and picture may even have been taken from different songs on the same occasion). The recording was done by AB Kinocentralen for a short film, celebrating the 20th anniversary of the Furuvik Park in 1956. Two copies of this film were found in the Gävle Town Archives and used for a TV programme in the 1980's. It has only been possible to examine the TV programme, where the second verse only was included [54 sec. song; 1 min. 20 sec. with applause], and it is uncertain if the first verse also exists.

5701
1957, January 5. Stockholm, Royal Opera House. Complete opera performance (recorded by Sw. Broadcasting Corp.). First broadcast: November 16, 1985. With Royal Orch. & Royal Opera Chorus, cond. Kurt Bendix. [Sw. Radio: MA 57/10410]

Rigoletto (Verdi), sung in It. by Eva Prytz (Gilda); Barbro Ericson (Giovanna), Judith Garellick (Countess Ceprano), Carrie Nilsson (Page); Kerstin Meyer (Maddalena); JB (Duke), Olle Sivall (Borsa); Erik Sundquist (Rigoletto), Georg Svedenbrant (Monterone), Carl-Axel Hallgren (Marullo); Sven-Erik Jacobsson (Sparafucile), Ingvar Wixell (Count Ceprano), Bertil Alstergård (Usher).

Complete:	[CD]	*Bluebell* ABCD 044

Excerpts:

(Act 1)	a. Della mia bella...Questa o quella; b. Signor nè principe...È il sol dell'anima;
(Act 2)	c. Ella mi fù rapita!...Parmi veder le lagrime;
(Act 3)	d. La donna è mobile; e. Un dì, se ben rammentomi...Bella figlia dell'amore.

(a-e)	[CD]	*Bluebell* ABCD 002
(a,c,d)	[CD]	*Legato* BIM 708-2
(d)	[33]	*Unique* UORC 197 // *Bluebell* BELL 196

This opera was played in four acts in Stockholm. Before the complete broadcast in 1985, excerpts from this performance may have been broadcast in 1960, and in 1977 "Parmi veder le lagrime" was used to illustrate an interview with the conductor Bendix.

5702
1957, January 26. Stockholm, Royal Opera House. Part of opera performance (privately recorded backstage). With Royal Orch. & Royal Opera Chorus, cond. Herbert Sandberg.
[Coll. M. Bergström]

Il trovatore (Verdi) [complete from scene 2]. Sung in It. by Aase Nordmo-Løvberg (Leonora), Ruth Moberg (Ines); Margareta Bergström (Azucena); JB (Manrico), Gösta Björling (Ruiz), Sture Ingebretzen (Messenger); Hugo Hasslo (Di Luna); Erik Saedén (Ferrando), Sven Wallskog (Gypsy).

The recording is complete from "Che più t'arresti" and consequently, everything sung by JB was preserved. The recording was made backstage by a member of the chorus for Margareta Bergström, who sang Azucena. On April 6, 1986, highlights from the recording were presented on the Swedish radio.

5703
1957, February 17. New York, CBS studio. *Ed Sullivan Show*, CBS television programme (black & white). With Hilde Güden (sop., in b), Thelma Votipka (m.-sop., in b) & Metropolitan Opera Orch., cond. Fausto Cleva.

a. La donna è mobile [It] (Verdi: *Rigoletto*)
b1. Giovanna, ho dei rimorsi... b2. Signor nè principe...È il sol dell'anima...Che m'ami [It] (Verdi: *Rigoletto*)

(a,b)	[33]	*Golden Age* EJS 367
(b2)	[33]	*Rococo* 1003 // *MDP* 026

An AV recording of this programme exists, and the part with JB was shown on Swedish television for the first time May 18, 1986.

5704
1957, August 5. Stockholm, Gröna Lund, Tivoli. Open-air recital (recorded by Gröna Lunds Tivoli AB). With Bertil Bokstedt, piano.

a.	Cielo e mar! [It] (Ponchielli: *La Gioconda*)
b.	Elle ne croyait pas [Sw: Hon kunde icke tro] (Thomas: *Mignon*)
c.	Di' tu se fedele [It] (Verdi: *Un ballo in maschera*)
d.	Morgen [Ger] (R. Strauss)
e.	Cäcilie [Ger] (R. Strauss)
f.	Mamma!...Quel vino [It] (Mascagni: *Cavalleria rusticana*)
g.	Till havs [Sw] (Nordqvist)

(b)	[33]	*ANNA* 1064 // *OASI* 660
	[CD]	*OASI* 7006

5705
1957, September 30. Malmö, Municipal Theatre (Malmö stadsteater). Part of opera performance (in-house recording). With Malmö Concert Hall Foundation Orch. & Malmö Municipal Theatre Chorus, cond. Sten-Åke Axelson.
[Malmö Municipal Theatre Archive: A40]

La bohème (Puccini): acts 1, 3 & 4. Sung in It. (JB throughout) & Sw. by Ethel Mårtensson (Mimì), Astri Herseth (Musetta); JB (Rodolfo); Nils Bäckström (Marcello), Arne Hasselblad (Schaunard); Bengt von Knorring (Colline), Karl-Fredrik Liljeholm, Carl-Johan Unger (Sergeants).

5706
1957, October 5. Stockholm, Concert Hall, Large Auditorium. Transcription of radio concert, pre-recorded without public. First broadcast: October 20, 1957. With Stockholm Philharmonic Orch., cond. Stig Westerberg. [Sw. Radio: Ma 57/10983]

a.	Trollsjön [Sw] (Söderman)
b.	Tristans död [Sw] (Rangström)
c.	Mamma!...Quel vino [It] (Mascagni: *Cavalleria rusticana*)
d.	Donna non vidi mai [It] (Puccini: *Manon Lescaut*)

(a)	[CD]	*Bluebell* ABCD 036
(b)	[33]	*RCA* (G) [1]HR 224, RL 43063 AS, (GB) RB 6620, (J) RA 2213, (SA) 30305, (US,Au,G?) LM 2784, (US) AGM1-4923 // *RCA* (GB) SER 5704/06

5707
1957, December 8. New York, Carnegie Hall. Sibelius Memorial Concert. With New York Philharmonic Orch., cond. Martti Similä. [Finnish Radio: V-14101]

a. Säv, säv, susa [Sw] (Sibelius)
b. Flickan kom ifrån sin älsklings möte [Sw] (Sibelius)
c. Var det en dröm [Sw] (Sibelius)
d. Svarta rosor [Sw] (Sibelius)
e. Demanten på marssnön [Sw] (Sibelius)

(a-e) [CD] *Bluebell* ABCD 050

It is not known how this recording, which was recently discovered in the Finnish Radio archive, was made (the concert was not broadcast). Two of the songs (b,e) were broadcast in Finland Oct. 26, 1991 (cf. No. 5105).

5801
1958, February 8. Stockholm, Cirkus. *Stora famnen* [A Big Hug], entertainment television programme including the drawing of lots for the World Football Championship. Host: Lennart Hyland. With Bertil Bokstedt, piano. [Sound recording: Sw. Radio: TAN 58/175]

a. Ein Traum [Nor: En drøm] (Grieg)
b. V molchan'i nochi taynoy [Eng: In the Silence of Night] (Rachmaninov)
c. Cäcilie [Ger] (R. Strauss)
d. Morgon [Sw] (Eklöf)

(a-c) [CD] *Bluebell* ABCD 050

After his performance, JB was presented with the first series of tickets for the championship by the secretary general, Holger Bergérus. An AV recording from this programme in the Sw. Television archive [137/58U] contains the drawing of lots only, not the artistic performances (which also included Kjerstin Dellert and Thomas Funck).

5802
1958, March 2. New York, Carnegie Hall. Recital (recorded by RCA for commercial publication). With Frederick Schauwecker, piano. [RCA: J 0063 (master tape?)]

a. Ingemisco [Lat] (Verdi: *Messa da Requiem*)
b. An die Leier [Ger] (Schubert)
c. Die Forelle [Ger] (Schubert)
d. Frühlingsglaube [Ger] (Schubert)
e. An Sylvia [Ger] (Schubert)
f. Die Allmacht [Ger] (Schubert)
g. Ständchen [Ger] (Schubert)
h. Adelaide [Ger] (Beethoven)
i. Ständchen [Ger] (Brahms)
j. Lensky's Aria: Kuda, kuda [Sw: Förbi, förbi] (Tchaikovsky: *Evgeny Onegin*)
k. Skogen sover [Sw] (Alfvén)
l. I drömmen du är mig nära [Sw] (Sjögren)
m. Jungfrun under lind [Sw] (Peterson-Berger)
n. Siren' [Eng: Lilacs] (Rachmaninov)
o. V molchan'i nochi taynoy [Eng: In the Silence of Night] (Rachmaninov)
p. Ein Traum [Nor: En drøm] (Grieg)

q. Nessun dorma! [It] (Puccini: *Turandot*)
r. Ideale [It] (Tosti)
s. La donna è mobile [It] (Verdi: *Rigoletto*)
t. E lucevan le stelle [It] (Puccini: *Tosca*)
u. Zueignung [Ger] (R. Strauss)

(a-u)	[CD]	*RCA* (G) [1]GD 60520, (US) 60520-2-RG
	[MC]	*RCA* (US) 60520-4-RG
(a,b,f,j,k,m,o-u)	[33]	*Cum Laude* KM 1001
(b,e,l,m,o,u)	[33]	*RCA* (G) [1]HR 224, RL 43063 AS, (GB) RB 6620, (J) RA 2213, (SA) 30305, (US,Au,G?) LM 2784, (US) AGMl-4923
(b,e,o,u)	[33]	*RCA* (J) RVC 7531/35
(b,o,u)	[33]	*RCA* (GB) SER 5704/06
(c,d,g,h,i,n)	[33]	*ANNA* 1069
(c,d,g,h,i)	[MC]	*Demand* DPC 504
(g,h,q,r)	[CD]	*Legato* BIM 708-2
(j,q,r)	[CD]	*OASI* 7006
(j)	[33]	*MDP* 035
(q,r)	[33]	*OASI* 660
(r)	[33]	*Unique* UORC 253

Excerpts from this recital have been sold on tape, labelled as an alleged Philadelphia recital in 1955.

5803
1958, June 26. Stockholm, Gröna Lund, Tivoli. Open-air recital (recorded by Gröna Lunds Tivoli AB). With Bertil Bokstedt, piano.

a. Dies Bildnis ist bezaubernd schön [Sw: Ack, detta är en ängels bild] (Mozart: *Die Zauberflöte*)
b. V molchan'i nochi taynoy [Eng: In the Silence of Night] (Rachmaninov)
c. La fleur que tu m'avais jetée [Fr] (Bizet: *Carmen*)
d. Aftonstämning [Sw] (Körling)
e. Till havs [Sw] (Nordqvist)
f. Ich hab' kein Geld, bin vogelfrei [Sw: Nu är jag pank och fågelfri] (Millöcker: *Der Bettelstudent*)
g. Land, du välsignade [Sw] (Althén)
h. Torna a Surriento [It] (E. de Curtis)

(b,c,f)	[CD]	*Bluebell* ABCD 042
(c,h)	[33]	*RCA* (Sw) VICS 1659

An excerpt from this recital was filmed for the Swedish TV programme *Vi går på Gröna Lund* [We Visit Gröna Lund], telecast August 3, 1958. The programme is preserved in the TV archive (830/58U) and includes the beginning [about 50 sec.] of the Carmen aria.

5804

1958, July 18. Stockholm, Concert Hall, Large Auditorium. *Sw. Broadcasting Corp. Public Summer Concert*. With Sw. Radio Orch. & Stockholm Philharmonic Orch., cond. Georg Ludwig Jochum. [Sw. Radio: Ma 58/679-80]

a. Säv, säv, susa [Sw] (Sibelius)
b. Svarta rosor [Sw] (Sibelius)
c. Morgen [Ger] (R. Strauss)
d. Ständchen [Ger] (R. Strauss)
e. La fleur que tu m'avais jetée [Fr] (Bizet: *Carmen*)
f. Mamma!...Quel vino [It] (Mascagni: *Cavalleria rusticana*)
g. Donna non vidi mai [It] (Puccini: *Manon Lescaut*)

(a-g) [CD] *Bluebell* ABCD 036

5805

1958, August 19. Stockholm, Stadion. *European Athletics Championship Opening Ceremony* (broadcast). With Stockholm Band of the Swedish Army, cond. Marc De la Berg. [Sw. Radio: TAN 58/860]

Morgon [Sw] (Eklöf)

5806

1958, December 2 (?). New York, Essex House Hotel (?). Interview [in Eng.; 9 min. 45 sec.] by Alan Wagner, host of WNYC radio programme *Living Opera*. First broadcast: December 14, 1958; rebroadcast: February, 1961.

Topics: JB's past opera and concert season; his type of voice; favourite roles; future recordings; concert and opera plans; his opera debuts in New York and Stockholm; his opera repertoire; favourite singers; problems with acting in *Aida*; favourite encore aria.

5807

1958, December 6. Stockholm, Cirkus (?). *För hela familjen* [For the Whole Family], entertainment television programme for NTF [The Swedish National Society for Road Safety]. With Bertil Bokstedt, piano.
[AV recording: Sw. Television: K 2995 (16 mm. film); L 2344 (magnetic soundtrack)]

Till havs [Sw] (Nordqvist)

5808

1958, December 11. Stockholm, Concert Hall, Large Auditorium. Transcription of radio concert, pre-recorded without public. First broadcast: December 25, 1958. With Stockholm Philharmonic Orch., cond. Stig Westerberg. [Sw. Radio: Ma 58/1113]

a. Kung Heimer och Aslög [Sw] (Söderman)
b. Till havs [Sw] (Nordqvist)
c. När jag för mig själv i mörka skogen går [Sw] (Peterson-Berger)
d. Bland skogens höga furustammar [Sw] (Peterson-Berger)
e. Sverige [Sw] (Stenhammar: *Ett folk*)

(a,c-e)	[CD]	*Bluebell* ABCD 036
(b)	[33]	*RCA* (G) [1]HR 224, RL 43063 AS, (GB) RB 6620, (J) RA 2213, (SA) 30305, (US,Au,G?) LM 2784, (US) AGM1-4923 // *RCA* (GB) SER 5704/06

The songs were broadcast in this order: a-e-c-d-b.

5901

1959, January 4. London, Palladium. *Sunday Night at the London Palladium*, ATV (Associated Television) programme. Host: Bruce Forsyth. With Ivor Newton, piano.

a. Mamma!...Quel vino [It] (Mascagni: *Cavalleria rusticana*)
b. E lucevan le stelle [It] (Puccini: *Tosca*)

Bridie Gallagher appeared as the other star on this programme. No AV recording was preserved by the producing company, and only audio recordings of the programme are known.

5902

1959, February 12. Stockholm, Royal Opera House. Part of opera performance (in-house recording: act 2 in mono, act 3 in stereo). With Royal Orch. & Royal Opera Chorus, cond. Nils Grevillius. [ALB, Stockholm: R88/0030]

Tosca (Puccini): acts 2 & 3, complete. Sung in It. (JB throughout) & Sw. by Kjerstin Dellert (Tosca); Barbro Ericson (Shepherd); JB (Cavaradossi), Anders Näslund (Spoletta); Arne Wirén (Scarpia), Bertil Alstergård (Sciarrone), Lennart Carlén (Jailer).

Complete acts: Not issued

Excerpts:
(Act 2) a. Vittoria!
(Act 3) b. Liberi!...Amaro sol per te.

(a,b)	[33]	*HMV* (Sw) 7C 153-35350/58*P // *ANNA* 1045
(b)	[33]	*Fischer* 101-3*

The ALB recording comprises act 3 only; act 2 is preserved in a private collection.

5903

1959, April 13. Atlanta (Georgia), Glenn Memorial Auditorium. Recital in 1958-59 Chamber Music Series for Students at Emory University (privately made in-house recording in stereo). With Frederick Schauwecker, piano. [Private US collection]

a. Frondi tenere...Ombra mai fù [It] (Handel: *Serse*)
b. Frühlingsglaube [Ger] (Schubert)
c. Die Forelle [Ger] (Schubert)
d. Ständchen [Ger] (Schubert)
e. Traum durch die Dämmerung [Ger] (R. Strauss)
f. Zueignung [Ger] (R. Strauss)

g. La fleur que tu m'avais jetée [Fr] (Bizet: *Carmen*)
h. Amor ti vieta [It] (Giordano: *Fedora*)
i. Siren' [Eng: Lilacs] (Rachmaninov)
j. V molchan'i nochi taynoy [Eng: In the Silence of Night] (Rachmaninov)
k. Skogen sover [Sw] (Alfvén)
l. I drömmen du är mig nära [Sw] (Sjögren)
m. Jungfrun under lind [Sw] (Peterson-Berger)
n. En svane [Nor] (Grieg)
o. Ein Traum [Nor: En drøm] (Grieg)
p. Tonerna [Sw] (Sjöberg)
q. Come un bel dì di maggio [It] (Giordano: *Andrea Chénier*)
r. Che gelida manina [It] (Puccini: *La bohème*)
s. Nessun dorma! [It] (Puccini: *Turandot*)

(a-s)	[CD]	*Bluebell* ABCD 020* // *Myto* 1MCD 912.39*
(a,g,n,r,s)	[CD]	*Gala* GL 315*
(b-f,h-j,l,m,o-q)	[CD]	*Verona* 28030/31*

5904
1959, April 27 [or a day or two earlier]. New York, Essex House Hotel (?). Interview [in Eng.; 6 min. 20 sec.] by Gene Fallon, host of WNYC radio programme *Around New York*. First broadcast: April 28, 1959.

Topics: JB's current recital tour; his return to the Met in the fall; the Bjoerling Male Quartet's US tour in 1919-21; JB's repertoire; comparative difficulty of concert and opera singing; JB's musical training.

5905
1959, June 16. Stockholm, Gröna Lund, Tivoli. Open-air recital (recorded by Gröna Lunds Tivoli AB). With Harry Ebert, piano.

a. Dies Bildnis ist bezaubernd schön [Sw: Ack, detta är en ängels bild] (Mozart: *Die Zauberflöte*)
b. Traum durch die Dämmerung [Ger] (R. Strauss)
c. Cäcilie [Ger] (R. Strauss)
d. Aftonstämning [Sw] (Körling)
e. När jag för mig själv i mörka skogen går [Sw] (Peterson-Berger)
f. Morgon [Sw] (Eklöf)
g. Till havs [Sw] (Nordqvist) [only a fragment recorded]
h. Ich hab' kein Geld, bin vogelfrei [Sw: Nu är jag pank och fågelfri] (Millöcker: *Der Bettelstudent*)

(a-f)	[CD]	*Bluebell* ABCD 042
(a,b,d,e)	[33]	*RCA* (Sw) VICS 1659

Bokstedt was erroneously given as accompanist on the sleeve of VICS 1659.

5906

1959, June 27. Siarö (Stockholm Archipelago), JB summer home. Telephone interview [in Sw.; 3 min. 50 sec.] by Eric Sandström on the radio programme *Medan vi väntar på Ingo* [While We Are Waiting for Ingo], commercial broadcast by Svenska AB Philips from Radio Luxembourg on the occasion of the heavyweight boxing championship fight between Ingemar Johansson and Floyd Patterson at Yankee Stadium, New York.

[Sw. Radio: TAN 59/683]

Topics: JB's impressions of Johansson; his thoughts about the fight; his own sporting habits.

5907

1959, August 20. Stockholm, Gröna Lund, Tivoli. Open-air recital (recorded by Gröna Lunds Tivoli AB). With Bertil Bokstedt, piano.

a. Verborgenheit [Ger] (Wolf)
b. Es muss ein Wunderbares sein [Ger] (Liszt)
c. Ständchen [Ger] (R. Strauss)
d. Som stjärnorna på himmelen [Sw] (Peterson-Berger)
e. Till havs [Sw] (Nordqvist)
f. Come un bel dì di maggio [It] (Giordano: *Andrea Chénier*)
g. Morgon [Sw] (Eklöf)
h. Torna a Surriento [It] (E. de Curtis)

(a-f,h) [CD] *Bluebell* ABCD 042

5908

1959, October 30. Stockholm, radio studio. Interview [in Sw.; 16 min. 10 sec.] by Bo Teddy Ladberg (Sw. Broadcasting Corp. Music Department). First broadcast: November 1, 1959 (during the first intermission of *Manon Lescaut* performance from the Royal Opera). [Sw. Radio: M 59/897:2]

Topics: JB's debut as the lamplighter in *Manon Lescaut*; John Forsell's significance for him; the Royal Opera in the thirties; the beginning of JB's American career and his tours in the US; mishaps during a *Ballo in maschera* performance in Philadelphia and *Bohème* performances in Stockholm; problems of singing in Italian in a Swedish ensemble; comparison of tenor roles in Puccini operas; memories of the soprano Nanny Larsén-Todsen.

The interviewer gave a detailed account of how this interview came about in *Jussi Björling: En minnesbok*, p. 125. According to that account (written in 1960), JB arrived at the studio at 17.25 p.m. on the day before the *Manon Lescaut* performance (thus on the 31). However, the date October 30, noted in the recording minutes, is confirmed by the fact that Ladberg in the interview refers to it as having been recorded "a few days in advance".

5909
1959, November 1. Stockholm, Royal Opera House. Complete opera performance (Sunday matinee; broadcast). With Royal Orch. & Royal Opera Chorus, cond. Nils Grevillius.
[Sw. Radio: M 59/897:1]

Manon Lescaut (Puccini). Sung in It. (JB throughout) & Sw. by Hjördis Schymberg (Manon); Margareta Bergström (Singer); JB (Des Grieux), Lars Billengren (Edmondo), Arne Ohlson (Dancing Master), Kolbjörn Höiseth (Lamplighter); Hugo Hasslo (Lescaut); Arne Tyrén (Geronte), Georg Svedenbrant (Sergeant), Sven-Erik Jacobsson (Innkeeper), Bo Lundborg (Sea Captain).

Excerpts:

(Act 1)	a1. Ma se vi talenta... a2. Tra voi, belle; b. Vedete? Io son fedele;
(Act 2)	c1. Senti, di qui partiamo... c2. Ah! Manon, mi tradisce;
(Act 3)	d1. Presto! In fila!... d2. Ah! non v'avvicinate!;
(Act 4)	e. Complete act.

(a2,b,c,d2,e)	[CD]	*Bluebell* ABCD 028
(a,c2,d2)	[CD]	*Legato* LCD 103-1
(c,d2)	[CD]	*Gala* GL 315 // *Myto* 2MCD 931.73
(d)	[CD]	*Legato* BIM 708-2

5910
1959, November 16. New York, Metropolitan Opera House. Complete opera performance (privately made in-house recording). With Metropolitan Opera Orch. & Chorus, cond. Nino Verchi.

Cavalleria rusticana (Mascagni), sung in It. by Giulietta Simionato (Santuzza), Rosalind Elias (Lola); Thelma Votipka (Lucia); JB (Turiddu); Walter Cassel (Alfio).

Complete: [33] *HRE* 301-2

Excerpts:
a. O Lola; b. Tu qui, Santuzza?...Ah! lo vedi; c. Comare Lola...Viva il vino spumeggiante...Mamma!...Quel vino.

(a-c)	[33]	*Golden Age* EJS 530
	[CD]	*Myto* 2MCD 931.73

5911
1959, November 21. New York, Metropolitan Opera House. Complete opera performance (privately made in-house recording). With Metropolitan Opera Orch. & Chorus, cond. Dimitri Mitropoulos.

Tosca (Puccini), sung in It. by Mary Curtis-Verna (Tosca); Peter Burke (Shepherd); JB (Cavaradossi), Paul Franke (Spoletta); Cornell MacNeil (Scarpia), Osie Hawkins (Sciarrone), Roald Reitan (Jailer); Lawrence Davidson (Sacristan), Norman Scott (Angelotti).

Complete:	[33]	*Unique* UORC 148

Excerpts:

(Act 1)	a1. Che fai?... a2. Recondita armonia... a3. Ma con quei cani...Mario, Mario, Mario!...Qual'occhio al mondo...È buona la mia Tosca [through "Se ci assalgon battaglia"];
(Act 2)	b. Tal violenza!...Ov'è Angelotti [through "...il Giudice v'aspetta"]; c. Floria! - Amore...Vittoria!;
(Act 3)	d. Vi resta un'ora...E lucevan le stelle...O dolci mani...Amaro sol per te...L'ora! - Son pronto.

(a-d)	[CD]	*Myto* 2MCD 916.47
(a2)	[33]	*HRE* 202-1

5912
1959, December 19. New York, Metropolitan Opera House. Complete opera performance (Saturday matinee, Texaco-Metropolitan broadcast). With Metropolitan Opera Orch. & Chorus, cond. Jean Morel.

Faust (Gounod), sung in Fr. by Elisabeth Söderström (Marguerite), Mildred Miller (Siebel); Thelma Votipka (Marthe); JB (Faust); Robert Merrill (Valentin), Roald Reitan (Wagner); Cesare Siepi (Méphistophélès).

Complete:	[33]	*Robin Hood* RHR 502-C
	[CD]	*Myto* 2MCD 906.33 // *Rodolphe* RPV 32702/03 // *Music & Arts* CD 701

Excerpts:

(Act 1-2)	a-c. [include all of Faust's part in these acts];
(Act 3)	d1. Quel trouble...Salut! demeure... d2. Alerte, la voilà!; e1. Prenez mon bras...Il était temps!... e2. Il se fait tard!...Ô nuit d'amour;
(Act 4)	f. Que voulez-vous;
(Act 5)	g. Arrête! N'as-tu pas promis; h. Va-t'en!... Alerte! alerte!

(a-h)	[33]	*Golden Age* EJS 210
(d1,e2)	[CD]	*Gala* GL 315
(d1,h)	[CD]	*Verona* 28030/31
(e2)	[CD]	*Verona* 28034/35

Both the Myto and the Rodolphe CD issues of this opera were originally mislabelled as No. 5010.

6001
1960, March 6. Stockholm, Royal Opera House. Complete opera performance (Sunday matinee; broadcast). With Royal Orch. & Royal Opera Chorus, cond. Herbert Sandberg. [Sw. Radio: MK 60/142]

Il trovatore (Verdi), sung in It. by Hjördis Schymberg (Leonora), Ingeborg Kjellgren (Ines); Kerstin Meyer (Azucena); JB (Manrico), Olle Sivall (Ruiz), Sture Ingebretzen (Messenger); Hugo Hasslo (Di Luna); Erik Saedén (Ferrando), Bertil Alstergård (Gypsy).

Complete:	[33]	*OASI* 656
	[CD]	*OASI* 7003-2 // *Bluebell* ABCD 045

Excerpts:

(Act 1)	a. Tacea la notte...Deserto sulla terra [to end of act];
(Act 2)	b1. Stride la vampa... b2. Non son tuo figlio?...Mal reggendo... b3. Inoltra il pie'... Perigliarti ancor languente;
(Act 3)	c1. Quale d'armi fragor... c2. Alto è il periglio... c3. Il presagio funesto...Ah sì, ben mio... c4. Manrico?...Di quella pira;
(Act 4)	d. Miserere...Quel suon...Ah, che la morte ognora; e. Madre? Non dormi?...Ai nostri monti [to end of opera].

(a-e)	[33]	*Golden Age* EJS 402
(b2,c,d,e)	[CD]	*Bluebell* ABCD 002
(c)	[CD]	*Gala* GL 315
(c2-3)	[33]	*HRE* 215-1
(c3-4)	[CD]	*Legato* LCD 103-1 // *Verona* 27068

6002
1960, July 5. Rättvik (Dalarna, Sweden), Persborg Hotel (?). Interview [in Eng.; 6 min.] by Anthony Baird for Sw. Broadcasting Corp. Foreign Programme (Radio Sweden) [recorded during a party?]. [Sw. Radio: UT 60/1174]

Topics: JB's reasons for singing at the US National Day celebration in Rättvik; his connections with the US; his opinion of contemporary artists; his early training and career; modern opera and composers.

[33] *MDP* 035 [2 min. 8 sec. excerpt only]

6003
1960, July 28. Stockholm, Gröna Lund, Tivoli. Open-air recital (recorded by Gröna Lunds Tivoli AB). With Bertil Bokstedt, piano.

a. Trollsjön [Sw] (Söderman)
b. Vladimir's Cavatina: Medlenno den' ugasal [Sw: Dagen gick långsamt till ro] (Borodin: *Knyaz* [*Prince*] *Igor*)
c. Ideale [It] (Tosti)
d. Till havs [Sw] (Nordqvist)
e. Land, du välsignade [Sw] (Althén)
f. Because [Eng] (d'Hardelot, pseud. of Rhodes)

(a-f)	[33]	*RCA* (Sw) VICS 1659
(a-c,e,f)	[CD]	*Bluebell* ABCD 042
(f)	[33]	*RCA* (J) RVC 7531/35

6004
1960, August 5. Gothenburg (Göteborg), Concert Hall. Radio concert. With Gothenburg Symphony Orch., cond. Nils Grevillius. [Sw. Radio: MO 60/416-17]

a. Lensky's Aria: Kuda, kuda [Sw: Förbi, förbi] (Tchaikovsky: *Evgeny Onegin*)
b. Donna non vidi mai [It] (Puccini: *Manon Lescaut*)
c. In fernem Land [Sw: I fjärran land] (Wagner: *Lohengrin*)
d. Säv, säv, susa [Sw] (Sibelius)
e. Svarta rosor [Sw] (Sibelius)
f. Skogen sover [Sw] (Alfvén)
g. Jag längtar dig [Sw] (Alfvén)

(a-g)	[33]	*RCA* (G) [1]HR 224, RL 43063 AS, (GB) RB 6620, (J) RA 2213, (SA) 30305, (US,Au,G?) LM 2784, (US) AGM1-4923
(a,c,e,f)	[33]	*RCA* (GB) SER 5704/06
(a,b)	[33]	*RCA* (G) KR 11014/1-2 (26.48016 DP)
(a,c)	[33]	*Golden Age* EJS 252
(b,c)	[CD]	*Legato* BIM 708-2
(c)	[33]	*RCA* (Fr) 731.006/10 // *RCA* (J) RVC 7531/35
	[CD]	*Gala* GL 315

Appendix: Performances Rumoured but not Proved to be Preserved; Broadcasts not Earlier Listed and Probably not Preserved

This list includes broadcasts for which there is no evidence that recordings have survived, even if they were sometimes recorded (for other broadcasts, see Section 1:B), as well as certain other JB performances rumoured to exist in recorded form. There seems to be a fair chance that recordings which may turn up in the future will be found on this list.

A01
1928, March 9. Stockholm, radio studio. *Varietéprogram* [Variety Programme]. With Sw. Radio Orch.
JB sang (according to his own recollections): For You Alone; I drömmen du är mig nära; aria from *Tosca*. Other soloists on this programme were S.-O. Sandberg (song), W. Witkowsky (piano) and C. Vitalis (xylophone). JB's fee for his first radio appearance was Kronor 30.

A02
1928, July. "Sång i radiokapellet" [Singing with the Radio Band].
According to a note in the Sw. Radio accounts, JB was paid for this on July 20, but his name is not found in the printed daily programme. The fee probably refers to a contribution to the regular programme "Underhållningsmusik av Radiokapellet" [Entertainment Music by the Radio Band], but there was no such broadcast on July 20. The latest possible date is the July 18.

A03
1930, April 3. Stockholm. Radio concert (joint with C. Christiansen, cello).
JB sang: 2 songs from "Fyra visor i svensk folkton" (Peterson-Berger); Jungfrun under lind; Mattinata; Questa o quella; Ch'ella mi creda.

A04
1930, December 25. Stockholm. Radio concert. Cond. I. Hellman.
Messiah, part 1. With G. Torpadie-Bratt, I. Aulin-Voghera, J. Berglund.

A05
1931, May 8. Helsinki. Broadcast perf. of Stockholm R. Opera on tour. Cond. N. Grevillius.
I cavalieri di Ekebù. With G. Pålson-Wettergren, B. Hertzberg, E. Beyron, J. Berglund and others.

A06
1931, September 16. Stockholm. Broadcast perf. of R. Opera. Cond. A. Järnefelt.
Saul og David. With K. Bernstein-Sundström, E. Larson, D. Stockman and others.

A07
1931, October 7. Stockholm. Broadcast perf. of R. Opera. Cond. N. Grevillius.
Roméo et Juliette (JB in role of Tybalt). With H. Görlin, E. Beyron and others.

A08
1932, February 29. Stockholm. Broadcast perf. of R. Opera. Cond. L. Blech.
Rigoletto. With I. Björck, A. Ohlson, E. Larson, L. Björker and others.

A09
1932, August 9. Stockholm. Partly broadcast perf. of R. Opera. Cond. H. Sandberg.
Tannhäuser: act 1. With I. Wassner, O. Ralf, C. Molin, L. Björker and others.

A10
1932, November 20. Stockholm. Broadcast perf. of R. Opera. Cond. H. Sandberg.
Mignon. With H. Görlin, A. Ohlson, J. Berglund and others.

A11
1932, December 12. Stockholm. Broadcast perf. of R. Opera. Cond. K. Bendix.
Rigoletto. With S. Andreva, I. Björck, E. Larson, L. Björker and others.

A12
1933, March 13. Stockholm. Broadcast perf. of R. Opera. Cond. N. Grevillius.
Knyaz Igor. With H. Görlin, G. Pålson-Wettergren, E. Larson, J. Berglund and others.

A13
1933, May 6. Copenhagen. Broadcast perf. of Stockholm R. Opera on tour. Cond. H. Sandberg.
Don Giovanni. With K. Bernstein-Sundström, I. Wassner, H. Görlin, J. Forsell, E. Stiebel and others.

A14
1933, August 23. Stockholm. Partly broadcast perf. of R. Opera. Cond. N. Grevillius.
I cavalieri di Ekebù: acts 1-2. With G. Pålson-Wettergren, B. Hertzberg, E. Beyron, J. Berglund and others.

A15
1933, September 14. Stockholm. Broadcast perf. of R. Opera. Cond. K. Bendix.
Djamileh. With B. Ewert, F. Cembraeus, G. Zettervall.

A16
1934, January 15. Stockholm. Partly broadcast perf. of R. Opera. Cond. H. Sandberg.
Arabella: act 1. With H. Görlin, S. Andreva, E. Larson, E. Stiebel and others.
[Fragments without JB preserved in Sw. Radio archive: L-B 266.]

A17
1934, March 22. Stockholm. Verdi radio concert. Cond. L. Blech.
JB sang: duet from *Un ballo in maschera* (w. I. Köhler).
[Excerpts without JB preserved in Sw. Radio archive: L-B 419.]

A18
1934, May 26. Oslo. Broadcast perf. of Stockholm R. Opera on tour. Cond. H. Sandberg.
Don Giovanni. With B. Hertzberg, I. Wassner, H. Görlin, J. Forsell, J. Berglund and others.

A19
1934, July 6. Malmö. Broadcast of festival concert, arranged by Svenska Musikerförbundet [The Swedish Musicians' Union]. Cond. O. Morales.
JB sang: Trollsjön; Kung Heimer och Aslög; Lindagull (Alfvén).

A20
1934, Aug. 19. Gothenburg. Broadcast concert with Västergötlands Sångarförbund [The Västergötland Singers' Union]. Cond. T. Rantzén.
JB sang: Che gelida manina; Aftonstämning; O paradiso; Serenad (Widéen).

A21
1934, August 28. Stockholm. Partly broadcast perf. of R. Opera. Cond. N. Grevillius.
Faust: acts 2-3. With H. Görlin, E. Ekendahl, J. Berglund, E. Larson and others.

A22
1934, September 7. Stockholm. Broadcast soiree at the Drottningholm Palace Theatre. Cond. H. Sandberg.
JB took part (with H. Schymberg & G. Allard) in a "divertissement" with music by Mozart.
[Excerpts from the soiree, without JB, preserved in Sw. Radio Archive: L-B 595.]

A23
1934, November 30. Stockholm. Partly broadcast perf. of R. Opera. Cond. H. Sandberg.
Kronbruden: acts 3-4. With B. Hertzberg, B. Ewert, J. Berglund, E. Larson and others.

A24
1934, December 10. Stockholm. Broadcast perf. of R. Opera. Cond. N. Grevillius.
Il tabarro. With G. Pålson-Wettergren, C. Molin and others.

A25
1935, February 11. Broadcast perf. of R. Opera. Cond. H. Sandberg.
Die Entführung aus dem Serail. With S. Andreva, H. Schymberg, S. Herdenberg, S. Edwardsen, L. Björker.

A26
1935, March 6. Stockholm. Broadcast perf. of R. Opera. Cond. N. Grevillius.
La fanciulla del West. With H. Görlin, J. Berglund and others.

A27
1935, May 23. Stockholm. Broadcast of Royal Wedding Gala [cf. note for Nos. 79-80] at R. Opera. Cond. N. Grevillius.
Roméo et Juliette: act 2. With H. Görlin and others.

A28
1935, July 2. Brussels. Broadcast of Swedish concert at World Exhibition (also relayed to Sweden). Cond. N. Grevillius.
JB sang: I männer över lag och rätt.

A29
1935, August 29. Stockholm. Broadcast perf. of R. Opera. Cond. S.-Å. Axelson. *Cavalleria rusticana*. With K. Rydqvist, B. Ewert, G. Allard, C. Molin.

A30
1936, January 4. Stockholm. Partly broadcast perf. of R. Opera. Cond. N. Grevillius. *Faust*: acts 1-2. With B. Hertzberg, J. Berglund, C. Richter and others.

A31
1936, January 26. *Från Strauss till Lehár*, radio concert (operetta medley) [cf. No. 3601]. Cond. N. Grevillius.
With N. Valdi, I. Köhler, G. Kjellertz.

A32
1936, March 4. Stockholm. Partly broadcast perf. of R. Opera. Cond. N. Grevillius. *La damnation de Faust*: acts 1-2. With H. Görlin, J. Berglund, E. Stiebel.

A33
1936, March 12. Vienna. Radio recital.
JB sang: Cielo e mar; Vallgossens visa (Geijer); Aftonklockan (Geijer); Ideale; Land, du välsignade; Che gelida manina.

A34
1936, May 12. Stockholm. Partly broadcast perf. of R. Opera. Cond. N. Grevillius. *Roméo et Juliette*: acts 1-2. With H. Schymberg, S. Herdenberg and others.

A35
1936, August 27. Stockholm. Partly broadcast perf. of R. Opera. Cond. N. Grevillius. *Fanal*: act 2. With H. Görlin, B. Ewert, J. Berglund and others.

A36
1936, September 15. Stockholm. Partly broadcast perf. of R. Opera. Cond. N. Grevillius. *La bohème*: acts 1-2. With H. Schymberg, I. Quensel, E. Larson, E. Stiebel, L. Björker and others.

A37
1936, November 1. Stockholm. Radio concert. Cond. A. Wiklund. [JB:s part in this concert was also transmitted to the US on the occasion of NBC's tenth anniversary. This was the first time Americans could hear him on radio in a live performance.]
JB sang: Trollsjön; Tonerna.
[Of this programme, only the introductory greeting to the American listeners by the deputy head of the Sw. Broadcasting Corp., Y. Hugo, has been preserved in the Sw. Radio archive: L-B 1693.]

A38
1936, November 1. Stockholm. Partly broadcast perf. of R. Opera. Cond. K. Bendix. *Il trovatore*: act 4. With I. Köhler, B. Ewert, E. Larson.

A39
1936, December 30. Stockholm. Broadcast perf. of R. Opera. Cond. S.-Å. Axelson.
L'illustre Fregona. With A. Ohlson, B. Ewert, C. Molin, S. Herdenberg and others.

A40
1937, January 29. Stockholm. Partly broadcast perf. of R. Opera. Cond. K. Bendix.
Faust: acts 1-3. With H. Görlin, E. Ekendahl, J. Berglund, C. Richter and others.

A41
1937, April 2. Stockholm. Non-public broadcast to Britain from R. Opera. Cond. N. Grevillius.
Fanal: act 2. With H. Görlin, B. Ewert, S. Edwardsen.

A42
1937, April 12. Stockholm. Partly broadcast perf. of R. Opera. Cond. N. Grevillius.
Madama Butterfly: act 1. With H. Görlin, S. Herdenberg and others.

A43
1937, April 28. Stockholm. Public radio concert. Cond. F. Busch.
Messa da Requiem (Verdi). With I. Souez, F. Elsta, L. Björker.

A44
1937, September 14. Stockholm. Partly broadcast perf. of R. Opera. Cond. H. Sandberg.
Don Giovanni: acts 1-2. With I. Köhler, I. Wassner, K. Rydqvist, E. Pinza (guest), E. Stiebel and others.

A45
1937, December 19. New York, Carnegie Hall. *General Motors Concert*: Christmas Music (broadcast by NBC). Cond. E. Rapee.
JB sang: Cielo e mar; "Traditional Swedish Christmas Carol"; "The Story of the Nativity" (probably a medley of Christmas music; with H. Jepson, sop.).

A46
1938, January 16. Stockholm. Radio interview after return from US tour.

A47
1938, February 17. Copenhagen. Radio concert, cond. N. Malko.
JB sang: Aria from *Don Giovanni*; Che gelida manina.

A48
1938, February 28. Stockholm. Partly broadcast perf. of R. Opera. Cond. K. Bendix.
Rigoletto: act 2. With H. Schymberg, E. Larson, L. Björker and others.

A49
1938, March 20. Stockholm. Popular radio concert. Cond. L.-E. Larsson.
JB sang: La fleur que tu m'avais jetée; Che gelida manina.

A50
1938, August 11. Stockholm. Partly broadcast perf. of R. Opera. Cond. K. Bendix.
Aida: act 4. With I. Köhler, B. Ewert, F. Jonsson.

A51
1938, November 13. Detroit, Masonic Temple Auditorium. *Ford Sunday Evening Hour*, CBS radio concert. Cond. J. Iturbi.
JB sang: Salut! demeure chaste et pure; En fermant les yeux; Sanctus (Gounod: *Messe Solennelle*); Flickan kom ifrån sin älsklings möte; Cäcilie.

A52
1939, January 15. Detroit, Masonic Temple Auditorium. *Ford Sunday Evening Hour*, CBS radio concert. Cond. F. Reiner.
JB sang: O paradiso; La danza; Flickan kom ifrån sin älsklings möte; Lenz (Hildach); Land, du välsignade; Funiculì, funiculà.

A53
1939, February 4. Stockholm. Partly broadcast perf. of R. Opera. Cond. N. Grevillius.
La bohème: act 1. With H. Schymberg, S. Herdenberg, C. Richter, L. Björker, F. Cembraeus.

A54
1939, April 9. Stockholm. *Svenska bilder* [Swedish Pictures], joint radio concert with K. Torlind (also transmitted to the US as part of greeting to the World Exhibition in New York). Cond. N. Grevillius.
JB sang: Serenad (Widéen); Tonerna.

A55
1939, May 3. Gothenburg. Partly broadcast perf. of Stockholm R. Opera on tour. Cond. N. Grevillius.
Roméo et Juliette: acts 1-2. With H. Schymberg, C. Molin, S. Edwardsen and others.

A56
1939, May 8. Gothenburg. Partly broadcast perf. of R. Opera on tour. Cond. N. Grevillius.
Faust: acts 1-2. With H. Görlin, J. Berglund, C. Richter and others.

A57
1939, May 23. London. Partly broadcast perf. of R. Opera (Covent Garden) [details see No. 3903].
Il trovatore: acts 1-2,4.

A58
1939. August 16. Lucerne, Jesuit Church. *Lucerne Festival Concert* (broadcast in Switzerland and may have been rebroadcast by NBC to the USA on the same day). Cond. A. Toscanini.
Messa da Requiem (Verdi). With Z. Milanov, K. Thorborg, N. Moscona.

A59

1939, October 28. Malmö. Radio concert. Cond. J. Fernström.
JB sang: Dalla sua pace; O paradiso; Che gelida manina; La donna è mobile.

A60

1940, September 26. Stockholm. Radio opera concert. Cond. N. Grevillius.
JB sang: Celeste Aida; Che gelida manina; Recondita armonia; E lucevan le stelle; La fleur que tu m'avais jetée.

A61

1942, April 9. Berlin, Philharmonie. Recital. Acc. M. Raucheisen.
[There are unconfirmed rumours that a recording of this recital does exist.]

A62

1942, November 28. Budapest. Recital (reported to have been recorded for broadcast to soldiers at the front).
JB sang: Una furtiva lagrima; Die Mainacht; Songs by Schubert, Sjögren, Alfvén, Sibelius etc. [The Hungarian Radio has not preserved a recording of this recital.]

A63

1943, October 7. Helsinki. Recital (partly recorded on tape by the Finnish Radio for broadcast on the following day). Acc. H. Ebert.
JB sang: Flickan kom ifrån sin älsklings möte; Svarta rosor; An die Leier; Frühlingsglaube; Zueignung; Ständchen (Strauss); Celeste Aida; La fleur que tu m'avais jetée; *Manon* aria; Amor ti vieta; Nessun dorma!; O paradiso; Two Puccini arias; Mattinata; La donna è mobile.

A64

1944, June 6. Stockholm, Stadion. *Swedish Flag Day ceremony* (broadcast).
JB sang: Land, du välsignade; Bisp Thomas' frihetssång.

A65

1944, before December 25 [broadcast date; recorded earlier]. Stockholm. Radio concert. Cond. N. Grevillius.
JB sang: Trollsjön; Sverige; Bisp Thomas' frihetssång; Cantique de Noël; Tonerna; Bön i ofredstid; Land, du välsignade.

A66

1945, April 18. Stockholm. Broadcast perf. of R. Opera. Cond. H. Sandberg.
Un ballo in maschera. With H. Guermant, G. Pålson-Wettergren, H. Schymberg, S. Björling and others.

A67

1945, June 6. Stockholm, Stadion. *Swedish Flag Day ceremony* (broadcast).
JB sang: Morgon; Nämner du Sverige.

A68
1945, September 23. Copenhagen. Partly broadcast perf. of R. Theatre. Cond. E. Tango. *Un ballo in maschera*: acts 2-3. With E. Schøtt, I. Steffensen, E. Oldrup, H. Skjær and others.

A69
1946, May 15. New York, Carnegie Hall. *Scandinavian "Pops" Music Concert* (broadcast by WNYC). Cond. S. Parmet.
JB sang songs by Sibelius, Grieg, Alfvén and Rangström.

A70
1947, November. Stockholm. Sound film recording for the motion picture *En svensk tiger* [A Swedish Tiger, or: A Swede Keeps Silent (double meaning)], in production from November 6 through December 15. Cond. S. Ehrling.
JB sang: O paradiso.
JB played the small role of the Opera Singer in this film, which was produced by Kungsfilm and released May 18, 1948. According to the Swedish Film Institute, only a fragment of the film is known to still exist, and this fragment does not contain any scene with JB.

A71
1950, (before?) September 1 (broadcast date). Stockholm. *Mitt allra bästa* [My Very Best], radio interview by G. Skoglund.

A72
1951, February 16. New York, NBC TV studio. *We, the People*, NBC television programme. Host: Dan Seymour. With piano.
JB sang: Vesti la giubba.
JB (in Canio costume) also took part in talk with Seymour and Enrico Caruso's widow Dorothy in which he describes why he never heard Caruso during his American tour with his brothers in 1919-21.

A73
1954, August 29. Johannesburg, City Hall. Radio concert. Cond. J. Schulman.
JB sang: Ombra mai fù; En svane; Jeg elsker dig; Ein Traum; Ingemisco; Una furtiva lagrima; Come un bel dì di maggio; Mamma!...Quel vino.
This broadcast was not preserved by the SABC.

A74
1954, November 11. Belgrade. Broadcast perf. of Belgrade Opera. Cond. K. Baranović. *La bohème*. With V. Heybalova, N. Sterle, S. Janković, Ž. Milosavljević, M. Čangalović and others.

A75
1954, November 15. Zagreb. Broadcast perf. of Croat National Opera. Cond. D. Žebre. *La bohème*. With B. Dežman, V. Grozaj, I. Francl, M. Kučić, T. Neralić and others.

A76
1954, December 10? (broadcast date Dec. 21). Stockholm. *Tomteluverött* [Red as Father Christmas' Cap]. Radio interview for this programme by B. Perrolf.

A77

1955, November 8. Chicago, Civic Opera House. Perf. of Lyric Theatre of Chicago (privately recorded - see below). Cond. N. Rescigno.

Il trovatore. With M. (Meneghini-)Callas, C. Turner, R. Weede and others.

For many years, there has been a persistent rumour that this performance was privately recorded in the opera house. In 1975, Henry Wisneski (*Maria Callas: The Art Behind the Legend*) wrote that "although one of the performances is rumoured to exist - taped by two Chicagoans who carried a tape recorder hooked up to a battery into the auditorium - it has not yet been made available to collectors". John Ardoin (*The Callas Legacy*, 1977) stated that the performance was recorded, but that the only known copy was destroyed. According to Stephen Stroff (*Guldstrupen*, 1981), the whole performance was recorded by the late William V. Arneth, who had a large collection of JB recordings; Stroff also stated in this book that he knew the name of a person who possessed a copy of the recording. Later, Stroff held the view that "the recording did exist at one time, but it was either lost or destroyed" (letter to the author, 1983).

It has been supposed that the performance was recorded in the box of the late Lawrence V. Kelly (one of the founders of the Chicago Lyric Theatre), but according to Hans H. Wurm, who was in the opera office at that time and was well acquainted with staff and artists (and who strongly doubted that the performance was recorded at all), a recording could not have been made in Kelly's box, for technical reasons.

There is now evidence that a copy of a recording was once in William Arneth's possession (however, Arneth reportedly stated that he had not been present at any of the two Chicago *Trovatore* performances). One of Arneth's friends, Otto Haberer, has described how Arneth in August 1958, during a party at his home at Metuchen, New Jersey, played as a surprise to Haberer and three other guests, acetates (transferred from tape) with excerpts from act 3 of this performance with acceptable sound (letter to the author, 1992).

If a recording was once in Arneth's possession, it has not been possible to find out whether it still exists or whether it was actually lost or destroyed, as supposed by Ardoin and Stroff. In addition, a singer who was a friend of Callas is reported to have claimed that she received a copy of the recording from her. Furthermore, a person claims to own a transcription of an unidentified radio programme where a short "Miserere" excerpt with Callas, supposedly taken from this performance, is played.

At last, it should be noted that a highly placed former employee of the Chicago Lyric Opera has stated that he unintentionally unplugged the recording machine during either the dress rehearsal or the first of the two *Trovatore* performances (on Nov. 5) (information from A. Farkas to the author, 1992).

A78

Mid-1950's. London, Albert Hall? BBC TV programme (*Tonight*?). Interview.

According to recollections of a man who saw the programme, this was an involuntary TV interview outside the dressing-room during which JB protested against the idea of conversation and refused to be interviewed. The *Tonight* programme began in 1957 and the only time JB gave a London recital parallel with the programme seems to have been on June 29, 1958, but there is no reference to him on the list of items shown June 30 - July 2.

A79

1958, May 20. Stockholm. Perf. of R. Opera. Cond. N. Grevillius.

Tosca: act 1. With B. Nilsson, S. Björling and others.

There are rumours that a private in-house recording was made of this performance, where JB had to be replaced after act 1 by Einar Andersson.

A80

1960, March 10, 12, 15 or 18. London. Perf. of R. Opera (Covent Garden) (privately recorded? - see below). Cond. E. Downes.

La bohème. With R. Carteri, M. Collier, J. Shaw, G. Evans, J. Rouleau and others.

There is evidence that one of these performances was privately recorded. The baritone John Shaw, who sang Marcello's role in this production, stated in a 1989 Australian radio interview that an unnamed person had recorded one of the performances and promised him a copy, which he never received. It has not been possible to find this person, so it is uncertain if a recording exists. However, it has also been reported that such a recording was advertised somewhere. None of the performances was recorded by the opera company or broadcast.

A81

1960, June 9. Stockholm, Gröna Lund, Tivoli. Open-air recital with Operasolisterna [The Royal Opera Soloists].

There was a tape from this performance in the now destroyed Gröna Lunds Tivoli collection (see note for No. 5106), and a private copy still exists. However, most of the original recording had been erased by another performance recorded on the same tape. Probably, the whole recital was originally recorded, but only the last part of the second section survives, and JB appeared as the last artist in the first section. At the end of the programme there were two short, improvised and unaccompanied tributes, sung by mostly unidentified soloists, to the accompanist Bertil Bokstedt and to the promoter of these recitals, the baritone Einar Larson, but it has not been possible to identify JB's voice in these ensembles. Thus it seems probable that he was not actually present for the final tributes and that no recording of his voice was preserved from the occasion.

C. Key to Index Numbers in the 1st and 2nd Edition of This Work and in "Jussi Björling: A Record List" (1969)

If nothing is written in the column for the 1st edition, the number has not been changed in the present edition. "A" numbers refer to the appendix on p. 227. A hyphen in the column for the 1st edition or for the JBRL indicates that the recording was not included in that work.

2nd	1st	JBRL
1-50		1-50
51A	51	51
B	51	51
52-55		52-55
56		55A
57		56
58		57
59		58
60		59
61		60
62		61
63		62
64		63
65		64
66		65
67		66
68		67
69		68
70A		69
B		-
71		70
72		71
73		72
74		73
75		74
76		75
77		76
78		77
79		78
80		79
81		80
82		81
83		82
84		83
85		84
86		85
87		86

2nd	1st	JBRL
88		87
89		88
90		89
91		90
92		91
93		92
94		93
95		94
96		95
97		96
98		97
99		98
100		99
101		100
102		101
103		-
104		103
105		-
106A	106	-
B	106	102
107A	107	-
B	107	104
108		105
109		105A
110A	110	106
B	110	-
111		107
112		108
113		109,109A
114A	110	
B		114
115		111
116		112
117		113
118		115
119		116
120		117

2nd	1st	JBRL
121		118,123
122		119
123		120
124		121-22
125		124
126		125
127		126
128		127
129		128
130		129
131		130
132		-
133		131
134		132
135		133
136		-
137		134
138		135
139A	139	136
B	139	-
140A		137
B		-
141		138
142		139
143		140
144		141
145		142
146		143
147A		144
B		144A
148		145
149		146
150		147
151A	151	-
B	151	148
152		149
153		150
154		151
155		152
156		153
157		154
158		155
159A	159	-
B	159	156
160A	160	-
B	160	157
161A	161	-

2nd	1st	JBRL
B	161	158
162A	162	159
B	162	-
163		160
164		161
165		162
166		163
167		164
168		165
169		166
170		167
171		168-69
172A		170
B		-
173		171
174		172
175		173
176		174
177		175
178		176
179		177
180		178
181		179
182		180
183		189
184		190
185		186
186		191
187		192
188		194
189		182
190		184
191		193
192		187
193		188
194		195
195		196
196		183
197		185
198		181
199		197
200		198
201		199
202		200
203		201
204		202
205		203

2nd	1st	JBRL
206		204
207		205
208		206
209		207
210		208
211		225
212		226
213		228
214		229,083
215		232
216A	216	231
B	216	231
217		230
218		227
219		233
220		234
221		235
222		236
223		237
224		238
225		239
226		240
227		244
228		241
229		245
230		242
231		243
232		263
233		267
234		268
235		269
236		270
237		264
238		266
239		265
240		271
241		272
242		274
243		273
3401		001
3601		003
3602		004,005
A37	3603	006
3701		008
3702		011
3703		007

2nd	1st	JBRL
3704		-
3705		009
3706		-
3707		010
3708		-
A45	3709	-
A51	3801	-
A52	3901	-
3901	3902	012
3902	3903	013
3903	3904	-
A58	3905	-
3904	3906	023
4001		014
4002		015
4003		016
4004		017
4005		018
4006		-
4007		019
4008		020
4101		021,038
4102		022
4201		024
4301		-
4302		025
4303		-
4401		026
4402		-
4501		027
4502		028
4503		029
4504		030
4505		-
4506		031
4601		033
4602		034
4603		035
4604		036
4605		037
4606		-
4701		039
A70	4702	-
4702	4703	041
4801		043
4802		044
4803		045

2nd	1st	JBRL
4804		046,047
4901		048
4902		049
4903		-
4904		052,054
4905		-
4907		050
4908		051
5001		053
5002		055
5003		-
5004		-
5005		-
5006		056,097b,c,e
5007		057
5008		058
5009		059
5010		060
5101		063,097a,d
A72	5102	-
5102	5103	064
5103	5104	-
5104	-	-
5105	-	-
5106	5105	-
5107	5106	-
5108	5107	065,071b
5109	5108	067,068b
5110	5109	066
5111	5110	061,068b
5201		069
5202		070
5203		-
5204		072
5301		073
5302		-
5303		-
53xx	-	-
5401		-
5402		-
5403		075
5404		076
5405		077
5406		-
5501		209-24
A77	5502	-
5502	5503	078
5601		079
5602		080
5603		081
5604		-
5605	-	-
5701		082
5702	-	-
5703	5702	084
5704	5703	-
5705	-	-
5706	5704	246,085
5707	-	-
5801		086
5802		247-61,087
5803		-
5804		088
5805		-
5806		-
5807		-
5808		262,089
5901		090
5902		-
5903		-
5904		-
5905		-
5906		-
5907	-	-
5908	5907	-
5909	5908	091
5910	5909	092
5911	5910	093
5912	5911	094
6001		095
A80	6002	-
A81	6003	-
6002	6004	-
6003	6005	-
6004	6006	275-81

Section 2: Disc and Tape Issues

A. Analogue Discs

1. 78 rpm.

Angel (EMI)

ARGENTINA; 10"/25 cm.

292708	>*HMV* DA 2039	?55

Columbia, USA [See note]

10"/25cm.

E 4547	4,5	20-05
E 4691	2,3	20-09
E 4768	1,6	20-11

Columbia (EMI)

ARGENTINA; 10"/25 cm.

292708	>*HMV* DA 2039	?54

Electrola, Germany (EMI) (Red label)

10"/25 cm.

DA 1548	>*HMV* DA 1548	a.50
DA 1582	>*HMV* DA 1582	38-04
DA 1584	>*HMV* DA 1584	38-01
DA 1701	>*HMV* DA 1701	a.50
DA 1841	>*HMV* DA 1841	a.50
DA 1908	>*HMV* DA 1908	a.50

12"/30 cm.

DB 3049	>*HMV* DB 3049	c.38
DB 3603	>*HMV* DB 3603	?
DB 3665	>*HMV* DB 3665 v.1	?
DB 21311	>*HMV* DB 21311	a.52
DB 21426	>*HMV* DB 21426	?53
DB 21563	>*HMV* DB 21563	53-10

The first label used for the acoustical recordings of Olle, Jussi and Gösta Björling in 1920 (gold on green background).

His Master's Voice [=*HMV*] (EMI)

NORWAY (Plum label); 10"/25 cm.

AL 2324	>*HMV* X 4720	a.38
AL 3096	>*HMV* X 6090	a.54

INTERNATIONAL SERIES (Red label); 10"/25 cm. [For local pressings, see note]

		Sw	*GB*
DA 1548	89,90	37-03	37-03
DA 1582	101,102	41-03	37-12
DA 1584	96,99	37-12	37-11
DA 1594	97,102	38-01	-
DA 1607	100,101	38-03	-
DA 1701	120,121	39-12	39-10
DA 1704	122,123	40-03	40-03
DA 1705	124	40-04/05	40-08
(DA 1797)	>*Vic.* 4531	(not issued)	
(DA 1818)	137,138	(not issued)	
DA 1836	141,142	45-02	46-06
DA 1837	145,148	44-09	46-04
DA 1841	143,146	44-07/08	45-12
DA 1890	155,156	48-12	-
DA 1902	159B,160B	49-07/08	49-02
DA 1908	161B,162A	49-09	49-09
DA 1931	165,166	50-05	50-02
DA 2025	200,202	-	53-01
DA 2039	199,201	53-09	53-07
DA 2068	188,191	54-11	-

NORWAY (Red label); 10"/25 cm.

DAN 1548	>*HMV* DA 1548	?
DAN 1582	>*HMV* DA 1582	?
DAN 1584	>*HMV* DA 1584	?
DAN 1836	>*HMV* DA 1836	?
DAN 1837	>*HMV* DA 1837	?
DAN 1841	>*HMV* DA 1841	?
DAN 1902	>*HMV* DA 1902	?
DAN 1931	>*HMV* DA 1931	?

INTERNATIONAL SERIES (Red label); 12"/30 cm. [For local pressings, see note]

			Sw	*GB*
DB 3049	87,88		37-03	37-06
DB 3302	95,98		37-12	38-01
DB 3603	112,113		38-10	38-12
DB 3665 v.1	114A,115		38-12	39-02
v.2	114B,115			
DB 3887	118,119		40-01	39-12
DB 5393 [Released in Italy only?]	87,95	41-04	-	-
DB 5759	>*Vic.*12725		42-10	41-03

DB 5787	>*Vic.*12831	?47-01	-
DB 6000 v.1 [See note]	139A,140A	41-12	-
v.2	139A,140B		
DB 6119 v.1	>*HMV* DB 6000 v.1	44-04	45-06
v.2	139B,140B		
DB 6163 v.1	144,147A	44-06	45-09
v.2	144,147B		
DB 6249	151B,152	46-02/03	(49-03)
DB 6714	153,157	48-10	(52-06)
DB 21311	173,174	51-12	51-09
DB 21426	172A,175	52-10	52-03
DB 21563	177,178	53-06	53-03
DB 21593	196,198	53-12	53-10
DB 21602	176,181	54-03	53-12
DB 21620 v.1	183-85	54-11	54-07
v.2	183-84,186		
DB 21621	179,180	54-10	54-10
DB 21622	171	54-11	54-07

NORWAY (Red label); 12"/30 cm.

DBN 3049	>*HMV* DB 3049	?
DBN 3603	>*HMV* DB 3603	?

AUSTRALIA (Red label)

10"/25 cm.

EC 60	>*HMV* X 4723	a.41
EC 89	>*HMV* DA 1704	42-11
EC 117	>*Vic.* 4531	?44
EC 143	>*HMV* DA 1841	a.49
EC 198	>*HMV* DA 2025	a.55
EC 207	>*HMV* DA 1837	55
EC 214	>*HMV* X 6090	55
EC 221	>*HMV* DA 2039	a.56

12"/30 cm.

ED 87	>*Vic.* 12725	42
ED 375	>*HMV* DB 6000 v.1	45-07
ED 1239	>*HMV* DB 6163 v.2	53

IRELAND

10"/25 cm.

IR 340	>*HMV* DA 1902	a.55
IR 344	>*HMV* DA 1931	a.55
IR 369	>*HMV* DA 1837	a.55
IR 370	>*HMV* DA 1841	a.55
IR 409	>*HMV* DA 1582	56-11
IR 420	>*HMV* DA 1548	?

12"/30 cm.

IRX 62	>*HMV* DB 21563	53/55
IRX 64	>*HMV* DB 3887	a.55
IRX 74	>*HMV* DB 3665 (v.2?)	a.55
IRX 77	>*HMV* DB 21602	a.55
IRX 87	>*HMV* DB 6000 v.1	a.55
IRX 91	>*HMV* DB 3603	a.55

FINLAND; 10"/25 cm.

TG 128	>*HMV* X 4716	?50/55
TG 129	>*HMV* X 6090	?50/55

SCANDINAVIAN SERIES (Plum label); 10"/25 cm. [See note]

		Int'l	*Sw*
X 3376	9,12	-	30-05
X 3377	10,11	-	30-04
X 3466	13,14	-	30-08
X 3556	20,21	-	30-12
X 3622	17,22	-	31-01
X 3628	15,16	-	31-02
X 3675	18,19	-	31-04
X 3683	26,28	-	31-03
X 3702	23,24	?	31-05
X 3724	25,27	-	31-06
X 3826	31	-	31-11
X 3829	29,30	-	31-12
X 3879	37,38	-	32-02
X 3880 ("Erik Odde")	36	-	32-02
X 3882 ("Erik Odde")	39	-	32-03
X 3885	34,35	?	32-03
X 3928	32,33	-	32-05
X 3992 ("Erik Odde")	42,43	-	32-10
X 3993	45,46	?	32-11
X 4011 ("Erik Odde")	47	-	32-11
X 4036 ("Erik Odde")	48	-	33-01
X 4095 ("Erik Odde")	49	-	33-03
X 4108 v.1	50,51A	-	33-05
v.2	50,51B	?	
(X 4121) [See note for Nos. 52-53]	52,53	(not issued)	
X 4127	57,58	-	33-08
X 4128	55,59	-	33-07
X 4133 ("Erik Odde")	60,62	-	33-09
X 4134 ("Erik Odde")	61	-	33-09
X 4176	63,64	-	33-11
X 4179	65,66	-	33-11
X 4192 ("Erik Odde")	67	-	33-12
X 4196 ("Erik Odde")	68	-	33-12
X 4204 v.1	69,70A	-	33-12
v.2	69,70B		

X 4205	71,72		-	34-01
X 4220	73,74		-	34-02
X 4265	75,76		-	34-04
X 4436	77,78		-	35-05
X 4449	79,80		-	35-06
X 4716	81,84		49-03	37-01
X 4720	82,83		36-10	37-02
X 4723	85,86		36-10	36-12
X 4777	91,92		49-03	37-05
X 4832	93,94		37-04	37-07
X 6090	107B,110A		49-03	38-08
X 6146	106B,111		38-10	39-01
X 6235	104,108		39-03	39-04
X 7077	149,150		-	44-07
X 7255 [Issued in Denmark only?]	104	50-04	-	-
X 7536	9,10		-	49-09
X 7947 [See note]	205,208		54-10	54-01
X 7964 [See note]	206,207		-	?54-03

Radiotjänst [Swedish Broadcasting Corp.]

10"/25 cm.

PR 5189 [Issued only as a lottery prize; see note]	4,5201	52-02

(RCA) Victor

USA (Red Seal) [some also pressed and issued in other countries]

10"/25 cm.

2136	>*HMV* DA 1701	41-01
2195	>*HMV* DA 1705	42-01
4372	>*HMV* DA 1548	37-11
4379	>*HMV* DA 1582	38-03
4408	>*HMV* DA 1584	38-11
4531	131,133	40-12

12"/30 cm.

12039 [+Canada]	>*HMV* DB 3049	37-09
12150	>*HMV* DB 3302	38-02
12635 [+Canada]	>*HMV* DB 3603	40-05
12725	125,126	40-06
12831	127,134,135	40-07
13588	>*HMV* DB 3665 v.2	41-04
13790 [+Canada]	>*HMV* DB 3887	41-11
15820 (in M 633)	87	40-02

10"/25 cm.

10-1200 [+Brazil]	143,145	46-02
10-1323	141,148	47-08
10-1477	>*HMV* DA 1908	49-09

12"/30 cm.

11-8440	>*HMV* DB 6000 v.1	43-06
11-9387 [+Canada]	>*HMV* DB 6163 v.2	47-02
12-0527	>*HMV* DB 6249	48-11
12-0674 (in MO 1275)	>*HMV* DB 3049	49-02
12-0675 (in MO 1275)	113,147B	49-02
12-0676 (in MO 1275)	>*HMV* DB 3887	49-02
12-3068 (in DM 1474)	145	51-01
12-3086	>*HMV* DB 6714	51-01

USA (Purple label, Swedish records); 10"/25 cm.

26-1093	>*HMV* X 3377	50-12
26-1095	83,84	51-01
26-1097	82,91	51-04
26-1098	92,108	51-07
26-1099	21,57	52-03
26-1105	>*Vic.* 26-1097	52-04
26-1111	46,104	52-11
26-1122	>*HMV* X 7964	54-10
26-1123	>*HMV* X 7947	54-11

ARGENTINA; 12"/30 cm.

66-6105	>*HMV* DB 21593	?
66-6143	>*HMV* DB 21621	?

BRAZIL; 12"/30 cm.

886-5031	>*HMV* DB 25163	?

USA (Red Seal set); 12"/30 cm.

DM 1474 (12-3064/68) "Verdi Commemorative Album"	145 [on 12-3068]	51-01

JAPAN

Victor Record Library for Every Home; 10"/25 cm.

HL 47	102	a.41
HL 54	89	a.41

12"/30 cm.

JD 1513	>*HMV* DB 3603	a.41

10"/25 cm.

JE 100	>*HMV* DA 1548	a.41
JE 149	>*HMV* DA 1582	a.41
JE 176	>*HMV* DA 1584	a.41

USA (Red Seal sets); 12"/30 cm.		
M 633 (15817/21) "Stars of the Metropolitan, vol. 2"	87 [on 15820]	40-02
MO 1275 (12-0674/76) "Jussi Bjoerling: Favorite Operatic Arias"	87,88,113,118,119,147B	49-02
JAPAN		
12"/30 cm.		
ND 139	>*HMV* DB 3603	c.50
ND 434	>*HMV* DB 3049	c.50
10"/25 cm.		
NF 4128	90,99	c.50
NF 4220	102 [>*Vic.* HL 47?]	a.55
Victor Record Lovers' Society; 12"/30 cm.		
RL 31	>*HMV* DB 3049	a.41
RL 42	>*HMV* DB 3302	a.41
RL 76	126	a.41
12"/30 cm.		
SD 199	179,181	?
10"/25 cm.		
SF 19	>*HMV* DA 1908	a.55
USA (Black Label, Swedish records); 10"/25 cm.		
V 24110	>*HMV* X 4720	39-01
V 24111	>*HMV* X 4777	39-01

V-Disc

USA (vinyl records not for sale, issued by Army Service Forces, Special Services Division); 12"/30 cm.

623	147B [See note]	46-05
863	4801a-c	48-09

2. 45 rpm.

Records are 7"/17 cm. normal play if not otherwise indicated.

Angel, Brazil (issued by EMI-Odeon)

TCB 02 "Jussi Bjorling: Cancões imortais"	>*HMV* 7EBS 13	58-07
TCB 13 "Recondita armonia"	>*HMV* 7ER 5087	59-01
TCB 26	143	60-05

CCGC [=Commissie Collectieve Gramofoonplaten Compagnie], Netherlands

PR 900 "Premieplaat 1967"	175	67

Disel, see *RCA* (65.xxx, 75.xxx, 95.xxx series)

Electrola, Germany (EMI)

7RW 110	>*HMV* 7R 124	a.54
7RW 131	>*HMV* 7R 106	a.54

His Master's Voice [=*HMV*] (EMI) [Includes translations of the label in France, Italy and Spain]

GREAT BRITAIN; extended play

7EB 6030 "Jussi Björling (Tenor)"	>*HMV* 7EBS 13	58-04

NEW ZEALAND; extended play

7EBM 6030 "Jussi Björling (Tenor)"	>*HMV* 7EBS 13	?62

AUSTRALIA; extended play

7EBO 6030 "Jussi Björling (Tenor)"	>*HMV* 7EBS 13	58-04

SWEDEN [& NORWAY, DENMARK; see note]; extended play

7EBS 1 "Jussi Björling"	81,82,91,92	54-08
7EBS 3 "Jussi Björling" [See note for *HMV* X 7947 & 7964]	205-08	56-06
7EBS 10 "Jussi Björling sjunger"	34,35,107B,110A	57-05
7EBS 11 "Jussi Björling sjunger"	83,84,93,94	57-05
7EBS 13 "Jussi Björling"	101,102,146,160B	58-03

ITALY ("*La Voce del Padrone*"); extended play

7EPQ 607 "Jussi Björling"	>*HMV* 7EBS 13	58-08

GREAT BRITAIN; extended play

7ER 5025 "Jussi Björling: Operatic Arias"	>*RCA* ERA 109	54-09
7ER 5055 "I Pagliacci (Excerpts)"	204a	55-11
7ER 5062 "I Pagliacci (Excerpts)"	204b2	56-03
7ER 5063 "Cavalleria Rusticana (Excerpts)"	>*HMV* 7ERQ 141	56-11
7ER 5079 "Cavalleria Rusticana (Excerpts)"	>*HMV* 7ERQ 143	57-06
7ER 5087 "Jussi Björling"	89,90,96,99	58-02
7ER 5179 "La Bohème: Excerpts No. 1"	211b2-5	60-09
7ER 5186 "La Bohème: Excerpts No. 2"	211e2-3,f	60-11
7ER 5189 "Jussi Björling"	>*HMV* 7EBS 13	60-12
7ER 5190 "La Bohème: Excerpts No. 3"	211g	61-01
7ER 5193 "Jussi Björling: Operatic Arias"	98,112,113,153	61-03
7ER 5196 "Jussi Björling: Operatic Arias"	87,152,161B,162A	61-06
7ER 5207 "Jussi Björling: Operatic Arias"	95,143-45	61-11
7ERC 1 "Jussi Björling"	188,191-93	54-12
7ERC 2 "Jussi Björling"	189,190,197	54-12

SPAIN ("*La Voz de su Amo*"); extended play

7ERL 1307	181	a.62
7ERL 1453 "La Bohème: Selección"	>*HMV* 7ER 5186	a.62

NEW ZEALAND; extended play

7ERM 5186 "Excerpts from 'La Bohème'"	>*HMV* 7ER 5186	?62
7ERM 5189 "Jussi Björling"	>*HMV* 7EBS 13	?62

AUSTRALIA; extended play

7ERO 5179 "La Bohème: Excerpts No. 1"	>*HMV* 7ER 5179	61-06
7ERO 5193 "Jussi Björling: Operatic Arias"	>*HMV* 7ER 5193	62-06
7ERO 5196 "Jussi Björling: Operatic Arias"	>*HMV* 7ER 5196	62-04

ITALY ("*La Voce del Padrone*"); extended play

7ERQ 136 "Pagliacci (Excerpts)"	>*HMV* 7ER 5055	56-01
7ERQ 140 "Pagliacci (Excerpts)"	>*HMV* 7ER 5062	56-03
7ERQ 141 "Cavalleria Rusticana (Excerpts)"	203a	?56-05
7ERQ 143 "Cavalleria Rusticana (Excerpts)"	203c,d	56-05
7ERQ 167	203a	57-06
7ERQ 229 "Jussi Björling"	>*HMV* 7ER 5087	60-08
7ERQ 251 "Jussi Björling: ..."	>*HMV* 7ER 5196	61-06
7ERQ 255	112	?61
7ERQ 258 "Jussi Björling: ..."	>*HMV* 7ER 5207	?61

NETHERLANDS (issued by EMI-Bovema)

7OPH 1004	139A,140A	58-08

GREAT BRITAIN

7P 208	>*HMV* 7R 106	59-09
7P 239	>*HMV* 7RQ 3128	59-11
7P 261	113,145	60-10
7P 330	97,159B	?63

NETHERLANDS (issued by EMI-Bovema)

7PH 1011	>*HMV* 7R 106	a.60
7PH 1013	>*HMV* 7RQ 3128	a.60

SOUTH AFRICA

7PJ 713	>*HMV* 7R 106	63-11
7PJ 736	>*HMV* 7P 261	64-07

AUSTRALIA

7PO 239	>*HMV* 7RQ 3128	60-08
7PO 330	>*HMV* 7P 330	64-10

GREAT BRITAIN

7R 106	143,146	52-10
7R 124	173,175	52-10
7R 160	177,178	53-11
7R 173	>*RCA* 447-0808	54-01

FRANCE ("*La Voix de son Maître*"; issued by EMI Pathé-Marconi)

7RF 115	145,148	51-12

AUSTRALIA

7RO 105	>*HMV* 7R 124	55-02

ITALY ("*La Voce del Padrone*")

7RQ 3007	>*HMV* 7R 106	53-06
7RQ 3008	>*HMV* 7R 124	53-06
7RQ 3128	87,88	?

DENMARK

45X 8433	104	61-04

FRANCE ("*La Voix de son Maître*"; issued by EMI Pathé-Marconi)

ROVL 9016	>*Pl.Mus.* 7ERF 17.121	?69
ROVL 9040	87,143	?69

Plaisir Musical, France (issued by EMI Pathé-Marconi)

7ERF 17.109 "Deux cavatines"	119,151B	62-04
7ERF 17.121 "Manon"	112,152	62-07

RCA (*Victor*)

AUSTRALIA; extended play

26012 "Bjoerling Favourites, vol. 1"	179,182d3,d5,203a	?
26019 "Bjoerling and Merrill in Opera"	>*RCA* ERA 134	?

AUSTRALIA or USA? [see note]; extended play

26044 "Jussi Bjoerling in Four Great Tenor Arias"	>*RCA* ERA 109	?56
26045 "Jussi Bjoerling in Song"	>*RCA* ERA 141	?56
26071 "Excerpts from 'Il Trovatore'"	>*RCA* ERA 112	?
26072 "Excerpts from 'Il Trovatore'"	>*RCA* ERA 113	?

SPAIN; extended play

3-26004	>*RCA* ERA 109	a.55
3-26068	>*RCA* ERA 141	a.60
3-26114 "Aida: Fragmentos"	210: excerpts	a.60
3-26178	5501i-1	a.60
3B 26035 (2) "Cavalleria Rusticana & I Pagliacci: Selección"	>*RCA* ERB 38	a.60

USA (Swedish records)

43-1105	>*RCA* 53-5004	52-04
43-1111	46,104	52-11
43-1122	206,207	54-10
43-1123	205,208	54-11

GERMANY (issued by Teldec)

47-0808 (=447-0808)		
47-9133	>*HMV* 7R 124	c.57-09
47-9149	>*RCA* 65.510	c.58-01
47-9150	170,204a	c.58-01
47-9155	>*RCA* 447-9155	c.65-03
47-9157	>*RCA* 447-9157	c.64-01
47-9159	>*RCA* 447-9159	c.64-03
47-9365	>*RCA* 447-9365	c.64-03

USA

Red Seal

49-0475	161B,162A	49-09
49-0621	143,145	49-10
49-3068 (in WDM 1474)	145	51-01
49-3086	153,157	51-01
49-3193/94 (in WDM 1495)	171	51-04
49-3374 (in WDM 1546)	179,181	51-10
49-3375 (" ")	169,170	51-10
49-3376 (" ")	176,180	51-10
49-3405 (in WDM 1565)	162	51-10
49-3409 (" ")	170	51-10
49-3667 (in WDM 1626)	180	52-03
49-3825 (in WDM 7007)	174,175	52-10
49-3826 (" ")	171 (beg.),173	52-10
49-3827 (" ")	171 (end),172B	52-10
49-3874/82 (WDM 6008)	182	52-10
49-4180/91 (WDM 6106)	203,204	53-09

Blue-green label (Swedish records)

53-5003	83,84	51-01
53-5004	82,91	51-04

BELGIUM (issued by Disel)

65.504	170(?),181	?c.55
65.505	169,180	?c.55
65.506	182d3,d5	?c.55
65.510	182e,f2	?c.55
65.511	176,179	?c.55
65.517	>*HMV* 7R 124	?c.55
65.519	114B,115	?c.55
75.532 "Your Favorite Music, vol. 2"	175	?c.55
75.534 "Your Favorite Music, vol. 4"	181,182d5	?c.55
75.537 "Your Favorite Music, vol. 7"	179	?c.55
75.542 "Your Favorite Music, vol. 10"	166	?c.55
75.543 "Your Favorite Music, vol. 11"	153	?c.55
95.250 [Extended play]	>*RCA* ERA 109	?c.55

USA & GERMANY (Golden Standard Series; issued by Teldec in Germany) [US release dates]

447-0808	176,181	57-09
447-0809	179,180	57-09

GERMANY (Golden Standard Series; issued by Teldec)

447-9133	>*HMV* 7R 124	c.58-03
447-9149	>*RCA* 65.510	c.58-03
447-9150	>*RCA* 47-9150	c.58-03
447-9155	162A,179	?58
447-9156	182d5,217	c.58-06
447-9157	180	c.58-03
447-9159	5501i	c.58-03
447-9167	5501c,d	c.58-03
447-9363	219a3,f1	c.61-09
447-9364	210a1,216A	c.61-09
447-9365	212d,213	c.61-09
447-9366	170,240d1	c.61-09

USA (Red Seal); extended play

549-0051 (in ERB 7027)	171 (beg.),172B	53-10
549-0052 (" ")	171 (end),173,182d5	53-10
549-5123 (in ERB 38)	204b	55-01
549-5124 (" ")	203d2,204a	55-01
549-5262 (in ERC 2045)	211a2,f3	57-01
549-5263 (" ")	211a3-4,f1-2	57-01
549-5264 (" ")	211c,d,e	57-01
549-5274 (in ERC 2046)	210a1,g3	57-01
549-5275 (in ERC 2046)	210g1-2	57-01

BRAZIL; extended play

585-0005 "Jussi Bjoerling"	>*RCA* ERA 109	?

ITALY; extended play

A72R 0086	>*RCA* ERA 109	a.58
A72R 0088	210a1 (?)	a.58
A72R 0090	203a,d	a.58

JAPAN; extended play

EP 3046 "Jussi Bjoerling in Four Great Tenor Arias"	>*RCA* ERA 109	?

ITALY; extended play

ERA 50-088	>*RCA* A72R 0088	a.62
ERA 50-090	>*RCA* A72R 0090	a.62
ERA 50-148	209d,e	a.62
ERA 50-151	222 (?)	a.62

USA & GERMANY (Red Seal; issued by Teldec in Germany); extended play

		US	*G*
ERA 109 "Jussi Bjoerling in Four Great Tenor Arias"	161B,162A, 179,181	53-11	55
ERA 112 "Gems from 'Il Trovatore'"	182f2	53-11	
ERA 113 "Three Selections from 'Il Trovatore"	182b,c1	53-11	c.59-03
ERA 134 "Bjoerling and Merrill in Opera"	145,157,173,175	53-11	c.65-08
ERA 141 "Jussi Bjoerling in Song"	183,184,187,191, 193	54-01	
ERA 209 "Arias Sung and Acted"	88,204a	54-06	c.54-05
ERA 245 "Three Arias by Jussi Bjoerling"	143,153,176	55-08	c.56-03

GERMANY (Red Seal; issued by Teldec); extended play

ERA 6052	219f1	?
ERA 6059-1	220b1	?
ERA 6149	240c1,e2	?
ERA 9509 "Jussi Bjoerling"	213,216A,217-18	c.57-08
ERA 9511 "Jussi Björling singt berühmte Opernarien"	162A,176,179,181	c.57-09
ERA 9513 "Your Favorites, vol. 1"	175	c.57-09
ERA 9515 "Your Favorites, vol. 2"	176,182e (abridged)	c.57-10
ERA 9516 "Your Favorites, vol. 3"	180	c.57-11
ERA 9548 "Wunschkonzert I"	>*RCA* ERA 9515	c.58-05
ERA 9574 "Wunschkonzert II"	180	c.58-06
ERA 9702 "Jussi Björling singt Beethoven und Schubert"	5501a-d	c.60-03
ERA 9791 "Belcanto in Opera: Jussi Björling"	219a3,f1,222,240d1	c.61-01
ERA 9795 "Belcanto in Opera: Renata Tebaldi"	240e	c.61-01

SWEDEN (made for Grammofon AB Electra by Teldec, Germany); extended play

ERAS 87 "Jussi Björling: Land, du välsignade"	227-31	57
ERAS 102 "Jussi Björling"	214,215	58
ERAS 113 "Jussi Björling: Trollsjön"	232,237-39	a.59-09

USA (Red Seal sets); extended play

ERB 38 (549-5123/24) "Highlights from 'Cavalleria Rusticana' & 'I Pagliacci'"	203d2,204a,b	55-01
ERB 7027 (549-0051/52) "Bjoerling and Merrill Sing Operatic Duets"	171,172B,174,182d5 [>33.*RCA* LRM 7027]	53-10
ERC 2045 (549-5262/64) "Highlights from 'La Bohème'"	211b2-4,d,e,f,g [>33.*RCA* SLP 20]	57-01
ERC 2046 (549-5274/76) "Highlights from 'Aida'"	210a1,g	57-01

JAPAN

ES 8510	179,219f1	?

GERMANY (Red Seal; issued by Teldec); extended play

ESC 9791* "Belcanto in Opera: Jussi Björling"	>*RCA* ERA 9791	c.61-01
ESC 9795* "Belcanto in Opera: Renata Tebaldi"	>*RCA* ERA 9795	c.61-01

SWEDEN (made for Grammofon AB Electra by Teldec, Germany)

FRS 569 "Jussi Björling: Två sånger av Sibelius"	235,236	a.59-09
FRS 576 "Jussi Björling: Adams julsång, Beethovens julsång"	233,234	59

FRANCE (issued by AREA)

FVA 630.255	>*RCA* 65.504	p.54
FVA 630.259	169,176,180	p.54

ITALY

NC 0060	222,226	a.62
NC 0061	223,224	a.62
NC 0080	240b2,e2	a.62
NSC 0060*	>*RCA* NC 0060	a.62
NSC 0061*	>*RCA* NC 0061	a.62
NSC 0080*	>*RCA* NC 0080	a.62

GREAT BRITAIN

Red Seal

RB 9271 "Pearl Fishers Duet" (Your Hundred Best Tunes, No. 1)	>*HMV* 7R 124	78-06

Extended play (issued by Decca)

RCX 150 "Highlights from 'Cavalleria Rusticana'"	220c	59-09

RCX 155 "Jussi Bjoerling: Recital"	222-25	59-10
RCX 206 "The Incomparable Bjoerling"	219a3,221,240b2,d1	62-04
RCX 7114 "Jussi Bjoerling and Robert Merrill: Operatic Arias"	>*RCA* ERA 134	63-06
SRC 7027* "Highlights from 'Cavalleria Rusticana'"	>*RCA* RCX 150	59-09
SRC 7031* "Jussi Bjoerling: Recital"	>*RCA* RCX 155	59-10
SRC 7042* "The Incomparable Bjoerling"	>*RCA* RCX 206	62-04
JAPAN		
SX 8536* "Tosca"	219a3,f1	?
USA (Red Seal sets); extended play		
WDM 1474 (49-3064/68) "Verdi Commemorative Album"	145 [>78.*Vic.* DM 1474]	51-01
WDM 1495 (49-3193/96) "Highlights from Verdi's 'Don Carlo'"	171 [>33.*RCA* LM 1128]	51-04
WDM 1546 (49-3374/76) "Great Tenor Arias by Jussi Bjoerling"	169,170,176,179-81 [>33.*RCA* LM 105]	51-10
WDM 1565 (49-3405/09) "Highlights from 'Cavalleria Rusticana', 'I Pagliacci'"	162A,170 [>33.*RCA* LM 1160]	51-10
WDM 1626 (17-0367+49-3664/67) "Ten Tenors - Ten Arias"	180 [>33.*RCA* LM 1202]	52-03
WDM 6008 (49-3874/82) "Il Trovatore"	182 [>33.*RCA* LM 6008]	52-10
WDM 6106 (49-4180/91) "Cavalleria Rusticana, I Pagliacci"	203,204 [>33.*RCA* LM 6106]	53-09
WDM 7007 (49-3825/27) "Operatic Duets by Jussi Bjoerling and Robert Merrill"	171,172B,173-75 [>33.*RCA* LM 7007]	52-10

3. 33 1/3 rpm.

Records are 12"/30 cm. if not otherwise indicated.

ABC Records, Australia (issued by Australian Broadcasting Corp.)

836 642-1 "John Cargher's Historic Singers of Renown"	96	88

ABC, USA (private issue by Edward J. Smith)

ABC 1001 (2) "Requiem"	4005	c.58

Accord, France (distributed by Musidisc)

ACC 1500 17 (4) "Jacques Offenbach 1880-1980"	110A	80

Ace of Diamonds (Decca)

GREAT BRITAIN & SPAIN		*Sp*	*GB*
GOS 617/18* "Requiem"	>*RCA* LD 6091	74	72-04
GOS 634/35* "Cavalleria Rusticana. [S.4] Jussi Bjoerling Operatic Recital = Recital de Opera por Jussi Bjoerling"	>*RCA* LM 6059	76	74-04

GREAT BRITAIN		
GOSB 636/38* "Grand Opera Festival"	221 [on GOSB 637]	73-10
GOSC 666/68* "Grand Opera Gala"	222 [on GOSC 667]	75-09

AD *(Archive Documents)*, see: *RRE*

Akkord, see: *Melodiya*

Angel (EMI)

ARGENTINA (issued by EMI-Odeon)		
5672/74 *? "Madama Butterfly"	>*HMV* ALP 1795/97	?
5675/76 "La Bohème"	>*RCA* LM 6042	?
6001/02 "La Bohème"	>*RCA* LM 6042	?
6083 "Jussi Bjoerling: Arias de Opera"	>*HMV* ALP 1620	?
6877/79 "Madama Butterfly"	>*HMV* ALP 1795/97	?

7059 "Jussi Bjoerling: Arias de Opera"(?)	?	a.80
10059 "Jussi Bjoerling: Opera Arias"	?	?

USA (issued by Capitol)

35821 "Madama Butterfly: Highlights"	>*Cap.* G. 7233	61-12
35824/26 (=CL 3604)		
36367 (in BL 3683)		

CHILE (issued by EMI-Odeon)

3ACX 47190 "Jussi Bjoerling: Arias de Opera"	>*HMV* ALP 1620	61
3ACX 47341 "Jussi Bjoerling: Recital de Opera"	>*Cap.* G 7248	64
3ACX 47365 "Jussi Bjoerling: Canciónes y Baladas"	>*Cap.* G 7247	62
3ACX 47530 "Jussi Bjoerling" (Voces de Oro No. 2)	>*HMV* HQM 1190	70

BRAZIL (issued by EMI-Odeon)

3BBX 21 "Vozes de Ouro"	101,143,146	61-08
3BBX 28 "Vozes de Ouro, vol. 2"	90,99	62-11
3CBX 322/24* "Madama Butterfly"	>*HMV* ALP 1795/97	62-07
3CBX 328 "Jussi Bjorling: Recital de Saudade"	>*Cap.* G 7248	82-08

CHILE (issued by EMI-Odeon)

3SACX 47406/08* (=SOA 539)

JAPAN (issued by Toshiba-EMI)

AA 8013* "Madama Butterfly: Highlights"	>*Cap.* G 7233	66-12
AA 9603/05*[?] "Madama Butterfly"	>*HMV* ALP 1795/97	c.66
AB 7123 "The Beloved Bjoerling, vol. 3: Songs and Ballads, 1936-1953"	>*Cap.* G 7247	65-11
AB 7127 "Jussi Bjoerling: Operatic Recital"	>*Cap.* G 7248	65-03
AB 7134 "The Beloved Bjoerling: Opera Arias"	>*HMV* ALP 1620	65-11
AB 9368/69 "La Bohème"	>*RCA* LM 6042	?

USA (issued by Capitol)

BL 3683 (36366/67) "The Genius of Puccini"	241c3-4,e [on 36367]	66-10
CL 3604 (35824/26) "Madama Butterfly"	>*HMV* ALP 1795/97	61-12
COLH 148 "The Beloved Bjoerling, vol. 1: Opera Arias 1936-1948" (Great Recordings of the Century)	>*HMV* ALP 1620	65-03
COLH 149 "The Beloved Bjoerling, vol. 2: Songs & Ballads 1936-1953" (Great Recordings of the Century)	>*Cap.* G 7247	65-03
COLH 150 "The Beloved Bjoerling, vol. 3: Opera Arias 1936-1945" (Great Recordings of the Century)	>*Cap.* G 7248	65-03

JAPAN (issued by Toshiba-EMI)		
GR 70085 "Jussi Björling: Opera Arias" (Great Recordings of the Century)	87-90,95,99,141,143, 147A,153,161B,162A	a.86
HA 5031 "The Beloved Bjoerling, vol. 2: Opera Arias 1936-1945"	>*Cap.* G 7248	62-04
HA 5032 "The Beloved Bjoerling, vol. 3: Songs and Ballads, 1936-1953"	>*Cap.* G 7247	62-05
HA 5085 "The Beloved Bjoerling [vol. 1]: Arias 1936-1948"	>*HMV* ALP 1620	62-10
ARGENTINA (issued by EMI-Odeon)		
LPC 12083 "Jussi Björling: Arias de Operas"	>*HMV* ALP 1620	?
LPC 12193 "Jussi Björling: Arias de Operas"	>*Cap.* G 7248	?
LPC 12243/44 "La Bohème"	>*RCA* LM 6042	
LPC 12337/39 "Madama Butterfly"	>*HMV* ALP 1795/97	?
USA (issued by Capitol)		
S 35821* "Madama Butterfly: Highlights"	>*Cap.* G 7233	61-12
S 35824/26* (=SCL 3604)		
S 36367* (in SBL 3683)		
SBL 3683* (36366/67) "The Genius of Puccini"	>*Angel* BL 3683	66-10
SCL 3604* (S 35824/26) "Madama Butterfly"	>*HMV* ALP 1795/97	61-12
CHILE (issued by EMI-Odeon)		
SOA 539* (3SACX 47406/08) "Madama Butterfly"	>*HMV* ALP 1795/97	c.65
URUGUAY (issued by Palacio de la Música R. & R. Gioscia)		
UAL 12211 "Jussi Bjorling: Operatic Arias" (?)	>*HMV* ALP 1620 or *Cap.* G 7248 ?	?
UAL 12513 "Jussi Bjorling"	>*HMV* HQM 1190	70-06

ANNA Record Company, USA (private issue by Edward J. Smith)

ANNA 1005 "Jussi Bjoerling, Tenor"	55,59,80,3707a-d, 3902a-f,5602a1-2,a5,c3,d2	78-05
ANNA 1006 "Jussi Bjoerling, Tenor"	5,10,11,13-16,34,50,63, 64,66,93,94,108,114A, 131,133	78-05
ANNA 1017 "Jussi Bjoerling Recital"	125-27,134,135,147B, 177,178,4904b,d-f, 5202c,5403a-c,5405b	78-09
ANNA 1040/41 "Elizabeth Rethberg"	4004a1 [on 1041]	79-05
ANNA 1045 "Jussi Bjoerling in Opera"	113,4002b,d2,4003a, 4502a-c,4904f,5902a,b	80-03
ANNA 1060 "La Bohème: Che gelida manina"	4804a2	81-09

ANNA 1064 "A Tenor Potpourri"	5003f,5704b	81-09
ANNA 1069 "Jussi Bjoerling (1937-1952)"	3704a,b,3708c,4605d, 4904a,g,4906a,b,d, 5001a,e,5005a-c, 5302b,5802c,d,g,h,i,n	83-10

*The **Arturo Toscanini Society***, USA (private issue for members only)

ATS 1005/06 "Requiem" [+rehearsal segment]	4005	70
ATS 1023/24 "Missa Solemnis"	4008	71-06
THS 65031/32 "Toscanini Conducts Verdi's Requiem Mass"	4005	?75

***BBC** Records*, Great Britain (issued by BBC Enterprises)

BBC REH 715(*) "Opera, vol. 1" (The Vintage Collection)	90	89

***Belvedere** Produktion*, Austria (issued by Teletheater; pressed in Germany)

76.23589 (76.41822) "Wiener Staatsoper 1936"	3602a,b1-2	87
76.23596/97 (76.28691) "Wiener Staatsoper 1937"	3702a-c	87

***Bluebell** of Sweden* (issued by Firma Frank Hedman, Solna)

BELL 116 "Gröna Lund sommaren 1950"	5003a-f	80-09
BELL 132 "Jussi Björling, alias Erik Odde 1932-1933"	31,36,39,42,43,47-49, 60-62,67,68	81-11
BELL 163 "Jussi Björling Live: Holland 1939, Norway 1954"	3902a-f,5403a-f,h	84-03
BELL 187 "Jussi Björling: Songs and Opera Arias 1940-1951"	125-27,131,133-35,149, 150,177,178,3903b,4102a,b	85-08
BELL 196 "Swedish Opera Singers in New York 1893-1947" [Label: "Swedish Opera Singers at the Metropolitan 1893-1947"]	5701d	86-08
BELL 198 "Jussi Björling, Hjördis Schymberg: La Bohème, Roméo et Juliette: Stockholm 1940"	4001a,4002a,b1,b2,c,d	86-08

***Bongiovanni** Records*, Bologna, Italy

GB 1035/36 "28 'Sogni' dalla Manon di Massenet" (Il mito dell'opera)	112 [on GB 1035]	85-12

Capitol, USA (EMI)

G 7233 "Madama Butterfly: Highlights"	241a,c3-4,d3,e	61-02
G 7239 "The Beloved Bjoerling, vol. 1: Opera Arias 1936-1948"	>*HMV* ALP 1620	61-02
G 7247 "The Beloved Bjoerling, vol. 2: Songs and Ballads 1936-1953"	81,82,91,92,97,101,102, 146,155,156,159B,160B, 205-08	61-05
G 7248 "The Beloved Bjoerling, vol. 3: Opera Arias 1936-1945"	88-90,99,119,121,139A, 141,142,147A,151B	61-05
GCR 7232 (3) "Madama Butterfly"	>*HMV* ALP 1795/97	61-02
SG 7233* "Madama Butterfly: Highlights"	>*Cap.* G 7233	61-02
SGCR 7232* (3) "Madama Butterfly"	>*HMV* ALP 1795/97	61-02

Cetra, Italy

LO 71 (3) "Il Trovatore" (Opera Live)	4101	78

Classics for Pleasure, Great Britain (EMI)

CFP 41 4498 1* "Duets from Famous Operas"	>*HMV* ASD 2382	86-02
CFPD 41 4446 3* (41 4446/47 1) "Madama Butterfly"	>*HMV* ALP 1795/97	85-06

Classics Record Library, USA (issued by Book-of-the-Month Club; made by London Records)

50-5552* (3) "A Grand Opera Gala"	220d2 [on record 1]	79-05

Club "99", USA (issued by The German News Co., New York)

CL 110 "Tales of Offenbach"	110A	77-11

Columbia (EMI)

GERMANY (issued by EMI Electrola)

1C 052-30174 "Holiday in Scandinavia"	82	?73

SWEDEN

4E 056-35326 "Värmland"	82	76-07

GERMANY (issued by EMI Electrola)

C 91296/97 (WCX 593/94) "Giuseppe Verdi 1813-1963" [Records also sold separately]	120 [on 91296]	63-12

AUSTRIA (issued by Donauland Record Club; made by EMI-Columbia)

Parnass 62528 (F 60828/29) "Unvergessene Stimmen: Die grossen Tenöre"	>*Parnass* 62528	c.76

SWEDEN

SPPH 016 "Together" [Special issue for SKTF [The Swedish National Union of Local Government Officers)]	81	c.80-05
SPPH 061(*) "Winds of Sweden" [Special issue for Johnson & Samco Chartering AB]	91	82-04

GERMANY (issued by EMI Electrola)

(33)WCX 593/94 (=C 91296/97)

Cum Laude, USA (private issue by Discount Records, Chicago)

KM 1001 "Jussi Bjoerling Recital"	5802a,b,f,j,k,m,o-u	c.65

Dacapo, Germany (issued by EMI Electrola)

1C 137 1009473M (1009471,-81) "Jussi Björling: Der Tenor des Nordens [Vol. 1]"	>*Dacapo* 1C 177-00947/48M	85
1C 137 1033543M (1033541,-51) "Jussi Björling: Der Tenor des Nordens, Folge 2"	>*Dacapo* 1C 147-03354/55M	83
1C 147-00947/48M "Jussi Björling: Der Tenor des Nordens [Vol. 1]"	>*Dacapo* 1C 177-00947/48M	71
1C 147-03354/55M "Jussi Björling: Der Tenor des Nordens, Folge 2"		78-11
-03354M	15,16,26,46,50,51B,73, 74,100,106B,107B,110A, 111,154,157,162A,164, 166-68	
-03355M	10,20,81-84,93,97,108, 155,156,159B,160B,165, 199,201,202	
1C 177-00947/48M "Jussi Björling: Der Tenor des Nordens" [Vol. 1]		70-07
-00947M	89,98,112,113,114B,115, 118-21,140A,145,148, 151B,152	
-00948M	87,88,95,96,99,101,102, 141-44,146,147A,153, 161B	

Decca [in the issues of "Die Fledermaus", JB is guest in act 2 gala only]

GERMANY

6.35107 EK* (3) "Die Fledermaus"	>*Decca* MET 201/03	75/76
6.35137 DX* (2) "Requiem"	>*RCA* LD 6091	75/76
6.35311 DX* (3) "25 Opernhits mit 25 Weltstars"	222 [on record 2]	76-05
6.35317 DX* (2) "Cavalleria Rusticana [S.4] Jussi Björling: Arien"	>*RCA* LM 6059	76-09
6.43585 AD* (=417 686-1)		
6.48138 DX* (2) "Die grossen Tenöre unserer Zeit, Vol. 1"	221 [on record 2]	c.80-10
6.48169 DM* (2) "Requiem"	>*RCA* LD 6091	82-09

GREAT BRITAIN

414 466-1* "Golden Operetta" (Jubilee)	243	85-10
417 686-1* "Puccini Weekend: Famous Arias from..." (Weekend Classics)	>*Decca* SPA 574	87-05

FRANCE

592 152* (3) "La Chauve-Souris"	>*Decca* MET 201/03	82-12
593 028* (2) "Requiem" (Noblesse)	>*RCA* LD 6091	c.82-05

GREAT BRITAIN

D247D 3* (3) "Die Fledermaus: Gala Performance"	>*Decca* MET 201/03	82-11
DJB 2003* (2) "Requiem" (Jubilee)	>*RCA* LD 6091	83-09

GERMANY

DK 11528/1-2* "Requiem"	>*RCA* LD 6091	72-09

GREAT BRITAIN

DPA 533/34* "Favourite Composers: Puccini"	222 [on DPA 534]	76-05

AUSTRALIA

DTS 533/34* "Private Collection: Puccini"	>*Decca* DPA 533/34	77

GREAT BRITAIN

GRV 4* "Jussi Björling" (Grandi Voci)	>*Rich.* SR 33254 [with arias in a different order]	81-12

GERMANY

LXT 2023/25-C "Die Fledermaus"	>*Decca* MET 201/03	60-11

GREAT BRITAIN

MET 201/03 "Die Fledermaus"	243 [on MET 202]	60-10

ITALY		
OCSI 14/15* "Favourite Composers: Puccini"	>*Decca* DPA 533/34	76/78
GREAT BRITAIN		
SET 201/03* "Die Fledermaus"	>*Decca* MET 201/03	60-10
GERMANY		
SMA 25051-D/1-3* "Die Fledermaus"	>*Decca* MET 201/03	70-10
GREAT BRITAIN		
SPA 574* "One Fine Day"	222	80-09
GERMANY		
SXL 20023/25-B* "Die Fledermaus"	>*Decca* MET 201/03	60-11
AUSTRALIA		
SXLA 7515* "Ten Famous Tenors"	>*London* OS 26207	a.76-04

Electrola, Germany (EMI)

29601-2(*) (2) "Die grossen Tenöre" [Special club issue]	88 [on record 1]	?76
1C 037-03071* "Madame Butterfly: Grosser Querschnitt"	241a,b2,c3-4,d3,e	77-04
1C 049-30659* "Die grosse Tenor-Star-Parade	241a	76-10
1C 063-00372* "Grosse Opern-Duette"	241c4	69-10
1C 187-30183/84* "Victoria de los Angeles: Arien, Duette und Szenen"	241c4 [on 187-30184]	c.74-02
ASDW 373/75* (=STE 91076/78)		
CSDW 7145* (=STE 80789)		
CSDW 7362* (=SME 80994)		
E 70412 [10"/25 cm.] "Das Sänger-Porträt: Jussi Björling 1"	87,98,113,143,144,152, 153,157,161B,162A	61-03
E 80789 (WCLP 844) "Madame Butterfly: Grosser Querschnitt"	241a1,b2,c3-4,d2-3,e	63-11
E 91076/78 (WALP 1795/97) "Madame Butterfly"	>*HMV* ALP 1795/97	60-11
SME 80789* (CSDW 7145) "Madame Butterfly: Grosser Querschnitt"	>*Elec.* E 80789	65
SME 80994* (CSDW 7362) "Weltstars singen berühmte Liebesduette"	241c4	66-07
STE 80789* (CSDW 7145) "Madame Butterfly: Grosser Querschnitt"	>*Elec.* E 80789	63-11
STE 91076/78* (ASDW 373/75) "Madame Butterfly"	>*HMV* ALP 1795/97	60-11
WALP 1112/13 "Der Troubadour"	>*RCA* LM 6008	a.55-06
WALP 1126/28 "Cavalleria Rusticana, Der Bajazzo"	>*RCA* LM 6106	a.55-06

WALP 1187 "Jussi Björling: Lieder"	>*RCA* LM 1771	a.55-06
WALP 1326/28 "Manon Lescaut"	>*RCA* LM 6116	a.58
WALP 1795/97 (=E 91076/78)		
WBLP 1053 [10"/25 cm.] "Opern-Szenen mit Jussi Björling und Robert Merrill"	>*RCA* LM 7007	a.55-06
WBLP 1055 [10"/25 cm.] "Jussi Björling singt Opern-Arien"	>*RCA* LM.105	a.55-06
WCLP 844 (=E 80789)		

EMI (Cf. also: *Angel, Capitol, Columbia, Dacapo, Electrola, Fame, His Master's Voice, Hör Zu, Music for Pleasure, Odeon, Plaisir Musical, Seraphim, Voix Illustres, World Record Club*)

SWEDEN

2600833 (2600831,-41) "Gyllene ögonblick på Gröna Lund"	92 [on 2600831]	84-05
7C 138-35580/81 "Scandinavia!: Music from Sweden, Norway and Finland"	82,91 [on -35580]	78-11

SOUTH AFRICA

CEY 247 "Nostalgic Moments"	>*EMI* SCA 016	82-08
EMCJ 6001 (2) "25 Stars That Shine Forever"	143 [on record 1]	73-11
EMGJ 6004 (2) "20 Magnificent Opera Arias"		74-04
(record 1)	145	
(record 2)	88,144	
EMGJ 6006 (2) "25 Songs That Live Forever"	160B [on record 2]	74-08

SWEDEN

EMISP 127 "Arias for Lovers of Opera" [Promotion record for Wallenius Lines (" The Opera Line")]	90,113,139A,143,145, 151B,153	87-09

GREAT BRITAIN

NTS 208 "Nostalgic Memories"	>*EMI* SCA 016	80

AUSTRALIA

SCA 016 "Nostalgic Memories [vol. 1]"	159B	77-06
SCA 034 "Nostalgic Memories, vol. 2"	102	?

Enharmonic, USA (issued by Ars Antiqua, Bloomington, Indiana)

EN 82-004 (2) "Collector's Choice: Rare Vocal Recordings 1895-1950"	147B	83-08

ERR *Historical Operatic Treasures*, USA (private issue by Ed Rosen)

ERR 109-3 (3) "Ballo in Maschera"	4007	73-12
ERR 121-1 "Jussi Björling 1937-1941"	3707a-c,3902a-f,4101c	74-09
ERR 145-1 "Roméo et Juliette, abridged"	4701a-f	77-04

Estro Armonico *Rare Opera Editions*, Belgium (private issue)

EA 020 (3) "Rigoletto" [JB on s.6 only: "J. Björling & L.Warren in Rigolettos Arias"]	4506a2,c,d	c.76-03

Eterna, East Germany (issued by VEB Deutsche Schallplatten, Berlin)

8 20 534 "Künstler der Welt bei uns zu Gast"	243	66-03
8 20 829 "Jussi Björling" (Grosse Sänger der Vergangenheit. 11)	50,51B,71-78,86,114B, 115,120,141,142,148	68-11
8 25 517/19* "Die Fledermaus" [JB guest in act 2 gala only]	>*Decca* MET 201/03	66-03

Eva *Records*, Sweden

304 391 (2) "Absolute Opera"	175,216B	91

Excellent, Sweden (issued and distributed by Nordiska Kompaniet AB & AB Turitz; made by EMI)

1286 001-18 "För dig allén"	12,17,34,35,45,46,51B, 85,93,94	70-09

Fabbri/ERI, Italy

V 21 "Grandi personaggi Verdiani: Azucena"	4101b5	83-03
V 30 "Grandi personaggi Verdiani: Manrico"	4101a1,c3	83-05

Fame, South Africa (EMI)

FAME 13 "25 Stars That Shine Forever, vol. 1"	143	83-07
FAME 19 "20 Magnificent Opera Arias, vol. 1"	145	83-07
FAME 20 "20 Magnificent Opera Arias, vol. 2"	88,144	83-07

FAME 22 "25 Songs That Live Forever, vol. 2"	160B	83-07

Fischer, Sweden (issued by "Fischer Vorlag" = T[omas] Fischer & Co. AB; distributed by EMI)

101-3* (101/03) "Kjerstin Dellert: Mina musikaliska memoarer"		85-11
(101*) "Kjerstin Dellert: Operaskivan"	5902b	

Fonit Cetra, Italy

DOC 9 (3) "Manon Lescaut" (Documents)	5602	c.82-02

Franklin Mint Record Society, USA (limited edition for subscribers only)

13/14* "Requiem" (The 100 Greatest Recordings of All Time)	>*RCA* LD 6091	78-10

Glendale, USA (issued by Legend Records)

GL 8006 "Jussi Bjoerling: Fabulous Radio Performances, 20th Anniversary Tribute 1911-1960"	4801a,d,4803b-d,4901a, 4907b,5006a,5101a, 5102c,5108d	81-04

The Golden Age of Opera, USA (private issue by Edward J. Smith)

EJS 154 (2) "Roméo et Juliette"	4701	59/60
EJS 168 "Potpourri (3)"	4004,5601a,b	59/60
EJS 207 "Excerpts from 'Trovatore'"	4101a-e	61-04
EJS 208 "Excerpts from 'Don Carlo'"	5008a-f	61-04
EJS 209 "Excerpts from 'Rigoletto'"	4506a-e	61-04
EJS 210 "Excerpts from 'Faust'"	5912a-h	61-04
EJS 230 (2) "Ballo in Maschera"	4007	62-02
EJS 251 "Manon Lescaut: Highlights"	4908a-g	62-11
EJS 252 "Jussi Bjoerling: Operatic Arias and Duets (1946-1960)"	4601a,4901c,4906c, 4907c,5001d,5010f, 5101a(aria only),5109b, 5110d,5111b,5202c, 6004a,c	62-11
EJS 279 "Jussi Bjoerling in Opera and Song, (1939-1954)"	3902a,e,f,4604c,4902c, d,f,5102a-c,5110e, 5202b,d,e,5403a,b	63-10

EJS 337 "Faust (Highlights). Jussi Bjoerling Recital"	16,76,3602a,3701a-f, 3702b,cl,3902b-e, 5006d,5101d	65-06
EJS 346 "Cavalleria Rusticana"	5404	65-11
EJS 347 "Aida, Fanal, Meistersinger (Highlights)" [JB in "Fanal" only]	3401	65-11
EJS 366 "Trovatore: Excerpts"	3901a-f	66-05
EJS 367 "Jussi Bjoerling in Opera and Song, vol. 2"	4602b,d,4801a-c,4803a, 4907a,b,5006a,c,d,5101 b-d,5108a,c,5403f,h, 5703a,b	66-05
EJS 384 "Bohème (act 1). Le canzoni dei ricordi" [JB in "Bohème" only]	4001	67-01
EJS 402 "Trovatore: Excerpts"	6001a-e	67-05
EJS 405 "Jussi Bjoerling in Opera (1936-48)"	3602a,b1-2,3707a-e, 4101c3,c4,4804a,5002d	67-09
EJS 406 "La Traviata: Excerpts"	3904a-g	67-09
EJS 468 "Ballo in Maschera (Highlights)"	5002a1,b2,b4,c1,d,e	69-05
EJS 530 "Cavalleria Rusticana (Highlights)" Jussi Bjoerling Recital"	141,4201a-c,4502a,c-e, 5910a-c	70-12

His Master's Voice [=*HMV*] (EMI) [includes translations of the label in France, Italy & Spain]

SWEDEN

1031401(*) "La Bohème [Excerpts]" (Operaklassiker)	>*HMV* ESD 7023	85-01
1359931 "Jussi Björling: 30-talsinspelningar på svenska"	13,14,29,30,32,33,37, 38,55,57,63-66,79,104	84-10

FRANCE ("*La Voix de son Maître*")

2905433(*) (2) "La Bohème" (Références)	>*RCA* LM 6042	a.85-09
2910753 (8) "Les Introuvables du chant Verdien"	121	86
7540161 "Tenorissimo"	87	90

FINLAND

7691751 "Jussi Björling: Suosituimmat aariat ja laulut = Mest älskade arior och sånger" (Toiveklassikot)	34,81,82,84(14?),88,89,92, 99,101,106B,107B,139A,143, 144	87-03

GREAT BRITAIN

0C 047-01948M (=HLM 7038)
0C 053-03140(*) (=ESD 7023)
0C 053-03596* (=SXLP 30306)
0C 145-78000* (=ASD 4076 in SLS 5233)
0C 155-06518/20M (=RLS 715)
0C 157-00183/85* (=SLS 5128)

0C 191-00126/27(*) (=SLS 896)
1E 047-01266M (=HLM 7004)
1E 053-01948M (=HQM 1190)

SPAIN ("*La Voz de su Amo*"; issued by EMI-Odeon)

1J 063-00372* "Great Operatic Duets"	>*HMV* ASD 2382	?
1J 163-00126/27(*) "La Bohème"	>*RCA* LM 6042	75-10

FRANCE ("*La Voix de Son Maître*"; issued by EMI Pathé-Marconi)

2C 061-01502* "Madame Butterfly: Extraits"	241a,c,d,e	74

ITALY ("*La Voce del Padrone*")

3C 061-00739M (=QALP 10402)		
3C 061-00740M (=QALP 5340)		
3C 061-17669M (=QALP 10305)		
3C 153-00126/27(*) "La Bohème"	>*RCA* LM 6042	c.76-04

SWEDEN

4E 153-34532/33M "Jussi Björling: 28 av de mest älskade ariorna och sångerna [vol. 1]"		71-12
-34532M	34,35,81-84,91-94,107B, 110A,205-08	
-34533M	87-89,95,119,121,143-45, 151B,157,162A	

NETHERLANDS (issued by EMI-Bovema)

5C 045-00191M "Jussi Björling zingt aria's van Verdi, Gounod..."	>*Cap.* G. 7248	76
5C 045-01715M "Jussi Björling zingt aria's van Puccini, Donizetti..."	87,95,96,98,112,113, 114B,115,120,143,145, 148,152,153,161B	76-03
5C 047-00191M "Jussi Björling zingt aria's van Verdi, Gounod..."	>*Cap.* G 7248	74-09
5C 047-01266M "Wereldberoemde tenoren"	>*HMV* HLM 7004	?74
5C 051-00243* "Madama Butterfly: Hoogtepunten"	>*HMV* ALP 2060	75-09
5C 181-25204/05(*) "25 maal goud in opera"	211b2 [on -25205]	75-05

SWEDEN

7C 037-35918M "Hjördis Schymberg: Hovsångerska"	139A,140A	82-08
7C 061-35731M "De 20 mest önskade med Jussi Björling"	20,23,34,81,82,84,87, 89-92,99,101,107B,110A, 143,145,146,205,208	80-10
7C 061-35822 "Operans svenska världsartister" (Önskeklassiker)	>*HMV* SPPH 030	81-05
7C 137-00947/48M "Önskeartisten (2): Jussi Björling"	>*Dacapo* 1C 177- -00947/48M	78-10

7C 153-06518/20M "The Art of Jussi Björling" (HMV Treasury)	>*HMV* RLS 715	78-03
7C 153-35350/58*p "Operan: Röster från Stockholmsoperan under 100 år"		76-12
-35355M	3401	
-35358*p	5902a,b	
7C 153-35445/46M "Jussi Björling: 28 av de mest älskade ariorna och sångerna, vol. 2"		77-10
-35445M	18-20,23-25,27,51B,77, 85,86,106B,108,111	
-35446M	90,97,99,101,102,139A, 141,142,146,147A,155, 156,159B,160B	
7C 191-00126/27(*) "La Bohème"	>*RCA* LM 6042	78-05

SPAIN ("*La Voz de su Amo*"; issued by EMI-Odeon)

10C 165-078000/02(*) "El Arte de Victoria de los Angeles"	>*HMV* SLS 5233	?83

GREAT BRITAIN

ALP 1112/13 "Il Trovatore"	>*RCA* LM 6008	54-03
ALP 1126/28 (RLS 610) "Cavalleria Rusticana, I Pagliacci"	>*RCA* LM 6106	54-04
ALP 1187 "A Song Recital by Jussi Björling"	>*RCA* LM 1771	54-11
ALP 1326/28 (RLS 635) "Manon Lescaut"	>*RCA* LM 6116	56-02
ALP 1388/90 (RLS 638) "Aida"	>*RCA* LM 6122	56-10
ALP 1391 "Highlights from 'Il Trovatore'"	>*RCA* LM 1827	57-02
ALP 1409/10 "La Bohème"	>*RCA* LM 6042	56-12
ALP 1481 "Excerpts from 'Cavalleria Rusticana', 'I Pagliacci'"	>*RCA* LM 1828	57-09
ALP 1620 "Jussi Björling: Operatic Arias"	87,95,98,112,113,143-145,152,153,157,161B, 162A	59-11
ALP 1795/97 (RLS 664) "Madama Butterfly"	241	60-11
ALP 1832/33 "Il Trovatore" (Memorial Edition: Jussi Björling)	>*RCA* LM 6008	61-05
ALP 1841 "Jussi Björling: Operatic Recital" [Two versions, see note]	>*Cap.* G 7248	61-07
ALP 1857 "Jussi Björling: Songs and Ballads"	>*Cap.* G 7247	61-10
ALP 1921 "La Bohème: Highlights"	211b2-5,e,f2,g	62-12
ALP 2060 "Highlights from 'Madama Butterfly'"	241a,b,c2-4,d3,e	64-11
ALP 2274 "Victoria de los Angeles: Favourite Arias"	241e	66-08
ASD 373/75* (SLS 759) "Madama Butterfly"	>*HMV* ALP 1795/97	60-11
ASD 609* "Highlights from 'Madama Butterfly'"	>*HMV* ALP 2060	64-11
ASD 2274* "Victoria de los Angeles: Favourite Arias"	>*HMV* ALP 2274	66-08

ASD 2382* "Great Operatic Duets"	241c4	68-07
ASD 3030/31(*) (=SLS 896)		
ASD 3532/34* (=SLS 5128)		
ASD 4076(*) (in SLS 5233)		
FRANCE (*"La Voix de Son Maître"*; issued by EMI Pathé-Marconi)		
ASDF 177/79* "Madame Butterfly"	>*HMV* ALP 1795/97	65-10
SOUTH AFRICA		
ASDJ 373/75* "Madama Butterfly"	>*HMV* ALP 1795/97	69-02
ASDJ 2382* "Great Operatic Duets"	>*HMV* ASD 2382	68-10
SPAIN (*"La Voz de su Amo"*)		
ASDL 977* "Great Operatic Duets"	>*HMV* ASD 2382	?
NEW ZEALAND		
ASDM 609* "Madama Butterfly: Highlights"	>*HMV* ALP 2060	?64
ITALY (*"La Voce del Padrone"*)		
ASDQ 5286/88* "Madama Butterfly"	>*HMV* ALP 1795/97	62-05
ASDQ 5304* "Madama Butterfly: Brani scelti"	>*Cap.* G 7233	62-05
GREAT BRITAIN		
BLP 1053 "Jussi Björling and Robert Merrill in Scenes from..." [10"/25 cm.]	>*RCA* LM 7007	54-10
BLP 1055 "Great Tenor Arias by Jussi Björling" [10"/25 cm.]	>*RCA* LM 105	55-01
CSLP 503 "50 Years of Great Operatic Singing, vol. 4: 1930-1940" (Golden Treasury of Immortal Performances)	>*RCA* LCT 6701-4	56-09
CSLP 504 "50 Years of Great Operatic Singing, vol. 5" (Golden Treasury of Immortal Performances)	>*RCA* LCT 6701-5	56-09
ESD 7023(*) "La Bohème" (HMV Greensleeve Opera Highlights Series)	211b,c,d,e1,f,g2-3	77-08
EX 29 0169 3 (E 29 0169/81 1) "The Record of Singing, vol. 3"	110A [on E 29 0176 1]	84-11
EX 7 69741 1 (E 7 69741/48 1) "The Record of Singing, vol. 4: From 1939 to the End of the 78 Era"	151B [on E 7 69747 1]	89-03
FRANCE (*"La Voix de Son Maître"*; issued by EMI Pathé-Marconi)		
FALP 301/03 "Cavalleria Rusticana, Paillasse"	>*RCA* LM 6106	54-09
FALP 554/55 "La Bohème"	>*RCA* LM 6042	58-10
FALP 629 "Jussi Björling: Airs d'opéras" (Gravures illustres)	>*HMV* ALP 1620	60-07
FALP 670/72 "Madame Butterfly"	>*HMV* ALP 1795/97	60-10

NETHERLANDS; 10"/25 cm.

GHLP 1027 "Jussi Björling"	87,98,113,143,144, 152,157,161B,162A	c.63

GREAT BRITAIN, AUSTRALIA, SOUTH AFRICA (HMV Treasury)

		Au	*GB*
HLM 7004 "Great Tenors of the World"	98,143	72-09	72-03 SA:81-06

GREAT BRITAIN, SOUTH AFRICA (HMV Treasury)

HLM 7038 "Jussi Björling: Arias & Songs by Beethoven, Elgar..."	>*HMV* HQM 1190	74-01 SA:81-06
HLM 7115/17 (=RLS 715)		

GREAT BRITAIN, AUSTRALIA

HQM 1190 "Jussi Björling: Songs and Arias by Beethoven, Elgar..." (Golden Voice Series No. 17)	22,96,114B,115,118, 120,122-24,140A,148, 165,166,199-202	70-03	69-11

SOUTH AFRICA

JALP 11 "Madama Butterfly: Highlights"	241: excerpts	62-06
JALP 29 "Jussi Björling" (Golden Voice Series)	>*HMV* HQM 1190	?71-05
JALP 1112/13 "Il Trovatore"	>*RCA* LM 6008	?
JALP 1126/28 "Cavalleria Rusticana, I Pagliacci"	>*RCA* LM 6106	?
JALP 1409/10 "La Bohème"	>*RCA* LM 6042	58-11
JALP 1620 "Jussi Björling: Operatic Arias"	>*HMV* ALP 1620	?
JALP 1841 "The Beloved Björling"	>*Cap.* G 7248	?
JALP 1921 "La Bohème: Highlights"	>*HMV* ALP 1921	66-02

SPAIN ("*La Voz de su Amo*"; issued by EMI-Odeon)

LALP 262/64 "Cavalleria Rusticana, I Pagliacci"	>*RCA* LM 6106	a.60
LALP 311/12 "La Bohème"	>*RCA* LM 6042	a.60

NEW ZEALAND

MALP 1409/10 "La Bohème"	>*RCA* LM 6042	?64
MALP 1481 "Excerpts from 'Cavalleria Rusticana', 'I Pagliacci"'	>*RCA* LM 1828	?64
MALP 1620 "Jussi Björling: Operatic Arias"	>*HMV* ALP 1620	?62
MALP 1841 "Jussi Björling: Operatic Recital"	>*Cap.* G 7248	?62
MALP 1857 "Jussi Björling: Songs and Ballads"	>*Cap.* G 7247	?63
MALP 1921 "Highlights from 'La Bohème'"	>*HMV* ALP 1921	?64
MALP 2060 "Madama Butterfly: Highlights"	>*HMV* ALP 2060	?64

AUSTRALIA		
OALP 1126/28 "Cavalleria Rusticana, I Pagliacci"	>*RCA* LM 6106	56-08
OALP 1409/10 "La Bohème"	>*RCA* LM 6042	57-05
OALP 1620 "Jussi Björling: Operatic Arias"	>*HMV* ALP 1620	60-01
OALP 1795/97 "Madama Butterfly"	>*HMV* ALP 1795/97	61-06
OALP 1841 "Jussi Björling: Operatic Recital"	>*Cap.* G 7248	61-12
OALP 1857 "Jussi Björling: Songs and Ballads"	>*Cap.* G 7247	62-04
OALP 1921 "Highlights from 'La Bohème'"	>*HMV* ALP 1921	63-06
OALP 2274 "Victoria de los Angeles: Favourite Arias"	>*HMV* ALP 2274	67-03
OALP 7521 "Highlights from 'Madama Butterly'"	>*HMV* ALP 2060	62-10
OALP 7534 "Great Tenors of the Century"	>*HMV* QALP 10402	68-03
OASD 373/75* "Madama Butterfly"	>*HMV* ALP 1795/97	61-06
OASD 2274* "Victoria de los Angeles: Favourite Arias"	>*HMV* ALP 2274	67-03
OASD 2382* "Great Operatic Duets"	>*HMV* ASD 2382	68-11
OASD 7521* "Highlights from 'Madama Butterfly'"	>*HMV* ALP 2060	62-10
OELP 9673 "Jussi Bjorling: Operatic Arias"	>*HMV* ALP 1620	71-03
OXLP 7586 "The Golden Age of Song, vol. 3"	90,99	75-02
OXLP 7617 "The Golden Age of Song, vol. 4"	110A,139A	76-06
OXLP 7633 "A Portrait of Jussi Bjorling"	87-89,96,113,114B,115, 119-21,141-43,147A, 148,151B	78-02
OXLP 7639 "The Golden Age of Song, vol. 7"	106B,107B	78-10
OXLP 7650 "The Golden Age of Song, vol. 10"	166	c.81
OXLP 7660 "Jussi Bjorling: Popular Songs and Encores"	20,81,85,86,101,102, 110A,122,124,146,159B, 160B,165,166	82-08
SWEDEN		
PRO 3034 (4E 153-34532/33M + 7C 153-35445/46M) "Jussi Björling 1930-1953" [Two albums issued together in a box with its own number]	>4E 153-34532/33M + 7C 153-35445/46M	c.78-11
PRO 3053 "The Voice of Sweden" [Promotion record for Läkerol (a lozenge)]	81	79-10
ITALY ("*La Voce del Padrone*")		
QALP 5340 "Omaggio a Umberto Giordano"	142	67
QALP 10050/52 "Cavalleria Rusticana, I Pagliacci"	>*RCA* LM 6106	54-07
QALP 10171/72 "La Bohème"	>*RCA* LM 6042	57-05
QALP 10212 "Cavalleria Rusticana, I Pagliacci: Brani scelti"	>*RCA* LM 1828	58-09

QALP 10266 "Jussi Björling: Recital operistico"	>*HMV* ALP 1620	60-04
QALP 10293/95 "Madama Butterfly"	>*HMV* ALP 1795/97	c.61
QALP 10305 "Ricordo di Giacomo Puccini"	96	62-09
QALP 10319 "Jussi Björling: Recital operistico"	>*Cap.* G 7248	c.62
QALP 10321 "Madama Butterfly: Brani scelti"	>*Cap.* G 7233	62-02
QALP 10402 "I grandi tenori del secolo"	87	66-04
GREAT BRITAIN (sets)		
RLS 610 (=ALP 1126/28)		
RLS 635 (=ALP 1326/28)		
RLS 638 (=ALP 1388/90)		
RLS 664 (=ALP 1795/97)		
RLS 715 (HLM 7115/17) "The Art of Jussi Björling" (HMV Treasury)		77-11
(HLM 7115) "The Early Swedish Recordings 1929-1936"	9-12,15,16,20,21,26,46, 50,51B,71-74,81-84	
(HLM 7116) "Italian Opera"	87-89,96,120,121,138, 141-44,147A,157,161B, 162A,164,167,168	
(HLM 7117) "French Opera and Operetta. Popular Songs and Encores"	93,97,100-02,106B,107B, 110A,111,119,146,151B, 154-56,159B,160B	
SWEDEN, NORWAY		
SCLP 1008 "Jussi Björling: Sånger och operaarior"	18-20,23-25,27,71-76, 78,108	61-01
SWEDEN		
SGLP 507 "Jussi Björling"	12,17,28,45,46,51B,69, 77,85,86,106,111	64-11
GREAT BRITAIN (sets)		
SLS 759* (=ASD 373/75)		
SLS 896(*) (ASD 3030/31) "La Bohème"	>*RCA* LM 6042	74-11
SLS 5128* (ASD 3532/34) "Madama Butterfly"	>*HMV* ALP 1795/97	78-09
SLS 5233(*) (ASD 4076/78) "The Art of Victoria de los Angeles"	211b3 [on ASD 4076]	82-03
SWEDEN		
SPPH 030 [Promotion record for Walleniusrederierna (a shipping company)]	87,88,99,119	80-09
GREAT BRITAIN		
SXLP 30306* "Madama Butterfly" (HMV Concert Classics Opera Highlights)	241a,c2-4,d3,e	79-09

NETHERLANDS (issued by EMI-Bovema)

SXLPH 1510* "Madama Butterfly: Hoogtepunten"	>*HMV* 2C 061-01502	?
XLPH 1002 "Jussi Björling, tenor: Operaaria's"	>*HMV* ALP 1620	66-04
XLPH 20010 "Jussi Björling" (Grote stemmen van onze tijd. 6)	>*Cap.* G 7248	68-04

Historical Opera Performances Edition, USA (private issue)

HOPE 204 (2) "Rigoletto"	4506	c.76-12
HOPE 221 (3) "Trovatore"	4101	c.76-12

Historical Recording Enterprises, see: HRE Recordings

Hör Zu, Germany (issued by EMI Electrola)

SHZE 184* "Weltstars singen berühmte Liebesduette"	>*Elec.* SME 80994	?

***HRE** Recordings* [formerly: Historical Recording Enterprises], USA (issued by Ed Rosen)

HRE 202-1 "Ten Tenors in Ten Live Performances [vol. 1]"	5911a2	77-05
HRE 210-1 "Jussi Bjoerling in 'Faust'"	5010a-h	77-06
HRE 214-2 (2) "The Great Jussi Bjoerling, vol. 1 (1945-1952): Arias from Live Radio-TV Performances"		77-09
(record 1)	4803b-d,4901a-c,4907a-c, 5006a,b,d,5101a,d	
(record 2)	3701a-f,3902e,4602b,d, 5102a,c,5110b,[abridged] e,5202a-c	
HRE 215-1 "Ten Tenors in Ten Live Performances, vol. 2"	6001c2-3	77-09
HRE 281-2 (2) "Jussi Bjoerling: Live Performance from Sweden 1940"		79-08
(record 1)	4002b,d2,4301a	
(record 2)	3904a,b,4001	
HRE 301-2 (2) "Cavalleria Rusticana" [S.4: Tancredi i Clorinda (non-JB)]	5910	79-12

HRE 376-2 (2) "Jussi Bjoerling in Vienna 1936-1937"		82-02
(record 1)	3602a,b1	
(record 2)	3602b2-3,3701a-f,3702a-c, 3902e	
HRE 377-1 "Recondita armonia"	5603a	82-02

***Impact** Music Promotions*, Roseville, Australia

IMA 011 "The World's Greatest Voices"	>*RCA* SP 185	81-07

***K-tel** International*, Australia

NA 468 "The World's Greatest Tenors"	175	a.76

K-West, Great Britain (issued by Kenwest Records, London)

KNEWLP 601* "A Night at the Opera, vol. 1"	219f1	88
KNEWLP 602* "A Night at the Opera, vol. 2"	219a2-3,240d1	88

***Legendary** Recordings*, USA (private issue)

LR 136 "An Operatic Christmas"	234	80-11
LR 137-2 (2) "Jussi Bjoerling: I Pagliacci plus [s.4] Bjoerling in Arias & Duets"	5101a,5102c,5405, 5601a,b	81-02
LR 138 "The Legendary Jussi Bjoerling in Song: Live Performances 1920-1952"	4,234,4006b-d,4602b, 4801a-c,4803c,4901a,b, 4907a,5110e,5201,5202a, b,d,f	81-02
LR 141 "Eleanor Steber: Live Performances 1940-1953"	4602b,d	81-02
LR 142-5 (5) "A Festival of Song"	5009e [on record 1]	81-06

London (cf. also *Richmond*) [In the issues of "Die Fledermaus", JB is guest in act 2 gala only]

BRAZIL

0417823-1* "Jussi Björling" (Grandi Voci)	>*Rich.* SR 33254	87

USA

A 4347 (X 5588/90) "Die Fledermaus"	>*Decca* MET 201/03	60-12

USA, CANADA

JL 42004* (2) "Requiem" (Jubilee)	>*RCA* LD 6091	82-04

USA

OS 25223* (in OSA 1319)		
OS 26207* "Ten Famous Tenors, Ten Famous Arias"	220d	71-07
OS 26268/69* (=OSA 1294)		
OS 26293* (in OSA 1441)		
OS 26363/64* (=OSA 12101)		
OSA 1294* (OS 26268/69) "Requiem"	>*RCA* LD 6091	72-12
OSA 1319* (OS 25222/24) "Die Fledermaus"	>*Decca* MET 201/03	60-12
OSA 1441* (OS 26293/96) "San Francisco Opera Gala"	225 [on OS 26293]	72-12
OSA 12101* (OS 26363/64) "Cavalleria Rusticana. [S.4] Jussi Bjoerling Operatic Recital"	>*RCA* LM 6059	74-01

JAPAN

SLA 7004/05* "Cavalleria Rusticana. [S.4] Jussi Bjoerling Operatic Recital"	>*RCA* LM 6059	76
SLC 7028/30* "Die Fledermaus"	>*Decca* MET 201/03	c.76

USA

X 5588/90 (=A 4347)

Magnavox, USA [unnumbered demonstration record]

G80P4323-5D [matrix] "Ezio Pinza Presents 'I Hear Music'"	204a2	c.53-09

Magnificent *Editions*, USA (issued by HRE Recordings)

ME 105-3 (3) "Don Carlo"	5008	79-09

Marcato, Germany (issued by ECI Book Club)

34399-6 (34400/02) "Tenöre des Jahrhunderts"	98 [on 34402-8]	78
34402-8 (in 34399-6)		
73667* (3) "Die Fledermaus" [JB guest in act 2 gala only]	>*Decca* MET 201/03	?65
75316 "Weltstars singen Lieder der Welt"	82	?
LPD 011556-7* "Gala Abend der leichten Muse"	>*Eterna* 8 20 534 (?)	?

MDP Collectors Limited Edition, USA (private issue)

MDP 004 (2) "Gina Cigna & Jussi Bjoerling in 'Il Trovatore'" [S.4: Cloe Elmo recital]	3901a-f	78-09
MDP 026 (2) "Bjoerling ... Live!" [vol. 1]		80-10
(record 1)	76,3602bl-2,3702b,3707 a,c-e,3902a-e,4301a, 4502a,c,4506d	
(record 2)	4902a-f,4904b,c,f,5108d, 5601b,5703b2	
MDP 034 "Elisabeth Rethberg: Great Scenes from Live Opera"	4004a1	80-10
MDP 035 "Bjoerling ... Live!, vol. 2"	4303a,b,4502b,4506c, 4702b,5110c,5111b, 5403a-f,h,5802j, 6002 [excerpt]	81-02

Melodiya, Soviet Union [Matrix numbers are given; no other record numbers were used. *Akkord* label was (also?) used for one of the issues. Identification of recordings partly uncertain.]

D 007487/88 [8"/20 cm.] "Yussi Byorling" [Issued on *Akkord* label]	203a,209b2,212c,213,218	61
D 00019605/06 [7"/17.5 cm.] "Yussi Byorling"	209b2,212c,170	67
D 21793/94 [10"/25 cm.] "Yussi Byorling"	169,170,176,180,209b2, 216A(?),224,240d1	68
D 030913/18*? (3) "Turandot"	>*RCA* LM 6149	?
D 033317/22 (3) "Trubadur"	>*RCA* LM 6008	72

Melodram, Milan, Italy

006 (3) "Missa Solemnis, Messa da Requiem"	4005,4008	80-02

MET, USA (made by RCA)

Metropolitan Opera Historic Broadcast Series [Available only for contribution to Metropolitan Opera Fund, New York, of $ 125 or more]

MET 8 (3) "Un Ballo in Maschera"	4007	81-01
MET 11 (3) "Roméo et Juliette"	4701	84-01

Issued by Metropolitan Opera Guild, New York:

MET 50 (3) "50 Years of Guild Performances at the Met"	161B [on record 1]	85-10

MET 100 (5) "Metropolitan Opera Historic Broadcast: Centennial Collection 1935-1939"		85-03
(record 2)	5008c	
(record 4)	5010f1-2	
MET 110 "Jussi Bjoerling at the Met" (Great Artists at the Met)	87,89,90,99,119-21,145, 147B,148,151B,162A, 171,209a,b2,f2-4	80-11
MET 404 (2) "The Johnson Years: 1935-1950" (One Hundred Years of Great Artists at the Met)	180 [on record 2]	84-04
MET 405 (2) "The Bing Years I: 1950-1961" (One Hundred Years of Great Artists at the Met)	209d	85-04

***Morgan** Records*, USA or Belgium (private issue)

3MOR 5601 (3) "Manon Lescaut"	5602	c.75-05

MR, USA (private issue by Steve Smolian)

MR 2000 (2) "Missa Solennis"	4008	a.69-02

Music for Pleasure, Sweden (EMI; made in Great Britain)

MFP 5571 "Jussi Björling"	>*HMV* SGLP 507	73

***Musik** AB Records*, Lövstabruk, Sweden

LPFG 001(*) "Tre generationer" [Reissued as: "Tre generationer Björling: Jussi, Raymond, Rolf"]	81,84,92,205	85

***OASI** Recordings*, USA (private issue)

OASI 656 (2) "Il Trovatore"	6001	84-06
OASI 660 "Jussi Bjoerling (Tenor) (1911-1960): Operatic and Song Recital"	110B,116,151A,172B, 4504b,4801a-c,5003f, 5004c, 5101c,5302b, 5406a,5704b,5802q-r	?86

Odeon (EMI)

ITALY

3C 061-00739M "I grandi tenori del secolo" >*HMV* QALP 10402 ?67

3C 061-00740M "Omaggio a Umberto Giordano" >*HMV* QALP 5340 ?67

SWEDEN

4E 054-34633M "Svenska filmschlager. 2" 92 73-01

USA [imported Swedish *HMV* records, distributed by P. I. Records, New York, with old label pasted over]

4E 153-34532/33M "Jussi Björling: 28 av de mest älskade ariorna och sångerna [vol. 1]" >*HMV* 4E 153-34532/33M c.72

SWEDEN

4E 154-34398/99M "Sweden!" 82,91 [on 154-34399] 71-08

7C 062-35947M "Odeonkavalkaden 1936-1945, del 4" 84 82-11

7C 138-35818/20 "Säg det i toner: En nostalgisk kavalkad" 81-11

-35819 >*Odeon* 4E 054-34633M

USA [imported Swedish *HMV* records, sold like 4E 153-34532/33M]

7C 153-35445/46M "Jussi Björling: 28 av de mest älskade..., vol. 2" >*HMV* 7C 153-35455/46M c.78

SWEDEN

7C 158-35912/13 "The Sounds of Sweden" 92 [on 158-35913] 82-06

USA [imported German *Columbia* records, sold like 4E 153-34532/33M]

C 91296/97 (WCX 593/94) "Giuseppe Verdi 1813-1963" 120 [on C 91296] 63

GERMANY (issued by EMI Electrola)

O 83343 "Die teuerste Operette der Welt [vol.] 1" 107B ?63

USA (made in Great Britain)

PHQM 1190 "Jussi Björling" (Golden Voice Series No. 17) >*HMV* HQM 1190 c.69-11

SWEDEN (some of the records made in Great Britain; NK = AB Nordiska Kompaniet, a Stockholm department store)

PMCS 303 "A Remembrance of Sweden" or [with Odeon sleeve but Parlophone label] "NK Presents Music from Creative Sweden" 82 64-06

PMCS 308 "En NK-skiva med Jussi Björling" [especially made for NK]	4,81,91,92,104,110A, 121,142,146,161B,205, 207,241a1,d2-3	65-11
PMES 507 "Jussi Björling"	>*HMV* SGLP 507	68
PMES 551 "Jussi Björling: Sånger och opera-arior"	>*HMV* SCLP 1008	68-08
PMES 560 "Sweden in Music"	82	68-06

ITALY

QALP 10402 "I grandi tenori del secolo"	>*HMV* QALP 10402	?

USA [imported Swedish *HMV* record, sold like 4E 153-34532/33M]

SGLP 507 "Jussi Björling"	>*HMV* SGLP 507	c.65

GERMANY

WCX 593/94 (=C 91296/97)

Operatic Archives, USA (private issue by William Seward, John Carreddu Press, New York)

OPA 1007 "La Bohème: Excerpts"	4804a-d	a.69
OPA 1008 "A Popular Concert with Bidú Sayão"	4701a2	a.69
OPA 1019/20 "Rigoletto"	4506	c.69-06
OPA 1036/37 "Bidú Sayão: Serata d'onore"	5108d [on 1037]	a.73-10
OPA 1051/52 "Elisabeth Rethberg: Golden Anniversary Issue 1922-1972"	4004a1-2 [on 1051]	a.73-10

Opus, Czechoslovakia (issued by Opus Record and Publishing House, Bratislava)

9112 0821/22(*) "Cavalleria Rusticana" [S.4: Milanov arias]	>*RCA* VIC 6044	a.79
9112 1251/53* "Turandot"	>*RCA* LM 6149	?

Parlophone, Sweden (EMI)

PMCS 303 (=Odeon PMCS 303)

Parnass, Germany (issued by P.P. Kelen Record Club; made by EMI Electrola)

62528 (62529/30) "Unvergessene Stimmen: Die grossen Tenöre"	88,121 [on 62529]	?77-06

Plaisir Musical, France (issued by EMI Pathé-Marconi)

CVPM 130.560* "Madame Butterfly: pages choisies"	241: excerpts	67

Prestige Musical Franklin, France (limited edition for subscribers only) [compare *Franklin Mint* Record Society]

13/14* "Requiem" (Les 100 Plus Grand Enregistrements de tous les temps)	>*RCA* LD 6091	81

RCA (Victor)

SOUTH AFRICA (Red Seal; issued by Teal)		
30019 "Jussi Bjoerling in Song"	>*RCA* LM 1771	56
30035 "Bjoerling Sings at Carnegie Hall"	>*RCA* LM 2003	57
30058 "Manon Lescaut: Highlights"	>*RCA* LM 2059	58
30061 "Highlights from 'Il Trovatore"'	>*RCA* LM 1827	58
30065 "Aida: Highlights"	>*RCA* SLP 19	58
30066 "Ten Tenors, Ten Arias"	>*RCA* LM 1202	58
30086 "Cavalleria Rusticana: Highlights"	>*RCA* LM 2243	59
30095 "Bjoerling in Opera"	>*RCA* LM 2269	59-05
30126 "Opera for People Who Hate Opera"	>*RCA* LM 2391	60-01
30170 "Turandot: Highlights"	>*RCA* LM 2539	61
30190/91 "Great Moments in Opera"	>*RCA* LM 6061	61
30209 "The Incomparable Bjoerling"	>*RCA* LM 2570	62
30231 "Great Tenor Arias"	>*RCA* LM 2631	62-11
30305 "Jussi Bjoerling in Concert"	>*RCA* HR 224	?c.63
FRANCE (issued by AREA)		
430.367 "Duos d'amour à l'opéra"	210g3,220b2 (?)	62-02
430.731 "Voix immortelles: 1896-1950"	170	67-07
530.268 "Airs célèbres de l'opéra francais"	180	62-03
530.269 "Ensembles célèbres de l'opéra"	182e,210b	62-09
530.271 "Les héros de Verdi"	210a1,225	63-01
630.344 "Le Trouvère: Sélections"	>*RCA* LM 1827	58-07
630.382 "Aida: Sélections"	>*RCA* SLP 19	58-05
630.383/84 "Cavalleria Rusticana. [S.4] Jussi Bjoerling Récital"	169,170,176,179-81,203	57
630.456/57 "La Tosca"	>*RCA* LM 6052	58
630.503 "Cavalleria Rusticana: Sélections"	>*RCA* LM 2243	59
630.537 "Les grandes heures de l'opéra par les plus grands ténors du monde"	>*RCA* LM 2372	60-05
630.559/60 "Cavalleria Rusticana"	220	?63
630.564/66 "Turandot"	>*RCA* LM 6149	61

630.577/78 "Paillasse" [S.4: Opera choruses]	>*RCA* LM 6084(?)	61
630.583 "Bjoerling à Carnegie Hall"	>*RCA* LM 2003	61
630.597/98 "Requiem"	>*RCA* LD 6091	61
630.826 "50 ans de belcanto"	>*RCA* LM 20083	?66
640.521/22* "Cavalleria Rusticana"	>*RCA* 630.559/60	?60-04
640.660/62* "Turandot"	>*RCA* LM 6149	61
640.682/83* "Requiem"	>*RCA* LD 6091	61
731.006/10 "Wagner: Inoubliables interprètes"	6004c	c.71-08
731.011/13(*) "Aida"	>*RCA* LM 6122	71-01
830.501 "Les grands ténors du siècle"	>*RCA* LM 2372	?67

GERMANY (Victrola) [see note]

26.35003 DM,DP (VIC 6008/1-2) "Der Troubadour = Il Trovatore"	>*RCA* LM 6008	75/76
26.35004 EA (VIC 6119/1-3) "Aida"	>*RCA* LM 6122	75/76
26.35116 EK* (PVL3-9041) "Turandot"	>*RCA* LM 6149	76-03
26.41213 AF* (VIP 2) "Puccini's Greatest"	>*RCA* LSC 5003	c.75-09
26.48001 DM,DP (VIC 6005/1-2) "Rigoletto"	>*RCA* LM 6051	75/76
26.48002 DM,DP (VIC 6027/1-2) "Manon Lescaut"	>*RCA* LM 6116	75/76
26.48009 DM,DP* (VICS 6000/1-2) "Tosca"	>*RCA* LM 6052	c.75-09
26.48016 DP*(*) (KR 11014/1-2) "Jussi Björling: Die grossen Opernerfolge = Jussi Björling in Opera"	>*RCA* KR 11014/1-2	75/76

BRAZIL

105.4004 "Dez tenores - dez árias"	182d5	?

SPAIN (Plum label)

3L 16153 "Aida: Selección"	>*RCA* SLP 19	a.61
3L 16174 "Il Trovatore: Selección"	>*RCA* LM 1827(?)	a.61
3L 16282 "Jussi Björling: Fragmentos de Opera"	>*RCA* LM 2269	a.61
3LB 16273 (2) "Rigoletto"	>*RCA* LM 6051	a.61
3LC 16076 (3) "Aida"	>*RCA* LM 6122	a.61
3LC 16269 (3) "Manon Lescaut"	>*RCA* LM 6116	a.61

FRANCE (issued by AREA)

A 630.255 "Jussi Bjoerling et Robert Merrill Récital"	>*RCA* LM 1841	55-06
A 630.361/62 "Le Trouvère"	>*RCA* LM 6008	57-03
A 630.373/75 "Aida"	>*RCA* LM 6122	57-03

USA (Gold Seal)

AGL2-4514* (2) "Tosca"	>*RCA* LM 6052	82-10
AGL3-3970* (3) "Turandot"	>*RCA* LM 6149	81-04
AGM1-4806 "Bjoerling in Opera"	>*RCA* LM 2269	83-08

AGM1-4889 "Jussi Bjoerling: Operatic Duets with Robert Merrill, Operatic Scenes with..."	>*RCA* LM 2736	84-02
AGM1-4923 "Jussi Bjoerling in Concert"	>*RCA* HR 224	84-03
AGM1-5277 "Jussi Bjoerling: Operatic Arias" (Legendary Performers No. 77)	203a,209b2,210a1, 212c,d,213,215,216B, 217-18,219a2-3,f1,f4, 240b2,d1	85-08
AGM3-4805 (3) "Opening Nights at the Met"	>*RCA* LM 6171	83-09
NETHERLANDS (Victrola; issued by Inelco Nederland))		
AVL 10906 "Aida: Highlights"	210a1,c,e,g2-3	76
AVL 10987 "Cavalleria Rusticana: Highlights"	203a,b,c2,d2	76
USA, AUSTRALIA (?) (Victrola)		
AVM2-0699 (2) "Il Trovatore"	>*RCA* LM 6008	US:74-10
SOUTH AFRICA (Red Seal; issued by Teal)		
B 30194 (2) "Cavalleria Rusticana. [S.4] Arias by Jussi Bjoerling"	>*RCA* LM 6059	61
B 30216 (2) "Pagliacci" [S.4: opera choruses]	>*RCA* LM 6084	61
ITALY		
B12R 0023/24 "Il Trovatore"	>*RCA* LM 6008	a.58
GERMANY		
BL 86587* "Aria"	>CD.*RCA* 6587-2-RC	87
BRAZIL (Red Seal)		
BRL 57 "Dez tenores - dez árias [vol. 1]"	>*RCA* LM 1202	?
BRL 100	>*RCA* LM 1160	a.56
BRL 173	>*RCA* LM 1847	a.56
BRL 181 "Aida: ..."	>*RCA* SLP 19	a.56
BRL 182 "Selecionador Sêlo Vermelho"	>*RCA* SRL 12-14	a.56
BRL 253 "Bjoerling in Opera"	>*RCA* LM 2269	?
BRL 3031 [10"/25 cm.] "Duetos operisticos"	>*RCA* LM 7007	?
SOUTH AFRICA (Red Seal; issued by Teal)		
C 30014 (3) "Aida"	>*RCA* LM 6122	56
C 30024 (3) "Turandot"	>*RCA* LM 6149	61
ITALY		
C12R 0164/66 "Manon Lescaut"	>*RCA* LM 6116	c.56
C12R 0175/77 "Aida"	>*RCA* LM 6122	c.57
USA (Red Seal)		
CRM8-5177*[p] (8) "*RCA*/Met: 100 Singers, 100 Years"		84-11
(record 5)	209f3-4	
(record 7*)	240c1	

GREAT BRITAIN

DPS 2004/1-2* "Opera Gala"	>*RCA* VCS 7061	70

NETHERLANDS

DVLB 16480 "A Treasury of Grand Opera in High Fidelity"	>*RCA* LM 1847	?
GL 43194 "Bjoerling Sings at Carnegie Hall" (Gold Seal: The Originals)	>*RCA* LM 2003	80-06

GERMANY

Gold Seal - DMM

GL 84889 "Jussi Bjoerling & Robert Merrill: The Pearl Fishers Duet and Other Famous Operatic Duets and Scenes"	>*RCA* LM 2736	85
GL 85277 "Bjoerling: Opera Arias = Opernarien = Airs d'opéra" (Legendary Performers)	>*RCA* AGM1-5277	86-09
GL 87799 "Jussi Bjoerling: The Pearl Fishers Duet (=Les Pêcheurs de Perles, duo) Plus Duets and Scenes by Puccini and Verdi"	>CD.*RCA* 7799-2-RG	88-09

Red Seal (issued by Teldec) [Records also have titles in English like corresponding LM issues. Dates for releases in Germany = TG; outside Germany = TO.]

		TG	*TO*
HR 210 "Berühmte Liebesduette"	>*RCA* LM 2628	65/66	62-09
HR 211 "Berühmte Tenöre singen neapolitanische Lieder"	>*RCA* LM 2630		62-09
HR 212 "Berühmte Tenor-Arien"	179,209b2	65/66	62-09
HR 224 "Jussi Bjoerling: Historische Aufnahmen 1958"	5706b,5802b,e,l, m,o,u,5808b, 6004a-g		65-01

JAPAN (Red Seal)

JRM5 7162 (=RVC 7531/35)

GERMANY (issued by Teldec)

KD 9 (5) "Mit Musik leben: Giacomo Puccini"	240b2,b4,c2,d1,f (?)	63-08

Victrola

KR 11014/1-2*(*) "Jussi Björling: Die grossen Opernerfolge = Jussi Björling in Opera"		71-09
11014-1	171,172B,173-74,176,212c, 219a2-3,f4,226,240b2,d1,6006b	
11014-2	175,203a,220c,224,5501 i-l,t-v,6004a	

ITALY (Victrola, Plum label)

KV 6005 (2) "Rigoletto"	>*RCA* LM 6051	66-01
KV 6008 (2) "Trovatore"	>*RCA* LM 6008	66-01
KV 6103 (3) "Aida"	>*RCA* LM 6122	66-02

KV 6110 (2) "Manon Lescaut"	>*RCA* LM 6116	66/68
KVS 6000* (2) "Tosca"	>*RCA* LM 6052	66/68
KVS 6011* (2) "Requiem"	>*RCA* LD 6091	66/68
KVS 6114* (3) "Turandot"	>*RCA* LM 6149	68-03

AUSTRALIA (Red Seal)

L 16098 "Bjoerling, Merrill: Great Operatic Arias"	>*RCA* LM 1841	58
L 16174 "Bjoerling in Opera"	>*RCA* LM 2269	59
L 16225 "Fifty Years of Great Operatic Singing: Tenors"	>*RCA* LM 2372	60
L 16237 "Artists and Arias"	>*RCA* LM 2391	60
L 16301 "60 Years of Best Loved Music, vol. 3"	>*RCA* LM 2574	61
L 16305 "The Incomparable Bjoerling"	>*RCA* LM 2570	61
L 16339 "Bjoerling Sings at Carnegie Hall"	>*RCA* LM 2003	62
L 16347 "Great Love Duets"	>*RCA* LM 2628	62
L 16349 "Great Tenors Sing Neapolitan Songs"	>*RCA* LM 2630	62
L 16352 "Great Tenor Arias"	>*RCA* LM 2631	62
L 16370 "Jussi Bjoerling"	>*RCA* LM 9884	62
L 17007 "Jussi Bjoerling in Song"	>*RCA* LM 1771	?62
LB 16012 (2) "Il Trovatore"	>*RCA* LM 6008	57
LB 16110 (2) "Tosca"	>*RCA* LM 6052	58
LB 16157 (2) "Cavalleria Rusticana. [S.4] Arias by Jussi Bjoerling"	>*RCA* LM 6059	59
LB 16193 (2) "Great Moments in Opera: Verdi, Puccini"	>*RCA* LM 6061	59
LB 16239 (2) "Rigoletto"	>*RCA* LM 6051	59
LB 16348 (2) "Summer Festival: 20 of the World's Greatest Artists"	>*RCA* LM 6097	62
LC 16134 (3) "Aida"	>*RCA* LM 6122	57
LC 16311 (3) "Turandot"	>*RCA* LM 6149	61

USA (Plum label)

LCT 6701 (5) "50 Years of Great Operatic Singing"		55-05
6701-4	120	
6701-5	143	

USA [& CHILE] (Red Seal, Soria series)

LD 6091 (2) "Requiem" [+Chile]	242	60-10
LDS 6091* (2) "Requiem"	>*RCA* LD 6091	60-10

USA (Red Seal); 10"/25 cm.

LM 105 "Great Tenor Arias by Jussi Bjoerling"	169,170,176,179-81	51-10

USA & OTHER COUNTRIES (Red Seal) [For explanation of German (Teldec) release dates and for information about pressings in other countries, see note]

		Teldec	*US*
LM 1128 "Highlights from 'Don Carlo'"	171	-	51-04
LM 1160(-C) "Highlights from 'Cavalleria Rusticana', 'I Pagliacci' = 'C.R.', 'Der Bajazzo': Arien und Szenen"	162A,170	(57-07)	51-10
LM 1202 "Ten Tenors, Ten Arias"	180	-	52-03
LM 1771 "Jussi Bjoerling in Song"	183-98	-	53-11
LM 1801 "Arias Sung and Acted"	88,204a	(56-10)	54-06
LM 1802 "An Adventure in High Fidelity"	184	57-11	54-09
LM 1827(-B,-C) "Highlights from 'Il Trovatore' = Der Troubadour: Arien und Szenen"	182c1,d3-5,e, f1-2	56-07	55-01
LM 1828 "Highlights from 'Cavalleria Rusticana', 'I Pagliacci'"	203a,b2,d2,204a,b	-	55-01
LM 1841(-C v.l) "Jussi Bjoerling, Robert Merrill: Great Operatic Arias = Berühmte Opernarien" [see note]	169,170,176, 179-81	(56-07)	54-11
LM 1841-C v.2 "...: Berühmte Opernarien"	170,176,179-81, 217		?58-03
LM 1847 "A Treasury of Grand Opera in High Fidelity"	182d5	-	55-01
LM 2003(-C) "Bjoerling Sings at Carnegie Hall"	5501a-1,t-w	57-01	56-08
LM 2045 "Highlights from 'La Bohème'"	>*RCA* SLP 20	-	57-01
LM 2046(-C) "Aida: Highlights = Arien und Szenen"	>*RCA* SLP 19	(57)	57-01
LM 2059(-C) "Manon Lescaut: Highlights = Arien und Szenen"	209b,c,d,f,g	57-03	57-01
LM 2243(-C) "Cavalleria Rusticana: Highlights = Arien und Szenen"	220a,b1,c,d	59	58-12
LM 2269(-C) "Bjoerling in Opera = Opernabend mit Jussi Björling"	203a,209b2, 210a1,212c,d, 213,215,216B, 217-18,219f1	59	59-03
LM 2372(-C) "Fifty Years of Great Operatic Singing: Tenors = 50 Jahre Oper: Grosse Tenöre der 'Met'"	223	c.60-04	60-02
LM 2391(-C) "Opera for People Who Hate Opera = Festliches Opernkonzert"	219f1	c.60-08	60-01
LM 2539 "Turandot: Highlights"	240b2-4,c,d1,e2,f	-	61-08
LM 2570(-C) "The Incomparable Bjoerling = Jussi Björling: In Memoriam"	219a2-3,f4, 220c,221-26, 240b2,d1,242a	(61-11)	61-11
LM 2574 "Sixty Years of Music America Loves Best, vol. 3"	176	-	61-08
LM 2628 "Great Love Duets"	209d,210e1	-	62-07

LM 2630 "Great Tenors Sing Neapolitan Songs"	5501t	-	62-08
LM 2631 "Great Tenor Arias"	>*RCA* HR 212	-	62-10
LM 2736(-C) "Jussi Bjoerling: Operatic Duets with Robert Merrill, Operatic Scenes with... = Jussi Bjoerling in berühmten Opernduetten"	171,172B,173-75, 182a,d1-3,d5, 209e,f2-4,210e3, 212a2,e	64-06	64-04
LM 2784 "Jussi Bjoerling in Concert"	>*RCA* HR 224	65-03	65-02
LM 6008(/1-2) "Il Trovatore = Der Troubadour"	182	(57)	52-10
LM 6042 (2) "La Bohème"	211	-	56-09
LM 6045 (2) "I Pagliacci" [S.4: opera choruses]	204	-	56-10
LM 6046(/1-2) "Cavalleria Rusticana" [S.4: Verdi opera choruses]	203	(57-03)	57-01
LM 6051(/1-2) "Rigoletto"	212	57-09	57-09
LM 6052(/1-2) "Tosca"	219	(58-03)	57-11
LM 6059(/1-2) "Cavalleria Rusticana. [S.4] Arias by Jussi Bjoerling = Jussi Björling singt italienische Opernarien"	220-26	?59	58-09
LM 6061 (2) "Great Moments in Opera: Verdi, Puccini"		-	58-10
(record 1)	211b4-5,212d,219f1		
(record 2)	172A,210g		
LM 6069 (2) "Aida (abridged)"		-	59-08
(record 1)	210a,f,g		
(record 2)	210d,e1		
LM 6084(/1-2) "Pagliacci = Der Bajazzo" [S.4: opera choruses (not same as in LM 6045)]	204	61	60-05
LM 6091/1-2 "Requiem"	>*RCA* LD 6091	61-10	-
LM 6097 (2) "Summer Festival: 20 of the World's Greatest Artists"	220b2	-	62-05
LM 6106 (3) "Cavalleria Rusticana, I Pagliacci"	203,204	-	53-09
LM 6116 (3) "Manon Lescaut"	209	-	55-09
LM 6122(/1-3) "Aida"	210	57	55-10
LM 6138 (3) "Vanessa" [JB in "Operatic Selections" on s.6 only]	220b2	-	58-08
LM 6149(/1-3) "Turandot"	240	(60)	60-08
LM 6171 (3) "Opening Nights at the Met"	171a2-3 [on record 1]	-	66-09

USA (Red Seal); 10"/25 cm.

LM 7007 "Operatic Duets by Jussi Bjoerling and Robert Merrill"	171,172B,173-75		52-10

GERMANY (Red Seal; issued by Teldec)

LM 9800-D,-E "Jussi Björling" [10"/25 cm.]	213-15,216A,217-18	57-05
LM 9811-C "Tosca: Arien und Szenen"	219a,b1-3,c3-4, f1-2,f4,f6,f8	(58-11)
LM 9823-E "Acht Tenöre, acht Arien = Eight Tenors, Eight Arias" [10"/25cm.]	216A	?59-07
LM 9844-E "Opernduette Björling - Merrill = Björling and Merrill in Duets" [10"/25cm.]	>*RCA* LM 7007 [Duets on s.2 in different order]	59-08
LM 9847-E "Rigoletto: Arien und Szenen = Highlights" [10"/25cm.]	212a,b,d,e2	(59-09)
LM 9872-C "Belcanto a Verona"	240c1,d1	(60-11)
LM 9875-C "Arien und Szenen aus 'Turandot'"	240a,b,d,e2,f2	61-05

SWEDEN, USA (Red label; Swedish issue made for Grammofon AB Electra by Teldec)

LM 9884 "Jussi Björling"	214,227-32,235-39	Sw:61-11 US:64-10

ITALY (Red Seal)

LM 20039 "Pagine scelte dalla 'Cavalleria Rusticana' e dai 'Pagliacci'"	204a,b,220b2	62-03
LM 20075 "Le romanze che voi preferite, vol. 1"	210a1	64-01
LM 20076 "Le romanze che voi preferite, vol. 2"	220d2,240e2	64-09
LM 20083 "50 anni di belcanto: Tenori, vol. 2"	180	65-12
LM 20129 "Celebri voci, famosi duetti"	171a2-3	70-09

BRAZIL

LMB 500 "Uma Aventura em Alta Fidelidade"	>RCA LM 1802	?

ITALY (Red Seal)

LMD 60005 (2) "Aida: Highlights. Incisioni 1911-1954"		71-03
(record 1)	210d	
(record 2)	210f	
LMD 67002 (5) "Belcanto"	221-26 [on record 4]	62-11

GREAT BRITAIN (Red Seal)

LP 3043 (=RCALP 3043)

ITALY; 7"/17 cm.

LRC 51-007 "Jussi Björling:..."	219a3,222-24, 226,240b2	a.63

USA (Red Seal); 10"/25 cm.

LRM 7027 "Bjoerling and Merrill Sing Operatic Duets"	171,172B,174, 182d5	53-10

USA & OTHER COUNTRIES (Red Seal) (For explanation of German (Teldec) release dates and for information about pressings in other countries, see note.]

		Teldec	*US*
LSC 2243(-B)* "Cavalleria Rusticana: Highlights = Arien und Szenen"	>*RCA* LM 2243	60	58-12
LSC 2391(-B)* "Opera for People Who Hate Opera = Festliches Opernkonzert"	>*RCA* LM 2391	60-08	60-01
LSC 2539* "Turandot: Highlights"	>*RCA* LM 2539	-	61-08
LSC 2570(-B)* "The Incomparable Bjoerling = Jussi Björling: In Memoriam"	>*RCA* LM 2570	(61-11)	61-11
LSC 5003* "Puccini's Greatest Hits"	219a3,f1,240d1	-	71-08
LSC 6052* (3) "Tosca" [S.6: Operatic Arias]	219,222,226	-	60-06
LSC 6052/1-2* "Tosca"	>*RCA* LM 6052	(60)	-
LSC 6059(/1-2)* "Cavalleria Rusticana. [S.4] Arias by Jussi Bjoerling = Jussi Björling singt italienische Opernarien"	>*RCA* LM 6059	60	58-09
LSC 6091/1-2* "Requiem"	>*RCA* LD 6091	?61-04	
LSC 6097* (2) "Summer Festival: 20 of the World's Greatest Artists"	>*RCA* LM 6097	-	62-05
LSC 6138* (3) "Vanessa" [JB in "Operatic Selections" on s.6 only]	>*RCA* LM 6138	-	58-08
LSC 6149(/1-3)* "Turandot"	>*RCA* LM 6149	(60)	60-08

GERMANY (Red Seal; issued by Teldec)

LSC 9811-B* "Tosca: Arien und Szenen"	219a,b3-5,c4,f1,f4-8	(58-11)
LSC 9875-B* "Arien und Szenen aus 'Turandot'"	>*RCA* LM 9875-C	61-05

SWEDEN, AUSTRALIA (Red Seal; Swedish issue made for Grammofon AB Electra by Teldec)

LSC 9884*(*) "Jussi Björling = Jussi Björling Sings Swedish Songs"	214,227-31,235-39	Sw:69-09

GERMANY (Red Seal; issued by Teldec)

LSC 9964-B* "Turandot: Arien und Szenen"	240b2,b4,c2,d1,f	67-01

ITALY (Red Seal)

LSC 20102* "Momenti magici del Melodramma"	240d1	69
LSC 20106* "Gran Gala all'Opera, vol. 1"	240c1	?69

BRAZIL

LVD 7064 "Famous Arias" (?)	?	?

ITALY (Victrola, Pink label)

MCV 533 (3) "Aida"	>*RCA* LM 6122	71-09
MCV 534 (2) "Cavalleria Rusticana" [S.4: Recital di Zinka Milanov]	>*RCA* VIC 6044	71-06
MCV 535* (2) "Tosca"	>*RCA* LM 6052	72-02
MCV 536 (2) "Il Trovatore"	>*RCA* LM 6008	72-02
MCV 537* (3) "Turandot"	>*RCA* LM 6149	72
MCV 540 (2) "Rigoletto"	>*RCA* LM 6051	72
MCV 544 (2) "Manon Lescaut"	>*RCA* LM 6116	72-10

GREAT BRITAIN (Red Seal)

PL 42146 (2) "A Century of Sound"	174 [on record 1]	77

GERMANY (Victrola, Pink label)

PVL3-9041* (=26.35116 EK)

JAPAN (issued by RVC)

RA 2203 "Bjoerling at Carnegie Hall"	>*RCA* LM 2003	?
RA 2213 "Jussi Bjoerling in Concert"	>*RCA* HR 224	?

GREAT BRITAIN (Red Seal; up to 1968 issued by Decca)

RB 6515 "Great Tenor Arias"	>*RCA* LM 2631	62-11
RB 6516 "Great Love Duets"	>*RCA* LM 2628	62-11
RB 6543 "Summer Festival, vol. 2"	220b2	63-07
RB 6585 "Jussi Bjoerling: Operatic Duets with Robert Merrill, Operatic Scenes with..."	>*RCA* LM 2736	64-10
RB 6620 "Jussi Bjoerling in Concert"	>*RCA* HR 224	65-07
RB 16011 "Bjoerling Sings at Carnegie Hall"	>*RCA* LM 2003	58-01
RB 16031/32 "Rigoletto"	>*RCA* LM 6051	57-11
RB 16051/52 "Tosca"	>*RCA* LM 6052	58-02
RB 16078 "Highlights from 'Manon Lescaut'"	>*RCA* LM 2059	58-11
RB 16081/82 "Cavalleria Rusticana. [S.4] Jussi Bjoerling Operatic Recital"	>*RCA* LM 6059	59-03
RB 16089 "Great Moments in Opera: Verdi"	172A?,210g	59-05
RB 16149 "Bjoerling in Opera"	>*RCA* LM 2269	59-05
RB 16198 "Fifty Years of Great Operatic Singing: Tenors"	>*RCA* LM 2372	60-05
RB 16267 "Turandot: Highlights"	>*RCA* LM 2539	62-02
RB 16268 "Golden Classics, vol. 2"	>*RCA* LM 2574	62-02
RCALP 3034 "The Pearl Fishers Duet and Other Famous Operatic Duets and Scenes" (Legacy)	>*RCA* LM 2736	a.83-06
RE 25020/22 "Turandot"	>*RCA* LM 6149	61-02
RE 25026/27 "Requiem Mass"	>*RCA* LD 6091	61-04

JAPAN (issued by RVC)		
RGC 1036/37 "Tosca"	>*RCA* LM 6052	?
RGC 1101/03 "Aida"	>*RCA* LM 6122	?
RGC 1106/07 "Il Trovatore"	>*RCA* LM 6008	?
GERMANY (Red Seal; Ullstein Musik)		
RL 42876 EF* (2) "Grand Gala in der Oper"	240c1	79-09
RL 43063 AS "Jussi Björling in Concert"	>*RCA* HR 224	80-04
RL 43077 EF (2) "Der unvergessliche Jussi Björling singt grosse Opernarien"		80-04
43077-1	>*RCA* SER 5704	
43077-2	>*RCA* SER 5705	
GREAT BRITAIN (Red Seal)		
RL 43243 "The Pearl Fishers Duet and Other Famous Operatic Duets and Scenes"	>*RCA* LM 2736	80-08
GERMANY, ITALY (Red Seal)		
RL 85177 (8) "RCA/Met: Hundert Sänger, Hundert Jahre = 100 Singers, 100 Years"	>*RCA* CRM8-5177	85
NEW ZEALAND (Red Seal)		
RSL 3519 "Bjoerling, Merrill: Great Operatic Arias"	>*RCA* LM 1841	58
RSL 3551/52 "Tosca"	>*RCA* LM 6052	?
JAPAN (Red Seal; issued by RVC)		
RVC 7531/35*p (JRM5-7162) "The Art of Jussi Bjoerling"		76
7531	171,172B?,174,182a,c1,d2-5, 210a1,e3,212a2,c,d,e	
7532	173,176,181,203a,b,c2, d2,209b2,d,217,219a2-3, f1,240d1	
7533	169,175,179,180,213,215, 216B,218,5501i,j,l,6004c	
7534	185-87,189,190,192-94, 196-98,5501a,b,f-h, 5802b,e,o,u	
7535*(*)	214,227-31,235-39,5501 t,v,w,6003f	
GREAT BRITAIN (Red Seal; up to 1968 issued by Decca)		
SB 2021/22* "Cavalleria Rusticana. [S.4] Jussi Bjoerling Operatic Recital"	>*RCA* LM 6059	59-02
SB 2138* "Turandot: Highlights"	>*RCA* LM 2539	62-02
SB 6543* "Summer Festival, vol. 2"	>*RCA* RB 6543	63-07
SER 4520/22* "Turandot"	>*RCA* LM 6149	61-02
SER 4526/27* "Requiem Mass"	>*RCA* LD 6091	61-04

SER 5643/45* "Turandot"	>*RCA* LM 6149	72-10
SER 5704/06 "The Golden Voice of Jussi Björling"		74-11
5704	170,171,203a,209b2,e, f2-4,212a2,c,d,e,213, 216B,217,219f1	
5705	169,172B,173-76,179-81, 182a,d1-3,d5,210a1,e3	
5706	218,5501a,c-e,h,t,v, 5706b,5802b,o,u,5808b, 6004a,c,e,f	
SER 5719*(*) "Jussi Björling Sings Swedish Songs"	>*RCA* LSC 9884	75-03
JAPAN (Red Seal; issued by RVC)		
SHP 2010/11* "Cavalleria Rusticana. [S.4] Jussi Bjoerling Operatic Recital"	>*RCA* LM 6059	a.75
SHP 2103* "The Incomparable Bjoerling"	>*RCA* LM 2570	a.75
GERMANY (issued by Teldec)		
SKD 9* (5) "Mit Musik leben: Giacomo Puccini"	>*RCA* KD 9	63-08
AUSTRALIA (Red Seal)		
SLB 16348* (2) "Summer Festival: 20 of the World's Greatest Artists"	>*RCA* LM 6097	62
SLC 16311* (3) "Turandot"	>*RCA* LM 6149	61
USA		
SLP 19 "Aida: Highlights"	210a1,e,g	56-11
SLP 20 "Bohème: Highlights"	211b2-5,d,e,f,g	56-11
GERMANY (issued by Teldec)		
SMR 8008* (2) "Tosca"	>*RCA* LM 6052	67-01
AUSTRALIA (Gold label)		
SP 185 "The World's Greatest Voices in Opera & Song"	175,210a1,212d	77
JAPAN (issued by RVC)		
SRA 2785/87* "Turandot"	>*RCA* LM 6149	?
SRA 3024/25* "Requiem"	>*RCA* LD 6091	?
USA (Red Seal)		
SRL 12-14 "RCA Victor Red Seal Selector"	209f2-4	55-09
SRL 12-28 "A Showcase in Sound"	211b4	56-09
EUROPE (Red Seal; issued by Teldec outside Germany)		
SVA 1010 "Bjoerling Sings at Carnegie Hall"	>*RCA* LM 2003	66-10

ITALY (Red Seal)

TRL1-7011* "Puccini 1924-1970: Un giorno a Torre del Lago"	240c1	74-03
TRL1-7055 "I grandi tenori: Da Caruso a Domingo"	182d2-3	76-06
TRL4-1173 (4) "Giuseppe Verdi: Una vita per la musica"		76
(record 2)	212d	
(record 4)	210d2	

USA (Red Seal)

VCS 7061* (2) "Opera Gala"		70-04
7061-1	240c1	
7061-2	240b2	

VARIOUS COUNTRIES (Victrola, Pink label) [Countries where this series was pressed and issued are indicated, with dates when available: Australia, Great Britain, USA (Series: Immortal Performances), Germany (TO = Teldec outside Germany, TG = Teldec in Germany)]

VIC 6000 (2) "Tosca"	>*RCA* LM 6052	US:64-03
VIC 6000/1-2 "Tosca"	>*RCA* LM 6052	TG+TO:64-08
VIC 6005/1-2 "Rigoletto"	>*RCA* LM 6051	TO:65-08 TG:72-10
VIC 6008/1-2 "Der Troubadour = Il Trovatore"	>*RCA* LM 6008	TO:65-11 TG:72-04
VIC 6027 (2) "Manon Lescaut"	>*RCA* LM 6116	US:69-08 GB:69 Au:?
VIC 6027/1-2 "Manon Lescaut"	>*RCA* LM 6116	TG+TO:73-07
VIC 6041 (2) "Rigoletto"	>*RCA* LM 6051	US:70-09 GB:71-06 Au:?
VIC 6044 (2) "Cavalleria Rusticana. [S.4] Milanov arias"	203	US:71-05 Au:?
VIC 6119 (3) "Aida"	>*RCA* LM 6122	US:69-07
VIC 6119/1-3 "Aida"	>*RCA* LM 6122	TG+TO:73-07

SWEDEN (Victrola; made for Grammofon AB Electra by Teldec)

VICS 1546(*) "Hovsångare på konsertestraden"	233,234	70-04
VICS 1659(*) "Jussi Björling på Gröna Lund"	5803c,h,5905a,b,d,e,6003a-f	72-03

VARIOUS COUNTRIES (Victrola, Pink label) [See note before VIC series]

VICS 1672(e)*(*) "Puccini's Biggest Hits"	209b2,219a3,f1	US:72-07 GB:73-07
VICS 1672(*) "Puccini's Biggest Hits"	>*RCA* VICS 1672(e)	Au:73-01
VICS 1740* "The Incomparable Bjoerling"	>*RCA* LM 2570	GB:73-07

VICS 6000* (2) "Tosca"	>*RCA* LM 6052	US:64-03 GB:64-04 Sp:65
VICS 6000/1-2* "Tosca"	>*RCA* LM 6052	TG+TO:64-08
VICS 6044(*) (2) "Cavalleria Rusticana. [S.4] Milanov Arias"	>*RCA* VIC 6044	GB:71-07

ITALY (Victrola)

VICS 6114* (=KVS 6114)

GERMANY (Pink label; issued by Teldec)

VIP 2* "Puccini's Greatest"	>*RCA* LSC 5003	72-07

ITALY

Victrola, Gold label

VL 42435 (2) "Aida: Highlights"	>*RCA* LMD 60005	78
VL 42436 "Jussi Björling: Registrazioni 1950-1959" (L'età d'oro del belcanto)	170,176,179,181, 182d3-5,209b2, d3-4,210a1,212c, 213,217,219f1, 240d1	78

Victrola, Pink label

VL 43533 (3) "Aida"	>*RCA* LM 6122	77
VL 43534 (2) "Cavalleria Rusticana. [S.4] Recital di Zinka Milanov"	>*RCA* VIC 6044	77
VL 43535* (2) "Tosca"	>*RCA* LM 6052	77
VL 43536 (2) "Il Trovatore"	>*RCA* LM 6008	77
VL 43537* (3) "Turandot"	>*RCA* LM 6149	77
VL 43540 (2) "Rigoletto"	>*RCA* LM 6051	77
VL 43544 (2) "Manon Lescaut"	>*RCA* LM 6116	77

GERMANY (Victrola)

VL 70190 (3) "Aida"	>*RCA* LM 6122	a.84-07

ITALY [half-speed mastering]

Victrola, Pink label

VLS 00699(*) (2) "Il Trovatore"	>*RCA* LM 6008	82-09
VLS 03970* (3) "Turandot"	>*RCA* LM 6149	82-09
VLS 43533(*) (3) "Aida"	>*RCA* LM 6122	82-09
VLS 43534(*) (2) "Cavalleria Rusticana. [S.4] Recital di Zinka Milanov"	>*RCA* VIC 6044	82-09
VLS 43535* (2) "Tosca"	>*RCA* LM 6052	82-09
VLS 43540(*) (2) "Rigoletto"	>*RCA* LM 6051	82-09
VLS 43544(*) (2) "Manon Lescaut"	>*RCA* LM 6116	82-09

Pink label

VLS 45510* "Tenorissimi" (First Class: Opera Series)	>*RCA* TRL1-7055	83-09

Reader's Digest

BRAZIL (made by RCA)

BMI 1966 (10) "La bella musica italiana"	>*Sel.Read.Dig.* BMI 1/10	?
BMIS 1966* (10) "La bella musica italiana"	>*Sel.Read.Dig.* BMI 1/10	?

AUSTRALIA & GREAT BRITAIN (made by RCA)

RD4-67-1/6,-1/7* "Command Performance: A Night at the Opera" [British edition has 7 records]		?
(Record 2)	219f1	
(Record 3)	219c2-4	

GREAT BRITAIN (made by RCA in Britain & Netherlands)

RDM 2678 + RDS 6671/77* (8) "Command Performance: A Night at the Opera"		?
(RDS 6672)	219f1	
(RDS 6673)	219c2-4	

The Record Collectors' Club, Peoria, Illinois, USA (private issue)

5	5010f2	a.69-02

Richmond, USA & Canada (issued by London; also pressed in Great Britain by Decca)

SR 33254* "The Voice of Jussi Bjoerling" (Treasury)	220b,c,d2,221-26, 242a,243	77-10

***Robin Hood** Records*, USA (private issue by BJR Enterprises, New York)

RHR 502-C (5021/23) "Faust"	5912	c.74-08
RHR 509-B (5091/92) "Il Trovatore"	4101	79-04
RHR 515-B (5151/52) "La Bohème"	4804	79-04
RHR 516-C (5161/63) "Un Ballo in Maschera. [S.6] Songs of Yugoslavia Sung by Zinka Milanov"	4007	80-12

***Rococo** Records*, Toronto, Canada (Series: Famous Voices of the Past)

1003 (3) "Un Ballo in Maschera & [S.6] Jussi Bjoerling in Rigoletto and Bohème"	4007,5601a,b,5703b2	73-07
5201 "Jussi Bjoerling" [vol. 2]	6,13,27,34,35,46,55,58, 65,66,69,70B,94,106B, 107B,110A,111	62-10

5231 "Jussi Bjoerling, vol. 3"	16,26,28-30,45,57,59-62,67,68,79,80,83	65-09
5237 "Jussi Bjoerling, vol. 4"	9,12,17,20,32,33,37-39,42,43,47-49,64,85	66-01
5304 "Jussi Bjoerling, vol. 5: Verdi and Puccini Recital"	4001a1,a3,4007a,4101b2-3,c2-3,c4,e1,4506d,4908c,e2,f,5202c	69
5329 "Jussi Bjoerling, vol. 6: Gounod Recital"	4604b,c,4701a2,b2,c,e,f	69
5341 "Jussi Bjoerling, vol. 7"	10,11,14,18,19,21,23,24,93,104,108,207,4605b,c,4801a-c,5202d,e	72
R 31 "Jussi Bjoerling" [vol. 1]	50,51B,71-78,86,114B,115,120,141,142,148,165	61-06

***RRE** Rare Recorded Editions*, Great Britain (issued by Michael Thomas, London)

AD 101/02 "Björling in Gounod's Roméo et Juliette"	4701	85-09

*The **Rubini** Collection*, Great Britain (issued by Syd Gray)

GV 21 "Jussi Bjorling: The Early Years"	10,11,15,16,23,24,81,82,84,91,92,104,108,110A	72

The Salvation Army, Western Territory, USA [16"/40 cm. transcription discs, with matrix numbers only]

CPM 16-1074 "An Army of Stars Salute the Salvation Army, Christmas 1951"	5108e	51-12
RR 17175 "An Army of Stars Salute the Salvation Army, Christmas 1949"	4905	49-12

Selezione dal Reader's Digest, Italy (made by EMI)

3C 147-52050/55*(*) "Puccini: Melodie eterne"		75-05
-52051	241c2-4	
-52054	211e3-4	
3C 147-52402/10 "Va pensiero: Le melodie immortali di G. Verdi"	89 [on -52410]	76-04
BMI 1/10 "La bella musica italiana"	223 [on record 10]	c.68
RDIS 212-1/8* "I grandi tenori"		?
(-6)	226	
(-7)	222	
(-8)	223	

RDP/T 1-2* (7) "Tre capolavori di Puccini"	219	64
RDS 13D*(*) (10) "13 Perle del Melodramma"		c.71
(record 8 = matrix RKBY 12665/66)	203b1,d2	
(record 10 = matrix RKBY 12669/70)	240b2,c1,e2	

Seraphim (EMI)

USA (issued by Capitol)		
60168 "The Art of Jussi Bjoerling [vol. 1]: Songs, Oratorio and Opera Arias" (Great Recordings of the Century)	>*HMV* HQM 1190	71-04
60206 "Great Tenors of the Century"	>*HMV* HLM 7004	74-01
60219 "The Art of Jussi Bjoerling [vol. 2]: Opera Arias" (Great Recordings of the Century)	88-90,95,98,99,112,113, 119,121,143,145,151B, 152,153	74-05
JAPAN (issued by Toshiba-EMI [label uncertain])		
EAC 30070* "Madama Butterfly: Highlights"	>*Cap.* G 7233	
EAC 30233/35* "Madama Butterfly"	>*HMV* ALP 1795/97	78-01
EAC 30239/40(*) "La Bohème"	>*RCA* LM 6042	78
EAC 40159* "Victoria de los Angeles: Opera Arias"	>*Sera.* S 60262 (?)	?
EAC 55101(*) "Angel Best Classics 1800"	211b2	?82
EAC 60178/82 "The Greatest Singers of the Century"	113 [on 60180]	a.81
USA (issued by Capitol)		
IB 6000 (2) "La Bohème"	>*RCA* LM 6042	66-10
IB 6058 (2) "I Pagliacci. [S.4] Bjoerling Arias"	141,142,146,147A,157, 161B,162A,204	70-04
IH 6150 (8) "The Record of Singing, vol. 4"	>*HMV* EX 7 69741 1	?89
IM 6143 (13) "The Record of Singing, vol. 3"	>*HMV* EX 29 0169 3	85
S 60262* "Victoria de los Angeles: Opera Arias"	241e	79-08
SIB 6000(*) (2) "La Bohème" [This number assigned by mistake, cp. SIB 6099]	>*RCA* LM 6042	75-04
SIB 6099(*) (2) "La Bohème"	>*RCA* LM 6042	75-05

SR Records, Sweden (issued by Sveriges Radio / Sveriges Riksradio, Stockholm)

RMLP 1272/73 "La Traviata"	3904	78-03
SRLP 1272/73 (=RMLP 1272/73)		
SRLP 1354/55 "Björling: Jussi, Olle, Gösta, kvartetten"		80-11
1354	1-6,4102c,4201a-c,4302c, 4502b,c,5204b,5301a	
1355	5201	

TAP [*Top Artists Platters*], USA (private issue by Edward J. Smith)

T 333 "Di quella pira: One Aria, 40 Tenors, 80 High C's"	75	62-01

Unique Opera Records, USA (private issue by Edward J. Smith)

UORC 110 (3) "Faust"	5010	72-04
UORC 115 (2) "Trovatore"	4101	72-05
UORC 121 (3) "Don Carlo"	5008	72-09
UORC 148 (2) "Tosca"	5911	73-03
UORC 176 (2) "Rigoletto"	4506	73-11
UORC 180 (2) "Bohème"	4804	73-12
UORC 197 "Potpourri No. 3"	5701d	74-03
UORC 207 (2) "Manon Lescaut"	4908	74-05
UORC 229 "Messa da Requiem"	4005	74-12
UORC 253 "Tosti Songs"	5802r	75-05
UORC 254 "Potpourri Four"	4006d(?),4301a	75-05
UORC 269 (2) "La Traviata"	3904	75-11
UORC 340 "Tenor Potpourri (1951-1952)"	5108a,b,d	77-05
UORC 350 "Jussi Bjoerling: Opera Recital (1937-1954)"	3707e,4004a1,4101c3-4, 4303a,c,4701b2,4801d, 4803d,4904c,d,5001c, 5101a,5102c,5108a,e, 5403c	77-09
UORC 376 "Jussi Bjoerling Recital (1955)"	5502a-r	77-12
UORC 377 "Jussi Bjoerling: Tenor"	4-6,9,21,26,34,35,63,64, 66,70B,79,93,94,104,149, 150,5201	77-12

United States Government (issued by various government offices) [16"/40 cm. transcription discs with matrix or master numbers only]

Department of State:		
17-3553 / QND6-MM-9414 "Concert Music Series, Program No. 8"	4603b,c,e	?
DS-1066 / D-45632 "Voice of America, Program No. 115"	4801c,4901a-c	?
DS-1401/02 "America Sings, Program No. 3/4"	4907a-c [on DS-1401]	?
DS-2334/45 "Voice of America, Program No. 32"	5008	?
DS-2451 "Voice of America, Concert Hall Program No. 70"	5006a,b,d,5101b,d	?

Office of War Information (Overseas Branch):

17-513 "Sweden Calls America, No. 13"	4303a-c	?

Valitut Palat, Finland (issued by Finnlevy)

VPS 1041/48* "Lauantain toivotut klassikot"	219f1 [on VPS 1047]	75

Victor, see: *RCA*

Victrola, see: *RCA* (series AVL, AVM, KR, KV, MCV, VIC, VICS, VL, VLS)

Vocal Record Collectors Society, USA (private issue by William Violi)

VRCS 1962 "Christmas 1962"	234	62-12

La ***Voce del Padrone***, see: *His Master's Voice* (series 3C, ASDQ, QALP)

Voce Records, USA

VOCE 88 "Great Singers: Previously Unpublished Recordings"	128-30	84-09
VOCE 95 "Jussi Bjoerling, Annalisa Bjoerling"	4801a-c,4904b,d-f,4906c,d, 5006b,c,5108a-c,5110c	85-09

La ***Voix de Son Maître***, see: *His Master's Voice* (includes series 2C, ASDF, FALP)

Voix Illustres, France (issued by EMI Pathé-Marconi)

50018 "Jussi Björling"	>*HMV* ALP 1620	63-11

La ***Voz de su Amo***, see: *His Master's Voice* (series 1J, 10C, LALP)

Westminster, Brazil

630501001/02* "Tosca"	>*RCA* LM 6052	78

World Record Club (EMI) [distributed to members only]

AUSTRALIA

3145 "Jussi Bjorling: Operatic Recital"	>*Cap.* G 7248	72-01
3199 "Jussi Bjorling: Songs and Ballads" (Retrospect Series)	>*Cap.* G 7247	74-02
3226 "Highlights from 'La Bohème'"	>*HMV* ALP 1921	?

NEW ZEALAND

CO 566 "Jussi Bjorling: Songs & Ballads"	>*Cap.* G 7247	75-02

AUSTRALIA

R 01933 "Highlights from 'La Bohème'"	>*HMV* ALP 1921	74-10
R 03176 "The Golden Age of Song, vol. 3"	>*HMV* OXLP 7586	c.77-07
R 03668 "The Golden Age of Song, vol. 4"	>*HMV* OXLP 7617	78-06
R 04467* "Great Operatic Duets"	>*HMV* ASD 2382	?78
R 05223/25 "The Art of Jussi Björling"	>*HMV* RLS 715	78-11
R 05957 "Songs from the World's Greatest Singers, vol. 1"	>*EMI* SCA 016 (?)	79
R 06137 "The Golden Age of Song, vol. 7"	>*HMV* OXLP 7639	c.79-08
R 06662* "Madama Butterfly: Highlights"	>*HMV* SXLP 30306	80-12
R 08064 "Songs from the World's Greatest Singers, vol. 2"	>*EMI* SCA 034 (?)	80-10
R 10033 "The World's Greatest Voices in Opera and Song"	>*RCA* SP 185	82-01
R 10132 "Great Tenors of the World"	>*HMV* HLM 7004	82-01
R 11409 "Jussi Björling: Popular Songs and Encores"	>*HMV* OXLP 7660	83-06
R 13509 (4) "The Golden Age of Song"	90,110A,139A	82
TE 241/42 "Pagliacci" [S.4: Operatic arias with Victoria de los Angeles]	204	c.78

NEW ZEALAND

WE 26451/53 "The Art of Jussi Bjorling"	>*HMV* RLS 715	79-11

Photo: Swedish Film AB

Jussi Björling in one of his films (Resan till dej [The journey...], 1953).

B. Compact Discs

***ABC** Records*, Australia (issued by Australian Broadcasting Corporation) - AAD

836 642-2 "Singers of Renown"	>33.*ABC* 836 642-1	88

Angel, see: *EMI*

*The **Arturo Toscanini Recordings Association***, USA (issued by Music & Arts Programs of America for The Arturo Toscanini Recordings Assn., Milan, Italy; pressed in Japan) - AAD

ATRA 240 "Toscanini: Historic Concert Performances from 1940: Requiem, Te Deum"	4005	86-08
CD 259 (2) "Arturo Toscanini: Missa Solemnis, Choral Fantasy"	4008	87-07

AS disc, Milan, Italy

AS 307 "Missa Solemnis"	4008	?91
AS 1110/11 "Il Trovatore (Hommage à Jussi Bjoerling)"	4101	91

Award, Australia (issued by Award International / Vogue Music)

AWCD 28600*? "Puccini: Favourite Arias"	?	?92
AWCD 28875* (2) "Requiem"	>33.*RCA* LD 6091	?92
AWCD 29115 "Jussi Björling: 'Nessun Dorma'" (The Greatest Tenors)	87,88,90,96,98,99,114B, 118,120,143,151B,223, 224	92

Axis, Australia (EMI) - AAD

7017672 "The Incomparable Jussi Bjorling"	87-90,95,96,98,99,112, 113,114B,118,121,139A, 143-45,147A,151B,153	c.92-04

***BBC** Records*, Great Britain (issued by BBC Enterprises)

BBC CD 715(*) "Opera, vol. 1" (The Vintage Collection)	>33.*BBC* REH 715	89

Bluebell, Sweden (issued by AB Frank Hedman, Ankdammsg. 13, S-17143 Solna) - ADD

ABCD 002 "Jussi Björling in Rigoletto, Il Trovatore: Royal Opera, Stockholm"	5701a-e,6001b2,c,d,e	87-02
ABCD 006 "Jussi Björling Live: Holland 1939, Norway 1954"	>33.*Bluebell* BELL 163	87-04
ABCD 013 "Jussi Björling, Hjördis Schymberg"	>33.*Bluebell* BELL 198	87-11
ABCD 016 "Jussi Björling: Rare and Alternative Recordings 1933-1949 + 'Juvenile Trio' 1920"	1-3,5-6,51A,52,53,70B, 80,106A,107A,110B, 114A,116,117,140B, 147B,151A,159A,160A, 161A,162B,163	88-07
ABCD 020* "Jussi Björling: The Atlanta Recital April 13, 1959"	5903a-s	89-02
ABCD 028 "Jussi Björling: Manon Lescaut, Cavalleria Rusticana, Pagliacci: Royal Opera, Stockholm"	5404a,b,5405a,b,5909a2, b,c,d2,e	90-05
ABCD 036 "Jussi Björling: Swedish Radio Concerts"	4502a-e,5204a,5706a, 5804a-g,5808a,c-e	90-11
ABCD 042 "Jussi Björling: Gröna Lund Recordings, vol. 1"	5803b,c,f,5905a-f,5907 a-f,h,6003a-c,e,f	92-03
ABCD 044 (2) "Rigoletto"	5701	92-06
ABCD 045 (2) "Il Trovatore"	6001	92-10
ABCD 050 "Jussi Björling in Song and Ballad"	125-29,131-36,4201a-c,5707a-e, 5801a-c	?93-05
ABCD 3001 "O Helga Natt"	234	91-10

Bongiovanni Records, Bologna, Italy (Series: Il mito dell'opera) - AAD

GB 1051-2 "34 'Di quella pira' da Il Trovatore di Giuseppe Verdi"	121	90
GB 1071-2 "23 'Vesti la giubba' da Pagliacci di Ruggero Leoncavallo"	144	c.92-12

Classics for Pleasure, Great Britain (EMI) - ADD

CD-CFP 9013* (CDB 7 62023 2) "Duets from Famous Operas"	>*HMV* ASD 2382	88-02

Club "99", USA - AAD

CL 511/12 "Tales of Offenbach"	110A	?90

CML (Classical Music Ltd.), Great Britain (issued by BMG Records)

CML 062/63* "Tosca, vol. 1/2" [Records sold separately]	>33.*RCA* LM 6052	?90

Conifer Records, Great Britain - AAD

TQ 305 "Golden Legacy of Legendary Singers" (The Compact Selection)	101	89

Decca - ADD

GERMANY

8.35828 ZT* (=421 608-2)
8.43585 ZG* (=417 686-2)
8.43907 ZG* (=421 018-2)
8.44333 ZS* (=421 316-2)

GREAT BRITAIN (some issues pressed in Germany)

417 686-2* "Puccini Weekend: Famous Arias" (or: "...Berühmte Arien") (Weekend Classics)	>33.*Decca* SPA 574	88-04
421 018-2* "Opera Weekend: Famous Arias" (Weekend Classics)	223	88-08
421 046-2* (2) "Die Fledermaus: Gala Performance" [JB guest in Act 2 gala only]	>33.*Decca* MET 201/03	87-07
421 316-2* "Jussi Björling" (Opera Gala)	>33.*Rich.* SR 33254	89-03
421 319-2* "Golden Operetta" (Opera Gala)	>33.*Decca* 414 466-1	89-06
421 608-2* (421 609/10-2) "Requiem" [+ Quattro pezzi sacri, cond. Mehta] (Jubilee)	242	89-02
421 869-2* "Great Tenor Arias" (Opera Gala)	>MC.*Decca* 417 534-4	90-06

FRANCE

425 878-2* (2) "Les grandes voix du siècle"	?	90

GREAT BRITAIN

425 985-2* "Cavalleria Rusticana" (Historic series)	220	91-05
433 064-2* "Your Hundred Best Opera Tunes I"	223	91-10
433 066-2* "Your Hundred Best Opera Tunes III"	221	91-10
433 069-2* "Your Hundred Best Opera Tunes VI"	222,224	91-10
433 636-2* "Puccini: Famous Arias" (Headline Classics)	>33.*Decca* SPA 574	92-03

433 755-2* "Operamania"	223	c.92-07
436 300-2* "Opera Gala!: An Introduction = Eine Einführung = Una Introduzione"	223	92-09
436 463-2* "Ten top Tenors"	221,224	c.93-01

EMI (*Classics*) - ADD
[Issues with "Angel" logo but only EMI text listed here. Cf. also *Axis, Classics for Pleasure*, *HMV*.]

GERMANY

1 59909 2* "Die grosse Tenor-Star-Parade"	>33.*Elec*. 1C 049-30659	?89

JAPAN

CC 30 3583/84 "La Bohème"	>33.*RCA* LM 6042	?

GREAT BRITAIN

CDC 7 49503 2 "Pagliacci"	204	89-06

FRANCE

CDC 7 54016 2 "Tenorissimo"	>33.*HMV* 7 54016 1	90

SWEDEN

CDC 7 61075 2 "Jussi Björling: På Svenska = The Swedish Recordings"	18-20,23-24,34-35,51B, 81-85,91-92,106B,107B, 108,110A,111,205-08	88-12

USA

CDCB 47235 (=CDS 7 47235 8)

GREAT BRITAIN (Series: Références; [sold in USA as] Great Recordings of the Century)

CDH 7 61053 2 "Jussi Björling: Airs d' opéras = Opera Arias = Opernarien" (version 1 = matrix AR 1:x:x)	87,88,90,96,98,99, 114B,118-20,142-44,148, 152,153,157,164	88-03
(version 2 = matrix AR 3:x:x)	(=version 1 except 139A instead of 164)	c.88-11
CDH 7 64707 2 "Jussi Björling: Opera Arias & Songs = Airs d'Opéras et mélodies = Opernarien & Gesänge, vol. 2" [Back: "Arias, Duets & Songs, vol. 2"]	51A,89,95,102,110A,112-13, 115,121-22,124,140A,141,145, 146,147A,151B,154-56,161B, 162,164	93-03

USA

CDHG 69741 (=CHS 7 69741 2)
CDMB 63634* (=CMS 7 63634 2)

GREAT BRITAIN

CDS 7 47235 8 (7 47235/36 2) (USA: CDCB 47235) (2) "La Bohème"	>33.*RCA* LM 6042	86-10
CDZ 7 62520 2* "Puccini: Arias and Duets = Arien und Duette = Airs et Duos" (Laser series)	241c4	88-07
CHS 7 69741 2 (CDH 7 69742/48 2) "The Record of Singing, vol. 4: From 1939 to the End of the 78 Era"	151B [on 7 69746 2]	91-08

SWEDEN (made in The Netherlands)

CMCD 6061 "Sweden"	91	92

GREAT BRITAIN

CMS 7 63634 2* (7 63635/36 2) (USA: CDMB 63634) "Madama Butterfly"	>*HMV* ALP 1795/97	90-10

Eva Records, Sweden

354 391 (2) "Absolute Opera"	>33.*Eva* 304 391	c.91-11

Evasound Music, Australia (issued by Laser Records, Sydney)

EMD 021 "The World's Greatest Voices, vol. 1"	159B	91

Gala, Portugal (issued by Movieplay S.A.)

GL 315*p "Jussi Björling: His Last Performances 1959-1960"	6,233-36,5903a,g,n,r,s, 5909c,d2,5912d1,e2, 6001c,6004c	92

HMV Classics, Great Britain (EMI)

7 67630 2* "Puccini: Arias, Duets & Choruses" (The HMV Collection. 26)	>*EMI* CDZ 7 62520 2	92

K-West, Great Britain (issued by Kenwest Records Ltd, London)

KNEWCD 601* "A Night at the Opera, vol. 1"	>33.*K-West* KNEWLP 601	88
KNEWCD 602* "A Night at the Opera, vol. 2"	>33.*K-West* KNEWLP 602	88

Laser Records, Sydney, Australia (pressed in USA)

LAS 4777 (6) "The Great Tenors Collection"	90,98,175 [on disc 6]	?

Legato Classics, USA (distributed by Lyric Distribution Inc., P.O. Box 235, Roslyn Heights, NY 11577; some issues pressed in Brazil. Cf. also *Standing Room Only*) - AAD

BIM 708-2 (2) "Jussi Bjoerling: The Swedish Caruso: Live Performances 1937-1960" (Biographies in Music)		?90-03
(record 1)	3708a-d,3902e,3903b, 4001a1,4002b1,d,4502c-e, 4801a-c,4803b,c, 4901c, 4907c,5006d	
(record 2)	4906d,5002a,5010d,5108a, c,5403c,5501i,j,l,5701a, c,d,5802g,h,q,r,5909d, 6004b,c	
BIM 712-1 "Eleanor Steber" (Biographies in Music)	4602b,d	?92
LCD 103-1 "Jussi Björling: Live Recordings 1929-1960"	9,34,3902a-f,4303c, 5110b,5202b,e,5403a,b, 5404b2,5909a,c2,d2, 6001c3-4	87
LCD 154-1 "Un Ballo in Maschera (Abridged)"	5002a-e	90
LCD 155-1 "Pagliacci"	3702a-c1,5405	92
LCD 164-1 "Cavalleria Rusticana"	5404	92

Legendary Recordings, USA

LR-CD 1004 "Tales of Offenbach"	110A	88-09

London - ADD

USA

417 686-2* "Puccini Weekend: Famous Arias" (Weekend Classics)	>33.*Decca* SPA 574	88-04
421 018-2* "Opera Weekend: Famous Arias" (Weekend Classics)	>*Decca* 421 018-2	89-01
421 046-2* "Die Fledermaus: Gala Performance" [JB guest in act 2 gala only]	>33.*Decca* MET 201/03	87-11
421 608-2* (2) "Requiem" [+ Quattro Pezzi Sacri, cond. Mehta] (Jubilee)	>*Decca* 421 608-2	89-04
421 869-2* "Great Tenor Arias" (Opera Gala)	>MC.*Decca* 417 534-4	a.92

425 985-2* "Cavalleria Rusticana" (Historic series)	>*Decca* 425 985-2	91-08

JAPAN

230E 1211/12* "Requiem"	>*Decca* 421 608-2	?
POCL 2278/79* "Die Fledermaus: Gala Performance" [JB guest in act 2 gala only]	>33.*Decca* MET 201/03	?
POCL 2449* "Jussi Björling"	>33.*Rich.* SR 33254	?

Melodram, Milan, Italy (pressed in Italy, Switzerland or Japan) - AAD / ADD

CD 27502 [on discs: MEL 27502] (2) "Manon Lescaut" (Connaisseur)	5602	90
CDM 27079 [on discs: MEL 27079] (2) "Rigoletto [+ Bidù Sayão canta Manon]"	4506	90
MEL 38006 (3) "Arturo Toscanini: Messa da Requiem, Missa Solemnis"	>33.*Melodram* 006	88-05

***Memoir** Classics* - AAD

GREAT BRITAIN (issued by Memoir Records, P.O. Box 66, Pinner, Middx HA5 2SA)

CDMCS 111 "Presenting Memoir Classics"	82	92

Series: Great Voices of the Century

CDMOIR 405 "Great Tenors"	90	c.91-01
CDMOIR 409 "Three Tenors: Björling, Gigli, Tauber"	82,98,101,102,107B, 119	c.91-12
CDMOIR 411 "Great Voices of the Century Sing Sacred Songs and Arias"	115	c.91-12
CDMOIR 412 "Great Voices of the Century Sing Puccini"	96	92

BRAZIL

RGE 342.8010 "Great Tenors"	>*Memoir* CDMOIR 405	?

MET, USA (issued by The Metropolitan Opera Guild, 70 Lincoln Center Plaza, New York, NY 10023-6593) - ADD

MET 110CD "Jussi Bjoerling at the Met" (Great Artists at the Met)	>33.*MET* 110	87-09
MET 207CD "Sunday Night Concert at the Met"	95	87-10
MET 210CD (2) "Songs Our Mothers Taught Us"	188 [on disc 1]	90-10

MET 501CD (2) "La Bohème" (Great Operas at the Met)	173,211a [on disc 2]	88-03
MET 509CD (2) "Il Trovatore" (Great Operas at the Met)	182f3	90-07
MET 512CD (2) "Cavalleria/Pagliacci" (Great Operas at the Met)	203b [on disc 1]	91-07
MET 516CD* (2) "Tosca" (Great Operas at the Met)	219a	92-08

Music & Arts Programs of America, P.O. Box 771, Berkeley, CA 94701, USA (cf. also *Arturo Toscanini Recordings Assn.*)

CD 636 (2) "Rigoletto"	4506	90
CD 701 (2) "Faust"	5912	92

Myto Records, Via Martiri Oscuri 27, I-20125 Milan, Italy

1MCD 912.39*p "Jussi Björling in Concert"	3902a,4906b-d,5903a-s	91
2MCD 89004 (2) "Roméo et Juliette [+ J.Björling canta arie]"	3902a,c,e,f,4701	89
2MCD 90317 (2) "Un Ballo in Maschera [+ J.Björling canta Verdi]"	3902a,4007,4101b2-5,c	90
2MCD 906.33 (2) "Faust"	5912	90
2MCD 911.35 (2) "Don Carlo"	5008	91
2MCD 916.47 (2) "La Bohème [+ J.Björling in Tosca, Met 1959]"	4804,5911a-d	91
2MCD 922.58 (2) "Faust"	5010	92-04
2MCD 931.73 (2) "Manon Lescaut [+ J. Björling in Cavalleria Rusticana, New York 1959, and Manon Lescaut, Stockholm 1959]"	4908,5909c,d2,5910a-c	93-01

Nickson Records, Rochester, NY, USA (private issue by N. Nickson) - AAD

NN 1003 "Dimitri Mitropoulos: Document Three"	147B	90

Nimbus Records, Wyastone Leys, Monmouth, Great Britain (Series: Prima Voce) - ADD

NI 7812 "Great Singers, vol. 2: 1903-1939"	124	c.90-07
NI 7835 "Björling [vol. 1]: The First Ten Years"	16,50,51B,71-78,82,83, 85,87,88,95,98,112, 114B,115,120-21	92-06

NI 7842 "Björling, vol. 2"	81,89,90,96,99,102,106B, 107B,110A,113,118-19, 123-27,131,133-35,139A,140A	93-01

OASI Recordings, P.O. Box 955, East Northport, NY 11731, USA

OASI 7003-2 (2) "Il Trovatore"	6001	c.90-11
OASI 7006 "Jussi Bjoerling (Tenor) (1911-1960) in Arias, Songs, & Duets"	110B,116,151A,172B, 4502b,4504b,4506c, 4702b,4801a-c,5003f, 5004c,5101c,5110c, 5111b,5302b,5406a, 5704b,5802j,q,r	91

Opera Now, London, Great Britain

[Record without number, presented with the Jan. 1991 issue of this magazine to illustrate Luciano Pavarotti's article "My Favourite Tenors"]	143	91-01

Operaviva, Italy (issued by Armando Curcio Editore, Rome)

OPV 017 "Manon Lescaut (selezione)"	5602a-e	89

Palette, Japan (issued by Crown Records)

PAL 3004/06 "Arturo Toscanini: Requiem, Missa Solemnis"	>33.*Melodram* 006	?

Parlophone, Great Britain (EMI)

CDP 7 91916 2 (CDPCS 73331) "Scandal: Music from the Motion Picture"	153	89

Pro Arte, USA (issued by Fanfare) - AAD

CDD 489 "20 Legendary Tenors" (The Original Recordings)	87	90

***RCA** (Victor)* (issued by RCA/Ariola, later BMG Music) - ADD

USA

4514-2-RG* (2) "Tosca" (The Victor Opera Series)	>33.*RCA* LM 6052	87-09
5932-2-RC* "Turandot" (Red Seal)	>33.*RCA* LM 6149	87-02
5934-2-RC*p "Jussi Bjoerling: Operatic Arias (Red Seal)	176,180,181,203a,209b2, 210a1,212c,d,213,215, 216B,217,218,219a2-3, f1,f4,240b2,d1	87-02
6510-2-RG "Cavalleria Rusticana" (The Victor Opera Series)	>MC.*RCA* RK 6046	87-09
6587-2-RC* "Aria"	240d1	87-10
6643-2-RG (2) "Il Trovatore" (The RCA Victor Opera Series)	>33.*RCA* LM 6008	88-09
6652-2-RG (3) "Aida" (The RCA Victor Opera Series)	>33.*RCA* LM 6122	88-03
7799-2-RG*p "The Pearl Fishers (= Les pêcheurs de perles = Die Perlenfischer): Jussi Bjoerling with..." (The RCA Victor Vocal Series)	171,172A,173-75,209d, 210g,219b3c,240b2-4	88-08
60172-2-RG (2) "Rigoletto" (Gold Seal: RCA Victor Opera Series)	>33.*RCA* LM 6051	90-03
60191-2-RG "Il Trovatore: Highlights..." (Gold Seal: RCA Victor Opera Series)	182c,d3-5,e,f2-3	90-06
60192-2-RG* "Tosca: Highlights..." (Gold Seal: RCA Victor Opera Series)	219a,b3-5,d,e,f	90-06
60201-2-RG "Aida: Highlights..." (Gold Seal: RCA Victor Opera Series)	210a1,e1,f,g	89-10
60520-2-RG "Jussi Bjoerling at Carnegie Hall" (Gold Seal: RCA Victor Vocal Series)	>*RCA* GD 60520	91-04
60573-2-RG (2) "Manon Lescaut" (Gold Seal: RCA Victor Opera Series)	>33.*RCA* LM 6116	90-11
60841-2-RG* "Opera Goes to the Movies" (60+)	240d1	91-09
09026-60935-2* "TV Classics" (60+)	240d1	92-05
09026-61440-2 "Opera's Greatest Moments"	175	92-09

GERMANY

BD 86587* "Aria"	>*RCA* 6587-2-RC	c.87-10
GD 60172 (2) "Rigoletto" (Gold Seal: RCA Victor Opera Series)	>33.*RCA* LM 6051	90-01
GD 60191 "Il Trovatore: Highlights = Querschnitt = Extraits = Brani scelti" (Gold Seal: RCA Victor Opera Series)	>*RCA* 60191-2-RG	90-09
GD 60192* "Tosca: Highlights = ..." (Gold Seal: RCA Victor Opera Series)	>*RCA* 60192-2-RG	90-06
GD 60201 "Aida: Highlights = ..." (Gold	>*RCA* 60201-2-RG	89-11

Seal: RCA Victor Opera Series)		
GD 60520 "Jussi Bjoerling at Carnegie Hall" (Gold Seal: RCA Victor Vocal Series)	5802a-u	90-10
GD 60573 (2) "Manon Lescaut" (Gold Seal: RCA Victor Opera Series)	>33.*RCA* LM 6116	90-10
GD 60841* "Opera Goes to the Movies" (60+)	>*RCA* 60841-2-RG	92
GD 60935* "TV Classics" (60+)	>*RCA* 09026-60935-2	92
GD 82059* "Opera's Greatest Hits"	?	?
GD 84514* (2) "Tosca" (The Victor Opera Series)	>33.*RCA* LM 6052	87-10
GD 85277*[p] "Jussi Bjoerling: Operatic Arias" (Gold Seal)	>*RCA* 5934-2-RC	89-03
GD 86510 "Cavalleria Rusticana" (The Victor Opera Series)	>MC.*RCA* RK 6046	87-10
GD 86643 (2) "Il Trovatore" (The RCA Victor Opera Series)	>33.*RCA* LM 6008	88-05
GD 86652 (3) "Aida" (The RCA Victor Opera Series)	>33.*RCA* LM 6122	88-05
GD 87799*[p] "Jussi Bjoerling: The Pearl Fishers Duet (= Les Pêcheurs de perles, duo), plus Duets and Scenes by Puccini and Verdi" (The RCA Victor Vocal Series)	>*RCA* 7799-2-RG	88-09

GREAT BRITAIN (pressed in Germany)

GD 89788* "Puccini's Greatest Hits"	>MC.*RCA* GK 89788	90

USA

RCD2-5932 (=5932-2-RC)

GREAT BRITAIN (Red Seal, single record) [see note]

RD 49524 "Jussi Bjoerling with Robert Merrill: The Pearl Fishers Duet"	172A,173-75	88-12

GERMANY (Red Seal)

RD 85932* (2) "Turandot"	>33.*RCA* LM 6149	87-05
RD 85934*[p] "Jussi Bjoerling: Operatic Arias"	>*RCA* 5934-2-RC	87

Rodolphe Productions, France (Series: Opera Viva)

RPV 32690/91 "Roméo et Juliette"	4701	a.91-02
RPV 32702/03 "Faust"	5912	91

*Selezione dal **Reader's Digest***, Italy

RDCD 101*p (6) "13 Perle del Melodramma: Le più grandi voci della Lirica"	>33.*Sel.Read.Dig.* RDS 13D	?

Standing Room Only, USA (issued by Legato Classics / Lyric Distribution) - ADD

SRO 832-2 (2) "La Traviata"	3904	91

***Swedish Society** Discofil*, Sweden (issued by Grammofon AB Electra, Solna; later by Prophone Music, Box 210, S-126 02 Hägersten) - ADD

SCD 1010*p "Jussi Björling: Songs in Swedish"	214[mono],227-31 [electr. stereo],232-34[mono], 235-39[stereo]	87-05

Symphony, The Netherlands (issued by Disky Communications, Hoorn)

SYCD 6159* "Tosca: Highlights" (The Grand Opera Collection)	>*RCA* 60192-2-RG	92

Testament, Great Britain - ADD

SBT 1005 "Ten Top Tenors"	89,95	91

Tring (issued by Tring International PLC; made in EEC)

TFP 013*p (VAR 059/62) "Opera: Favourite Highlights"		91
VAR 059 "The Great Tenors"	87,175	
VAR 060 "Puccini Highlights"	171a1-2,210g1-2,219b3-4	
VAR 061 "Verdi Highlights"	172A,174,219c	
VAR 062 "Bizet - Gounod - Rossini"	175	

Verona, Luxembourg (issued by Compact Music GmbH; pressed in Belgium or Great Britain) - AAD

2700 "Opera and Other Vocal Works: Catalogue CD Sampler"	3902b	90
27022 "Jussi Björling: Recital [vol. 1]"	3902a,e,f,4801a,5101a, 5110b-e[e abridged], 5202b-e	?89

27068 "Jussi Björling: Recital, vol. 2"	3902b,c,4702a,5403a-f, h,6001c3-4	90
28030/31*p "Jussi Björling Recital: Opera Arias and Songs"		c.92-11
(28030)	162,4701b2,e,5404a,b, 5602a2,a4-5,5912d1,h	
(28031)	227-29,231,4906d,5108a, 5602b,c1,d2,5903b-f,h-j, l,m,o-q	
28034/35 "Famous Duets: Opera Arias and Scenes"	5912e2 [on 28034]	c.92-11

Victorie Music, France

290 222 "Londres: Ses grands interprètes: Covent Garden"	119	90

Voce Records, USA - AAD

VOCE 119CD "Great Duets"	5108d,e	88-10
VOCE 120CD "Noël: Christmas Greetings from..."	4606	89-12

C. Audio Tapes

1. Open Reel

Speed is 7 1/2 ips. / 19 cm./sec. if not otherwise indicated.

Angel (EMI), USA (issued by Capitol)

L 35821* "Highlights from 'Madama Butterfly'"	>33.*Cap.* G 7233	a.69-02
ZC 3604* (2) "Madama Butterfly"	>33.*HMV* ALP 1795/97	a.69-02
ZS 35821* "Highlights from 'Madama Butterfly'"	>33.*Cap.* G 7233	

His Master's Voice [=*HMV*] (EMI), Great Britain

HTA 9/10 "Il Trovatore"	>33.*RCA* LM 6008	55-02
HTA 34/35 "La Bohème"	>33.*RCA* LM 6042	57-11

London, USA

K 490250* "Cavalleria Rusticana. A Jussi Bjoerling Recital"	>33.*RCA* LM 6059	74-07
K 90215* "Requiem Mass"	>33.*RCA* LD 6091	75-06
L 90184* "Ten Famous Tenors, Ten Famous Arias"	>33.*London* OS 26207	73-09
R 90030* (2) "Die Fledermaus" [JB guest in act 2 gala only]	>33.*Decca* MET 201/03	73-10
R 490219* (2) "San Francisco Opera Gala"	>33.*London* OSA 1441	74-07
SRO 33254-A* "The Voice of Jussi Bjoerling" (Treasury)	>33.*Rich.* SR 33254	78-09

RCA (Victor)

USA (Red Seal)

DC 34 "Highlights from 'Il Trovatore'"	>33.*RCA* LM 1827	57-04
DC 45/46 "La Bohème"	>33.*RCA* LM 6042	57-03
EC 42 "Aida, act 3-4"	210: last part	57-03
FC 41 "Aida, act 1-2"	210: first part	57-03
FTC 2039* "Opera for People Who Hate Opera"	>33.*RCA* LM 2391	60-12
FTC 2065* "Turandot: Highlights"	>33.*RCA* LM 2539	61-09
FTC 7001* "Requiem Mass"	>33.*RCA* LD 6091	62-03
FTC 8001* (2) "Turandot"	>33.*RCA* LM 6149	61-01

MT 101 (=DC 45/46)
MT 103 (=EC 42 + FC 41)

USA (Red Seal); 3 3/4 ips. / 9.5 cm./sec.		
TR3-5005* "Great Moments from Grand Opera [vol. 1]"	219a3,221	67-03
TR3-5035 "The Immortal Jussi Bjoerling: Operatic Scenes" (Collector's Series)	171,172B,173-75,181, 182a,d1-3,d5,203a, 209b2,e,f2-4,210a1,e3, 212a2,c,d,e,213,215,216B, 217-18,219f1	68-09
TR3-5042* "Great Moments from Grand Opera, vol. 2"	225	69-03

2. Cassette

ABC Records, Australia (issued by Australian Broadcasting Corporation)

836 642-4 "John Cargher's Historic Singers of Renown"	96	88

Ace of Diamonds, Great Britain (issued by Decca)

K2C 7* (2) "Grand Opera Festival"	>33.*Ace Diam.* GOSB 636/38	75-09

Angel (EMI), USA (issued by Capitol)

4X3S 3604* (3) "Madama Butterfly"	>33.*HMV* ALP 1795/97	77-05
4XS 35821* "Madama Butterfly: Excerpts"	>33.*Angel* 35821	71-04

BBC Records, Great Britain (issued by BBC Enterprises)

BBC ZCF 715(*) "Opera, vol. 1" (The Vintage Collection)	>33.*BBC* REH 715	89

Bluebell, Sweden (issued by AB Frank Hedman, Solna)

CELL 3001 "O Helga Natt"	>CD.*Bluebell* ABCD 3001	91-10

Classics for Pleasure, Great Britain (EMI)

CFP 41 4498 4* "Duets from Famous Operas"	>33.*HMV* ASD 2382	86-02
CFPD 41 4446 5* (2) "Madama Butterfly"	>33.*HMV* ALP 1795/97	85-06

Columbia (EMI)

GERMANY (issued by EMI Electrola)

1C 228-30174 "Holiday in Scandinavia"	>33.*Col.* 1C 052-30174	a.76

SWEDEN

4E 246-35326M "Värmland"	>33.*Col.* 4E 056-35326M	76-08
TC-SPPH 036 [Special issue for Tipstjänst AB (The Swedish Football Pools Service)]	107B	82-02
TC-SPPH 061(*) "Winds of Sweden" [Special issue for Johnson & Samco Chartering AB]	>33.*Col.* SPPH 061	82-04

Conifer Records, Great Britain

TQC 305 "Golden Legacy of Legendary Singers" (The Compact Selection)	>CD.*Conifer* TQ 305	89

Decca

GERMANY

4.35107 MH* (3) "Die Fledermaus" [JB guest in act 2 gala only]	>33.*Decca* MET 201/03	c.77
4.43346 OG* (=417 173-4)		
4.43541 OG* (=417 534-4)		
4.43585 AD* (=417 686-4)		

GREAT BRITAIN

410 217-4* "Puccini: Arias & Duets" [90 min.]	222	83-12
414 466-4* "Golden Operetta" (Jubilee)	>33.*Decca* 414 466-1	85-10
417 173-4* "Puccini: Great Arias = Airs célèbres = Grosse Arien" (Opera Gala)	222	86-04
417 534-4* "Great Tenor Arias = Grands airs de ténor = Grosse Tenorarien" (Opera Gala)	223,224	87-03
417 686-4* "Puccini Weekend: Famous Arias..." (Weekend Classics)	>33.*Decca* SPA 574	87-05

421 018-4* "Opera Weekend: Famous Arias" (Weekend Classics)	>CD.*Decca* 421 018-2	87-10
421 316-4* "Jussi Björling" (Opera Gala)	>33.*Rich.* SR 33254	89-03

ITALY (issued by Fabbri Editore, Rome; made in The Netherlands)

424 040-4* "Jussi Björling in 'Cavalleria Rusticana'" (Le interpretazioni indimenticabili, vol. 3) [Special issue included with the magazine Lirica No. 73]	220a,b,cd	89-02

GREAT BRITAIN

433 064-4* "Your Hundred Best Opera Tunes I"	>CD.*Decca* 433 064-2	91-10
433 066-4* "Your Hundred Best Opera Tunes III"	>CD.*Decca* 433 066-2	91-10
433 069-4* "Your Hundred Best Opera Tunes VI"	>CD.*Decca* 433 069-2	91-10
433 636-4* "Puccini: Famous Arias" (Headline Classics)	>33.*Decca* SPA 574	92-03
436 300-4* "Opera Gala! An Introduction..."	>CD.*Decca* 436 300-2	92-09
436 463-4* "Ten top Tenors"	>CD.*Decca* 436 463-2	c.93-01
K247K 32* (2) "Die Fledermaus: Gala Performance" [JB guest in act 2 only]	>33.*Decca* MET 201/03	82-11
KCSP 574* "One Fine Day"	>33.*Decca* SPA 574	80
KDJBC 2003* (2) "Requiem" (Jubilee)	>33.*RCA* LD 6091	83-09
KDPC 533/34* "Favourite Composers: Puccini"	>33.*Decca* DPA 533/34	76-06
KGRC 4* "Jussi Björling" (Grandi Voci)	>33.*Rich.* SR 33254	82-10

AUSTRALIA

TC-DTS 533/34* "Private Collection: Puccini"	>33.*Decca* DPA 533/34	77

Demand Performance Cassettes, Glendale, USA

DPC 504 "Jussi Bjoerling: The Tenor of Our Times"	4904a,4906a,b,d,5802c, d,g,h,i	85

Electrola, Germany (EMI)

1C 225-30659* "Die grosse Tenor-Star-Parade"	>33.*Elec.* 1C 049-30659	76-10
1C 237-03071* "Madame Butterfly: Grosser Querschnitt"	>33.*Elec.* 1C 037-03071	77-04

EMI

SWEDEN (Series: Music from Sweden)

1362734 "A Remembrance of Sweden"	>33.*Odeon* PMCS 303	87-06
1362744 "Värmland"	>33.*Col.* 4E 056-35326M	87-06
1362764 "A Musical Journey"	>33.*Odeon* PMES 560	87-06
1362774 "The Sounds of Sweden"	>33.*Odeon* 7C 158-35912/13	87-06

GERMANY

1 59909 4* "Die grosse Tenor-Star-Parade"	>33.*Elec.* 1C 049-30659	?89

SOUTH AFRICA

L4CEY 247 "Nostalgic Moments"	>33.*EMI* SCA 016	82-08
L4EMCJ 6001 (2) "25 Stars That Shine Forever"	>33.*EMI* EMCJ 6001	73-11
L4EMGJ 6004 (2) "20 Magnificent Opera Arias"	>33.*EMI* EMGJ 6004	74-04
L4EMGJ 6006 (2) "25 Songs That Live Forever"	>33.*EMI* EMGJ 6006	74-08

GREAT BRITAIN

LZ 7 62520 4* "Puccini: Arias and Duets..." (Laser series)	>CD.*EMI* CDZ 7 62520 2	88
TC-NTS 208 "Nostalgic Memories"	>33.*EMI* SCA 016	80

AUSTRALIA

TC-SCA 016 "Nostalgic Memories"	>33.*EMI* SCA 016	?77-06

Emidisc, Sweden (EMI)

4E 278-51009M "Sweden!"	>33.*Odeon* 4E 154-34398/99M	72-11

***ERR** Historical Operatic Treasures*, USA (private issue by Ed Rosen)

ERRC 121 "Jussi Bjoerling: Live Concerts 1936-1941"	>33.*ERR* 121-1	74-09

Eva Records, Sweden

504 391 (2) "Absolute Opera"	>33.*Eva* 304 391	c.91-11

Evasound *Music*, Australia (issued by Laser Records, Sydney)

EMC 021 "The World's Greatest Voices, vol. 1"	>CD.*Evasound* EMD 021	91

Fame, South Africa (EMI)

L4FAME 13 "25 Stars That Shine Forever, vol. 1"	>33.*Fame* 13	83-07
L4FAME 19 "20 Magnificent Opera Arias, vol. 1"	>33.*Fame* 19	83-07
L4FAME 20 "20 Magnificent Opera Arias, vol. 2"	>33.*Fame* 20	83-07
L4FAME 22 "25 Songs That Live Forever, vol. 2"	>33.*Fame* 22	83-07

Franklin Mint *Record Society*, USA (limited edition for subscribers only)

13/14* "Requiem"	>33.*RCA* LD 6091	78-10

His Master's Voice [=*HMV*] (EMI) [includes translations of the label in Spain & Italy]

SWEDEN

1031404(*) "La Bohème [Excerpts]" (Operaklassiker)	>33.*HMV* ESD 7023	85-01

FRANCE (*"La Voix de son Maître"*)

7540164 "Tenorissimo"	>33.*HMV* 7540161	90

FINLAND

7691754 "Jussi Björling: Suosituimmat aariat ja laulut..." (Toiveklassikot)	>33.*HMV* 7691751	87-03

GREAT BRITAIN

0C 285-78000* (=TC-ASD 4076 in TC-SLS 5233)
0C 543-00126/27(*) (=TC-SLS 896)
1E 245-00372* (=TC-ASD 2382)

SPAIN (*"La Voz de su Amo"*; issued by EMI-Odeon)

1J 245-00126/27(*) "La Bohème"	>33.*RCA* LM 6042	75-10

SWEDEN

4E 278-51007M "Jussi Björling: 28 av de mest älskade ariorna och sångerna [vol. 1]"	>33.*HMV* 4E 153-34532/33M	72-11

7C 237-00947M "Önskeartisten 2: Jussi Björling, vol. 1"	>33.*Dacapo* 1C 177-00947M	78-11
7C 237-00948M "Önskeartisten 2: Jussi Björling, vol. 2"	>33.*Dacapo* 1C 177-00948M	78-11
7C 253-35445/46M (1) "Jussi Björling: 28 av de mest älskade ariorna och sångerna, vol. 2"	>33.*HMV* 7C 153-35455/46M	77-12
7C 261-35731M "De 20 mest önskade med Jussi Björling"	>33.*HMV* 7C 061-35731M	80-10
7C 261-35822 "Operans svenska världsartister" (Önskeklassiker)	>33.*HMV* SPPH 030	81-12

ITALY ("*La Voce del Padrone*")

CV 5003 "I grandi tenori del secolo"	>33.*HMV* QALP 10402	a.75-06

SOUTH AFRICA

L4HLM 7004 "Great Tenors of the World"	>33.*HMV* HLM 7004	81-06
L4HLM 7038 "Jussi Björling: Arias & Songs..."	>33.*HMV* HQM 1190	81-06

GREAT BRITAIN

TC-ASD 2382* "Great Operatic Duets"	>33.*HMV* ASD 2382	a.74-08
TC-ASD 4076* (in TC-SLS 5233)		
TC-ESD 7023(*) "La Bohème" (HMV Greensleeve Opera Highlights Series)	>33.*HMV* ESD 7023	77-08
TC-HLM 7004 "Great Tenors of the World"	>33.*HMV* HLM 7004	79-05

AUSTRALIA

TC-OXCP 7660 "Jussi Björling: Popular Songs and Encores"	>33.*HMV* OXLP 7660	?82-08

GREAT BRITAIN

TC-SLS 896(*) (2) "La Bohème"	>33.*RCA* LM 6042	75-10
TC-SLS 5128* (3) "Madama Butterfly"	>33.*HMV* ALP 1795/97	78-09
TC-SLS 5233* (TC-ASD 4076/78) "The Art of Victoria de los Angeles"	>33.*HMV* SLS 5233	82-03

AUSTRALIA & NEW ZEALAND

TC-SMP 0046* "Highlights from 'Madama Butterfly'" (Masterpiece II)	>33.*HMV* SXLP 30306	81-12

GREAT BRITAIN

TC-SXLP 30306* "Madama Butterfly" (HMV Concert Classics Opera Highlights)	>33.*HMV* SXLP 30306	79-09
TC2-MOM 120* "Italian Operatic Favourites" (Miles of Music)	241c4	83

K-West, Great Britain (issued by Kenwest Records, London)

KNEWMC 601* "A Night at the Opera, vol. 1"	>33.*K-West* KNEWLP 601	88
KNEWMC 602* "A Night at the Opera, vol. 2"	>33.*K-West* KNEWLP 602	88

Laser Records, Sydney, Australia

LASC 4777 (6) "The Great Tenors Collection"	>CD.*Laser* LAS 4777	?

London

USA		
414 085-4* "The Great Voice of Jussi Björling" (Jubilee)	>33.*Rich.* SR 33254	84-10
414 356-4* "Ten Famous Tenors, Ten Famous Arias" (Jubilee)	>33.*London* OS 26207	?
417 825-4* (2) "Requiem"	>33.*RCA* LD 6091	88
D 31215* (2) "Requiem"	>33.*RCA* LD 6091	73-02
D 31250* (2) "Cavalleria Rusticana. A Jussi Bjoerling Operatic Recital"	>33.*RCA* LM 6059	74-08
USA, CANADA		
JLS 42004* (2) "Requiem" (Jubilee)	>33.*RCA* LD 6091	82-04
USA		
M 31184* "Ten Famous Tenors, Ten Famous Arias"	>33.*London* OS 26207	72-02
OSA5 1319* (2) "Die Fledermaus" [JB guest in act 2 gala only]	>33.*Decca* MET 201/03	78-02
P 31219* (3) "San Francisco Opera Gala"	>33.*London* OSA 1441	73-04

Marcato, Germany (issued by ECI Book Club)

33332-8 (33333/35) "Tenöre des Jahrhunderts"	>33.*Marcato* 34399-6	78

Memoir Classics, Great Britain (Series: Great Voices of the Century)

CMOIR 405 "Great Tenors"	>CD.*Memoir* CDMOIR 405	c.91-01
CMOIR 409 "Three Tenors: Björling, Gigli, Tauber"	>CD.*Memoir* CDMOIR 409	c.91-12

CMOIR 411 "Great Voices of the Century Sing Sacred Songs and Arias"	>CD.*Memoir* CDMOIR 411	c.91-12
CMOIR 412 "Great Voices of the Century Sing Puccini"	>CD.*Memoir* CDMOIR 412	92

MET, USA (issued by the Metropolitan Opera Guild; made by RCA) [For series titles, see corresponding 33 rpm./CD issues]

MET 50C (3) "50 Years of Guild Performances at the Met"	>33.*MET* 50	85-10
MET 110C "Jussi Bjoerling at the Met"	>33.*MET* 110	81-11
MET 207C (2) "Sunday Night Concert at the Met"	>CD.*MET* 207CD	87-12
MET 210C (2) "Songs Our Mothers Taught Us"	>CD.*MET* 210CD	90-10
MET 404C (2) "The Johnson Years: 1935-1950"	>33.*MET* 404	84-04
MET 405C (2) "The Bing Years I: 1950-1961"	>33.*MET* 405	85-04
MET 501C (2) "La Bohème"	>CD.*MET* 501CD	88-05
MET 509C (2) "Il Trovatore"	>CD.*MET* 509CD	90-07
MET 512C (2) "Cavalleria / Pagliacci"	>CD.*MET* 512CD	91-07
MET 516C* (2) "Tosca"	>CD.*MET* 516CD	92-08

Nimbus Records, Monmouth, Great Britain (Series: Prima Voce)

NC 7812 "Great Singers, vol. 2: 1903-1939"	>CD.*Nimbus* NI 7812	?90-07
NC 7835 "Björling: The First Ten Years"	>CD.*Nimbus* NI 7835	92-06

Odeon (EMI)

SWEDEN

1359474 "Odeonkavalkaden 1936-1945, del 4"	>33.*Odeon* 7C 062-35947M	83-11
4E 254-34402 "Sweden in Music"	>33.*Odeon* PMES 560	71-04
4E 254-34403M "A Remembrance of Sweden"	>33.*Odeon* PMCS 303	71-04
4E 278-51009M [see: *Emidisc*]		
7C 254-34205M "A Remembrance of Sweden"	>33.*Odeon* PMCS 303	76-10
7C 254-34206 "Sweden in Music"	>33.*Odeon* PMES 560	76-10
7C 458-35914 "The Sounds of Sweden"	>33.*Odeon* 7C 158-35912/13	82-06

ITALY

MC 5003 "I grandi tenori del secolo"	>33.*HMV* QALP 10402	a.75-06

USA (issued by P.I. Records, New York)

MCPF 6031(*) "Jussi Bjoerling: Opera Arias & Songs, vol. 1"	>33.*HMV* SCLP 1008	73-06
MCPF 6032(*) "Jussi Bjoerling: Opera Arias & Songs, vol. 2"	>33.*HMV* SGLP 507	73-06

Prestige Musical Franklin, France (limited edition for subscribers only)

13/14* "Requiem"	>33.*RCA* LD 6091	81

RCA (issued by RCA/Ariola, later BMG Music) [For series titles, see generally corresponding 33 rpm./CD issues]

GERMANY

24.48009 CT* (2) (PVK2-9005) "Tosca"	>33.*RCA* LM 6052	75-05

USA

4514-4-RG* (2) "Tosca"	>33.*RCA* LM 6052	87-09
6587-4-RC* "Aria"	>CD.*RCA* 6587-2-RC	87-10
7799-4-RG*p "The Pearl Fishers..."	>CD.*RCA* 7799-2-RG	88-08
60172-4-RG (2) "Rigoletto"	>33.*RCA* LM 6051	90-03
60191-4-RG "Il Trovatore: Highlights"	>CD.*RCA* 60191-2-RG	90-06
60192-4-RG* "Tosca: Highlights"	>CD.*RCA* 60192-2-RG	90-06
60201-4-RG "Aida: Highlights"	>CD.*RCA* 60201-2-RG	89-10
60520-4-RG "Jussi Bjoerling at Carnegie Hall"	>CD.*RCA* GD 60520	91-04
60573-4-RG (2) "Manon Lescaut"	>33.*RCA* LM 6116	90-11
60841-4-RG* "Opera Goes to the Movies"	>CD.*RCA* 60841-2-RG	91-09
09026-60935-4* "TV Classics"	>CD.*RCA* 09026-60935-2	92-05
09026-61440-4 "Opera's Greatest Moments"	>CD.*RCA* 09026-61440-2	92-09
AGK1-4806 "Bjoerling in Opera"	>33.*RCA* LM 2269	83-08

CANADA (Gold Seal)

AGK1-4889 "Bjoerling: Operatic Duets & Scenes"	>33.*RCA* LM 2736	?84

USA

AGK1-5277 "Jussi Bjoerling: Operatic Arias" (Legendary Performers)	>33.*RCA* AGM1-5277	85-08
AGK2-4514* (2) "Tosca"	>33.*RCA* LM 6052	82-10
AGK3-3970* (3) "Turandot"	>33.*RCA* LM 6149	81-04
AGK3-4805 (3) "Opening Nights at the Met"	>33.*RCA* LM 6171	83-09
ALK3-5380 (3) "Aida"	>33.*RCA* LM 6122	a.85-04
ARK3-2537* (3) "Turandot"	>33.*RCA* LM 6149	77-11

GERMANY

BK 86587* "Aria"	>33.*RCA* 6587-2-RC	87

USA

CLK2-5377 (2) "Il Trovatore"	>33.*RCA* LM 6008	a.85-04
CRK8-5177 (8) "RCA/Met: 100 Singers, 100 Years"	>33.*RCA* CRM8-5177	84-11

GERMANY

GK 60172 (2) "Rigoletto"	>33.*RCA* LM 6051	90-01
GK 60191 "Il Trovatore: Highlights"	>CD.*RCA* 60191-2-RG	90-09
GK 60192* "Tosca: Highlights"	>CD.*RCA* 60192-2-RG	90-06
GK 60201 "Aida: Highlights"	>CD.*RCA* 60201-2-RG	89-11
GK 60841* "Opera Goes to the Movies"	>CD.*RCA* 60841-2-RG	92
GK 60935* "TV Classics"	>CD.*RCA* 09026-60935-2	92
GK 82059* "Opera's Greatest Hits"	?	?

GREAT BRITAIN

GK 84889 "Jussi Bjoerling & Robert Merrill: The Pearl Fishers Duet..."	>33.*RCA* LM 2736	85

GERMANY

GK 85277 "Bjoerling: Opera Arias..." (Legendary Performers)	>33.*RCA* AGM1-5277	86-09
GK 87799*p "Jussi Bjoerling: The Pearl Fishers Duet..."	>CD.*RCA* 7799-2-RG	88-09
GK 89788* "Puccini's Greatest Hits"	219a2-3,f1,240d1	88-11

GREAT BRITAIN

MCK 570*(*) "Puccini's Biggest Hits"	>33.*RCA* VICS 1672(e)	c.73

GERMANY

PVK2-9005* (24.48009 CT) "Tosca"	>33.*RCA* LM 6052	75-05

GREAT BRITAIN

RCAK 3043 "The Pearl Fishers Duet and Other Famous Operatic Duets and Scenes"	>33.*RCA* LM 2736	a.83-06

USA

RK 1195* "Puccini's Greatest Hits"	>33.*RCA* LSC 5003	72-04

ITALY

RK 6046 "Cavalleria Rusticana"	203	76
RK 6149/1-2* "Turandot"	>33.*RCA* LM 6149	72-10

SWEDEN (made for Grammofon AB Electra by Teldec, Germany)

RK 9884*(*) "Jussi Björling"	>33.*RCA* LSC 9884	75

GERMANY

RK 42876 CF* (2) "Grand Gala in der Oper"	>33.*RCA* RL 42876 EF	79
RK 43077 CF "Der unvergessliche Jussi Björling singt grosse Opernarien"	>33.*RCA* RL 43077 EF	80-04

GREAT BRITAIN

RK 43243 "The Pearl Fishers Duet and Other Famous Operatic Duets and Scenes"	>33.*RCA* LM 2736	80-08

AUSTRALIA

SPK 185 "The World's Greatest Voices in Opera & Song"	>33.*RCA* SP 185	?77

ITALY

VK 43535* (2) "Tosca"	>33.*RCA* LM 6052	77
VK 43537* (2) "Turandot"	>33.*RCA* LM 6149	77

Victrola; half-speed mastering

VKS 00699(*) (2) "Il Trovatore"	>33.*RCA* LM 6008	82-09
VKS 03970* (3) "Turandot"	>33.*RCA* LM 6149	82-09
VKS 43533(*) (3) "Aida"	>33.*RCA* LM 6122	82-09
VKS 43534(*) (2) "Cavalleria Rusticana and Zinka Milanov's Recital"	>33.*RCA* VIC 6044	82-09
VKS 43535* (2) "Tosca"	>33.*RCA* LM 6052	82-09
VKS 43540(*) (2) "Rigoletto"	>33.*RCA* LM 6051	82-09
VKS 43544(*) (2) "Manon Lescaut"	>33.*RCA* LM 6116	82-09

Half-speed mastering

VKS 45510(*) "Tenorissimi"	>33.*RCA* TRL1-7055	83-09

Seraphim (EMI), USA (issued by Capitol)

4X2G 6099(*) (2) "La Bohème"	>33.*RCA* LM 6042	a.78-11
4XG 60168 "The Art of Jussi Bjoerling [vol. 1]: Songs, Oratorio & Opera Arias" (Great Recordings of the Century)	>33.*HMV* HQM 1190	79-04
4XG 60219 "The Art of Jussi Bjoerling, Album 2: Opera Arias" (Great Recordings...)	>33.*Sera.* 60219	79-08
4XG 60262 "Victoria de los Angeles: Opera Arias"	>33.*Sera.* S 60262	79-08

Svenska Favoriter, Storvreta, Sweden (distributed by mail order)

SFMC 1057 "Svenska favoriter nr 57"	83	89
SFMC 1063 "Svenska favoriter nr 63"	208	90

Swedish Society, Sweden (issued by Prophone Music)

SSC 1010*p "Jussi Björling: De vackraste sångerna"	>CD.*Sw.Society* SCD 1010	91-12

Utbildningsradion [Swedish Educational Broadcasting Co.], Stockholm, Sweden

26-92299-1 (2) "Viva l'Opera" [Appendix to Italian language course]	144	c.92-10

Verona, Luxembourg (issued by Compact Music GmbH; made in The Netherlands)

427022 "Jussi Björling: Recital [vol. 1]"	>CD.*Verona* 27022	?89

Vogue Music, Mortlake, Australia

VM 23C (2) "Great Voices of the Century"	159B,175	?

Westminster, Brazil

630701016/17 "Tosca"	>33.*RCA* LM 6052	78

World Record Club (EMI), Australia [distributed to members only]

C 03176 "The Golden Age of Song, vol. 3"	>33.*HMV* OXLP 7586	c.77-07
C 03668 "The Golden Age of Song, vol. 4"	>33.*HMV* OXLP 7617	78-06
C 04467* "Great Operatic Duets"	>33.*HMV* ASD 2382	c.78
C 05223/25 "The Art of Jussi Bjoerling"	>33.*HMV* RLS 715	78-11
C 05957 "Songs from the World's Greatest Singers, vol. 1"	>33.*EMI* SCA 016 (?)	79
C 06137 "The Golden Age of Song, vol. 7"	>33.*HMV* OXLP 7639	c.79-08
C 06662* "Madama Butterfly: Highlights"	>33.*HMV* SXLP 30306	80-12
C 08064 "Songs from the World's Greatest Singers, vol. 2"	>33.*EMI* SCA 034 (?)	80-10
C 10033 "The World's Greatest Voices in Opera and Song"	>33.*RCA* SP 185	82-01

3. Cartridge

Angel (EMI), USA (issued by Capitol)

8XS 35821* "Highlights from 'Madama Butterfly'"	>33.*Cap.* G 7233	71-04

EMI, South Africa

L8EMGJ 6004(*) (2) "20 Magnificent Opera Arias"	>33.*EMI* EMGJ 6004	74-04

His Master's Voice [=HMV], Great Britain (EMI)

8X-ASD 2382* "Great Operatic Duets"	>33.*HMV* ASD 2382	?71

London, USA

M 69184* "Ten Famous Tenors, Ten Famous Arias"	>33.*London* OS 26207	c.71-07

Odeon, USA (issued by P.I. Records, New York)

8PF 6031(*) "Jussi Bjoerling:..., vol. 1"	>33.*HMV* SCLP 1008	73-06
8PF 6032(*) "Jussi Bjoerling:..., vol. 2"	>33.*HMV* SGLP 507	73-06

RCA

USA (Red Seal)		
R8S 1195* "Puccini's Greatest Hits"	>33.*RCA* LSC 5003	71-06
R8S 5044* (2) "Great Moments from Grand Opera [vol. 1]"	219a3,221	66-12
R8S 5053* (2) "Great Moments from Grand Opera, vol. 2"	225	67-12
ITALY		
R8S 6149/1-2* "Turandot"	>33.*RCA* LM 6149	72-10
USA		
V8S 1022* "Tosca: Highlights"	219a2-3,b2-5,c2-3,f1,f4-6	70-03
V8S 1048*(*) "Puccini's Biggest Hits"	>33.*RCA* VICS 1672(e)	72-07

D. Video Tapes

VAI, USA (issued by on VHS video, NTSC or PAL system, by Video Artists International, P.O. Box 153, Ansonia Station, New York, NY 10023) (Series: Voice of Firestone Classic Performances)

69101 "Jussi Bjoerling in Opera and Song [vol. 1]"	5001a-e,5110a-f	90-08
69111 "Jussi Bjoerling in Opera and Song, vol. 2"	5009a-f	c.90-11

Virgin

VVD 546* "Aria" [film directed by R. Altman; JB not in picture] (Modern Classics. 18)	240d1	?

Notes for Section 2

A1. 78 rpm. discs

Columbia E series

Three of the four inspected copies of E 4547 (including the two with the alleged Take 2 of 85799 and the "combined" record E 4528/E 4547 [see below]) bear a label of a type not listed in Pekka Gronow's detailed surveys 1973 (*American Columbia Scandinavian "E" and "F" Series*; Helsinki) and 1977 (*Studies in Scandinavian-American Discography 2;* Helsinki). This label belongs to the group of light green Columbia labels with text in gold, used up to 1923. However, it has five patent dates (from the years 1902, 1906, 1908, 1908, 1909) and the price 85c./90c. This indicates that the label was used after Gronow's type 4.1.1 (1973) / 2.2.1 (1977) but before his type 4.1.2 / 2.2.2. The copy marked 1-28 bears a "flag" label (Gronow's type 5.2 / 3.2). As the "flag" label was introduced in the last months of 1923, this copy must have been pressed later (note the high number of the stamper) and shows a continuing demand for the record. The checked copies of E 4691 & E 4768 (three of each) bear light green labels of Gronow's type 4.1.2 / 2.2.2. All three Björling records were still listed in the Columbia Scandinavian catalogue for May 1924. Probably, they were deleted from the catalogue when the electrical recording process was introduced in 1925 (Gronow, personal communication).

In a Swedish collection (T. Franzén), there is a curious Columbia record which has "Sommarglädje" (matrix 85798 2-A-2) and label for E 4547 on one side but on the reverse a Hungarian comic song, "A tót elvtárs" (matrix 85779 1-A-14) and label for E 4528.

HMV DA/DB series

Swedish release dates are generally taken from the HMV monthly supplements. Sales statistics for the series in the Swedish HMV archive give further information which seems in a few cases not to be in accordance with the release dates in the supplements. According to the statistics, DA 1594 was sold already in 1937, but DA 1582 not until 1943 (though a handwritten note in the latter case confirms the release date in the supplement). DB 5787, which could be found for the first time in the supplement for January, 1947, was according to a similar note issued in 1944, but the first copies sold were entered for 1946. Up to September, 1939, JB's records in these series had a total sale of more than 60.000 copies in Sweden; DB 3049 was by far the most popular record.

With a few exceptions, British release dates are taken from the HMV numerical catalogue. DB 6249 and DB 6714 were available on special order only and not dated in the catalogue; the dates given for them in parenthesis are the months when they were reviewed in *The Gramophone*. British pressings have been noted for all issued records except DB 5393 and DB 6000. Listed below by country are records which are known to exist in local pressings (numbers bold) and records issued in countries where it seems probable that they were also pressed.
Australia: DA **1548,1582,1584,1701,1705**; DB **3049,3302,3603,3665v.1,3887**; Chile: DA 1548,1584,1701,1836; DB 3049,3302,3665; Denmark: DA **1705,1908**; DB 21311; Italy (La Voce del Padrone): DA **1548,1584,1701,1836**; DB 3049,**3302,3665v.1,5393**,

21311,21426; Netherlands: DB **3049,3887,6119,21311,21426**; South Africa: DB **3887,21311,21563**; Sweden: DA **1548,1705,1836,1841**; DB **3302,3603,3887,5759, 6000 (v.1+2),6163v.2**; Switzerland (?): DB **6163v.1**

HMV DB 6000

This number was also used for a Swiss issue with recordings by Szantho. The Swedish record was renumbered as DB 6119.

HMV X series

In the right column are Swedish release dates; X 7255 seems to have been issued in Denmark only. The left date column indicates records also found in the international catalogue. The X series was for the most part (except the last issues) pressed in Britain. British pressings have been found of all examined discs except X 7255, 7536 & 7964, Danish pressings of X 3724, 6090, 6146, 7255, 7947 & 7964 and Swedish pressings of X 4716, 4777, 6090, 6235, 7077, 7536, 7947 & 7964.

In this series, JB appeared on several discs only as a "refrain singer", mostly under his pseudonym "Erik Odde". These have non-JB material on the reverse side (generally the same orchestra with or without a singer). Those sides contain the following tunes: X 3826, En kärleksnatt vid Öresund (Winter); X 3880, Tumme Tott (Armand); X 3882, Förlåt mig (Sahlberg); X 4011, Die Sache, die man Liebe nennt (Straus); X 4036, Romany (Gavroche); X 4095, Det är jag som går vägen uppför stegen (Axelson); X 4134, Någon gång, någonstans på vår jord (Ahlin); X 4192, En stilla flirt (Sylvain); X 4196, Det är min charme (Winter). The reverse side of X 7255 contains a Danish song, Hellige Flamme (Weyse).

Labels on Jussi Björling's first issued record as a tenor (X 3377, April 1930) and his first "Erik Odde" record (X 3880, February 1932).

HMV X 7947 & X 7964 (& 45 rpm., *HMV* 7EBS 3)

The original issues of Nos. 205-08 on these records were sold for the benefit of Stadsbuds-kåren ["Town-Messengers' Union"], an exclusive charitable organization in Stockholm, of which JB and the shipowner Sven Salén (composer of Nos. 206 and 207) both were members.

Radiotjänst PR 5189

This was not a regular release [see also No. 5201]. One copy of the record was put up as the prize in an "American" lottery, arranged by the very popular radio programme "Karusellen". The listeners were to send in their contributions, between one and fifty Kronor, to Radiohjälpen [The Radio Relief Fund] for the fight against cancer. The one coming closest to the predetermined price of the record was to win it, and the winner is reported to have been a sewing club in the village of Södra Möinge in Skåne, which got the record for Kronor 8.28.

(RCA) Victor records

When the American records are known also to have been pressed in Canada, this is noted after their number. At least two Victor records have also been reported as pressed in Mexico, but their numbers are not known.

V-Disc 623

According to Richard S. Sears (*V-Discs: A History and Discography*, Westport, Conn., 1980), the *Cavalleria* aria sung by JB on this disc was taken from the Telephone Hour concert on October 7, 1945, conducted by Mitropoulos (No. 4503), but there is no evidence that JB sang the aria on that occasion. JB's *Cavalleria* aria taken from the V-Disc record was also used for the Nickson CD issue NN 1003 and there presented as a Mitropoulos recording.

A2. 45 rpm. discs

HMV 7EBS series

Records in this series have been found pressed in Sweden (all except 7EBS 13), Norway (all except 7EBS 10) and Denmark (7EBS 1, 10 & 11).

RCA 26000 series

While the two first listed numbers in this series were pressed and issued by Australian RCA, that company cannot give any information about the other numbers. American RCA states that the series was not issued in the US, although JBRL listed four of the records as American and American pressings of the two last numbers are reported to exist. 26044 & 26045 were advertised in The Netherlands in 1956 (together with RCA LP records with Australian numbers).

A3. 33 rpm. discs

Angel

From Chile, a JB record ("Opera Arias") is known, which was probably issued on this label and with the number 7025 or 107025.

The Beautiful Music Company

This US company issued in 1992 a 4LP / 3CD / 3MC set, distributed by mail order: "50 Great Moments in Opera". It contains 139A(?) and 113 or 169.

Electrola

The following LP and MC issues were probably made for record clubs or other special purposes by EMI Electrola:
BE 60828 "Unvergessene Stimmen"
CS 26011 / MC 23260 "Romeo und Julia"
F 666371 / MC 661201 / MCCS 33335 "Tenöre des Jahrhunderts" [>*Marcato* 34399-6?]

HMV ALP 1841

A complete retransfer of this record was done, with the original matrix numbers 2XSB 5-2N & 2XSB 6-2N changed to -6N & -4N, respectively. As there was a note about the planned retransfer in *The Gramophone* for October, 1961 (in E. Greenfield's review of ALP 1857), the retransfer probably took place in the autumn of 1961.

RCA 26.00000 series

Except 26.35116, these numbers constitute renumberings of earlier issues whose numbers were also retained on the sleeves and are here listed in parenthesis; both numbers are given in Section 1. Two price suffixes indicate that the suffix was changed in 1977.

RCA LM/LSC 1000/2000/6000 series

The list gives detailed information (titles in the respective language and release dates) for the US and Teldec versions only. Release dates given by Teldec refer to the *first* publication by that company; dates in brackets mean that the records were first released by them either outside Germany (LM/LSC 2570, LM 6046, LM 6052, LM/LSC 6149, LM/LSC 9811, LM 9847, LM 9872) or for the US Army (LM 1160, 1801, 1841, 2046, 6008, LSC 6052). Teldec records may not always have been released on the German market. The Teldec numbers for separate discs often (but not always) have a suffix letter to indicate the price. Teldec set numbers have a numerical suffix to show how many records are included in the set (/1-2, etc.). In Section 2, these suffixes (disregarded in listing of foreign / US Army releases above) are given in parenthesis when the record was issued both in the US (without suffix) and by Teldec, without parenthesis when there is only a Teldec suffix number. In Section 1, numbers with and without suffixes are treated as separate numbers.

The following pressings are noted from other countries: *Argentina*, LM 6008, LSC 6149; *Australia*, LM 2736, LM 2784 (issued 1965), LSC 5003 (issued 71-11); *Brazil*, LM 2372 "Dez tenores, dez árias, vol. 2", LM 6059(?), LM 6061, LSC 6052; *Canada*, LM 2059, LM 6116, LM 6149; *Chile*, LM 6051, LM 6116, LM 6122, LM 6149; *Spain*, LM 2372 "50 Años de Opera", LM 2630 "Canciónes Napolitanas por Grandes Tenores" (issued 1964), LM 6008, LSC 6149 (issued 1976). This is probably only a small random selection of local pressings, which may have been made also in other countries. The following numbers are known to have been issued in countries where they also may have been pressed: *Argentina*, LM 105, 2003, 2570, 6051, 6052, 6059, 6116, 6122, 6149; *Brazil*, LM 1847, 2046, 2269, 2628, 6051, 6052, 6084, 6122, 6149, LSC 6149; *Chile*, LM 105, 1128, 1771, 2269, 6008, 6052, 6059, 6106; *Italy*, LM 1802, 2372, 2359, 2570, 6008, 6046, 6052, 6059, 6116, 6122, 6149, LSC 2539, 6059, 6149.

RCA LM 1841-C

Concerning the difference between LM 1841 (USA) & LM 1841-C (Teldec), JBRL quoted a letter from Teldec (transl.): "...could not be published by us with this aria [= No. 169, the Flower Song]; since we had no license for it, publication was not allowed. Our issue is from March, 1958." In fact, there is one version of LM 1841-C with the Flower Song [here: "v.1"] and one [here: "v.2"] where it has been replaced by "Come un bel dì di maggio" (new label, but appropriate parts of the old sleeve only printed over). The record has even been sold with "Come un bel dì" but with label erroneously giving the French aria.

RCA LM 2269

In 1959, this record received a Grammy Award from the US National Academy of Recording Arts and Sciences for "Best Classical Performance, Vocal Soloist". (In 1960 & 1961, the same award - for best opera recording - was given to the complete recordings of *Turandot* and *Madama Butterfly*, in which JB took part.)

B. Compact Discs

Bluebell

Among the CD issues planned on this label are "Gröna Lund Recordings, vol. 2" (a selection from 5003, 5106, 5107, 5604 & 5704) and "Four Singing Brothers Björling" (JB recordings: 4, 3703a,b, 4102a-c, 5201, 5204b, 5705c,d). ABCD 050 had not yet been issued when this manuscript was sent to press.

EMI CDH 7 61053 2

The two versions of this issue have the same text, according to which the *Bohème* duet with Schymberg was included. This is not correct for version 1, and the wrong take numbers are also indicated for "Una furtiva lagrima" and "Cujus animam".

Pearl

Pavilion Records, Sparrows Green, Wadhurst, East Sussex TN5 6SJ, Great Britain, prepares a 3-CD JB issue on this label which will preliminarily contain the following recordings:
Vol.1, "Scandinavian Songs and German Lieder": 4,10,11,18,19,81-84,91-92,122-29,131-36; Vol. 2, "Operetta and Song": 12,13,25-28,34,35,37-39,45,46,58,63,65,86,93,94,97, 100,106,107,110,111; Vol. 3, "Songs and Arias": 9,15-17,20,24,50,51B,75,77,87,89,90, 95,96,98,99,101-02,112,114B,115,118,119,121.

RCA RD 49524

There are two versions of this disc, one made in Britain and distributed with the magazine *Opera Now*, Dec. 1989, one made in Germany and sold commercially.

C2. Cassette tapes

Johnston Cassettes

Eight audio cassettes, sold by mail order by Johnston Cassettes, March, Cambridgeshire, Great Britain (1987) under the title "Great Opera Stars Sing Light Music" but without printed labels, have not been regarded as regular issues and are therefore only mentioned in this note. The cassettes contain: No. 1: 3704a,e; No. 2: 4803a,5101c,5102b; No. 3: 4006b,4601b,4604b,4605d; No. 4: 4303a; No. 5: 4503d,4802; No. 6: 4006d,4301a; No. 7: 93,100,155; No. 8: 36,39,42,47

D. Video tapes

Bel Canto Society

These four video cassettes sold by mail order by Bel Canto Society, USA, without printed labels, are only mentioned in this note: No. 7, "Opera Titans", contains 5703; No. 10, "Great Tenors, vol. 1", contains 5302b; No. 12, "Great Tenors, vol. 2", contains 3704e; No. 527, "Fram för framgång", contains 3704.

Section 3: Indexes

The indexes refer to the recordings in Section 1:A-B only, not to the performances in the Appendix to Section 1:B (with a few exceptions in the Title Index) or in the Chronological Table.

A. Composer Index

Numbers in italics indicate recordings with instrumental accompaniment (usually piano) or without accompaniment; other recordings are with orchestra. Numbers in brackets indicate commercial recordings which are known or supposed to have been destroyed, or individual items from concerts etc. of which recordings have not been located and which therefore may or may not exist.

1. Works with Known Composer

Abraham, Paul (Ábrahám, Pál; 1892-1960) Hungarian

Die Blume von Hawaii (1931). Text: Alfred Grünwald & Fritz Löhner-Beda; [Sw] Anita & Björn Halldén (pseud.: S.S.Wilson & Nalle Halldén).

Kann nicht küssen ohne Liebe (act 2)
[Sw] Kyssar utan kärlek (Aldrig forska, aldrig spörja...) 38

Du traumschöne Perle der Südsee (act 2)
[Sw] En skimrande pärla i havet (Het och röd solens glöd...) 37

Adam, Adolphe (1803-1856) French

Cantique de Noël ["O Holy Night"]. Text: Placide Cappeau de Roquemaure.
[Sw] Julsång (O helga natt...). Text: Augustin Kock. 234, *4505, 4606, 5406*

Ahlberg, Gunnar (1886-1943) Swedish (pseud.: Guy Ammandt)

Slut dina ögon [Close Your Eyes] (Allt jag drömt...), waltz. Text [Sw]: Hadar Hellerstedt (pseud.: Gösta Sölwe). [41], 45

Alfvén, Hugo (1872-1960) Swedish

Endräkt [Concord] (Det är fullkomnat...). Text [Sw]: Anders Grape. 5301

Jag längtar dig [I Long for You] (...), Op. 28 No. 5. Text [Sw]: Ernest Thiel. 239, 6004

Så tag mit hjerte [Now Take My Heart] (...). Text [Dan]: Tove Ditlevsen. 238

Skogen sover [The Forest Asleep (also: The Sleeping Forest)] (...), Op. 28 No. 6. Text [Sw]: Ernest Thiel. 134, *4902*, 5403, *5802*, *5903*, 6004

Almroth, Knut O. W. (1900-1971) Swedish (pseud.: K.O.W.A.)

Tangoflickan [The Tango Girl] (Skönaste señorita...). Text [Sw]: Composer [see note]. [54], 59

Althén, Ragnar (1883-1961) Swedish

Land, du välsignade [Thou Blessed Land]. Text [Sw]: Elisabet Björklund. 92, 228, 3703, 3704, 3707, *3903*, *4302*, 4605, *5203*, *5604*, *5803*, *6003*

Ammandt, Guy (pseudonym; see: **Ahlberg, Gunnar**)

Armand, Jacques (pseudonym; see: **Thiel, Olof**)

Arthur, Gerald [No information available; possibly pseudonym]

To-day. Text: ?.
[Sw] I dag (Himmelens tungsinta skyar flytt...). Text: Berndt Carlberg (pseud.: Berco). 21

Åström, Axel (1872-1940) Swedish

I lyckans tempelgård [In the Sanctuary of Happiness] (Vårt liv en ständig kamp ju är...). Text [Sw]: Gunnar Ahlberg. 29

Atterberg, Kurt (1887-1974) Swedish

Fanal, Op. 35 (1934). Text [Sw]: Composer (after "Flammendes Land" by Oscar Ritter & Ignaz Michael Welleminsky).

I männer över lag och rätt [Ye men of law and justice], Martin Skarp's aria (act 1) 77

Nu, bröder, ändas våra strider [Now, brothers, let us end this strife], finale (act 3) 3401

Ball, Ernest R. (1878-1927) American

Love Me and the World Is Mine. Text: Dave Reed Jr.
[Sw] Bliv min, så är världen min (Jag vandrar som i drömmar hän...). Text: Sven Nyblom. 25

Bartlett, James Carroll (1850-1929) American

A Dream (Last night I was dreaming of thee...). Text: Charles B. Cory. 4006

Baumann, Erik (1889-1955) Swedish

Läppar som le så röda [Smiling Red Lips] (Lyckan som all världens skalder...), waltz from the motion picture "Fridolf i lejonkulan" [Fridolf in the Lion's Den]. Text [Sw]: Nils Perne & Georg Eliasson (pseud.: Nils-Georg). 49

Beach, Amy Marcy Cheney (Beach, Mrs. H.H.A.; 1867-1944) American

Ah, Love, but a Day (...). Text: Robert Browning. 202, 5110

Beethoven, Ludwig van (1770-1827) German

Adelaide (Einsam wandelt dein Freund...), Op. 46. Text: Friedrich von Matthisson. *124*, 4904, *5501*, *5802*

Die Ehre Gottes aus der Natur, Op. 48 No. 4. Text: Christian Fürchtegott Gellert. [Sw] Lovsång (I himlar sjungen...). Text: Jacob Axel Josephson (?). 233

Missa Solemnis, Op. 123 (1824). Text: liturgical [Lat].

Complete 4008

Beneken, Friedrich Burkhard (1760-1818) German

Der Gottesacker. Text: August Cornelius Stockmann.
[Sw] O, hur stilla [Oh, How Peacefully] (O, huru ljuvligt...), also called "Vid graven" [At the Grave]. Text: ? *1*

Bick, Eva Swedish [No other information available; probably real name of the pseudonym "Bickvor"]

Min sommarmelodi [My Summer Tune] (Sommarns vackra bilder draga...). Text [Sw]: The Composer. 33

Bickvor (pseudonym; see: **Bick, Eva**)

Bizet, Georges (1838-1875) French

Carmen (1875). Text: Henri Meilhac & Ludovic Halévy.

La fleur que tu m'avais jetée, Don José's "Flower Song" (act 2)
113, 169, 3902, 4102, 4803, 5005, 5009, *5106*, *5501*, *5502*, 5803 5804, *5903*

Les pêcheurs de perles (1863). Text: Michel Carré & Pierre-Étienne Piestre (pseud.: E. Cormon).

Au fond du temple saint, duet Nadir - Zurga (act 1) 175

Je crois entendre encore, Nadir's romance (act 2) 154, 4502

Bode, Johnny (1912-1983) Swedish

Min längtan är du [You Are My Yearning] (Morgonhimlens stjärnor mot mig glimma...), tango-serenade. Text [Sw]: Roland Levin (pseud.: Roland). 63

Borganoff, Igor (pseudonym; see: **Njurling, Sten**)

Borodin, Alexander (1833-1887) Russian

Knyaz Igor [*Prince Igor*] (1890). Text: Vladimir Stasov & Composer; [Sw] G. von Kraskowski & Ture Rangström.

Medlenno den' ugasal [Daylight is fading away], Vladimir's recitative & cavatina (act 2) [abridged]
[Sw] Dagen gick långsamt till ro 51, 218, *6003*

Brahms, Johannes (1833-1897) German

Die Mainacht (Wann der silberne Mond...), Op. 43 No. 2. Text: Ludwig Hölty *185*

Ständchen (Der Mond steht über dem Berge...), Op. 106 No. 1. Text: Franz Kugler. *5501*, *5802*

Campbell-Tipton, Louis (1877-1921) American

A Spirit Flower (My heart was frozen...). Text: Martin Stanton. *201*

Carsten, Bert (pseudonym; see: **Nordlander, Bert Carsten**)

Caruso, Enrico (1873-1921) Italian

Dreams of Long Ago. Text: Earl Carroll.
[Sw] Ungdomsdrömmar (Allt är så stilla...). Text: Abraham Lundquist. 93

Christgau, Michael Danish

Bryllupsvalsen [The Wedding Waltz]. Text: Flemming Geill.
[Sw] Bröllopsvalsen (Vitröda flaggor nu fladdra för vinden...). Text: Tor Bergström & Gösta Stenberg (pseud.: Dardanell & Dix Dennie). 79

Cilea, Francesco (1866-1950) Italian

L'arlesiana (1897). Text: Romualdo Marenco.

È la solita storia, Federico's recitative & aria (Lamento di Federico, act 2)
157, 224, 4502

Dahl, Adrian (1864-1935) Swedish

Bachanal [Bacchanal] (Jag vill leva, jag vill älska...). Text [Sw]: Fredrik Nycander.
52, 57, *3704*, *5004*

De Curtis, Ernesto (1875-1937) Italian

Torna a Surriento (Vide 'o mare quant'è bello...). Text: Giambattista de Curtis.
[It] *5803*, *5907*
[Sw] Gondolsång (Se ett ensamt mörkrött segel...). Text: Sven Nyblom. 9

De Curtis, Giambattista (1860-1926) Italian (pseud.: Totò)

Carmela. Text: The Composer.
[Sw] Carmela (Ibland blommor och grönskande lunder...). Text: ? 24

Denza, Luigi (1846-1922) Italian-British

Funiculì, funiculà. Text [Neapolitan]: Giuseppe Turco.
[It] Funiculì, funiculà (Stasera, Nina mia...). Text: Angelo Zanardini. 4006

D'Hardelot, Guy (pseudonym; see: **Rhodes, Helen**)

Di Capua, Eduardo (1865-1917) Italian

'O sole mio (Che bella cosa...). Text: Giovanni Capurro. 101

Donizetti, Gaetano (1797-1848) Italian

L'elisir d'amore (1832). Text: Felice Romani.

Una furtiva lagrima, Nemorino's romance (act 2)
153, [158], 216, 4402, 4502, 5204

Dresser, Paul (1857-1906) American

On the Banks of the Wabash, Far Away. Text: The Composer.
[Sw] Barndomshemmet [My Childhood Home] (Där som sädesfälten böja sig för vinden...). Text: Karl-Ewert Christenson (pseud.: Karl Ewert) [see note]. *5*

Eklöf, Ejnar (1886-1954) Swedish

Morgon [Morning] (Här är stigen...). Text [Sw]: Karl Gustav Ossiannilsson.
135, 3703, *4302*, *5107*, *5801*, 5805, *5905*, *5907*

Elgar, Edward (1857-1934) British

Salut d'amour, Op. 12
[Sw] Violer [Violets] (Daggstänkta, doftande violer små...). Text: Carl Gehrman.
22

Enders, Georg (1898-1954) Austrian-Swedish

Lilla prinsessa [Little Princess], Prinsessan Ingrids förlovningsvals (Sagor det finns så många...), waltz. Text [Sw]: Nils Perne & Georg Eliasson (pseud.: Nils-Georg). 80

Fall, Leo (1873-1925) Austrian

Die geschiedene Frau (The Girl in the Train; 1908). Text [Ger]: Victor Leon; [Sw]: ?

Kind, Du kannst tanzen wie meine Frau, (excerpt from) duet Karel - Jana (act 2)
[Sw] Barn, du kan dansa såsom min fru 3601

Firestone, Idabelle (Firestone, Mrs. Harvey S.; 1874-1954) American

If I Could Tell You (...). Text: Madeleine Marshall.
[4504, 4602], 4603, 4604, 5001, 5009, 5110, 5202

In My Garden (And now each flower...). Text: Lester O'Keefe.
[4504, 4602], 4603, 4604, 5001, 5009, 5110, 5202

Flotow, Friedrich von (1812-1883) German

Martha (1847). Text [Ger]: Friedrich Wilhelm Riese (pseud.: Wilhelm Friedrich); [It]: Achille de Lauzières.

Ach, so fromm, Lyonel's aria (act 3)
[It] M'apparì tutt'amor 118, 213, 4504, *5604*

Foster, Stephen (1826-1864) American

Jeanie with the Light Brown Hair (I dream of Jeanie...). Text: The Composer.
159, [4504], 4907, *5501*

Friml, Rudolf (1879-1972) Czech-American

The Vagabond King (1925). Text: Brian Hooker & William H. Post.

Only a Rose (Red rose out of the east...) (act 1) 100

Geehl, Henry Ernest (1881-1961) British

For You Alone (Take thou this rose...). Text: P.J. O'Reilly.
[Eng] 97, [4601, 4602], 4803, 5101
[Sw] För dig allén (Tag denna ros...). Text: Anita Halldén (pseud: A.W). [7], 12

Giordano, Umberto (1867-1948) Italian

Andrea Chénier (1896). Text: Luigi Illica.

Come un bel dì di maggio, Chénier's aria (act 4)
141, 217, *5003*, 5006, *5107*, *5502*, *5903*, *5907*

Fedora (1898). Text: Arturo Colautti.

Amor ti vieta, Loris Ipanoff's aria (act 2) 142, 223, *5501*, *5502*, *5903*

Glover, Charles W. (1806-1863) British

The Rose of Tralee (The pale moon was rising...). Text: E. Mordaunt Spencer.
5102

Godard, Benjamin (1849-1895) French

Jocelyn (1888). Text: Armand Silvestre & Victor Capoul.

Cachés dans cet asile...Oh! ne t'éveille pas encor, Jocelyn's berceuse (act 2)
[Eng] Concealed in this retreat...Oh! wake not yet ("Angels Guard Thee"). Text: Nathan Haskell Dole. 166, 4603

Gounod, Charles (1818-1893) French

Faust (1859). Text: Jules Barbier & Michel Carré; [Sw] Ernst Wallmark.

Complete [Fr] 5010, 5912

Excerpts from acts 1-3 & 5 [JB in Sw., rest of ensemble in Ger.] 3701

Excerpts from act 3, incl. cavatina [JB in Fr., rest of ensemble in Sw.] 4401

Salut! demeure chaste et pure, Faust's cavatina (act 3)
[Fr] 119, 180, [4605], 5001
[Sw] Var hälsad, dygdens kyska boning 3902

Quittons ce lieu sombre...Anges purs, trio (act 5, finale) [JB in Sw., rest of ensemble in Fr.] 3708

Messe Solennelle à Sainte Cécile (1855). Text: liturgical [Lat].

Sanctus 4604

Repentir. Text: ?
[Eng] O Divine Redeemer (Ah! turn me not away...). Text: A. Phillips. 4604

Roméo et Juliette (1867). Text: Jules Barbier & Michel Carré; [Sw] Ernst Wallmark.

Complete
[Fr] 4701
[Sw] 4002

Ange adorable, duet Roméo - Juliette ("Madrigal", act 1)
[Fr] 163, 4904, 5108, 5109
[Sw] Helgon, du ljuva 4102

Ah! lève-toi, soleil!, Roméo's cavatina (act 1)
[Fr] 151
[Sw] Höj dig, du klara sol 15

Act 2, complete [Sw] 4301

Va! je t'ai pardonné...Nuit d'hyménée, duet Roméo - Juliette (act 4)
4904, 4906, 5108

Grieg, Edvard (1843-1907) Norwegian

Jeg elsker dig [I Love Thee] (Min tankes tanke...), Op. 5 No. 3. Text [Dan]: Hans Christian Andersen [see note]. 4503, 4603, 5403

En svane [A Swan] (Min hvide svane...), Op. 25 No. 2. Text [Nor]: Henrik Ibsen.
183, *53xx*, 5403, *5501*, *5903*

Ein Traum, Op. 48 No. 6. Text: Friedrich von Bodenstedt.
[Nor] En drøm (Jeg så engang i drømmesyn...). Text: Nordahl Rolfsen.
184, *53xx*, [5403], *5501*, *5502*, *5801*, *5802*, *5903*

Gruber, Franz (1787-1863) Austrian

Stille Nacht, heilige Nacht. Text: Josef Mohr.
[Sw] Stilla natt, heliga natt (...). Text: ? [see note]. *4505*

Gustaf (1827-1852) Prince of Sweden and Norway

Sjung om studentens lyckliga dag [Let's Sing about the Happy Days of Students] (...); also called "Studentsång". Text [Sw]: Herman Sätherberg. 104

Gyldmark, Hugo (1899-1971) Danish

Gitarren klinger [Sounds of Guitar], serenata [dedicated to JB]. Text: Alfred Kjærulf.
[Sw] Gitarren klingar (Matt lagunens vågor glimma (...). Text: Oscar Ralf. 66

Handberg-Jørgensen, Michael (d. 1972) Danish

Klovnens tango [The Clown's Tango]. Text: Bøhling Pedersen
[Sw] Klownens tango (Hör, musiken kallar...). Text: Oscar Ralf. 64

Handel, George Frideric (1685-1759) German-English

Serse (1738). Text [It]: Niccolò Minato.

Frondi tenere...Ombra mai fù, Serse's [Xerxes's] recitative & aria ("Largo", act 1) 4904, 5403, *5502*, *5903*

Hansson, Stig (1900-1968) Swedish (pseud.: Jules Sylvain)

Det är något som binder mitt hjärta vid dig [Something Is Tying My Heart to You] (Säg mig, minns du liksom jag...), waltz from the motion picture "Hans livs match" [His Life's Match]. Text [Sw]: Fritz-Gustaf Sundelöf (pseud.: Fritz Gustaf). 36

Dina blåa ögon lova mer, än dina röda läppar ger [Your Blue Eyes Promise More than Your Red Lips Give] (Om månen har sagt att jag håller dig kär...), tango from the motion picture "En stilla flirt" [A Quiet Flirtation]. Text [Sw]: Gösta Stevens. 67

Säg, att Du evigt håller mig kär [Say That You Will Love Me Forever] (Uti det blå...), from the motion picture "Två man om en änka" [Two Men and One Widow]. Text [Sw]: Åke Söderblom. 69

Hardelot, Guy d' (pseudonym; see: **Rhodes, Helen**)

Henrikson, Alice (1906-1977) Swedish (pseud: Alice LeBeau)

Kärlekens sång [Song of Love] (Den är död, romantiken...), waltz. Text [Sw]: Ejnar Westling. 68

Herbert, Victor (1859-1924) Irish-American

Naughty Marietta (1910). Text: Rida Johnson Young.

Ah! Sweet Mystery of Life, Captain Dick's song
[Sw] Liv, du är ej längre en mystär (Ja, du liv, din gåta...). Text: Sven Lindström. 13

Princess Pat (1915). Text: Henry Blossom.

Neapolitan Love Song ('Tis ev'ning and the sun is at rest...)
4603, 4901, 5001, 5009, 5109, 5202

Heymann, Werner R. (1896-1961) German

Es führt kein andrer Weg zur Seligkeit, from the motion picture "Der Sieger" (in Sweden: Hoppla, här är jag). Text: Robert Gilbert.
[Sw] Den enda väg, som för till salighet (Drömmar jag drömmer dag och natt...). Text: Nils Perne & Georg Eliasson (pseud.: Nils-Georg). [40, *44*]

Irgendwo auf der Welt, slow foxtrot from the motion picture "Der goldene Traum" (in Sweden: En gyllene dröm). Text: Robert Gilbert & The Composer.
[Sw] Någonstans på vår jord (Jag alltid drömmer och hoppas...). Text: Nils Perne & Georg Eliasson (pseud.: Nils-Georg). 48

Jurmann, Walter (1903-1971) Austrian [Joint composer with Bronislaw Kaper of the following song]

Ninon, from the motion picture "Ein Lied für Dich" (in Sweden: En sång till dig). Text: Fritz Rotter & Ernst Marischka.
[Sw] Ninon (Att ett leende kan vara nog...) [see note]. Text: Einar Rosenborg (pseud.: Arne Olovson). 65

Kálmán, Emmerich (Imre) (1882-1953) Hungarian

Die Csárdásfürstin (The Gypsy Princess; 1915). Text: Leo Stein & Bela Jenbach; [Sw] Björn "Nalle" Halldén (?).

Tanzen möcht' ich...Tausend kleine Engel singen, (excerpt from) duet Edwin - Sylva (act 2)
[Sw] Dansa vill jag...Tusen röster hör jag sjunga 3601

Das Veilchen vom Montmartre (Paris in Spring; 1930). Text: Julius Brammer & Alfred Grünwald.

Du Veilchen vom Montmartre (act 1)
[Sw] Du går som en liten prinsessa (...). Text: Arvid Englind (?) [see note].
26

Heut' Nacht hab' ich geträumt von dir, tango (inserted for Raoul in this operetta; also used in *Die Csárdásfürstin*)
[Sw] Jag drömmer varje natt om dig (Alltid för dig, förtjusande kvinna...). Text: Anita Halldén (pseud.: S.S. Wilson). 46

Kaper, Bronislaw (1902-1983) Polish-American (See: **Jurmann, Walter**)

Körling, August (1842-1919) Swedish

Aftonstämning [Evening Mood] (Mörkgrön granskog skuggar över viken...). Text [Sw]: Daniel Fallström. 237, *5803*, *5905*

Vita rosor [White Roses] (Jag vet en fager rosenlund...). Text [Sw]: Karl Alfred Melin. 11

K. O. W. A. (pseudonym; see: **Almroth, Knut O.W.**)

Kremser, Edward (1838-1914) Austrian

Prayer of Thanksgiving (see: Section 3:A2, Wilt heden nu treden)

Laparra, Raoul (1876-1943) French

L'illustre Fregona (1931). Text: The Composer; [Sw] Moses Pergament.

Mélancolique tombe le soir, Tomas's serenade
[Sw] Serenad (Fylld av vemod sänker sig natten...) 50

LeBeau, Alice (pseudonym; see: **Henrikson, Alice**)

Lehár, Franz (1870-1948) Hungarian-Austrian

Das Land des Lächelns (The Land of Smiles; 1929). Text: Ludwig Herzer & Fritz Löhner; [Sw] Carl Johan Holzhausen.

Von Apfelblüten einen Kranz, Sou-chong's song (act 1)
[Sw] Av äppelblommor jag binder en krans 35

Dein ist mein ganzes Herz, Sou-chong's song (act 2)
[Ger] 243
[Sw] Du är min hela värld 34, 243

Leoncavallo, Ruggero (1858-1919) Italian

Mattinata (L'aurora di bianco vestita...). Text: The Composer.
[It] 146, 4503, 4801, 5009, *5106*
[Sw] Mattinata (I öster nu dagern bebådar...). Text: Sven Nyblom. [8], 17

Pagliacci (1892). Text: The Composer; [Sw] Ernst Wallmark.

Complete
[It] 204
[Sw: *Pajazzo*] 5405

E voi, piuttosto, final part of Tonio's prologue
[Sw] Och ni, långt hellre *5004*

A ventitre ore!, fragment (Canio, act 1)
[Sw] Kommen väl ihåg! 3702

Recitar!...Vesti la giubba...Ridi Pagliaccio, Canio's recitative & aria (act 1)
[It] 144, 181, 5102, 5110
[Sw] Spela komedi!...Pudra ditt anlet...Skratta, Pajazzo 74, 3702

O Colombina, Harlequin's serenade (act 2)
[Sw] O Colombin *5003*

No! Pagliaccio non son, Canio's aria (act 2)
[Sw] Nej, Pajazzo är jag ej 3702

Lesso-Valerio, P. (pseudonym; see: **Plessow, Erich**)

Lindberg, Helge (1898-1973) Swedish

Bagdad (Orientens sagostad ännu...), foxtrot. Text [Sw]: Nils Perne & Georg Eliasson (pseud.: Nils-Georg). 39

Liszt, Franz (Ferenc) (1811-1886) Hungarian-German

Es muss ein Wunderbares sein (...). Text: Oskar von Redwitz. 192, *5907*

Mascagni, Pietro (1863-1945) Italian

Cavalleria rusticana (1890). Text: Guido Menasci & Giovanni Targioni-Tozzetti; [Sw] Helmer Key.

Complete
[It] 203, 220, 5910
[JB in It.; rest of ensemble in Sw.] 5404

O Lola c'hai di latti, Turiddu's serenade (siciliana)
[It] O Lola, bianca 162
[Sw] O Lola, bort till dig 76, 3703

Bada, Santuzza, schiavo non sono...Ah! lo vedi, duet Turiddu - Santuzza.
[Sw] Jag är ej slav, förgäves du gråter...Å! där ser du [Santuzza in German, scene with Lola omitted] 3707

Mamma!...Quel vino, Turiddu's farewell scene (Addio alla madre)
147, 170, 4402, 4501, 4601, 4901, 5005, *5106*, 5204, *53xx*, *5501*, *5704*, 5706, 5804, *5901*

Massenet, Jules (1842-1912) French

Élégie. Text: Louis Gallet. [Sw] Elegi (O min ungdoms saliga vår...). Text: ? 4502

Manon (1884). Text: Henri Meilhac & Philippe Gille.

Instant charmant...En fermant les yeux, Des Grieux's recitative & aria (Le Rêve; The Dream) (act 2) 112, 4504, 5101, *5501*

En fermant les yeux (aria only) 3902

Je suis seul!...Ah! fuyez, douce image, Des Grieux's recitative & aria (act 3) 152, 4502, 4601, 4801, 4906

Meyerbeer, Giacomo (1791-1864) German

L'africaine (1865). Text: Eugène Scribe; [It] ?

Pays merveilleux... Ô Paradis, Vasco da Gama's recitative & aria (act 4)
[It] Mi batte il cor...O Paradiso 98, 179, 3708, 3902, *5003*, 5006, *5203*

Millöcker, Karl (1842-1899) Austrian

Der Bettelstudent (The Beggar Student; 1882). Text: Camillo Walzel (pseud.: F. Zell) & Richard Genée; [Sw] Ernst Wallmark.

Soll ich reden...Ich setz' den Fall, duet Symon - Laura (act 2)
[Sw] Skall jag tala...Antag det fall 111

Dich nur lieb' ich so inniglich, excerpt from above
[Sw] Dig blott älskar jag 3601

Ach, er hat sie ja nur auf die Schulter geküsst, excerpt (solo with chorus) from finale of act 2
[Sw] Ack, han gav henne blott uppå skuldran en kyss 3601

Ich hab' kein Geld, bin vogelfrei, Symon's song (act 3)
[Sw] Nu är jag pank och fågelfri [105], 107, *5203*, *5604*, *5605*, *5803*, *5905*

Morgan, Orlando (1865-1956) British

Clorinda (Clorinda is dainty and winsome...). Text: John Bledlowe. 4801, *5502*

Mozart, Wolfgang Amadeus (1756-1791) Austrian

Don Giovanni (1787). Text: Lorenzo da Ponte.

Il mio tesoro, Don Ottavio's aria (act 2) *5501*

Die Zauberflöte (1791). Text: Emanuel Schikaneder; [Sw] Herman Anders Kullberg.

Dies Bildnis ist bezaubernd schön, Tamino's aria (act 1)
[Sw] Ack, detta är en ängels bild *5803*, *5905*

Nedbal, Oskar (1874-1913) Czech

Polenblut (1913). Text: Leo Stein; [Sw] ?

Alle Achtung, alle Achtung, (excerpt from) duet Helena - Bolo ("Ihr seid ein Kavalier", act 2)
[Sw] Så betänksam, så betänksam 3601

Niedermeyer, Louis (1802-1861) Swiss-French

Pietà, Signore (Se i miei sospiri...), aria da chiesa [see note]. Text: ? 5403

Njurling, Sten (1892-1945) Swedish (pseud.: Igor Borganoff)

När rosorna vissna och dö [When the Roses Wither and Die] (En mollmelodi, en falsk elegi...). Text [Sw]: Ejnar Westling (pseud.: Stefan Kamensky) & The Composer. 31

Nordlander, Bert Carsten (1905-1989) Swedish (pseud.: Bert Carsten)

Varje litet ord av kärlek [Every Little Word of Love] (Sommarens vind smeker min kind...), waltz from the motion picture "Moderna fruar" [Modern Wives]. Text [Sw]: Gösta Stevens. 42

Nordqvist, Gustaf (1886-1949) Swedish

Bisp Thomas' frihetssång [Bishop Thomas' Song of Liberty] (Frihet är det bästa ting...). Text [Sw]: Thomas Simonsson (d. 1443). 150

Bön i ofredstid [Prayer in Time of War] (Du, som skapade med ditt ord...). Text [Sw]: Folke Personne. 149

Till havs [Toward the Sea] (Nu blåser havets friska vind...). Text [Sw]: Jonathan Reuter. 205, 5302, *53xx*, *5406*, *5704*, *5803*, *5807*, 5808, *5905*, *5907*, *6003*

Nyblom, Carl Göran (1867-1920) Swedish

Brinnande gula flod [Flaming Golden Stream] (Skimrande gula saft...). Text [Sw]: The Composer. 53, 58

Offenbach, Jacques (1819-1880) German-French

La belle Hélène (1864). Text: Henri Meilhac & Ludovic Halévy; [Sw] Frans Hedberg.

Au mont Ida trois déesses, Paris' Entrance Song (act 1)
[Sw] Uti en skog på berget Ida 110

Pérez-Freire, Osman (1880-1930) Chilean-French

Ay, ay, ay. Text: Robert Valaire
[Sw] Ay, ay, ay (Träd fram till din fönsterkarm...). Text: Ragnar Hyltén-Cavallius. 86

Peterson-Berger, Wilhelm (1867-1942) Swedish

Bland skogens höga furustammar [Among the High Fir-Trees in the Forest] (...), Op. 5 (=Fyra visor i svensk folkton) No. 4. Text [Sw]: "H" [see note]. 19, 231, *4302*, 5808

Jungfrun under lind [The Maiden under the Linden Tree] (I våren knoppas en lind så grön...), Op. 10 No. 1. Text [Sw]: The Composer, after Danish original by Ernst von der Recke. 208, *3903*, 4605, *4902*, 5101, *5107*, *5802*, *5903*

När jag för mig själv i mörka skogen går [When I Walk Alone in the Dark Forest] (...), Op. 5 No. 1. Text [Sw]: "H". 18, 230, *4302*, *5406*, 5808, *5905*

Som stjärnorna på himmelen [Like Stars in the Heavens] (...), Op. 5 No. 3. Text [Sw]: "H". *4302*, *5907*

Plessow, Erich (b. 1899) German (pseud.: P. Lesso-Valerio)

Warum, tango. Text: ?
[Sw] Varför? (Varför har du mig kysst...). Text: Carl Johan Holzhausen. 47

Ponchielli, Amilcare (1834-1886) Italian

La Gioconda (1876). Text: Arrigo Boito (pseud.: Tobia Gorrio).

Cielo e mar!, Enzo Grimaldo's aria (act 2)
95, 178, 221, *5106*, 5108, *5203*, *5704*

Puccini, Giacomo (1858-1924) Italian

La bohème (1896). Text: Giuseppe Giacosa & Luigi Illica; [Sw] Sven Nyblom.

Complete [It] 211, 4804

Acts 1, 3 & 4, complete [JB in It.; rest of ensemble in Sw.] 5705

Act 1, complete [Sw] 4001

Oh! sventata, sventata!...Che gelida manina...Sì. Mi chiamano Mimì, scene Mimì - Rodolfo (with Rodolfo's aria) (act 1) 5601

Che gelida manina, Rodolfo's aria (act 1)
[It] 87, 176, 3707, 3902, [4006], 4102, 4501, [4503], 4904, 4906, 4907, 5104, *5604*, *5903*
[Sw] Så kall ni är om handen 3703

O soave fanciulla, duet Rodolfo - Mimì (act 1)
139, 164, 4501, 4904, 4905, 4906, 5001, 5601

In un coupè?...O Mimì, tu più non torni, duet Rodolfo - Marcello (act 4) 173

La fanciulla del West (1910). Text: Guelfo Civinini & Carlo Zangarini; [Sw] Oscar Ralf.

Ch'ella mi creda, Dick Johnson's aria (act 3)
[It] 96, 222
[Sw] Låt henne tro 78

Madama Butterfly (1904). Text: Giuseppe Giacosa & Luigi Illica.

Complete [It] 241

Manon Lescaut (1893). Text: Marco Praga, Domenico Oliva, Luigi Illica, Giulio Ricordi & Giuseppe Giacosa.

Complete
[It] 209, 4908, 5602
[JB in It.; rest of ensemble in Sw.] 5909

Tra voi, belle, brune e bionde, Des Grieux's aria (act 1) 226

Donna non vidi mai, Des Grieux's aria (act 1) 161, 5101, 5706, 5804, 6004

Tosca (1900). Text: Giuseppe Giacosa & Luigi Illica; [Sw] Sven Nyblom.

Complete [It] 219, 5911

Acts 1 & 2, excerpts (JB's part complete) [It] 5603

Recondita armonia, Cavaradossi's aria (act 1)
[It] 90, 168, 3708
[Sw] Det sköna står att finna 71

Acts 2 & 3, complete [JB in It.; rest of ensemble in Sw.] 5902

E lucevan le stelle, Cavaradossi's aria (act 3)
[It] 99, 167, 4303, 5005, 5108, *5501*, *5802*, *5901*
[Sw] Jag minns stjärnorna lyste (Sången till livet) 72

Turandot (1926). Text: Giuseppe Adami & Renato Simoni.

Complete [It] 240

Nessun dorma!, Calaf's aria (act 3)
143, 4303, 4402, 4904, 5104, *5106*, 5202, *5802*, *5903*

Rachmaninov, Sergey (1873-1943) Russian-American

Siren', Op. 21 No. 5. Text: Ekaterina Beketova.
[Eng] Lilacs (Morning skies are aglow...). Text: Henry G. Chapman.
156, *194*, 4801, *5502*, *5802*, *5903*

V molchan'i nochi taynoy, Op. 4 No. 3. Text: Afanasy Fet.
[Eng] In the Silence of Night (Oh, in the silent night...). Text: George Harris & Deems Taylor. 155, 5006, *5502*, *5801*, *5802*, *5803*, *5903*

Rangström, Ture (1884-1947) Swedish

En ballad om god sömn [A Ballad about Good Sleep] (Fru Lust, hett är din fests behag...). Text [Sw]: Frans G. Bengtsson. 4201

En ballad om Lameks söner [A Ballad about Lamech's Sons] (Jabal och Jubal gå fromma och snälla...). Text [Sw]: Frans G. Bengtsson. 4201

En ballad om Narren och Döden [A Ballad about the Jester and Death] (Bjällrorna, den röda kammen...). Text [Sw]: Frans G. Bengtsson. 4201

Tristans död [Tristan's Death] (Har ödets skepp från min kärleks jord...), No. 4 from the cycle "Trots allt" [After All]. Text [Sw]: Bo Bergman. *4902*, 5706

Ray, Lilian (d. 1949) British

The Sunshine of Your Smile. Text: Leonard Cooke.
[Sw] Säg mig godnatt (Dagen har flytt...). Text: Oscar Ralf. 27

Reidarson, Per (1879-1954) Norwegian

Sommerens melodi [Summer's Melody], waltz. Text: Alf Rød.
[Sw] Sommarens melodi är som poesi (...). Text: ? 62

Rhodes, Helen (Guy) (Rhodes, Mrs. W.I.; 1858-1936) French (pseud.: Guy d'Hardelot)

Because. Text: The Composer.
[Eng] Because (Because you come to me...). Text: Edward Teschemacher.
160, 4603, *6003*

Rimsky-Korsakov, Nikolay (1844-1908) Russian

Sadko (1897). Text: The Composer & Vladimir Belsky.

Ne shchest' almazov, The Hindu Merchant's "Song of India" (scene 4)
[Sw] I söderns hav (Chanson hindoue). Text: Ture Rangström. 85
[Eng] My heathen guests. Text: ? 4803

Romberg, Sigmund (1887-1951) Hungarian-American

The Desert Song (1926). Text: Otto Harbach, Oscar Hammerstein II & Frank Mandel; [Sw] Carl Johan Holzhausen.

The Desert Song (Blue Heaven) (act 1)
[Sw] Från öknen det brusar 28

Maytime (1917). Text: Rida Johnson Young & Cyrus Wood.

Will You Remember (Our love is so sweet...), duet Richard - Ottilie (Sweethearts Duet, act 1) 4602, 5111

Rossini, Gioacchino (1792-1868) Italian

La danza, tarantella napoletana. Text: Carlo Pepoli.
[Sw] Tarantella (Ja, hela natten sjöng för mig...). Text: Alf Henrikson. 3704, 4006

Stabat mater (1842). Text: liturgical [Lat].

Cujus animam, tenor aria 114

Sahlberg(-Knoop), Sonja (1902-1968) Swedish

Aj, aj, aj du [Now, Now, Boy] (Varje man kan en gång falla...), foxtrot from the motion picture "Moderna fruar" [Modern Wives]. Text [Sw]: Gösta Stevens. 43

Salén, Sven (1890-1969) Swedish

Sången till havet [Song to the Sea] (Flyg ut, min sång...). Text [Sw]: The Composer. 206

Visa kring slånblom och månskära [Song of Blackthorn and Crescent Moon] (Drömmarnas vindar och skyarnas gång...). Text [Sw]: Nils Thorén. 207

Schrader, Mogens (d. 1934) Danish

I de lyse nætter [In the Bright Nights], serenade. Text: Dagmar Schrader.
[Sw] Sommarnatt [Summer Night] (Midsommarnätternas dämpade ljus...). Text: Gösta Stevens. 14, 84

Schubert, Franz (1797-1828) Austrian

Die Allmacht (Gross ist Jehovah, der Herr...), D. 852 (Op. 79 No. 2). Text: Johann Ladislaus Pyrker. *189*, 4604, *5802*

An die Leier (Ich will von Atreus Söhnen...), D. 737 (Op. 56 No. 2). Text: Franz Seraph von Bruchmann (after Anacreon). *127*, *5802*

An Sylvia (Was ist Silvia...), D. 891 (Op 106 No. 4). Text: Eduard von Bauernfeld (after William Shakespeare).
[Ger] *125*, 5009, *5802*
[Eng] Who is Silvia 4504

Die böse Farbe (Ich möchte ziehn in die Welt hinaus...), D. 795:17 (Op. 25, "Die Schöne Müllerin", No. 17). Text: Wilhelm Müller. *128*, *197*, *5003*, *5501*

Die Forelle (In einem Bächlein helle...), D. 550. Text: Christian Friedrich Daniel Schubart. *198*, *5501*, *5502*, *5802*, *5903*

Frühlingsglaube (Die linden Lüfte sind erwacht...), D. 686 (Op. 20 No. 2). Text: Ludwig Uhland. *129*, *5501*, *5502*, *5802*, *5903*

Ständchen (Leise flehen meine Lieder...), D. 957:4 (from "Schwanengesang"). Text: Ludwig Rellstab. *126*, *196*, 4901, *5501*, *5502*, *5802*, *5903*

Wandrers Nachtlied (Über allen Gipfeln ist Ruh...), D. 768 (Op. 96 No. 3). Text: Johann Wolfgang von Goethe. *130*, *136*, *190*

Sibelius, Jean (1865-1957) Finnish

Demanten på marssnön [The Diamond on the March Snow] (På drivans snö där glimmar...), Op. 36 No. 6. Text [Sw]: Josef Julius Wecksell.
235, *53xx*, *5501*, *5502*, *5604*, 5707

Flickan kom ifrån sin älsklings möte [The Maiden Came from Her Lover's Tryst (also: The Tryst)] (...), Op. 37 No. 5. Text [Sw]: Johan Ludvig Runeberg. 5105, 5707

Säv, säv, susa [Sigh, Rushes, Sigh (also: Murmuring Reeds; Ingalill)] (...), Op. 36 No. 4. Text [Sw]: Gustaf Fröding.
133, 236, 5105, 5204, *53xx*, 5403, *5501*, 5707, 5804, 6004

Svarta rosor [Black Roses] (Säg, varför är du så ledsen idag...), Op.36 No. 1. Text [Sw]: Ernst Josephson. *131*, *191*, 5105, 5204, *5501*, *5502*, 5707, 5804, 6004

Var det en dröm [Was It a Dream] (...), Op. 37 No. 4. Text [Sw]: Josef Julius Wecksell. 5105, 5204, 5707

Sjöberg, Carl (1861-1900) Swedish

Tonerna [Music (also: Visions)] (Tanke, vars strider blott natten ser...). Text: Erik Gustaf Geijer.
[Sw] 81, *188*, 227, 3703, 4303, 4601, *5107*, *53xx*, *5501*, *5502*, *5903*
[Eng] I Bless Ev'ry Hour (Loved one, I bless ev'ry hour...). Text: Fred S. Tysh [independent of Swedish text]. *200*

Sjögren, Emil (1853-1918) Swedish

I drömmen du är mig nära [You Are Near in My Dreams] (...). Text [Sw]: Tor Hedberg (after a Danish original). 10, *4902*, *5106*, *5802*, *5903*

Ich möchte schweben (...), Op. 12 No. 6 (from "Lieder aus Tannhäuser"). Text [Ger]: Julius Wolff. *132*, *5106*

Söderman, August (1832-1876) Swedish

Kung Heimer och Aslög [King Heimer and Aslaug] (Det skiner sol över dal och fjäll...). Text [Sw]: Frans Hedberg. 214, 5808

Trollsjön [The Enchanted Lake] (Högt upp bland bergets granar...). Text [Sw]: Edvard Bäckström, after "Der Mummelsee" [The Water-lily Lake] by Alois Schreiber [see note]. 232, *4902*, 5706, *6003*

Speaks, Oley (1874-1948) American

Sylvia (Sylvia's hair is like the night...). Text: Clinton Scollard. *199*, 5202

Stenhammar, Wilhelm (1871-1927) Swedish

Ett folk [A People], cantata op. 22 (1905). Text [Sw]: Verner von Heidenstam.

Sverige [Sweden] (Sverige, Sverige, Sverige, fosterland...)
91, 229, 4802, *5106*, 5808

Stradella, Alessandro

Pietà, Signore (see: **Niedermeyer, Louis**)

Straus, Oscar (1870-1954) Austrian

Rund um die Liebe (1914). Text: Robert Bodanzky & Friedrich Thelen; [Sw] ?

Es gibt Dinge, die muss man vergessen, (excerpt from) duet Hans - Stella (act 2)
[Sw] Det finns ting vilka äro för sköna 3601

Strauss, Johann (II) (1825-1899) Austrian

Der Zigeunerbaron (The Gypsy Baron; 1885). Text: Ignaz Schnitzer; [Sw] Sven Nyblom.

Wer uns getraut?, duet Barinkay - Saffi (act 2)
[Sw] Vem oss har vigt [103], 106

Strauss, Richard (1864-1949) German

Cäcilie (Wenn du es wüsstest...), Op. 27 No. 2. Text: Heinrich Hart.
123, *5501*, *5704*, *5801*, *5905*

Morgen (Und morgen wird die Sonne wieder scheinen...), Op. 27 No. 4. Text: John Henry Mackay. *122*, *187*, *5704*, 5804

Ständchen (Mach' auf, mach' auf...), Op. 17 No. 2. Text: Adolf Friedrich von Schack. *186*, 4601, 4907, *5003*, 5110, *5604*, 5804, *5907*

Traum durch die Dämmerung (Weite Wiesen im Dämmergrau...), Op. 29 No. 1. Text: Otto Julius Bierbaum. *5501*, *5502*, *5903*, *5905*

Zueignung (Ja, du weisst es, teure Seele...), Op. 10 No. 1. Text: Hermann von Gilm. 4503, 5006, *5502*, *5802*, *5903*

Sylvain, Jules (pseudonym; see: **Hansson, Stig**)

Tchaikovsky, Petr (1840-1893) Russian

Evgeny Onegin (Eugene Onegin; 1879). Text: Konstantin Shilovsky & The Composer; [Sw] Ernst Wallmark.

Kuda, kuda, Lensky's aria (act 2)
[Sw] Förbi, förbi 215, *5802*, 6004

Thiel, Olof (1892-1978) Swedish (pseud.: Jacques Armand)

Var det en dröm [Was It a Dream] (Ensam i dagens larm...). Text [Sw]: Axel Berggren. 70

Thomas, Ambroise (1811-1896) French

Mignon (1866). Text: Jules Barbier & Michel Carré; [Sw] Frans Hedberg.

Elle ne croyait pas, Wilhelm's romance (act 3)
[Sw] Hon kunde icke tro *5704*

Tilling, Erik (b. 1908) Swedish

Kanske att vi på samma drömmar bär [Maybe We Are Dreaming the Same Dreams] (Kanske att vi denna minut...), waltz. Text [Sw]: Nils Perne & Georg Eliasson (pseud.: Nils-Georg). 61

Tognarelli, Umberto Danish

Alt, hvad der er dejligt [Everything Beautiful]. Text: Mogens Dam.
[Sw] Allting som är vackert, minner mig om dig (...). Text: Nils Perne & Georg Eliasson (pseud.: Nils-Georg). 60

Törnquist, Folke (1899-1981) Swedish

O, milda sång [Oh, Sweet Song] (Varthän uti den vida världen vi två...). Text [Sw]: Fritz Stenfelt. 30

Toselli, Enrico (1883-1926) Italian

Serenata, Op. 6 No. 1. Text: Alfredo Silvestri.
[Sw] Serenata (Kom, det skymmer re'n...). Text: Sven Lindström. 20

Tosti, Francesco Paolo (1846-1916) Italian-British

L'alba separa dalla luce l'ombra (...). Text: Gabriele d'Annunzio.
165, 4803, *4902*, *5003*, *5107*, 5108, 5111, 5202, *53xx*, *5501*, *5502*

Ideale (Io ti seguii...). Text: Carmelo Errico. 102, *195*, *5501*, *5502*, *5802*, *6003*

Tours, Frank E. (1877-1963) British

Mother o'Mine (If I were hanged...). Text: Rudyard Kipling. 4605

Verdi, Giuseppe (1813-1901) Italian

Aida (1871). Text: Antonio Ghislanzoni, after French libretto by Camille du Locle; [Sw] Hjalmar Sandberg.

Complete [It] 210

Act 1, complete [Sw] 4003

Se quel guerrier...Celeste Aida, Radamès' recitative & aria (act 1)
[It] 88, 177, 3707, 5102, 5104, *5604*
[Sw] Vore jag utkorad...Ljuva Aida 3602

Celeste Aida [last part of aria only] 5302

Pur ti riveggo, duet Radamès - Aida (act 3)
[Sw] Jag ser dig åter [incomplete; Aida in German] 3602

Un ballo in maschera (1859). Text: Antonio Somma; [Sw] Ernst Wallmark.

Complete [It] 4007, 5002

Di' tu se fedele, Riccardo's barcarolle (act 1)
[It] 137, 148, 225, *5704*
[Sw] O säg, när på skummande vågor 3704

Act 2, first part [It] 4004

Don Carlo (1867 [1884; see note]). Text: Achille de Lauzières & Angelo Zanardini, after Joseph Méry & Camille du Locle.

Complete [It] 5007, 5008

Io l'ho perduta...Qual pallor...Dio, che nell'alma infondere, Don Carlo's scene & duet with Rodrigo (act 1) 171

La forza del destino (1862). Text: Francesco Maria Piave & Antonio Ghislanzoni.

Solenne in quest'ora, duet Carlo - Alvaro (act 3) 174, 3708

Messa da Requiem (1874). Text: liturgical [Lat].

Complete 242, 4005

Ingemisco, tenor aria 115, 3902, 5104, 5403, *5802*

Otello (1887). Text: Arrigo Boito.

O! mostruosa colpa!...Sì, pel ciel marmoreo giuro, duet Otello - Iago (Oath Duet, act 2) 172

Rigoletto (1851). Text: Francesco Maria Piave; [Sw] Ernst Wallmark.

Complete [It] 212, 4506, 5701

Questa o quella, The Duke's ballad (act 1)
[It] 138, 145, 5104
[Sw] O, I kvinnor 16

Giovanna, ho dei rimorsi...È il sol dell'anima...Che m'ami, (scene Gilda - Giovanna &) duet Duke - Gilda (act 1) 5703

È il sol dell'anima, duet Duke - Gilda (act 1) 140

Act 3, first part (up to quartet) [It] 5402

La donna è mobile, The Duke's aria (act 3)
[It] 89, 3707, *5107*, *5604*, 5703, *5802*
[Sw] Ack, som ett fjun så lätt 73

La traviata (1853). Text: Francesco Maria Piave; [Sw] Ernst Wallmark.

Complete [Sw: *Den vilseförda*] 3904

Il trovatore (1853). Text: Salvatore Cammarano & Francesco Maria Piave; [Sw] Oscar Ralf.

Complete [It] 182, 3901, 4101, 4702, 5702, 6001

Ah sì, ben mio, Manrico's aria (act 3) 116, 120

Di quella pira, Manrico's aria ("stretta") (act 3)
[It] 117, 121
[Sw] Skyhögt mot himlen 75

Quel suon...Ah! che la morte ognora, duet Leonora - Manrico (act 4) 4602

Wagner, Richard (1813-1883) German

Lohengrin (1850). Text: The Composer; [Sw] Frans Hedberg.

In fernem Land, Lohengrin's Narrative (Gralserzählung, act 3)
[Sw] I fjärran land 5204, *53xx*, *5406*, 6004

Wennerberg, Gunnar (1817-1901) Swedish

Psalm IV (Hör mig när jag ropar...), from "Stycken ur Davids psalmer". Text [Sw]: Holy Bible, Ps. 4:1-2. *6*

Wide, Eric (pseudonym; see: **Widestedt, Ragnar**)

Widestedt, Ragnar (1887-1954) Swedish (pseud.: Eric Wide)

Nämner du Sverige [If You Mention Sweden] (...). Text [Sw]: John Coldén. 108, 5301

Sjung din hela längtan ut [Sing Your Whole Yearning Out] (Se, nu gömmer solen sina strålar...). Text [Sw]: Nils Perne & Georg Eliasson (pseud.: Nils-Georg). 94

Wolf, Hugo (1860-1903) Austrian

Verborgenheit (Welt, o Welt, o lass mich sein...). Text: Eduard Mörike. *193, 5907*

2. Works without Known Composer

Ack Värmeland, du sköna [Oh Värmland, Thou Fairest] (...); also called "Värmlandsvisan". Swedish folk tune (probably of Dutch origin), arranged by Andreas Randel. Text [Sw]: Anders Fryxell (& Fredrik A. Dahlgren?). 82, [abridged] 3706

Allt under himmelens fäste [Beneath the Dome of the Sky] (...). Swedish folk-tune (from Gotland). Text [Sw]: ? 83

Hej dunkom, så länge vi levom [Come, Let Us Have a Gay Time As Long As We Live] (...). Swedish folk tune (from Bohuslän?). Text [Sw]: ? *3704, 5004*

I himmelen [In Heaven] (...). Norwegian folk tune. Text [Nor]: after Laurentius Laurinus the Elder (Swedish clergyman, 17th century). *2*

O Lamm Gottes unschuldig. German hymn tune. Text: Nikolaus Tech (Decius).
[Sw] Guds rena lamm oskyldig (...). Text: Olavus Petri. *3*

Ochi chernye [Dark Eyes]. Russian Gypsy tune.
[Sw] Svarta ögon (Vid din lägereld...). Text: Oscar Ralf. 55

Sommarglädje [Summer Joy] (Nu ä' dä sommar, nu ä' dä sol...). Tune of unknown origin. Text [Sw]: Eric Engstam. *4, 5201*

Tantis serenad [Tanti's Serenade] (Månstrålar klara glimma...). Tune of unknown origin [see note]. Text [Sw]: Arvid Ödmann. 23

Varför älskar jag? [Why Do I Love?] (Du så grymt söndersliter mitt bröst...). Gypsy tune (?). Text [Sw]: Sven Algot [= Sven-Olof?] Sandberg. 32

Wilt heden nu treden. Dutch hymn tune. Text: Adriaen Valerius (?).
[Eng] We Gather Together (Prayer of Thanksgiving). Musical arr.: Eduard Kremser. Text: Theodore Baker. 5110

Notes for Composer Index

Almroth, Tangoflickan

According to an article (of unknown date) in the Swedish popular magazine *Året Runt*, JB himself is noted as text author on the manuscript of this song. The composer's widow has not been able to confirm this.

Dresser, Barndomshemmet (On the Banks of the Wabash, Far Away)

"Barndomshemmet" is a free adaptation of Dresser's song. Karl Ewert's text, dealing with a Swedish immigrant in the US remembering the "red little cottage" of his childhood, was written for the popular singer Ernst Rolf. When Rolf published the song as sheet music, an otherwise unknown P. Würck was given as the composer and may perhaps have arranged the original music.

Grieg, Jeg elsker dig

It seems most correct to regard this song as sung in Norwegian, although (as remarked by J.W. Porter in JBD) H.C. Andersen's poem is written in Danish and the text has not been modified. In Andersen's days, the two written languages were practically identical, but JB uses Norwegian pronunciation.

Gruber, Stilla natt, heliga natt (Stille Nacht, heilige Nacht)

There are several Swedish text versions of this song, all beginning with the indicated four words. The author of the text used by the Björling couple (continuing "...världen all slumrar still") is not known.

Jurmann & Kaper, Ninon

This song was published as sheet music with the same text but with the title "En sång till dig".

Kálmán, Du går som en liten prinsessa (Du Veilchen vom Montmartre)

Englind was indicated on the original label as author of the Swedish text. However, in 1954 this tune was published as sheet music with the same text but with the title "Violen från Montmartre", and then Björn & Anita Halldén (pseud.: Nalle Halldén & S.S. Wilson) were named as text authors.

Körling, Vita rosor

The original spelling "Hvita rosor" is now antiquated.

Mascagni, *Cavalleria rusticana*: O Lola

The version in Sicilian dialect (O Lola, c'hai di latti) was used by JB in the complete recordings.

Niedermeyer, Pietà, Signore

This composition has often been attributed to the Italian 17th century composer Alessandro Stradella (e.g. in the programme of JB's Bergen concert, at which the song was recorded), sometimes also to Rossini. Donaudy was stated as the composer in a list of JB live recordings for sale. However, "Pietà, Signore" (the text used by JB does not include these words) is now generally assumed to be a work by Niedermeyer.

Peterson-Berger, Fyra visor i svensk folkton

According to B. Carlberg, *Peterson-Berger* (Stockholm, 1950), the composer found the poems by "H" which he set to music in a short story which was published in a popular weekly magazine. The texts have been attributed both to Helena Nyblom (the songs were dedicated to her by the composer) and to Vendela Hebbe, but no certain evidence for these attributions has been found.

Rossini, La danza

This song was also used for B. Paumgartner's opera *Rossini in Neapel*, the title role of which JB sang at the Royal Opera in Stockholm in 1936/37.

Sibelius, Säv, säv, susa

The original spelling "Säf, säf, susa" is now antiquated.

Söderman, Trollsjön

This song was actually composed to Schreiber's German text (Der Mummelsee), but since it has become known exclusively in the Swedish version, it is here treated as a Swedish original.

Verdi, *Un ballo in maschera*

Riccardo's aria in act 3, "Ma se m'è forza perderti", is missing in both complete recordings with JB.

Verdi, *Don Carlo*

Originally presented in a French 5-act version as *Don Carlos*, this opera was revised and abridged to four acts by the composer for a production in Italian in 1884. JB sang in the abridged Italian version, and most of the scene with Posa which he recorded had been rewritten by Verdi for this version (the duet "Dio che nell'alma infondere" was directly taken from act 2 of the original version). The opera is here treated as an Italian work.

Tantis serenad

The title alludes to the clown and circus manager Tanti (real name: Constantino Vulgo Bedini, 1861-1900), who was born in Italy but spent the last part of his life in Sweden. The song was originally published in Sweden in 1902 as "Månstrålar klara", but with "Tantis serenad" also noted on the cover. This sheet, which did not indicate any origin of words or music, also had a Danish version of the text. The text author's (translator's?) name was noted in the publisher's archive (Ödmann was one of the most famous tenors in the history of the Royal Opera). It seems probable that the tune is identical with an allegedly Italian one which Tanti used to sing with the refrain "Evviva Stoccolma" to his own concertina accompaniment, but there is no proof that he ever saw this text.

B. Title Index

This index lists alphabetically musical titles (with reference numbers for separate songs only), radio and television programmes, films, opera companies, concert institutions, etc. For reference numbers for operas, operettas, oratorios, etc., and excerpts from these, see under the composer's name in the Composer Index.

C. *Performer Index*

1. Conductors

2. Piano Accompanists

3. Singers

4. Interviewers

Section 4: Bibliography

A. Books and articles of discographical interest

Albert, Jürgen, "Erinnerung an Jussi Björling", *Collegium Musicum* 1971:3 (March), pp. 19-22. [Discussion of recordings, followed by one-page list of LP issues.]

The Art of Jussi Björling: [Discographical appendix, in Japanese]. In booklet accompanying *RCA* RVC 7531/35 (Tokyo, 1976), pp. 18-21. [This discography gives information about all relevant labels on the Japanese market.]

Bergquist, C. Hilding, "Jussi Björling", *Record Research*, 129-30 (Oct./Nov. 1974), p. 5. [Information about *Col.* E 4547.]

Björling, Anna-Lisa, *Mitt liv med Jussi* [My Life with Jussi]. Stockholm, Bonniers, 1987. 311 pp. [This book does not have any discographical appendix, but it includes, for example, a chapter about the deleted *Ballo* recording in 1960.]

Björling, Gösta, *Jussi: Boken om storebror* [Jussi: The Book About My Elder Brother]. Stockholm, Steinsvik, 1945. 223 pp. [Includes on pp. 186-89 a list of records made by JB as a solo artist under his own name.]

Björling, Jussi, *Med bagaget i strupen* [My Throat is My Traveling Bag]. Stockholm, Wahlström & Widstrand, 1945. 175 pp. [On pp. 118-22 is found a discography similar to that in Gösta Björling's book.]

Clough, F.F., & ***Cuming, G.J.***, "Jussi Bjoerling: A Discography", *American Record Guide*, vol. XII:4 (December 1945), pp. 87-90, 95. [The first JB discography in English, similar in scope to those in the Swedish books from 1945, and supplemented by a short biography.]

Clough, F.F., & ***Cuming, G.J.***, "Diskography", *Gramophone Record Review*, 55 (May 1958), pp. 572, 633-35, Addenda: 56 (June 1958), p. 706. [Second part of an article "The Great Interpreters, No. 15: Jussi Bjoerling", also including "Appreciation" by Robert Boas. This discography was the first one to list the acoustical and "Erik Odde" records.]

Douglas, Nigel, *Legendary Voices*. London, André Deutsch, 1992. 305 pp. [The chapter "Jussi Björling" on pp. 1-23 includes a discussion of many of JB's commercial recordings.]

Elfström, Mats, "Swedish National Discography: Jussi Bjorling and Related Research", *Record Research*, 125-26 (February 1974), p. 11. [Discussion of JB's acoustical Columbia records.]

Elfström, Mats, "Erik Odde", *Skivsamlaren*, 1 (November 1975): p. 4. [Anonymously published discography of records made under JB's pseudonym.]

Elfström, Mats, "Jussi Björling: First Records and Research on the Comedian Harmonists and von Eichwald Labels", *Record Research*, 137-38 (February/March 1976), p. 13. [Discography of JB's acoustical Columbia records.]

Goldberg, Don, "The Masked Ball Mystery", *Opera News*, vol. 55:9 (Jan. 19, 1991), pp. 34-35. [Discusses the *Ballo* recording project in 1960 (No. 244).]

Hagman, Bertil, editor, *Jussi Björling: En minnesbok* [JB: A Memorial Book]. Stockholm, Bonniers, 1960. 212 pp. [Several chapters in this book contain material of discographical interest, among them the following contributions: ***Bruun, Carl L.***, "Diskografi" [Discography], pp. 187-208 (includes all recordings which were issued by the time of JB's death); ***Ebert, Harry***, "Resor i krigstid" [Travels in Time of War], pp. 139-43; ***Ladberg, Bo Teddy***, "Jussi Björling och radion" [JB and the Radio], pp. 117-26.]

Hamilton, David, "A New Jussi Bjoerling Discography", *ARSC* [Association of Recorded Sound Collections] *Journal*, vol. XIV(1983):4, pp. 98-99. [A review of JBD, which also contains information about the existence of a few test pressings.]

Henrysson, Harald, *Förteckning (till sin huvuddel engelskspråkig) över ljudupptagningar med Jussi Björling och utgåvor av dessa* [A List (mainly in English) of JB Sound Recordings]. Borås, Bibliotekshögskolan, 1975. 54 pp. (mimeographed). [This examination paper from the Swedish College of Librarianship contains an earlier version of Section 1 of the present work.]

Himmelein, Fred T, "The Bjoerling Recordings: A Selective Discography", *Le Grand Baton*, vol. IV:l (February 1967), pp. 13-18. [Appendix to a biographical article by the same author.]

Kesting, Jürgen, *Die grossen Sänger*. Düsseldorf, Claassen, 1986. [The chapter "Der Tenor des Nordens: Jussi Björling" on pp. 1598-1606 includes information of discographical interest.]

Kesting, Jürgen, "Konkretisierte Erinnerung an bessere Tage des Gesangs: Jussi Björling und seine Schallplatten", *Opernwelt*, 1973:4 (April), pp. 43-47. [This analytical article also contains a discography of LP issues.]

Letchford, Michael, "Jussi Björling", in booklet accompanying record album *HMV* RLS 715 "*The Art of Jussi Björling*" (London, 1977), pp. 4-6. [Includes information about never realized recordings.]

Liliedahl, Karleric, *His Master's Voice: Elektriska inspelningar i Skandinavien och för den skandinaviska marknaden 1925-1934* [HMV: Electrical Recordings in Scandinavia and for the Scandinavian Market 1925-1934]. Stockholm, Arkivet för ljud och bild, 1990. 304 pp.

Natan, Alex, *Primo Uomo: Grosse Sänger der Oper*. Basel, Basilius Presse, c. 1963. [The biographical article about JB is supplemented by a "Diskothek" on pp. 112-13, listing LP records.]

Pease, Edward, "A Jussi Bjoerling Discography, Part I: Low-priced Recordings Currently Available from Normal Retail Sources in the United States; Part II: Full-priced Recordings, etc.", *NATS* [National Association of Teachers of Singing] *Bulletin*, vol. XXIX:2 (December 1972), pp. 12-15; vol. XXXII:2 (December 1975), pp. 6-11. [Discussion of commercial issues.]

Porter, Jack W., & ***Henrysson, Harald***, *A Jussi Bjoerling Discography*. Indianapolis, Jussi Bjoerling Memorial Archive, 1982. 190 pp. [Regarding this edition (here referred to as "JBD"), see the forewords to the first edition of the present work.]

Scott, Michael, "Jussi Björling 1908-1960", *Opera Now,* 9 (Dec. 1989), pp. 54-59. [Includes a short discography.]

Seemungal, Rupert P, *A Complete Discography of Jussi Björling*. 1st - 3rd ed. Trinidad, 1959-64. 55 pp. [=3rd ed.] (mimeographed). [The first list to include live recordings; matrix and take numbers (all speeds) are given for commercial recordings.]

Skandrup Lund, Eyvind, & ***Rosenberg, Herbert***, *Jussi Björling: A Record List*. Copenhagen, Nationaldiskoteket, 1969. 82 pp. (Nationaldiskoteket Discographies; 209). [This important publication for JB discography is here referred to as "JBRL". Cf. also the foreword to the first edition of the present work and the Key to Index Numbers, which includes the JBRL.]

Steane, J.B., *The Grand Tradition: Seventy Years of Singing on Record*. London, Duckworth, 1974. 628 pp. [JB's recordings are treated on pp. 371-74 in the chapter "Opera at Home".]

Tesoriero, Michael, & ***Rossell, David***, "A Tribute to Jussi Björling (1911-1960)", *2MBS-FM* [Australia], vol. 18:4 (April 1992), pp. 3-15. [The last page contains a "Jussi Björling CD Discography".]

B. Sleeve texts and record booklets dealing with Jussi Björling

This list is in no way complete. Only signed contributions are listed, which devote a major part of the text to JB.

Alexander, G.C.	*Angel* COLH 149; *Cap.* G 7247; *HMV* ALP 1857 [Eng]
Alfano, Vincent	*Legendary* LR 137-2 [Eng]
Bareis, Arbe	*Biog.Music* BIM 708-2; *Legato* LCD 154-1 [Eng]
Bicknell, J.D.	*HMV* ALP 1841 [Eng]
Blyth, Alan	*Decca* GRV 4; *EMI* CDH 7 61053 2 [Eng]
Bokstedt, Bertil	*RCA* VICS 1659 [Sw]
Bruun, Carl L.	*Rococo* 5231, 5237, R 31 [Eng]
Caputo, Pietro	*RCA* VL 42436 [It]
Court, L.D.	*Rococo* 5201, 5329 [Eng]
Douglas, Nigel	*Nimbus* NI 7835, 7842 [Eng,Ger,Fr]
Fitzgerald, Gerald	*Rich.* SR 33254 [Eng]
Freeman, John W.	*MET* 110, 110CD [Eng]
Friedner, Calle	*SR* SRLP 1354/55 [Sw,Eng]
Gédéon, Antoine	*RCA* LM 2736-C [Fr]
Goodwin, Noël	*HMV* ALP 1620 [Eng]
Gotwalt, John M.	*Legato* LCD 103-1 [Eng]
Grevillius, Nils	*RCA* HR 224, LM 2784 [Eng]
Guy, Rory	*Sera.* 60168 [Eng]
Hagman, Bertil	*RCA* SER 5704/06 [Sw,Eng]
Hague, Robert A.	*RCA* LM 1771 [Eng]
Hatton, Helen E.	*Rococo* 5304 [Eng]
Hedman, Frank	*Bluebell* ABCD 002, 006, 013, 020, 028, 036; BELL 132, 163, 187, 198 [Eng]; *RCA* LSC 9884 [Sw,Eng], SER 5719 [Eng]; *Sw. Society* SCD 1010 [Eng]
Henrysson, Harald	*Bluebell* ABCD 002, 006, 013, 020, 028, 036 [Sw], 042, 050 [Sw,Eng]; BELL 132, 163, 187, 198 [Sw]; *HMV* 1359931 [Sw]; *Sw.Society* SCD 1010 [Sw]
Höslinger, Clemens	*Dacapo* 1C 147-03354/55M; *EMI* CDH 7 61053 2 [Ger]
Hyatt, Fred	*Glendale* GL 8006 [Eng]
Kesting, Jürgen	*Dacapo* 1C 177-00947/48M [Ger,Eng]
Koeltzsch, Hans	*RCA* KR 11014/1-2 [Ger,Eng,Fr]
Kolodin, Irving	*Angel* COLH 150; *Cap.* G 7248 [Eng]
Kruijff, Jan de	*HMV* XLPH 20010 [Dutch]
Kupferberg, Herbert	*RCA* LM 2003, RB 16011 [Eng], SVA 1010 [Eng,Ger]
Laskowski, Klaus	*RCA* RL 43077 [Ger]

Letchford, Michael	*HMV* RLS 715 [Eng]
Limansky, Nicholas E.	*Legendary* LR 138 [Eng]
Martens, H.G.	*RCA* LM 2736-C [Ger]
Matthew-Walker, Robert	*RCA* GL 85277 [Eng,Fr,Ger,It]
Mohr, Richard	*RCA* AGM1-5277, GD 87799, RD 85934 [Eng,Fr,Ger,It]
Pfeiffer, John	*RCA* 60520-2-RG, GD 60520 [Eng,Ger,Fr,It]
Price, Walter	*RCA* LM/LSC 2570 [Eng,Ger,Fr], VICS 1740 [Eng]
Reimers, Lennart	*EMI* CDC 7610752 [Sw,Eng]
Riemens, Leo	*Rococo* 5341 [Sw]
Robinson, Francis	*RCA* GL 84889, LM 2736, RB 6585, RCALP 3043 [Eng]
Rose, Bob	*Voce* 95 [Eng]
Schonberg, Harold C.	*Angel* COLH 148; *Cap.* G 7239 [Eng]
Simon, Henry	*RCA* LM 2269 [Eng]
Smith, Edward J.	*ANNA* 1069 [Eng]
Steane, John	*Decca* 421 316-2 [Eng]
Tubeuf, André	*EMI* CDH 7 61053 2 [Fr]
Uekermann, Gerd	*Decca* 421 316-2 [Ger]